TRAVEL GEOGRAPHY

From THE TRAVEL TRAINING SERIES

Claudine Dervaes

First Printing August-September 1997
Published by Solitaire Publishing, P.O. Box 14508,
Tampa, FL 33690-4508. (813) 876-0286.

Materials available from Solitaire Publishing include:

ISBN 0-933143-50-8	The Travel Training Series
ISBN 0-933143-52-4	Travel Geography
ISBN 0-933143-51-6	Domestic Travel and Ticketing
ISBN 0-933143-36-2	Selling Tours and Independent Travel
ISBN 0-933143-24-9	International Travel
ISBN 0-933143-23-0	Selling Cruises
ISBN 0-933143-22-2	Sales and Marketing Techniques
ISBN 0-933143-53-2	The Travel Dictionary
ISBN 0-933143-40-0	Map Transparencies Set
ISBN 0-933143-41-9	ARC Forms Transparencies Set
ISBN 0-933143-42-7	Training Specifics Transparencies Set
ISBN 0-933143-08-7	TEACHING TRAVEL: A Handbook for the Educator
ISBN 0-933143-54-0	CAREERS IN TRAVEL (video tape)
ISBN 0-933143-18-4	The U.K. to U.S.A. Dictionary

Plus many other travel education products. Please contact us for a current catalog.

The author-publisher would like to thank John Stuart Hunter for editing assistance and display work.

TABLE OF CONTENTS

CHAPTER 10 - CARIBBEAN AND BERMUDA

CHAPTER 11 - SOUTH AMERICA

CHAPTER 12 - EUROPE

CHAPTER 1

Introduction to Travel

Highlights of this chapter include:

- *CAREERS IN TRAVEL*
- *JOB REQUIREMENTS, SALARIES BENEFITS AND OPPORTUNITIES*
- *MAJOR TRAVEL INDUSTRY ASSOCIATIONS*
- *TRAVEL AGENCY OPERATIONS*

WELCOME TO THE WORLD OF TRAVEL

Travel has interested people in all walks of life at all periods of history. Travel is an activity in which most people participate daily. People travel for business; pleasure; military, educational, family reasons; and for beginning a new life. Travel is an integral part of life for many people in the United States as well as the world. Travel contributes to the revenues of all levels of government in addition to contributing to the balance of trade between nations. With travel the people of the world get to know each other, to share and benefit by the exchange of ideas and ways. A better understanding of cultures and hope for a better world is provided through the experiences of travel - through books, magazines, news reports - and through visiting places and people.

Having "travel geography" skills means knowing transportation specifics, destinations, resorts, climate, sights, languages, currencies, cultures and experiences. A travel professional must "qualify" the client - get to know the individual's likes/dislikes, past travel experiences, travel preferences, budget, and the basic questions of when, where, how many, etc. This manual is designed to familiarize you with all areas of the world and to help you retain an understanding and knowledge of destinations. Other manuals from **The Travel Training Series** provide training in domestic and international ticketing, hotels, tours, cruises, etc. Complete details and the specifics of sales techniques and business communications are in the **Sales and Marketing Skills** manual.

Becoming a specialist in travel geography takes time, a solid background of study and research, and continual updating and review. The learning will never stop! You can complete this manual, read maps, travel guides, references, tour brochures, and magazines. You can watch TV programs and videos, attend travel shows and seminars, take courses and talk with experienced travelers. Develop a reference library with books, tapes, videos, software, files of articles and information, and subscribe to a computer database service. The public library, bookstores, and Solitaire Publishing can assist you with information on materials available.

There are so many travel products, destinations and many more sophisticated and experienced travelers - all requiring greater skills from today's travel professional. The growth of the travel industry has been phenomenal within the past century and will continue to expand. I welcome you to share and experience the influence and growth of this exciting, challenging and ever-changing industry!

NOTES

CAREERS IN TRAVEL

This section on careers provides information on the specifics of travel agency positions and operations, plus airline, hotel, car rental, tour, cruise, and other employment opportunities.

TRAVEL AGENTS

A travel agent is involved in a variety of activities. The agent provides information, advises clients, plans itineraries, makes hotel, car, tour, cruise, and rail reservations, and prints airline and other types of documentation. A travel agent must be knowledgeable, organized, and accurate. Furthermore, an agent must be able to work with people, speak effectively, and learn and adapt quickly as the industry changes so rapidly. The work can be quite hectic, especially during busy seasons of the year. Overtime may be required. In addition, some agencies are open at least one evening a week as well as Saturday (half/full day). You do not have to relocate as most agencies hire on a local basis. There are a number of job opportunities since most cities have a number of travel agencies and there is a fairly constant turnover in employees.

Most agencies offer their employees some basic benefits such as medical insurance, one to two weeks vacation, five to seven sick days, seven legal holidays, and one to two weeks time off for a familiarization or "fam" trip. The "fam" trip allows an agent to experience a cruise, tour, or airline sponsored trip to a destination in promotion of the sale of that product. Most "fam" trips are very inexpensive and for travel agents only, although some accept spouses or guests. The agency may pay for familiarization trips or just allow the time off. Discount tickets or airline passes are usually available after the agent has been employed for at least one year. Other discounts extended to agents include special hotel and car rental rates, complimentary or discounted admission to attractions, and other bonuses. Many suppliers offer free trips or cabins on cruises when a certain number/volume of sales has been booked by the agency or agent.

The travel agent's position has generally been low paying, especially as an entry level employee. An agency normally has a limited number of positions available. Most agencies consist of one or two travel agents, a manager and an owner. Larger agencies have other positions such as an accountant, receptionist, secretary, commercial agent, leisure sales agent, group sales agent, outside sales agent, ticket delivery staff, etc. The vast majority of agencies are computerized so there is a possible extension to jobs in computer technology relative to the travel industry. Most agents work on a salary, and many agencies provide a salary plus commission. Starting salaries vary greatly - depending on the area of the country and the qualifications of the individual. Starting pay can be as low as $15,000 a year, if you are inexperienced. However, it's possible to make $20,000 to $30,000 annually or more if you have an established clientele, can speak several languages, can sell or do presentations to groups, have travel experience and other qualifications. Generally, salaries are improving because the complexity of the job has increased. The professional agent today is a counselor, psychologist, and skilled salesperson who provides information as well as service. The agent is an educator and the "bridge" between the supplier and the public. Many tour and cruise companies sell their product only through travel agencies; and in some cases travel agencies sell 80% or more of an airline's tickets. Sales techniques, computerization, and good communication skills are necessary.

There are many products to sell, many destinations, better educated and more sophisticated travelers - requiring greater skills from the travel agent. There are hundreds of airline fares, and the availability of a seat at a particular fare changes by the minute. Work is doubled when fares are lowered and the agent has to rebook/reticket a client. The commission the agency earns on the sale of tickets and tours is roughly 10%. And the commission "caps" placed on certain domestic airline tickets by several major carriers has reduced commissions to a maximum of $25.00 or $50.00. However, the larger agencies and agencies belonging to consortiums can benefit from overrides and bonus commissions.

Primary is the need to understand the role played by the travel agent. Without travel agencies, the airline, hotel, car rental, tour and cruise companies would have to hire many more salespeople and open many more offices. Presently there are about 37,000 travel agencies in the United States alone, encompassing as many as 370,000 travel agents. Agency jobs have attracted people who are changing careers, women who are reentering the work force after raising a family, retirees, and young people. The idea of traveling all over the world and the "glamour" of the industry attracts many. However, the "real" job entails problem-solving, research, and sometimes very frustrating work, with the opportunities for travel occurring just a few times a year. A tremendous responsibility falls on the agent, because a small error - like booking the wrong date - can result in disastrous consequences. And if the tour, cruise, or airline company's operations are at fault, the client may still feel the agent is accountable. The rewards come from the challenge and interest of the job, the personal growth, the opportunity to travel, and the satisfaction of providing professional services to your clients, many of whom express their gratitude for your help.

With two years' experience as travel agent, you can move up to senior sales and managerial positions. There is also the opportunity to move from travel agency operations to some other component of the industry, such as tour company, airline, or cruise company operations.

Large travel agencies have agents who specialize in commercial/business travel as opposed to those working with leisure/vacation travel. A ***COMMERCIAL TRAVEL AGENT***, or an agent who works with business people, is sometimes responsible for acquiring and maintaining commercial accounts and may visit companies with a prepared package of details on what the agency provides in sales/services. Services can include lowest fare search, obtaining corporate rates for hotels and car rentals, delivering tickets, free passport photos, travel bags, or other amenities. Agencies may offer tracking of employee expenditures, billing on a monthly basis, etc. The commercial travel agent is expected to work very quickly and efficiently and maintain profiles of the specific needs and expectations of the individual business traveler, such as hotel preferences, seat assignment requests and other considerations. There may not be a great deal of creativity and consultation in the commercial agent's duties, since business travelers have more definitive requests. But if the agent is responsible for obtaining new accounts, there is an opportunity "to get out from behind the desk" to make sales calls.

The ***LEISURE TRAVEL AGENT*** or vacation travel agent works with individuals (and sometimes groups) and spends a great deal of time going over the details of a cruise or a trip to the Orient, for example. It is more of a "counseling" position, and the agent must ask many questions, know many different types of travel products, and be able to make appropriate recommendations for the needs and components of the vacation.

GROUP SALES TRAVEL AGENTS

An agency can have a department or agents specializing in groups. Reservations, travel specifics, itineraries, manifests, deposits, final payments, contract negotiations with suppliers, and the group's specific needs are all handled by the group sales travel agent. In addition, the agent may be responsible for securing groups and doing presentations to clubs, organizations, apartment and retirement communities. Important qualities of a group sales travel agent include: an outgoing personality, good organizational and sales skills, personal contacts and management responsibility. These agents may work entirely on commission or they may use the opportunity of obtaining groups in order to be the tour escort or tour guide. Most tour companies offer a "conductor discount," such as one passenger free for every 15 paying passengers. The position of tour escort or guide is discussed in more detail in the section on tour operations and jobs.

OUTSIDE SALES TRAVEL AGENTS OR INDEPENDENT CONTRACTORS

One way to get into the travel business if you don't have experience is to become an outside sales agent. Agencies contract outside salespeople as a marketing effort to secure new business. Since the average profit margin of the travel agency is low, agencies cannot afford a great deal of advertising. Therefore, outside sales agents represent the agency for acquiring new clients and work on commission. They contact potential customers and possibly groups. The outside sales agent needs to negotiate and legitimize with a contract the amount of commission split and other concerns. Outside sales travel agents may get 20% - 30% of the commission if they only refer the clients. If they make the reservations, process payments and ticketing, they may get half or more of the commission. The cost of business cards, reference books, mailings, and presentations are additional expenses for the outside sales agent. Outside agents must keep records of their contacts and log the sales in a step by step fashion. The agent usually gets paid after the clients have completed the trip because the arrangements could be cancelled. Outside agents must be organized, very self-motivated, outgoing, and not dependent on a continual income. Some travel training is necessary to be able to properly represent the services and skills of the travel agency. This is the area of the industry that has been growing dramatically in the last few years, as agents can work from their home by taking advantage of the recent advances in technology and communication (fax, phone, pagers, computers, the Internet, E-mail, etc.).

MAKE SURE YOU CHECK INTO STATE REQUIREMENTS FOR LICENSING OR REGISTRATION. SOME STATES REQUIRE SELLERS OF TRAVEL TO REGISTER AS WELL AS OBTAIN BONDS AND MEET OTHER STANDARDS.

CORPORATE TRAVEL AGENTS

Large corporations that have many employees traveling may choose to operate a travel agency themselves rather than giving their business to an outside travel agency. Corporate travel agencies (sometimes called "inplant" travel agencies) can have a different commission basis; and opportunities for a job as a corporate travel agent would be limited to cities where large companies are headquartered. The benefits are usually very good since the agent is entitled to the company benefits, higher pay scales, plus the travel agency benefits.

OPENING YOUR OWN TRAVEL AGENCY

If you choose to open your own travel agency it is a fairly inexpensive business to initiate, but it can be unprofitable for the first two to three years. A medium sized agency would require about $60,000 in capital. The Airlines Reporting Corporation (ARC) sets rules for the appointment of agencies to issue airline tickets. International Airlines Travel Agency Network (IATAN) sets standards for a group of international airlines. Once an agency has appointments, other suppliers normally recognize the agency for commissions on the sales of their products.

The ARC sets bond requirements, requires industry experience or skills for management, and must approve the location along with other standards. Some states require licensing or registration of travel agents. You can also choose to open a "Cruise Only" agency, which may not require the standards for airline ticketing appointment. However, "Cruise Only" agencies usually contract with an ARC agency in order to provide airline tickets for their customers when necessary. Instead of opening an agency you could buy an existing agency or a franchise travel agency. The Travel Dictionary contains lists of trade associations, consortiums, and franchises.

AIRLINE OPERATIONS

Now we will cover airline operations. Job opportunities with the airlines include ***PILOTS, FLIGHT ATTENDANTS, CUSTOMER SERVICE REPRESENTATIVES, TICKET AND GATE AGENTS, RESERVATIONISTS, MECHANICS, AND ENGINEERS.*** The positions of captain, co-pilot, and engineer all require FAA (Federal Aviation Administration) certification, and the jobs are somewhat limited, competitive, and require a college degree plus flight time - normally necessitating a previous military career. ***FLIGHT ATTENDANTS*** serve meals and drinks and are responsible for the comfort and safety of the passengers. Job requirements include: two/four years of college, public contact work experience, psychology, first aid, languages, home economics, and public speaking. Most airlines have a training program for the flight attendants and they usually require that you be willing to relocate.

RESERVATION AGENTS are telephone and computer operators responding to calls from the public and/or travel agents. Candidates should have a high school diploma or some college, work experience, and excellent communication skills. Starting pay ranges from $14,000 to $18,000 a year and there is overtime and bonus pay available.

TICKET AGENTS handle reservations and sell tickets at city ticket offices or at the airports. ***CUSTOMER SERVICE AGENTS*** assist customers at boarding and deplaning or at baggage and ticket counter areas. ***GATE AGENTS*** handle boarding procedures and other services for passengers.

There are positions available in District Marketing or Sales Offices of the airlines, such as ***SECRETARIES, SALES REPRESENTATIVES, MARKETING and OPERATIONS MANAGERS***, etc. Many carriers will fill their managerial positions from within.

The airline sponsored computer reservation systems are also large companies that will have a need for employees in programming, sales and marketing, operations, etc.

Airline operations are vulnerable due to the fact that their product - a seat on a plane - is a quickly perishable product. Competition, fuel prices, management and labor disputes, currency exchange rates, interest rates, strikes, accidents, terrorism, and economic decline all impact the airlines' operations. And yet there is no shortage of people wanting a job with an airline. The airlines receive hundreds of applications every day.

Shift work, relocation, and instability of the job are some of the disadvantages of working for the airlines. Generally however, the benefits are very good. Most airlines allow their employees, as well as their immediate families, to travel on space-available passes on most of the airline routes. A small service charge such as $25.00 is assessed for this privilege. The number of passes varies with the airline. There are also reciprocal agreements available with other airlines, allowing travel all over the world. There is reduced rate travel available on a confirmed basis - usually at 25% to 50% of the normal fare. Other suppliers may extend discounts and benefits to airline employees on their tour, cruise, and other travel products.

HOTELS AND THE HOSPITALITY INDUSTRY

Hoteliers and the hospitality or lodging industry offer the widest range of employment opportunities. Many people have risen to management in five to ten years. It's a lot more than bed and breakfast when the hotel business encompasses real estate, finance, food and beverage, meetings and conventions, design, maintenance, sales, administration, computerization, and public relations. New types of hotel properties have been built and the marketplace has become very competitive. Hotel industry candidates should be hard-working, service-oriented, self-disciplined, and willing to relocate to progress within the company. Depending on the size of property, hotels will have ***FRONT OFFICE STAFF*** consisting of a ***MANAGER, ROOM CLERK, RESERVATIONS CLERK, CASHIER, and TELEPHONE/COMPUTER OPERATOR.*** Salaries range from $13,000 to $25,000 a year. The ***SERVICE STAFF*** includes the ***CONCIERGE, BELL CAPTAIN, BELL PERSONS,*** **and** ***PORTERS***. There are quite a few positions in accounting available - such as ***CONTROLLER, CREDIT MANAGER, CASHIER, ACCOUNTS PAYABLE, ACCOUNTS RECEIVABLE, PAYROLL SUPERVISOR, AUDITOR***, etc. In ***FOOD SERVICE,*** there is ***BANQUET DIRECTOR, CATERING MANAGER, MAITRE D', WINE STEWARDS, CAPTAIN, SERVERS, BARTENDERS, BUSPERSONS, and CASHIERS***. There is the ***FOOD PREPARATION STAFF*** under the chef's supervision. ***HOUSEKEEPING STAFF, SALES AND MARKETING POSITIONS, MAINTENANCE AND OPERATIONS*** offer other opportunities. There are so many positions in this industry and "moving up" or laterally is feasible enough that taking any position with a hotel is a good way to start. The Educational Institute of the American Hotel and Motel Association (AH & MA) can provide you with resources and training, as well as many colleges and universities that offer hospitality management programs.

CAR RENTAL COMPANIES

There are about ten major and hundreds of smaller car rental companies. ***RESERVATIONISTS, COUNTER RENTAL AGENTS, STATION MANAGERS, SALES REPRESENTATIVES, DRIVERS, AND MAINTENANCE*** comprise some of the positions available. Shift work and relocation may be necessary. Entry level salaries are slightly better than minimum wage, but there are bonuses offered for performance in most positions.

TOUR COMPANIES

In the U.S., there are hundreds of tour companies. Major tour companies are usually headquartered in gateway cities such as New York, Seattle, Los Angeles, San Francisco, and Miami. Tour companies hire ***RESERVATIONISTS, MARKETING AND SALES STAFF, ACCOUNTANTS, TOUR ESCORTS, and TOUR OPERATIONS STAFF.*** Candidates for the job of ***TOUR ESCORT*** should be neat, personable, courteous, outgoing, organized, patient, fluent in a few languages, responsible, skilled in life-saving, CPR, and basic first aid. If you are interested in becoming a tour escort, start by volunteering locally as a guide/docent in a museum or attraction, and contact the Visitor's and Convention Bureau to find out about other possible tour guide opportunities. The Travel Industry Personnel Directory is an excellent resource as it lists tour companies alphabetically as well as by destinations. Contact the tour companies, send them your resume and follow with a phone call.

CRUISE LINES

Most cruise lines are located in the major port cities of Miami, Ft. Lauderdale, San Francisco, and New York. With cruise lines, the career opportunities are in ***RESERVATIONS, SALES, MARKETING, and OPERATIONS.*** There are relatively few positions on board the ships because most of the lines employ crews from Greece, Italy, the Bahamas, Philippines, Korea, and Indonesia. The shops and the casinos on board the cruise ships are usually operated by separate concession companies. There are some opportunities for work in the entertainment staff, purser's office, child care staff, facility and activity areas on the ships. The Cruise Lines International Association (CLIA) can provide addresses for many of the cruise lines. How to Get a Job with a Cruise Line is an excellent resource for "insider's tips" to the jobs on the ships.

SPECIALTY AREAS

There are also some jobs in specialty areas such as meeting and convention planners, multi-line representatives, and incentive travel planners. Some references are listed at the end of this chapter.

TRAVEL AND TOURISM

Travel and tourism offices also have staffing needs in meeting and convention planners, sales, marketing, and management. In addition, the travel industry has many support services, such as research and marketing firms, advertising, travel writing, financial services, trade associations, travel clubs, attractions and theme parks.

For training there are hundreds of travel schools, colleges, universities, vocational-technical centers, and travel agency affiliated schools. The public library, local travel agencies, and travel organizations are sources for lists of schools. You should talk to recent graduates of the school and to travel industry companies that you're interested in working for, to see if they recognize the training the school offers.

Overall, the travel industry offers many different professional skills and opportunities. Career paths can cross from segment to segment of the industry as well as within one company's operations.

TO WORK IN THE TRAVEL INDUSTRY MEANS SELLING DREAMS AND EXPERIENCES. IT MEANS HARD WORK, CHALLENGE, FRUSTRATION - AS WELL AS CREATIVITY, INSIGHT, PERSONAL GROWTH AND EXPRESSION. IT OFFERS THE OPPORTUNITY TO FULFILL YOUR OWN DREAMS!

NOTES

SOME POSITIONS IN TRAVEL

TRAVEL AGENCIES:

Receptionist
Ticket Delivery
Clerical
Accounting
Outside Sales
Travel Agent - Domestic
Commercial Travel
Representative
Group Sales

AIRLINES:

Reservationist
Ticket Agent
Flight Attendant
Passenger Service
Clerical/Secretarial
Operations
Accounting
Maintenance

HOTELS:

Reservationist
Reception/Desk Staff
Housekeeping
Bellpersons
Bell Captain
Porters
Cashier
Accounting

Agency Sales Manager
Night Auditor
Concierge/Guest Services
Telephone Operator
Food Service Staff
Maitre D'
Waitpersons
Wine Stewards
Bartenders
Maintenance

TOUR COMPANIES:

Receptionist
Reservationist
Clerical/Secretarial
Mail Manager
Accounting
Tour Escort/Guide
Marketing Assistant

CAR RENTAL COMPANIES:

Reservationist
Counter Rental Agents
Drivers
Maintenance
Passenger Service

CRUISE LINES:

Reservationist
Clerical/Secretarial
Accounting
Mail Manager
Passenger Service

ON-BOARD SHIPS:
Casino Operations Staff
Casino Manager
Beautician
Gift Shop Staff
Fitness/Dance Instructor
Entertainer
Cruise Staff/Hostess
Guest Lecturer

TRAVEL AND TOURISM OFFICES, CONVENTION AND VISITOR BUREAUS:

Receptionist
Clerical/Secretarial
Accounting

Marketing Director
Public Relations Director
Promotions Director
Research Director

REVIEW

NOTE: These can also be used as discussion questions if this manual is used in a training program/classroom environment.

1. Why do people travel? ____________________

2. What changes have you seen in the travel industry? ______

3. Name some of the differences in selling travel products versus other types of products. ____________

4. Name ten job titles in the hotel and hospitality industry.

5. Do you think there should be a federal/standardized licensing/certification program for travel agents? Why or Why not? ____________

MAJOR TRAVEL INDUSTRY ASSOCIATIONS

AAA - AMERICAN AUTOMOBILE ASSOCIATION--This is the largest of all travel clubs, and one of the largest publishers of travel maps and tour books. Emphasis of the association is on the auto travel aspect of tourism, but it has a strong travel agency operation through its World Wide Travel outlets. Services included with membership cover free maps and tour books, free travelers checks, emergency road service, and various other discounts and services (insurance, auto-buying services, etc.). The services may vary according to location, and there are reciprocal AAA affiliated organizations overseas.

ABA - AMERICAN BUS ASSOCIATION--Association of American bus companies. Companies must carry appropriate insurance and bonding.

ABTA - ASSOCIATION OF BRITISH TRAVEL AGENTS--Association of travel industry agents within United Kingdom. Similar to the American Society of Travel Agents.

ACTA - ALLIANCE OF CANADIAN TRAVEL ASSOCIATIONS--Association of Canadian travel agencies and other travel industry companies. It represents the interests of its members to the public, governments, suppliers and others. ACTA also develops high professional membership standards.

AH & MA - AMERICAN HOTEL AND MOTEL ASSOCIATION--Trade association covering the lodging industry in the U.S., Canada, Mexico, Central and South America.

AMTRAK - Also known as the National Railroad Passenger Corporation. AMTRAK coordinates the passenger railway system in the U.S.

ARC - AIRLINES REPORTING CORPORATION--A corporation of most of the scheduled airlines in the U.S. that establishes requirements for travel agencies to sell airline tickets.

ARTA - ASSOCIATION OF RETAIL TRAVEL AGENTS--An organization for retail travel agencies.

ASI - AMERICAN SIGHTSEEING INTERNATIONAL--Composed of local tour operators offering sightseeing tours, transfers, and charter transportation. A tariff book is published and available to travel agencies.

ASTA - AMERICAN SOCIETY OF TRAVEL AGENTS--One of the largest industry associations whose membership encompasses both U.S. and international travel agencies, airlines, hotels, tour companies and other entities.

ATA - AIR TRANSPORT ASSOCIATION--Trade association of U.S. and Canadian airlines.

CHRIE - COUNCIL ON HOTEL, RESTAURANT, AND INSTITUTIONAL EDUCATION--Fosters the advancement and standards of professionalism of hospitality and tourism management programs around the world.

CITC - CANADIAN INSTITUTE OF TRAVEL COUNSELLORS - A non-profit organization that encourages professionalism in the travel industry and promotes personal development through quality education and training.

CLIA - CRUISE LINES INTERNATIONAL ASSOCIATION--Association of cruise lines promoting professionalism and productivity in the selling of cruises. Travel agencies may join to receive training manuals and discounts on seminars.

CTO - CARIBBEAN TRAVEL ORGANIZATION --Organization supported by various Caribbean governments to promote travel and tourism to their area.

DOT - DEPARTMENT OF TRANSPORTATION--Responsible for consumer protection with regard to airline and other transportation operations. The CAB - Civil Aeronautics Board was dissolved after the Federal Act of Deregulation and the authority was transferred to the DOT.

FAA - FEDERAL AVIATION ADMINISTRATION--Government agency under the Department of Transportation that is responsible for airline and aircraft safety, airport operations, testing and licensing pilots.

FMC - FEDERAL MARITIME COMMISSION--An independent agency of the U.S. government in charge of foreign and domestic offshore commerce. It approves sailing rules, accepts or rejects tariffs, administers law for those suffering an injury or death through maritime operations, and investigates fishing law violations.

FTC - FEDERAL TRADE COMMISSION--Designed to protect the consumer by the regulation of commerce; establishes rules for trade operations.

IATAN - INTERNATIONAL AIRLINES TRAVEL AGENCY NETWORK--International airlines who set up rate structures and regulate procedures, avoiding unfair competition and unethical business practices. Known internationally as IATA - International Air Transport Association.

ICC - INTERSTATE COMMERCE COMMISSION--Approves operations providing travel between states of the U.S. and licenses these operations.

ICTA - INSTITUTE OF CERTIFIED TRAVEL AGENTS--Offers certification and several "designation" programs for individuals who complete applicable coursework and exam requirements.

ISMP - INTERNATIONAL SOCIETY OF MEETING PLANNERS--Organization that provides training and education plus networking opportunities for those involved in international meeting planning.

MPI - MEETING PROFESSIONALS INTERNATIONAL--Association offering networking opportunities and assistance in meeting planning and management.

NBTA - NATIONAL ASSOCIATION OF BUSINESS TRAVEL AGENTS--Association of business travel executives that maintains high levels of professionalism and communication between the buyers and suppliers through education, representation, and public relations.

NTA - NATIONAL TOUR ASSOCIATION--U.S. tour operators and wholesalers.

PATA - PACIFIC AREA TRAVEL ASSOCIATION--Promotes travel to the islands and countries of the Pacific region.

PCMA - PROFESSIONAL CONVENTION MANAGEMENT ASSOCIATION--Industry association for convention and meeting planners and suppliers.

TIAC - TOURISM INDUSTRY ASSOCIATION OF CANADA--A representative body for the travel industry in Canada.

TTRA - TRAVEL AND TOURISM RESEARCH ASSOCIATION--Provides study and research on travel and tourism details.

UFTAA - UNIVERSAL FEDERATION OF TRAVEL AGENTS ASSOCIATIONS--A world-wide organization representing all national travel agent associations.

USTOA - UNITED STATES TOUR OPERATORS ASSOCIATION--Association of tour operators that meet bonding and other requirements.

WATA - WORLD ASSOCIATION OF TRAVEL AGENTS--Brings representatives from travel agencies together in worldwide cooperation and growth.

WHO - WORLD HEALTH ORGANIZATION--Agency of the United Nations that reports on communicable diseases and advises governments on vaccination requirements.

WTO - WORLD TOURISM ORGANIZATION--Works with tourism agencies and strengthens international cooperation.

This is not an all-inclusive list or an endorsement of any organization.

The Travel Dictionary, available from Solitaire Publishing, lists travel industry associations with addresses and phone numbers. In addition, public libraries have resources such as the Gale Research Encyclopedia of Associations.

There may be local organizations not listed in the references of the library. Check with local travel agencies or other travel businesses for local associations offering membership opportunities. Also, many national organizations may have local chapters available.

MATCH THE FOLLOWING ACRONYMS WITH THEIR ASSOCIATIONS

_____ 1. FAA
_____ 2. ARC
_____ 3. IATAN
_____ 4. WTO
_____ 5. FMC
_____ 6. CLIA
_____ 7. ARTA
_____ 8. MPI
_____ 9. USTOA
_____10. NTA
_____11. ABA
_____12. TIAC
_____13. ISMP
_____14. ASTA
_____15. CHRIE
_____16. ICTA
_____17. ICC
_____18. DOT
_____19. AAA
_____20. PATA

A. AMERICAN AUTOMOBILE ASSOCIATION
B. FEDERAL MARITIME COMMISSION
C. INTERSTATE COMMERCE COMMISSION
D. INTERNATIONAL AIRLINES TRAVEL AGENCY NETWORK
E. INSTITUTE OF CERTIFIED TRAVEL AGENTS
F. AMERICAN SOCIETY OF TRAVEL AGENTS
G. ASSOCIATION OF RETAIL TRAVEL AGENTS
H. WORLD TOURISM ORGANIZATION
I. DEPARTMENT OF TRANSPORTATION
J. FEDERAL AVIATION ADMINISTRATION
K. MEETING PROFESSIONALS INTERNATIONAL
L. UNITED STATES TOUR OPERATORS ASSOCIATION
M. AIRLINES REPORTING CORPORATION
N. NATIONAL TOUR ASSOCIATION
O. AMERICAN BUS ASSOCIATION
P. INTERNATIONAL SOCIETY OF MEETING PLANNERS
Q. COUNCIL ON HOTEL, RESTAURANT, AND INSTITUTIONAL EDUCATION
R. CRUISE LINES INTERNATIONAL ASSOCIATION
S. PACIFIC AREA TRAVEL ASSOCIATION
T. TOURISM INDUSTRY ASSOCIATION OF CANADA

SOME REFERENCES AND RESOURCES

The Travel Training Series and The Travel Dictionary - by Claudine Dervaes
How to Get a Job with a Cruise Line - by Mary Fallon Miller
Home-Based Travel Agent - by Kelly Monaghan
The Official Outside Sales Travel Agent Manual - by Gary Fee and Alexander Anolik
Insiders Guide to Air Courier Bargains - by Kelly Monaghan
A Coach Full of Fun - by Jeanne Klender
The Travel Industry Personnel Directory - published by Fairchild Books
How to Open Your Own Travel Agency - by Douglas Thompson
Travel Agency Bookkeeping Made Simple - by Douglas Thompson and Mary Miller Marshall
A Personnel and Operations Manual for Travel Agencies - by Douglas Thompson and Alexander Anolik
Building Profits with Group Travel - by Carol Goldsmith and Ann Waigand
VIDEOS from Solitaire Publishing: Careers in Travel, Tour Leadership, Tour Welcome, Sales and Marketing Skills

CHAPTER 2

Basic World Geography

Highlights of this chapter include:

- ♦ *OCEANS, SEAS, GULFS, BAYS, AND RIVERS*
- ♦ *CONTINENTS, HEMISPHERES, LATITUDE AND LONGITUDE*
- ♦ *PRIME MERIDIAN, INTERNATIONAL DATE LINE, AND TIME ZONES*
- ♦ *FACTORS AFFECTING CLIMATE*
- ♦ *KINDS OF MAPS & GEOGRAPHIC TERMS*
- ♦ *THE 24 HOUR CLOCK*

NOTES

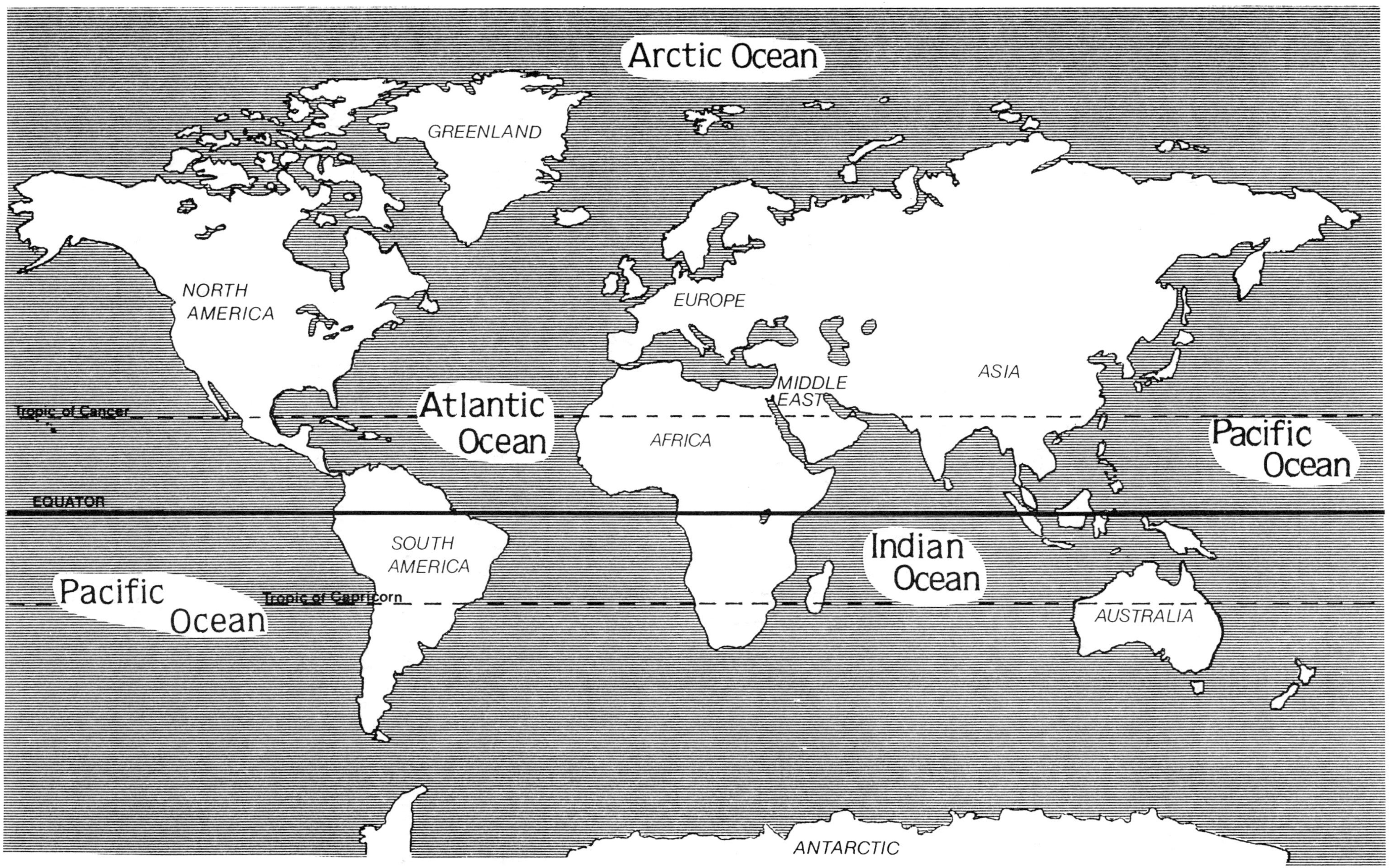

Outline Map of the World

BASIC WORLD GEOGRAPHY

One of the most important attributes of a travel industry employee is having a good working knowledge of geography. Don't concern yourself with how little geography you know right now, but resolve to learn and retain the coursework that will be presented in this manual. Practice is a most viable tool, so make a point of applying yourself to constant review on your own.

To begin with a basic understanding of the earth, you should know that the earth is one of nine planets revolving around the sun and they are (in order from the sun): Mercury, Venus, Earth, Mars, Jupiter, Saturn, Uranus, Neptune and Pluto. Earth is the fifth largest planet in the solar system with a diameter of about 8,000 miles. The circumference (distance around the surface) is about 25,000 miles. About 70% of the earth's surface is water and the oceans, from largest to smallest, are:

PACIFIC OCEAN

ATLANTIC OCEAN

INDIAN OCEAN

ARCTIC OCEAN

Some geographers also recognize the body of water around Antarctica as the Antarctic Ocean. However, as the area comprises the southern reaches of the Pacific, Atlantic, and Indian Oceans we will not consider it a separate ocean.

The heating and cooling of oceans are major influences on climate and weather patterns. Ocean currents generally revolve clockwise in the northern hemisphere and counter-clockwise in the southern hemisphere. More on ocean currents will be presented later.

In addition to the oceans, there are the many seas, bays, gulfs and rivers. The Mediterranean and the Caribbean are probably the two most popular for tourism. Other seas include: Baltic, North, Irish, Coral, Red, Weddell, Timor, Barents, Bering, Arabian, Black, East China, South China, Adriatic, Caspian, Tasman, Aegean, Ionian, Tyrrhenian, Beaufort, Ligurian, Philippine, and the Dead Sea.

Gulfs and bays are described as parts of an ocean or sea extending in-land. There is the Gulf of Mexico, the Gulf of Oman, the Persian Gulf, and the Gulf of Alaska - to name a few. There is Hudson Bay, Baffin Bay, and the Bay of Bengal.

The major rivers of the world include: Nile, Amazon, Mississippi, Volga, Yellow, Niger, Yukon, and Rio Grande.

CONTINENTS, HEMISPHERES, LATITUDE AND LONGITUDE

In the U.S., the continents are classified as the following seven:

NORTH AMERICA

SOUTH AMERICA

EUROPE

AFRICA

ASIA

AUSTRALIA

ANTARCTICA

In other countries, North and South America may be grouped as "America." Also, as Europe and Asia are basically connected, some people may refer to the area as Eurasia. In general geographic terms, the two halves of the earth divided by the equator (0 degrees latitude) are the Northern and Southern Hemisphere. The seasons are reversed on opposite sides of the equator (when it's summer in the U.S., it is winter in Australia). The two halves of the earth divided by the prime meridian (0 degrees longitude) are the Western Hemisphere (North and South America) and the Eastern Hemisphere (most of Europe, Africa, Asia and Australia). Imaginary lines circling the globe in a north/south or east/west direction divide the surface into zones and help determine exact locations.

Lines of **latitude:** circle the globe in an east/west direction and are measured in degrees north or south of the equator

Lines of **longitude:** circle the globe in a north/south direction and are measured in degrees east or west of the prime meridian

The lines of longitude and latitude are measured in degrees, and are subdivided into minutes, and into seconds. Therefore, an exact location might be designated as 28 12'10" N. and 83 48'38" W (the apostrophe stands for minutes and the quotes signify seconds).

EXERCISE:
Use an atlas and determine the latitude and longitude of your city. Give the degrees with their measurement (latitude lines go east/west but are measured as north or south; longitude lines go north/south but are measured east or west).

THE PRIME MERIDIAN, INTERNATIONAL DATE LINE, TIME ZONES

The prime meridian - 0 degrees longitude, is also called GMT (Greenwich Mean Time). The meridian on the opposite side of the globe - 180 degrees longitude - is called the IDL (International Date Line). The globe is divided into 24 theoretical time zones, each zone being the area that passes under the sun in one hour. Time zones are related to the prime meridian - stated as a time zone either east or west of GMT. However, since the actual "world clock" is no longer coordinated from Greenwich, England you may see the code UTC (Universal or Uniform Time Coordinated) eventually replace GMT. Military and other personnel may refer to the GMT as Z-time or Zulu time.

One of the best tools for determining relative time is the International Standard Time Chart, and thinking of the time zones as points on a line may help you in understanding the number of hours difference between places on the globe. The + (plus) zones are east/later zones and the - (minus) zones are west/earlier zones. During U.S. standard time, the points of -5, -6, -7, and -8 correspond to the time zones Eastern, Central, Mountain, and Pacific respectively. Comparing Miami, FL (Eastern time zone, -5) to Denver, CO (Mountain time zone, -7), there would be two hours difference and local time in Miami is two hours later than Denver. Comparing London, U.K. (0 time zone) to Los Angeles, CA (-8), it is eight hours earlier in Los Angeles.

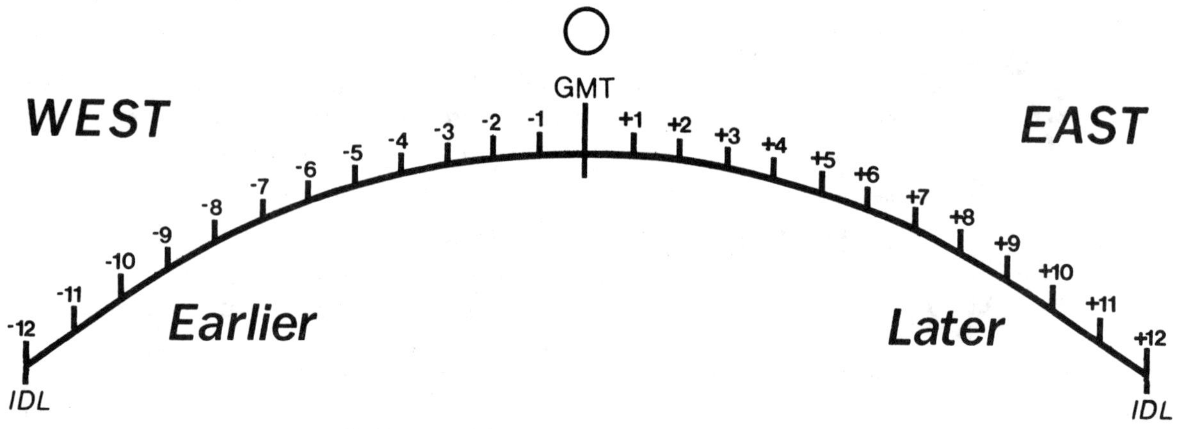

For reference, use the U.S. map of time zones on the next page, which is followed by a listing of countries, time zones, and if applicable, the approximate dates for daylight savings time.

TIME ZONES OF THE WORLD

Here are some of the time zones for many countries of the world. If you wish to know what time it is in a country, first find out your area's time zone. Then look up the time zone of the other country or area. Add the hours difference if the destination is in a later time zone, subtract the difference if the destination is in an earlier time zone.

For example, it's 1:00 p.m. in New York City and you want to know what time it is in Zurich, Switzerland. First, look up the time zone of New York (U.S. - Eastern), which would be -5 during standard time. Then look up Switzerland, which is +1 during standard time. The difference is 6 hours, and Switzerland is in a later time zone. When it's 1:00 p.m. in New York, it would be 7:00 p.m. in Switzerland.

	Standard time	Daylight savings	effective period for daylight savings time*
Afghanistan	+4 1/2		
Albania	+1	+2	Mar. (last) - Oct. (last)
Algeria	+1		
American Samoa	-11		
Andorra	+1	+2	Mar. (last) - Oct. (last)
Angola	+1		
Anguilla	-4		
Antigua(see Leeward Is.)			
Argentina	-3		
Armenia	+3		
Aruba	-4		
Australia-			
Lord Howe Is.	+10 1/2	+11	Oct. (last) - Mar. (last)
New South Wales	+10	+11	Oct. (last) - Mar. (last)
Northern Terr.	+9 1/2		
Queensland	+10		
South Australia	+9 1/2	+10 1/2	Oct. (last) - Mar. (last)
Tasmania	+10	+11	Oct. (last) - Mar. (last)
W. Australia	+8		
Victoria, Cap.Territory	+10	+11	Oct. (last) - Mar. (last)
Austria	+1	+2	Mar. (last) - Oct. (last)
Azerbaijan	+4		
Bahamas	-5	-4	Apr. (first) - Oct. (last)
Bahrain	+3		
Bangladesh	+6		
Barbados	-4		
Belarus	+2	+3	Mar. (last) - Oct. (last)
Belgium	+1	+2	Mar. (last) - Oct. (last)
Belize	-6		
Benin	+1		
Bermuda	-4	-3	Apr. (first) - Oct. (last)
Bhutan	+6		
Bolivia	-4		
Bosnia Herzegovina	+1	+2	Mar. (last) - Oct. (last)
Botswana	+2		
Brazil-East#	-3	-2	Oct. (second) - Feb. (second)
West	-4	-3	Oct. (second) - Feb. (second)
Territory-Acre	-5		
Fernando De Noronha	-2		
Br. Virgin Is.	-4		
Brunei	+8		
Bulgaria	+2	+3	Mar. (last) - Oct. (last)
Burkina Faso	GMT(0)		
Burma(see Myanmar)			
Burundi	+2		
Cambodia	+7		
Cameroon	+1		
Canada -			
Newfoundland	-3 1/2	-2 1/2	Apr. (first) - Oct. (last)
Atlantic area	-4	-3	Apr. (first) - Oct. (last)
Eastern area	-5	-4	Apr. (first) - Oct. (last)
Central area	-6	-5	Apr. (first) - Oct. (last)
Mountain area	-7	-6	Apr. (first) - Oct. (last)
Pacific area	-8	-7	Apr. (first) - Oct. (last)
Yukon terr.	-8	-7	Apr. (first) - Oct. (last)
Cape Verde Is.	-1		
Cayman Is.	-5		
Cntrl.African Rep.	+1		
Chad	+1		
Chile(continental)	-4	-3	Oct. (second) - Mar. (second)
Easter Is.	-6	-5	Oct. (second) - Mar. (second)
China	+8		

*Parentheses indicate the week in which change normally occurs.

	Standard time	Daylight savings	effective period for daylight savings time*
C.I.S. (Commonwealth of Independent States) - see individual states - such as Russia, Azerbaijan, Armenia, Belarus, etc.			
Cocos Is.	+6 1/2		
Colombia	-5		
Comoros	+3		
Congo	+1		
Cook Is.	-10		
Costa Rica	-6		
Cote d'Ivoire	GMT(0)		
Croatia	+1	+2	Mar. (last) - Oct. (last)
Cuba	-5	-4	Apr. (first) - Oct. (first)
Cyprus	+2	+3	Mar. (last) - Oct. (last)
Czech Republic	+1	+2	Mar. (last) - Oct. (last)
Denmark	+1	+2	Mar. (last) - Oct. (last)
Djibouti	+3		
Dom. Republic	-4		
Ecuador(continen.)	-5		
Galapagos Is.	-6		
Egypt	+2	+3	Apr. (last) - Sep. (last)
El Salvador	-6		
Eq. Guinea	+1		
Eritrea	+3		
Estonia	+2	+3	Mar. (last) - Oct. (last)
Ethiopia	+3		
Falkland Is.	-4	-3	Sep. (second) - Apr. (third)
Faroe Is.	GMT(0)	+1	Mar. (last) - Oct. (last)
Fiji	+12		
Finland	+2	+3	Mar. (last) - Oct. (last)
France	+1	+2	Mar. (last) - Oct. (last)
French Guiana	-3		
French Polynesia			
Gambier Is.	-9		
Marquesas Is.	-9 1/2		
Society Is., Tahiti	-10		
Gabon	+1		
Gambia	GMT(0)		
Georgia	+4	+5	Mar. (last) - Oct. (last)
Germany	+1	+2	Mar. (last) - Oct. (last)
Ghana	GMT(0)		
Gibraltar	+1	+2	Mar. (last) - Oct. (last)
Greece	+2	+3	Mar. (last) - Oct. (last)
Greenland			
West coast	-3	-2	Mar. (last) - Oct. (last)
East Greenland	GMT(0)		
Scoresby Sound	-1	GMT(0)	Mar. (last) - Oct. (last)
Thule	-4	-3	Apr. (first) - Oct. (last)
Grenada, St. Lucia	-4		
Guadeloupe	-4		
Guam	+10		
Guatemala	-6		
Guinea	GMT(0)		
Guinea-Bissau	GMT(0)		
Guyana	-4		
Haiti	-5	-4	Apr. (first) - Oct. (last)
Honduras	-6		
Hong Kong	+8		
Hungary	+1	+2	Mar. (last) - Oct. (last)
Iceland	GMT(0)		
India	+5 1/2		
Indonesia			
Central	+8		
East	+9		
West(Jakarta)	+7		
Iran	+3 1/2	+4 1/2	Mar. (third) - Sep. (third)

*Parentheses indicate the week in which change normally occurs.

	Standard time	Daylight savings	effective period for daylight savings time*
Iraq	+3	+4	Apr. (first) - Sep. (last)
Ireland, Rep. of	GMT(0)	+1	Mar. (last) - Oct. (last)
Israel	+2	+3	Mar. (last) - Aug. (last)
Italy	+1	+2	Mar. (last) - Oct. (last)
Jamaica	-5		
Japan	+9		
Jordan	+2	+3	Apr. (first) - Sep. (third)
Kazakhstan	+6	+7	Mar. (last) - Oct. (last)
Kenya	+3		
Kiribati, Rep. of	+12		
Canton,Enderbury	-11		
Christmas Is.	-10		
Korea, Dem. Rep.	+9		
Korea, Rep. of	+9		
Kuwait	+3		
Kyrgyzstan	+5	+6	Apr. (second) - Sep. (last)
Laos	+7		
Latvia	+2	+3	Mar. (last) - Oct. (last)
Lebanon	+2	+3	Mar. (last) - Oct. (last)
Leeward Is. (Antigua, Dominica Montserrat, Nevis, St. Kitts, Anguilla)	-4		
Lesotho	+2		
Liberia	GMT(0)		
Libya	+1	+2	Mar. (last) - Sep. (last)
Liechtenstein	+1	+2	Mar. (last) - Oct. (last)
Lithuania	+2	+3	Mar. (last) - Oct. (last)
Luxembourg	+1	+2	Mar. (last) - Oct. (last)
Macedonia	+1	+2	Mar. (last) - Oct. (last)
Madagascar	+3		
Malawi	+2		
Malaysia	+8		
Maldives	+5		
Mali	GMT(0)		
Malta	+1	+2	Mar. (last) - Oct. (last)
Martinique	-4		
Mauritania	GMT(0)		
Mauritius	+4		
Mexico			
Southern Baja & N. Pacific coast	-7		
Northern Baja	-8	-7	Apr. (first) - Oct. (last)
General Mexico	-6		
Midway Is.	-11		
Moldova	+2	+3	Mar. (last) - Oct. (last)
Monaco	+1	+2	Mar. (last) - Oct. (last)
Mongolia	+8	+9	Mar. (last) - Oct. (last)
Morocco	GMT(0)		
Mozambique	+2		
Myanmar	+6 1/2		
Namibia	+1	+2	Sep. (first) - Mar. (last)
Nauru, Rep. of	+12		
Nepal	+5 3/4		
Netherlands	+1	+2	Mar. (last) - Oct. (last)
Neth. Antilles	-4		
New Caledonia	+11		
New Zealand (except Chatham Is.)	+12	+13	Oct. (first) - Mar. (third)
Chatham Is.	+12 3/4	+13 3/4	Oct. (first) - Mar. (third)
Nicaragua	-6		
Niger	+1		
Nigeria	+1		
Niue Is.	-11		
Norfolk Is.	+11 1/2		
Norway	+1	+2	Mar. (last) - Oct. (last)
Oman	+4		
Pacific Trust Territory -			
Caroline Is.	+11		
Marshall Is.	+12		
Kwajalein	-12		
Mariana Is.	+10		
Belau Is.	+9		
Ponape(Pohnpei)	+11		
Pakistan	+5		
Panama	-5		
Papua New Guinea	+10		
Paraguay	-4	-3	Oct. (first) - Feb. (last)
Peru	-5		
Philippines	+8		
Poland	+1	+2	Mar. (last) - Oct. (last)
Portugal -			
Azores	-1	GMT	Mar. (last) - Oct. (last)
Madeira Is.	GMT	+1	Mar. (last) - Oct. (last)
the mainland	+1	+2	Mar. (last) - Oct. (last)
Puerto Rico	-4		
Qatar	+3		
Reunion	+4		

*Parentheses indicate the week in which change normally occurs.

	Standard time	Daylight savings	effective period for daylight savings time*
Romania	+2	+3	Mar. (last) - Oct. (last)
Russia (major cities)			
Moscow,St. Petersburg, Murmarsk	+3	+4	Mar. (last) - Oct. (last)
Samara,Izhevsk	+4	+5	Mar. (last) - Oct. (last)
Chelyabinsk,Perm, Nizhnevartovsk	+5	+6	Mar. (last) - Oct. (last)
Omsk	+6	+7	Mar. (last) - Oct. (last)
Novosibirsk,Krasnojarsk, Norilsk	+7	+8	Mar. (last) - Oct. (last)
Irkutsk,Ulan-ude, Bratsk	+8	+9	Mar. (last) - Oct. (last)
Chita,Yakatsk	+9	+10	Mar. (last) - Oct. (last)
Khabarovsk	+10	+11	Mar. (last) - Oct. (last)
Magadan	+11	+12	Mar. (last) - Oct. (last)
Petropavlovsk	+12	+13	Mar. (last) - Oct. (last)
Rwanda	+2		
St. Pierre & Miquelon	-3	-2	Apr. (first) - Oct. (last)
St. Vincent & the Grenadines	-4		
Samoa(western)	-11		
San Marino	+1	+2	Mar. (last) - Oct. (last)
Sao Tome & Principe Is.	GMT		
Saudi Arabia	+3		
Senegal	GMT		
Seychelles	+4		
Sierre Leone	GMT		
Singapore	+8		
Slovak Rep.	+1	+2	Mar. (last) - Oct.(last)
Slovenia	+1	+2	Mar. (last) - Oct.(last)
Solomon Is.	+11		
Somalia	+3		
South Africa	+2		
Spain -			
Canary Is.	GMT	+1	Mar. (last) - Oct. (last)
Continental, Balearic Is.,	+1	+2	Mar. (last) - Oct. (last)
Sri Lanka	+5 1/2		
Sudan	+2		
Suriname	-3		
Swaziland	+2		
Sweden	+1	+2	Mar. (last) - Oct. (last)
Switzerland	+1	+2	Mar. (last) - Oct. (last)
Syria	+2	+3	Apr. (first) - Sep. (last)
Taiwan	+8		
Tajikistan	+5		
Tanzania	+3		
Thailand	+7		
Togo	GMT		
Tonga	+13		
Trinidad & Tobago	-4		
Tunisia	+1		
Turkey	+2	+3	Mar. (last) - Oct. (last)
Turkmenistan	+5		
Turks & Caicos Is.	-5	-4	Apr. (first) - Oct. (last)
Tuvalu	+12		
Uganda	+3		
Ukraine	+2	+3	Mar. (last) - Oct. (last)
United Arab Emirates	+4		
United Kingdom	GMT	+1	Mar. (last) - Oct. (last)
U.S.A. -			
Eastern#	-5	-4	Apr. (first) - Oct. (last)
Central	-6	-5	Apr. (first) - Oct. (last)
Mountain#	-7	-6	Apr. (first) - Oct. (last)
Pacific	-8	-7	Apr. (first) - Oct. (last)
#Arizona and parts of Indiana don't observe Daylight Savings Time			
Alaska	-9	-8	Apr. (first) - Oct. (last)
Aleutian Is.	-10	-9	Apr. (first) - Oct. (last)
Hawaii	-10		
U.S. Virgin Is.	-4		
Uruguay	-3		
Uzbekistan	+5		
Vanuatu	+11		
Venezuela	-4		
Vietnam	+7		
Wake Is.	+12		
Wallis and Futuna	+12		
Yemen	+3		
Yugoslavia	+1	+2	Mar. (last) - Oct. (last)
Zaire -			
Kinshasa Mbandaka	+1		
Kasai, Kivu, Shaba and Haut-Zaire	+2		
Zambia	+2		
Zimbabwe	+2		

*Parentheses indicate the week in which change normally occurs.

TIME ZONES EXERCISE

Using the time zones list, work the following problems. For every answer provide the date and the time.

1. When it's 10:00 am, June 1, in Denver, CO, it is ________________ in Rome, Italy.
2. If it is 2:00 pm on January 15 in Frankfurt, Germany, what time is it in Hong Kong?________________
3. What time is it in Athens, Greece when it is 3:00 pm on August 3 in Los Angeles, CA?________________
4. At 12:00 noon, July 5 in Anchorage, AK, it would be ______________ in Glasgow, Scotland (U.K.).
5. When it is 4:30 pm, Feb. 4 in Lisbon, Portugal, it would be _______ ___________in Atlanta, GA.
6. If it is 12:30 am on September 10 in Sydney, Australia, what time is it in Nassau, Bahamas?__________________
7. At 3:30 pm in Moscow, U.S.S.R. on May 1, it would be _____________ ______________in Santiago, Chile.
8. On October 29 at 9:00 am in Paris, France it would be ____________ ______________in Istanbul, Turkey.
9. When it is 2:15 pm, March 28 in Bombay, India, it is _____________ ______________in Wellington, New Zealand.
10. If it is 7:30 pm on April 30 in Mexico City, Mexico, what time is it in Cape Town, South Africa?______________________

WORLD FACTS AND TRIVIA

OCEANS

The largest ocean by surface area is the Pacific Ocean. It has a maximum depth of 36,200 feet. Next largest is the Atlantic, with a maximum depth of 30,246 feet. The Indian Ocean has a maximum depth of 24,442 feet.

10 HIGHEST WATERFALLS OF THE WORLD

WATERFALL	LOCATION	HEIGHT feet	HEIGHT meters
Angel	Venezuela	3,281	1,000
Tugela	Natal, S.Africa	3,000	914
Cuquenan	Venezuela	2,000	610
Sutnerland	South Is., New Zealand	1,904	580
Takkakaw	British Columbia	1,650	503
Ribbon (Yosemite)	California	1,612	491
Upper (Yosemite)	California	1,430	436
Gavarnie	Southwest France	1,384	422
Vettisfoss	Norway	1,200	366
Widow's Tears (Yosemite)	California	1,170	357

OTHER NOTABLE WATERFALLS

WATERFALL	LOCATION	HEIGHT feet	HEIGHT meters
Kaieteur	Guyana	822	251
Bridal Veil (Yosemite)	California	620	189
Victoria	Zimbabwe-Zambia border	355	108

Notes: Iguassu Falls on the border of Brazil, Paraguay, and Argentina features 275 falls that drop from 120 to 240 feet. Niagara Falls on the New York-Ontario border has tremendous volume but only drops a height of between 158 and 167 feet.

LARGEST ISLANDS

	AREA sq.mi.	AREA sq.km.
Greenland	840,000	2,175,600
New Guinea	306,000	792,540
Borneo	280,100	725,459
Madagascar	226,658	587,044
Baffin	195,928	507,454
Sumatra	165,000	427,350
Honshu	87,805	227,415
Great Britain	84,200	218,078
Victoria	83,896	217,291
Ellesmere	75,767	196,237
Celebes	69,000	178,710
South Is. (NZ)	58,305	151,010
Java	48,900	126,651
Cuba	44,218	114,525
North Is. (NZ)	44,035	114,051
Newfoundland	42,030	108,858

DESERTS OF THE WORLD

The largest desert is the Sahara, with an area greater than the contiguous United States. The driest place on earth is in the Atacama Desert of Chile - no rainfall was recorded between 1570 and 1971. The highest temperature ever recorded was 136 degrees Farenheit (58 degress Centigrade) - in the Libyan Desert at Al-Aziziya.

FACTORS AFFECTING CLIMATE

The major ocean currents are important factors affecting climate. The **GULF STREAM**, for example, is a major ocean current that carries the warmer waters of the Atlantic Ocean (originating in the Caribbean) and helps moderate temperatures as far away as Great Britain and Norway. The **HUMBOLDT CURRENT**, flowing northward along the coast of Chile and Peru, produces cooler temperatures and causes a lot of cloud and fog. Additional factors that help determine the relative water temperature are the season of the year and the latitude of the destination. Generally the ocean water on the east side of the continents is warmer than on the west side. A map showing ocean currents is provided below:

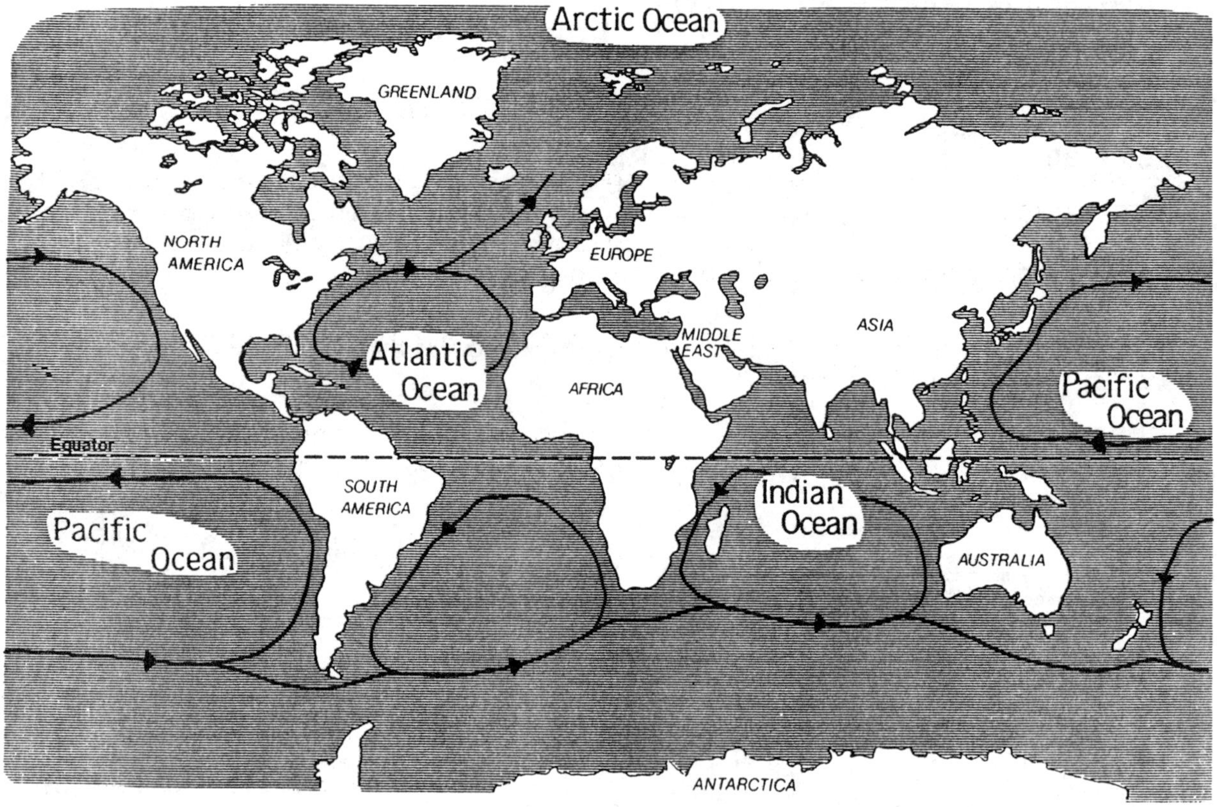

WINDS are another feature affecting climate and weather. The winds that tend to blow around the earth from west to east, generally in the temperate zone (between 30 and 60 degrees latitude, north and south of the equator) are called the **WESTERLIES**. The high altitude, high velocity center of these westerlies accounts for the **JET STREAM**, which makes flights from east to west longer. The **TRADE WINDS** are humid breezes that tend to blow from east to west. North of the equator the trade winds tend to come from the **northeast** and south of the equator they tend to come from the **southeast**. The trade winds are mostly prominent in the band between 25 degrees north and 25 degrees south of the equator. However, the east to west trade wind pattern is NOT the norm through much of Africa and parts of Asia.

HURRICANES are violent storms (called typhoons in the Pacific). The hurricane season is from June to November. Monsoons are lengthy, rainy seasons that happen in certain parts of the world during the summer. For example, India's monsoon season is from June to September and China's is from May to September.

MOUNTAINS are an important factor to climate. The world's major mountain chains include: the Appalachians and Rockies in the U.S., the Alps in Europe, the Andes in South America, and the Himalayas in Asia. The altitude in mountainous areas will lower temperatures and prevent weather patterns from crossing.

The **windward*** side of mountains is usually more lush and green as it receives more rainfall. The **leeward*** side tends to be dry, as less moisture is likely to make it over the top of the mountains. However, wind patterns can influence the terrain and climate. The forces of wind, rain, water, ice, and human activity continue to erode the earth's landscape.

*windward is towards the wind and leeward is the direction away from the wind

WEATHER VS. CLIMATE

The **weather** is what is happening in the atmosphere at a given time - the temperature, precipitation, humidity, wind, barometric pressure, and cloudiness conditions. The **climate** is the typical weather pattern or what to expect at a specific location.

Polar and mountainous regions of perpetual <u>ice and snow</u> cover one-tenth of the earth's land areas.

A place of mosses, lichens, and stunted trees and plants describes a <u>tundra</u> area. Beneath the surface the ground remains frozen.

As favorable climates produce an abundance of vegetation, the <u>mid-latitude forest</u> regions of the world serve as home for a majority of the world's people.

The <u>tropical forest</u> areas are known for their wide variety of insects, birds, and small animals. They range from the luxuriant vegetation of rain forests to scrub-like woodlands in drier areas.

The <u>savanna or tropical grassland</u> is an area with tall grass and very few trees. It is a place of winter droughts and summer rainfall.

The <u>mid-latitude grasslands</u> are where the sheep and cattle ranches proliferate and where land has been successfully cultivated for grain fields.

The <u>deserts</u> of the world are inhabited mainly by livestock-herding nomads and wildlife capable of surviving in such moisture-deficient areas.

Generally climates get colder as you travel north from the Tropic of Cancer and south from the Tropic of Capricorn. However, the altitude has a further cooling effect on climates - as snow may appear on the mountains in areas where the valleys may have none.

The **ADIABATIC RATE** is a general rule that for every 1,000 feet of altitude the temperature will be 3.5 degrees Farenheit cooler.

THE EQUINOXES, SOLSTICES, AND CLIMATIC ZONES

The relative positions of the sun and the earth thoroughout the year determine the seasons. On approximately March 21 and September 23 the sun is directly overhead at midday on the equator, called the vernal and autumnal equinox, respectively. On these equinox dates virtually all points on the earth have 12 hours of sunlight and 12 of darkness. And on approximately June 21 and December 21 the sun is at its most northerly or southerly position. Called the summer and winter solstice these dates correspond to the longest and shortest days of the year, respectively. Of course, the seasons are reversed in the Southern Hemisphere.

The five basic climatic zones are shown on the globe below:

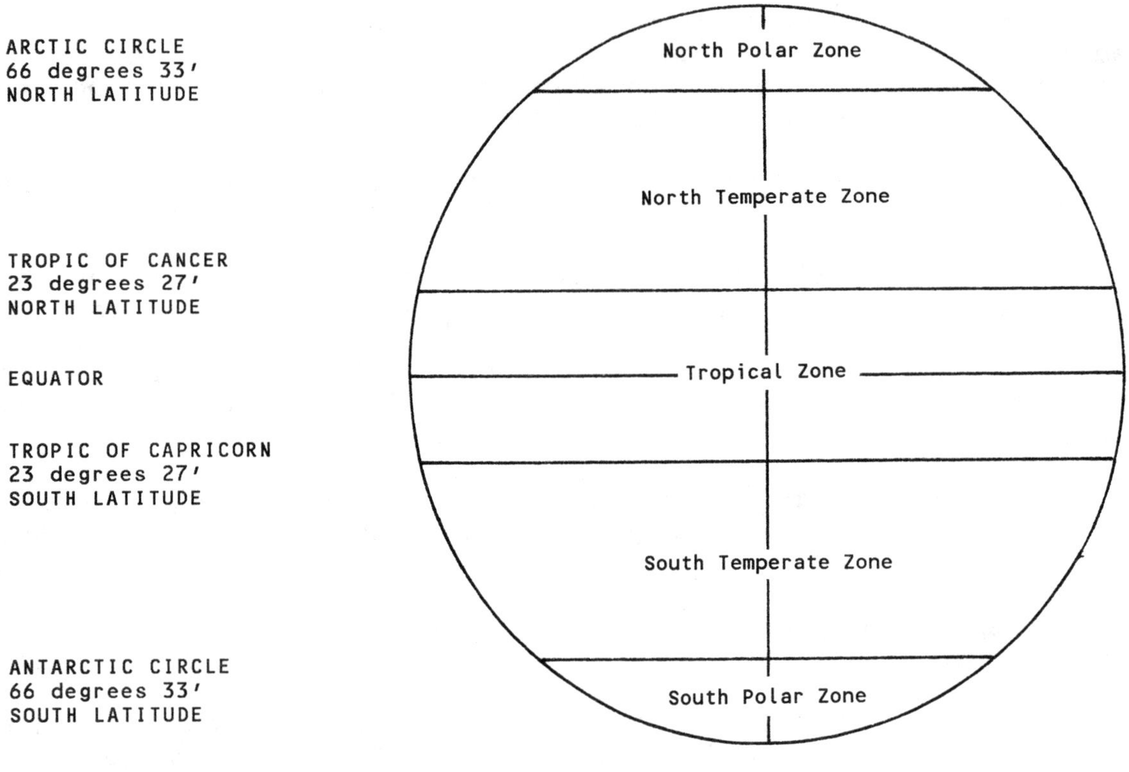

So far we have talked about oceans, rivers, continents, latitudes and longitudes, time zones, and the factors affecting climate (ocean currents, winds, mountains, altitudes, etc.).

A variety of maps are necessary to understand more about the specifics of climates, topography and other destination particulars.

Maps differ by the type of projection (the system by which the curved lines of longitude and latitude are translated onto a flat surface), by the scale (the relationship between distances on the map and the corresponding distance on earth - such as "one inch = 1000 miles"), and by the type or reference involved (historical, topographical/ physical, political).

KINDS OF MAPS

A few types of projections:

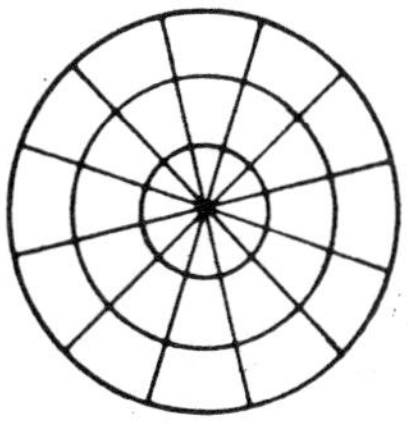

AZIMUTHAL - in this group of projections, a part of the globe is projected from an eyepoint onto a plane. When centered on the North or South Pole, these maps are sometimes called "polar projections."

Note: There are several types of azimuthal projections.

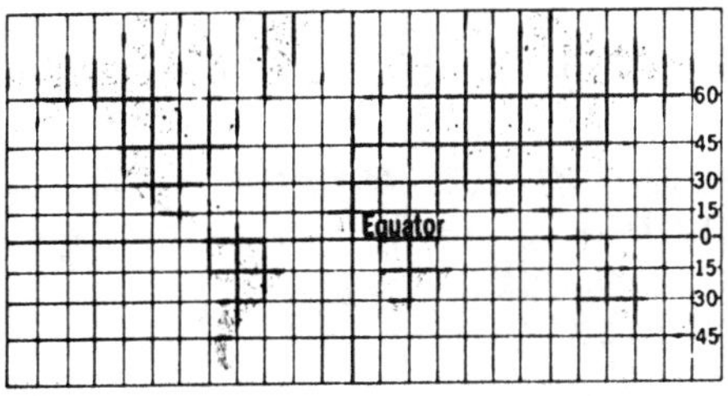

MERCATOR - all the meridians and parallels are shown as straight lines at right angles to one another.

GOODE'S INTERRUPTED PROJECTIONS - popular for world maps, it makes an equal-area map with little distortion of shape.

These are just a few types of map projections. Only on a globe can the meridians and the parallels be true, as the scale on a flat map cannot be true everywhere. In addition to the projection, the scale of the map must be considered to understand true distances and sizes. And there are certain TYPES OF MAPS:

POLITICAL - Concentrate on the boundaries of countries, states, etc., with very little (if any) details on surface features such as mountains, swamps, etc.

THEMATIC - Feature a theme such as languages, vegetations, population, climates, religions, etc. Usually color-coded.

PHYSICAL OR TOPOGRAPHICAL - Show mountains, lakes, swamps, rivers, and other surface features.

HISTORICAL - Political in nature but specifying empires, boundaries, and events in history.

SOME GEOGRAPHIC TERMINOLOGY

Altitude - The height of an object or elevation above a given level.

Antipodes - Two places on the earth's surface that are diametrically opposite one another (such as the North Pole and the South Pole).

Archipelago - A group of islands.

Atoll - An island made of a ring or strip of coral.

Axis - The line around which a thing rotates (the earth's axis runs through the poles).

Azimuth - A great circle direction, or the angle measured clockwise between a meridian and an intersecting great circle.

Basin - A portion of land lower than its surrounding areas; also an area drained by a river and its tributaries.

Bayou - A marshy creek or sluggish river tributary.

Butte - A conspicuous, isolated hill or mountain, usually with steep sides and a flat top.

Canal - An artificial watercourse for inland navigation/irrigation.

Canyon - A deep, narrow valley with steep sides.

Cape - A point of land projecting out into a body of water.

Cartography - Map making.

Continental Drift - The slow movement of the continents to their present position.

Continental Shelf - The submerged edge of a continent.

Contour Map - A map showing topographical features by the relative spacing of lines known as contour lines.

Cyclone - A circular storm revolving around a calm center. See also typhoon, tornado, and hurricane.

Delta - A land area formed by the sediment of a river.

Doldrums - A region of calms, sudden storms, and variable winds near the equator.

Estuary - The wide mouth of a river where the tide meets the currents.

Firth - See estuary.

Fjord - A narrow sea inlet usually bordered by steep cliffs.

Geyser - A natural fountain of hot water and steam, characterized by periodic bursts or eruptions.

Glacier - A field or body of ice formed in a region where snowfall exceeds melting.

Gorge - A particularly deep and narrow canyon.

Great Circle - The line of intersection of the surface of a sphere and any plane which passes through the sphere.

Horse Latitudes - Belt of calms at the northern edge of the north-east trade winds.

Hurricane - A tropical storm with winds greater than 75 miles per hour, usually accompanied by rain, thunder, and lightning.

Isobar - A line drawn on a map connecting places where the barometric pressure is the same.

Isthmus - A narrow strip of land between two larger land masses.

Meridians - The lines of longitude on the earth's surface.

Mesa - A high, steep-sided, rock plateau.

Parallels - The lines of latitude on the earth's surface.

Plateau - A broad, flat area of land, somewhat elevated.

Roaring Forties - Either of two ocean areas between 40 and 50 degrees latitude north and south where strong winds prevail.

Savanna - Grassy portion of land with few trees.

Small Circle - Any circle on a sphere smaller than a great circle (all parallels on the earth except the equator).

Steppe - A vast, treeless plain found in Southeast Europe or Asia.

Strait - Narrow body of water connecting two larger bodies of water.

Topography - The physical features of a place - such as mountains, lakes, glaciers, etc.

Tornado - A violent squall or whirlwind, a funnel cloud, causing severe damage in some cases.

Torrid Zone - The area between the Tropic of Cancer and the Tropic of Capricorn.

Tundra - Plains area having the ground frozen beneath the surface even in summer.

Typhoon - A hurricane occurring in the Pacific, usually during the summer and fall.

REVIEW ON TERMINOLOGY

Using the information in the chapter and the terminology list, define the following:

1. savanna ______________________________
2. typhoon ______________________________
____
3. vernal equinox ______________________________
____
4. adiabatic rate ______________________________
____
5. windward side ______________________________
6. mesa ______________________________
7. Gulf Stream ______________________________
____
8. political map ______________________________
____
9. isobar ______________________________
____
10. torrid zone ______________________________
____
11. atoll______________________________
12. delta______________________________
13. archipelago______________________________
14. bayou______________________________
15. isthmus______________________________

USING THE OUTLINE MAP BELOW AND AN ATLAS IF NECESSARY, ANSWER THE QUESTIONS THAT FOLLOW:

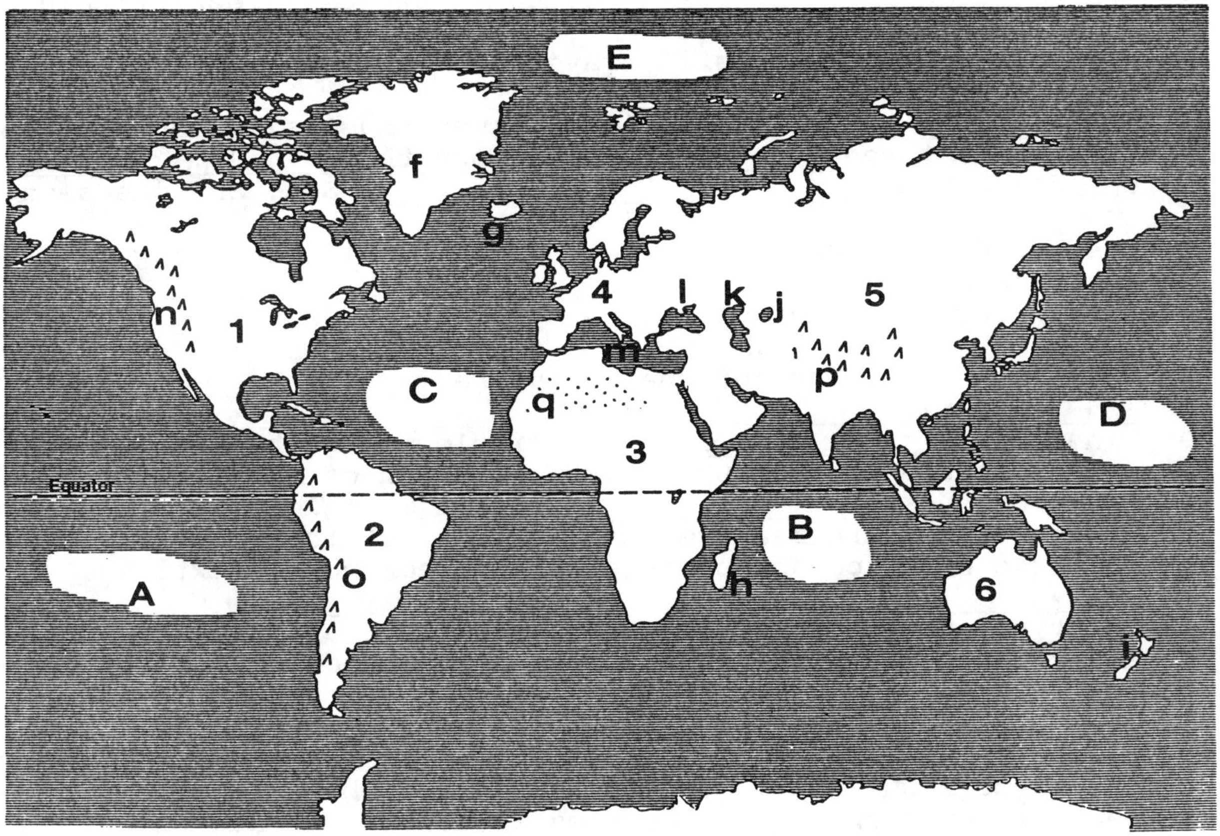

1. Identify continent #2____________________, #4__________________, #5__________________,#1___________________, #3____________, and #6____________________.
2. Identify ocean A____________, B______________, C___________, D______________, and E__________________.
3. Identify islands/countries labeled f_________________________, g_______________________, h______________________________, and i____________________________.
4. Identify the seas marked j________________, k________________, l____________________, and m____________________________.
5. Identify the mountain ranges marked n____________________, o_______________________, and p__________________________.
6. The desert marked q is the ______________________.
7. The equator passes through the South American countries of ______ ______________, ______________________and _________________.

BASIC WORLD GEOGRAPHY REVIEW

NOTE: AN ATLAS MAY BE NECESSARY ANSWERING SOME OF THE QUESTIONS.

1. The ________________ is the largest ocean.
2. The ________________ Sea is situated between Great Britain and Jutland of Denmark.
3. What bay does one cross if traveling from India to Myanmar by ship? ______________________________
4. The ________________ Sea lies between Australia and New Zealand.
5. Turkey has three coastlines, one along the ________________ Sea, one along the __________________________ Sea, and one along the ________________________ Sea.
6. One would cross the ________________ Sea if traveling from Wales to Ireland.
7. Baffin Bay is situated between northern Canada and ____________ ________________.
8. The seven continents of the world are ____________________ ____.
9. Lines of ____________________ circle the globe in an east/west direction and are measured north or south of the equator.
10. Lines of ____________________ circle the globe in a north/south direction and are measured east or west of the prime meridian.
11. What two major ocean currents were named in the text? ____
12. The type of map projection that shows the meridians and parallels as straight lines at right angles to one another is called the __________________________________ projection.
13. The jet stream makes flights from east to west shorter. True or False ______________
14. The trade winds are most prominent in the band between ______ degrees north and ______ degrees south of the equator.
15. Polar and mountainous regions of perpetual ice and snow cover one-fifth of the earth's land areas. True or False ____________
16. The adiabatic rule states that for every ___________ feet of altitude, the temperature will be _______ degrees Farenheit cooler.
17. The leeward side of a mountain tends to be more ______(wet/dry).
18. Define "tundra." ____ ____
19. Hurricanes are called ____________ in the Pacific and hurricane season is from ____________________ to ____________________.
20. Name five conditions that indicate the weather. ______________ ____

OPTIONAL EXERCISE: Using an atlas, locate the following seas: Laptev, Ross, Scotia, Kara, Timor, Aral, and the Sea of Okhotsk. Locate the Gulf of California and the Gulf of Carpenteria. See how many deserts you can identify on the continent of Australia. Where are the Drakensburg Mountains? Where are the Caribou Mountains?

IF IN A CLASSROOM ENVIRONMENT, HERE ARE SOME DISCUSSION QUESTIONS:
- Why is it important for anyone to study geography?
- What types of resources are available in the area you live?
- What type of climate typifies your area?
- Discuss the impact of technology and industry on environments.
- Why have some nations advanced more rapidly than others in technology?
- Discuss the difference between the standard of living in the U.S. and a country like Afghanistan, for example. Does a higher standard of living automatically mean a better quality of life?

THE TWENTY-FOUR HOUR CLOCK

Most of the world uses the twenty-four hour clock, as do the military forces, so that "am" or "pm" does not have to be specified. Since it is a universal way of showing schedules, it is important to be able to convert AM or PM time into the twenty-four hour clock and vice versa.

0000 is the start of the day, 1200 is 12:00 noon/12:00 pm, and 2400 is 12:00 midnight. No schedule will ever use 0000 or 2400, since a date would have to be specified (they may use 0001 which is 12:01 am, or 2359 which is 11:59 pm).

HINT: If a 24 hour time given is less than 12, it is AM (0815= 8:15 am, 1145 = 11:45 am, 0011 = 12:11 am). If a 24 hour time is 12 or more, it's PM and you MAY HAVE TO subtract 12 to determine the PM hour (12:05 = 12:05 pm because 12 stays the same, 16:22 = 4:22 pm because 16-12=4, 2300 = 11:00 pm because 23-12=11).

Change the following AM or PM times into the twenty-four hour clock. You do not need to indicate colons (:) in twenty-four hour time.

EXERCISE

CHANGE THE FOLLOWING INTO 24 HOUR TIME:

1. 4:56 pm = ______________
2. 7:18 pm = ______________
3. 11:23 pm = ______________
4. 12:22 pm = ______________
5. 9:40 pm = ______________
6. 11:07 pm = ______________
7. 7:50 pm = ______________
8. 3:12 am = ______________
9. 10:29 am = ______________
10. 12:44 am = ______________

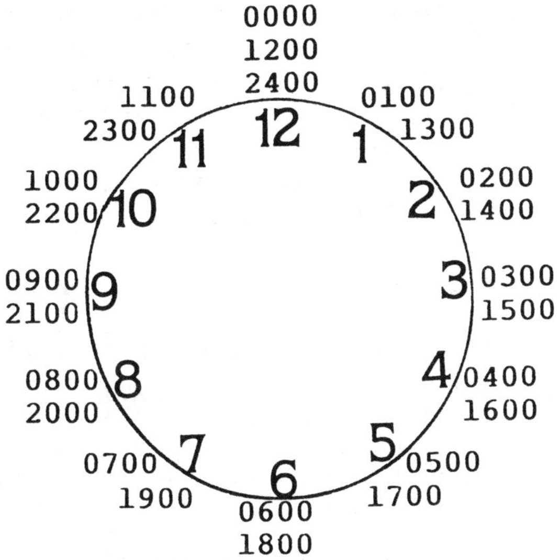

CONVERT THE FOLLOWING 24 HOUR TIMES INTO AM OR PM:

11. 1222 = ________________
12. 1458 = ________________
13. 1818 = ________________
14. 2203 = ________________
15. 1514 = ________________
16. 0455 = ________________
17. 1111 = ________________
18. 0815 = ________________
19. 0108 = ________________
20. 0026 = ________________

HERE IS SOME ADDITIONAL PRACTICE IN TIME CONVERSIONS:

CONVERT INTO AM OR PM

1. 0010 = ____________
2. 1752 = ____________
3. 1345 = ____________
4. 0532 = ____________
5. 1421 = ____________
6. 1903 = ____________
7. 2212 = ____________
8. 2009 = ____________
9. 1601 = ____________
10. 0941 = ____________
11. 1115 = ____________
12. 1310 = ____________
13. 2105 = ____________
14. 2032 = ____________
15. 1218 = ____________

CONVERT INTO 24 HOUR TIME

16. 10:12 am = ____________
17. 12:20 pm = ____________
18. 9:15 am = ____________
19. 8:45 pm = ____________
20. 6:20 am = ____________
21. 1:43 pm = ____________
22. 11:14 pm = ____________
23. 7:23 am = ____________
24. 4:52 pm = ____________
25. 9:50 pm = ____________
26. 12:01 am = ____________
27. 11:16 am = ____________
28. 5:42 pm = ____________
29. 6:35 pm = ____________
30. 8:05 pm = ____________

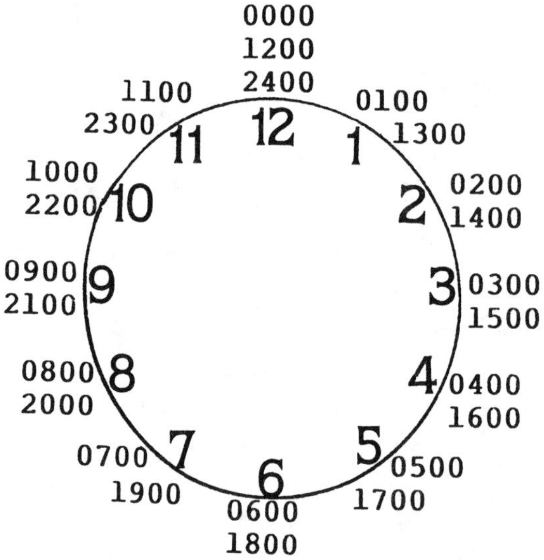

KNOWLEDGE OF GEOGRAPHY AND DESTINATIONS

In order to be proficient in your knowledge of destinations, you need to read a variety of guidebooks and publications, complete map practices and tests, and do exercises on destination information.

You may wish to start a travel library and subscribe to consumer and industry publications in order to have resources and be aware of trends and information. Contact state and country tourist offices to receive maps, brochures and pamphlets for help in your study and for reference. Organize files of this information. Maybe ask a travel agency if you can have any of their extra or old tour brochures, which can be very useful in learning about countries and destinations. Visit bookstores and perhaps purchase some current or sale-priced travel guides. In addition, there are many travel videos available for rental or sale, and numerous TV programs that you should watch (National Geographic, other specials on wildlife studies, destinations, etc.).

The study and practice for knowing about each area, country, city, etc. should include research and usage of atlases, travel guides, references such as the World Travel Guide, tour and cruise brochures, and access to the information resources on the Internet if possible.

You may already know some areas and be able to answer questions without using a resource. Questions may be repeated for emphasis. If you finish an area of study easily, fill out profiles and do extra study on areas with which you are not that familiar. There are so many countries, states, cities, and areas of the world - you can never know too much!

In this manual areas of the world and destinations are covered first with a brief description and some information, followed by blank profile forms, map exercises, and pages of reviews and tests on destination information.

If this manual is used in a travel school or college curriculum, other assignments and projects should be given for further depth and study. If used in an all-inclusive travel training program, the other sections of The Travel Training Series can be included in the curriculum (start with Geography, then use Domestic Travel and Ticketing, then return to Geography, then use Cruises or another manual, and back to Geography, etc.).

The world is constantly changing with political, social, economic and cultural events. It is important to keep current with world happenings by subscribing to local and national newspapers and watching and listening to the news.

OVERVIEW OF WORLD AREAS AND DESTINATIONS

NORTH AMERICA

The continent of North America includes the U.S., Canada, Mexico, and the Caribbean islands.

The destinations of the contiguous U.S. will be covered first, followed by Hawaii and Alaska. Individual map practices and tests on Hawaii and Alaska are provided because of their importance as tourist destinations and because of their geographical position.

CANADA

The second largest country in the world by area, Canada contains vast areas of unspoiled wilderness (Northwest Territories) and major cities such as Montreal, Quebec, Toronto, and Vancouver.

MEXICO

From the popular resorts of Cancun, Cozumel, Puerto Vallarta, Acapulco, and Ixtapa, to colonial Mexican cities such as Guadalajara and Morelia, to rustic adventure areas such as the Copper Canyon, Mexico offers a variety of scenery and vacation activities.

CENTRAL AMERICA

Central America bridges North America to South America and is comprised of Guatemala, Belize, Honduras, Nicaragua, El Salvador, Costa Rica and Panama.

CARIBBEAN

Alike but also different, the hundreds of Caribbean islands offer a wide variety of languages, cultures, foods, history, and topography. Some are mountainous, others flat, some lush and some arid. Bermuda is covered in this section although it is located off the coast of the Carolinas and is a more seasonal destination (the best time to visit Bermuda is from April to October).

SOUTH AMERICA

South America offers a full range of features which include jungles, deserts, mountains, rivers, lakes, and beaches. There's skiing in the Andes Mountains when it's summer in the U.S., there's magnificent Iguassu Falls, and there's the mighty Amazon River with excursions from the Brazilian or Peruvian side. Inca history is at its strongest with the archaeological ruins of Machu Picchu in Peru.

EUROPE

It may be small in area - a couple of hours drive may take you through several countries - but it is not lacking in its attractions, cultures, histories, landmarks, and travel experiences. Big Ben, the Eiffel Tower, famous cathedrals, museums, rivers, lakes, mountains, cities, gardens, beaches - Europe really does have it all.

AFRICA

It may not be everyone's dream to go to Africa, but this phenomenally large continent (four times the size of the U.S.) contains such diverse tribes, cultures, terrains, wildlife, and regions that it cannot be overlooked. Maybe it's the Sphinx, Pyramids, and Nile River that you would like to see, or go on a safari to see lions, wildebeests, elephants and other wildlife found elsewhere only in a zoo.

MIDDLE EAST AND ASIA

Israel, home to three world religions; the Blue Mosque in Istanbul, Turkey; the Taj Mahal in India; shopping in Hong Kong; walking on the Great Wall in China; trekking near Mt. Everest in Nepal; from experiencing interesting cultures, to sightseeing and shopping, these are just a few particulars of travel to the Middle East and Asia.

AUSTRALIA AND THE SOUTH PACIFIC

To go "down under" means having the opportunity to visit Ayers Rock, the Sydney Opera House and Harbor, the wine country of Adelaide, the yachting center of Hobart, the Great Barrier Reef off the coast of Australia. Touring New Zealand's North and South Islands means visiting Auckland, Wellington, Christchurch and the Southern Alps. The South Pacific conjures up pictures of idyllic islands, crystal blue waters, and peaceful island lifestyles and cultures (Tahiti, Bora Bora, Tonga, Fiji, etc.).

You might have already starting dreaming about places you have been or would like to visit. Travel means fulfilling dreams and experiences, learning about the peoples and cultures of the world. Every place has something to offer and it is important for the tourist to have compassion and understanding for the different peoples, customs, lifestyles of the world, and to consider the environment and ecology.

The world can be a better place if people learn about one another, benefiting from the exchange of ideas and ways, caring about and perhaps initiating problem-solving efforts to relieve the poverty, malnutrition, disease, homelessness, strife, and struggles of the world's peoples.

COUNTRY CODES - NAMES, CURRENCY NAMES, ISO* CODES

Note: Some country codes were not available.
*International Standards Organization

Abu Dhabi (see United Arab Emirates)		
AF-Afghanistan	Afghani	AFA
AL-Albania	Lek	ALL
DZ-Algeria	Algerian Dinar	DZD
AD-Andorra	Andorra Pesetas	ADP
AO-Angola	Kwanza Reajustado	AOR
AI-Anguilla	East. Carib.Dollar	XCD
AQ-Antarctica	-	
AG-Antigua	East. Carib.Dollar	XCD
AR-Argentina	Peso	ARS
AM-Armenia	Luma	AML
AW-Aruba	Aruban Guilder	AWG
AU-Australia	Australian Dollar	AUD
AT-Austria	Austrian Schilling	ATS
AZ-Azerbaijan	Manat	AZM
BS-Bahamas	Bahamian Dollar	BSD
BH-Bahrain	Bahraini Dinar	BHD
BD-Bangladesh	Taka	BDT
BB-Barbados	Barbados Dollar	BBD
BY-Belarus	Belarussian Ruble	BYB
BE-Belgium	Belgian Franc	BEF
BZ-Belize	Belize Dollar	BZD
BJ-Benin	CFA Franc	XOF
BM-Bermuda	Bermudian Dollar	BMD
BT-Bhutan	Ngultrum	BTN
BO-Bolivia	Bolivanio	BOB
BA-Bosnia Hercegovina	Dinar	BAD
BW-Botswana	Pula	BWP
BR-Brazil	Real	BRL
BN-Brunei	Brunei Dollar	BND
BG-Bulgaria	Lev	BGL
BF-Burkina Faso	CFA Franc	XOF
BU-Burma (see Myanmar)		
BI-Burundi	Burundi Franc	BIF
KH-Cambodia Dem.	Riel	KHR
CM-Cameroon	CFA Franc	XAF
CA-Canada	Canadian Dollar	CAD
CV-Cape Verde	Cape Verde Escudo	CVE
KY-Cayman Is.	Cayman Is. Dollar	KYD
CF-Central African Republic	CFA Franc	XAF
TD-Chad	CFA Franc	XAF
CL-Chile	Chilean Peso	CLP
CN-China	Yuan Renminbi	CNY
CX-Christmas Is.	Australian Dollar	AUD
CC-Cocos Is.	Australian Dollar	AUD
CO-Colombia	Colombian Peso	COP
KM-Comoros	Comoro Franc	KMF
CG-Congo	CFA Franc	XAF
CK-Cook Is.	New Zealand Dollar	NZD
CR-Costa Rica	Costa Rican Colon	CRC
CI-Cote D'Ivoire	CFA Franc	XOF
HR-Croatia	Kuna	HRK
CU-Cuba	Cuban Peso	CUP
CY-Cyprus	Cyprus Pound	CYP
Note: The area controlled by the Turkish Cypriot Community uses the Turkish Lira.		
CS-Czech Republic	Koruna	CZK
DK-Denmark	Danish Krone	DKK
DJ-Djibouti	Djibouti Franc	DJF
DM-Dominica	East. Carib.Dollar	XCD
DO-Dominican Rep.	Dominican Peso	DOP
Dubai (see United Arab Emirates)		
East. Caribbean	E.Carib.Dollar	XCD
TP-East Timor	Escudo	TPE
EC-Ecuador	Sucre	ECS
EG-Egypt	Egyptian Pound	EGP
SV-El Salvador	El Salvador Colon	SVC
GQ-Equatorial Guinea	CFA Franc	XAF
ER-Eritrea	Ethiopian Birr	ETB
EE-Estonia	Kroon	EEK
ET-Ethiopia	Ethiopian Birr	ETB
European Monetary Cooperation Fund	European Currency Unit	XEU
FK-Falkland Is.	U.K. Pound	FKP
FO-Faroe Is.	Danish Krone	DKK
FJ-Fiji	Fiji Dollar	FJD
FI-Finland	Markka	FIM
FR-France	French Franc	FRF
GF-French Guiana	French Franc	FRF
PF-French Polynesia	CFP Franc	XPF
TF-French Southern Territories	French Franc	FRF
GA-Gabon	CFA Franc	XAF
GM-Gambia	Dalasi	GMD
GE-Georgia	Lary	GEL
DE-Germany	Deutsche Mark	DEM
GH-Ghana	Cedi	GHC
GI-Gibraltar	Gibraltar Pound	GIP
GR-Greece	Drachma	GRD
GL-Greenland	Danish Krone	DKK
GD-Grenada	East. Carib.Dollar	XCD
GP-Guadeloupe, including St. Barthelemy, French St.Martin	French Franc	FRF
GU-Guam	U.S. Dollar	USD
GT-Guatemala	Quetzal	GTQ
GN-Guinea	Guinea Franc	GNF
GW-Guinea-Bissau	Guinea-Bissau Peso	GWP
GY-Guyana	Guyana Dollar	GYD
HT-Haiti	Gourde	HTG
HM-Heard and McDonald Islands	Australian Dollar	AUD
HN-Honduras	Lempira	HNL
HK-Hong Kong	Hong Kong Dollar	HKD
HU-Hungary	Forint	HUF
IS-Iceland	Iceland Krona	ISK
IN-India	Indian Rupee	INR
ID-Indonesia	Rupiah	IDR
IR-Iran	Iranian Rial	IRR
IQ-Iraq	Iraqi Dinar	IQD
IE-Ireland	Irish Pound(Punt)	IEP
IL-Israel	Shekel	ILS
IT-Italy	Italian Lira	ITL
JM-Jamaica	Jamaican Dollar	JMD
JP-Japan	Yen	JPY
JO-Jordan	Jordanian Dinar	JOD
KZ-Kazakhstan	Tenge	KZT
KE-Kenya	Kenyan Shilling	KES
KI-Kiribati	Australian Dollar	AUD
KP-Korea, Dem. People's Rep.	N. Korean Won	KPW
KR-Korea, Rep. of	Won	KRW
KG-Kyrgystan	Som	KGS
KW-Kuwait	Kuwaiti Dinar	KWD
LA-Laos People's Dem. Rep.	Kip	LAK
LV-Latvia	Lat	LVL
LB-Lebanon	Lebanese Pound	LBP
LS-Lesotho	Loti	LSL
LR-Liberia	Liberian Dollar	LRD
LY-Libyan Arab Jamahiriya	Libyan Dinar	LYD
LI-Liechtenstein	Swiss Franc	CHF
LT-Lithuania	Litas	LTL
LU-Luxembourg	Luxembourg Franc	LUF

MO-Macau	Macau Pataca	MOP
MK-Macedonia	Macedonia Denar	MKD
MG-Madagascar	Malagasy Franc	MGF
MW-Malawi	Kwacha	MWK
MY-Malaysia	Malaysian Ringgit	MYR
MV-Maldives	Maldivian Rufiyaa	MVR
ML-Mali	CFA Franc	XOF
MT-Malta	Maltese Lira	MTL
MH-Marshall Is.	U.S. Dollar	USD
MQ-Martinique	French Franc	FRF
MR-Mauritania	Ouguiya	MRO
MU-Mauritius	Mauritius Rupee	MUR
XM-Mayotte	French Franc	FRF
MX-Mexico	Nuevo Peso	MXN
FM-Micronesia, including Caroline Is., Ponape & Kosrae	U.S. Dollar	USD
MD-Moldova	Leu (plural Lay)	MDL
MC-Monaco	French Franc	FRF
MN-Mongolia	Tugrik	MNT
MS-Montserrat (see Eastern Caribbean)		
MA-Morocco	Moroccan Dirham	MAD
MZ-Mozambique	Metical	MZM
MM-Myanmar	Kyat	MMK
NA-Namibia	Namibian Dollar	NAD
NR-Nauru	Australian Dollar	AUD
NP-Nepal	Nepalese Rupee	NPR
NL-Netherlands	Neth. Guilder	NLG
AN-Neth. Antilles	Neth. Ant. Guilder	ANG
Nevis (see Eastern Caribbean)		
NC-New Caledonia	CFP Franc	XPF
NZ-New Zealand	New Zealand Dollar	NZD
NI-Nicaragua	Cordoba Oro	NIO
NE-Niger	CFA Franc	XOF
NG-Nigeria	Naira	NGN
NU-Niue	New Zealand Dollar	NZD
NF-Norfolk Is.	Australian Dollar	AUD
MP-Northern Mariana Is., incl. Mariana Is., except Guam	U.S. Dollar	USD
NO-Norway	Norwegian Krone	NOK
OM-Oman	Rial Omani	OMR
PK-Pakistan	Pakistan Rupee	PKR
PW-Palau	U.S. Dollar	USD
PA-Panama	Balboa	PAB
PG-Papua New Guinea	Kina	PGK
PY-Paraguay	Guarani	PYG
PE-Peru	Nuevo Sol	PES
PH-Philippines	Philippine Peso	PHP
PL-Poland	Zloty	PLZ
PT-Portugal	Portuguese Escudo	PTE
PR-Puerto Rico	U.S. Dollar	USD
QA-Qatar	Qatari Riyal	QAR
RE-Reunion	French Franc	FRF
RO-Romania	Leu	ROL
RU-Russia	Ruble	RUR
RW-Rwanda	Rwanda Franc	RWF
SH-St. Helena	Pound	SHP
KN-St. Kitts & Nevis (see Eastern Caribbean)		
LC-St. Lucia (see Eastern Caribbean)		
PM-St. Pierre & Miquelon		FRF
VC-St. Vincent & Grenadines (see E. Caribbean)		
AS-Samoa(American)	U.S. Dollar	USD
WS-Samoa(Western)	Tala	WST
SM-San Marino	Italian Lira	ITL
ST-Sao Tome & Principe	Dobra	STD
SA-Saudi Arabia	Saudi Riyal	SAR
SN-Senegal	CFA Franc	XOF
SC-Seychelles	Seychelles Rupee	SCR
Sharjah (see United Arab Emirates)		
SL-Sierra Leone	Leone	SLL
SG-Singapore	Singapore Dollar	SGD
SK-Slovakia	Koruna	SKK
SI-Slovenia	Tolar	SIT
SB-Solomon Is.	Solomon Is. Dollar	SBD

SO-Somalia	Somali Shilling	SOS
ZA-South Africa	Rand	ZAR
ES-Spain	Spanish Peseta	ESP
LK-Sri Lanka	Sri Lanka Rupee	LKR
SD-Sudan	Dinar	SDD
SR-Suriname	Suriname Guilder	SRG
SZ-Swaziland	Lilangeni	SZL
SE-Sweden	Swedish Krona	SEK
CH-Switzerland	Swiss Franc	CHF
SY-Syrian Arab Rep.	Syrian Pound	SYP
TW-Taiwan	New Taiwan Dollar	TWD
TJ-Tajikistan	Ruble	RUR
TZ-Tanzania	Tanzanian Shilling	TZS
TH-Thailand	Baht	THB
TG-Togo	CFA Franc	XOF
TK-Tokelau	New Zealand Dollar	NZD
TO-Tonga	Pa'anga	TOP
TT-Trinidad & Tobago	Trinidad & Tobago Dollar	TTD
TN-Tunisia	Tunisian Dinar	TND
TR-Turkey	Turkish Lira	TRL
TM-Turkmenistan	Manat	TMM
TC-Turks & Caicos	U.S. Dollar	USD
TV-Tuvalu	Australian Dollar	AUD
UG-Uganda	Uganda Shilling	UGX
UA-Ukraine	Karbovanet	UAK
AE-United Arab Emirates (comprised of Abu Dhabi, Ajman, Dubai, Fujairah, Ras-al-Khaymah, Sharjah, Umm Al Qaiwain	UAE Dirham	AED
GB-United Kingdom	Pound Sterling	GBP
US-United States, incl. Midway Is., Johnson Atoll, Wake Is.	U.S. Dollar	USD
UY-Uruguay	Peso Uruguayo	UYU
UZ-Uzbekistan	Sum	UZS
VU-Vanuatu	Vatu	VUV
VA-Vatican City	Italian Lira	ITL
VE-Venezuela	Bolivar	VEB
VN-Vietnam	Dong	VND
VG-Virgin Is.(Br.)	U.S. Dollar	USD
VI-Virgin Is.(U.S.)	U.S. Dollar	USD
WF-Wallis & Futuna	CFP Franc	XPF
YE-Yemen	Rial	YER
YU-Yugoslavia	New Dinar	YUG
ZR-Zaire	New Zaire	ZRN
ZM-Zambia	Kwacha	ZMK
ZW-Zimbabwe	Zimbabwe Dollar	ZWD

NOTE: CURRENCIES AND CURRENCY CODES ARE SUBJECT TO CHANGE AT ANY TIME.

COUNTRIES/TERRITORIES AND CAPITALS

Afghanistan	Kabul
Albania	Tirana
Algeria	Algiers
American Samoa	Pago Pago
Andorra	Andorra-la-Vella
Angola	Luanda
Antigua & Barbuda	St. John's
Argentina	Buenos Aires
Armenia	Yerevan
Aruba	Oranjestad
Australia	Canberra
Austria	Vienna
Azerbaijan	Baku
Bahamas	Nassau
Bahrain	Manama
Bangladesh	Dhaka
Barbados	Bridgetown
Belarus	Minsk
Belgium	Brussels
Belize	Belmopan
Benin	Porto-Novo
Bermuda	Hamilton
Bhutan	Thimphu
Bolivia	La Paz
Bosnia Hercegovina	Sarajevo
Botswana	Gaborone
Brazil	Brasilia
British Virgin Islands	Road Town, Tortola
Brunei	Bandar Seri Begawan
Bulgaria	Sofia
Burkina Faso	Ouagadougou
Burundi	Bujumbura
Cambodia	Phnom Penh
Cameroon	Yaounde
Canada	Ottawa
Cape Verde	Praia
Central African Republic	Bangui
Chad	N'Djamena
Chile	Santiago
China	Beijing
Colombia	Bogota
Comoros	Moroni
Congo	Brazzaville
Costa Rica	San Jose
Cote d'Ivoire	Yamoussoukro
Croatia	Zagreb
Cuba	Havana
Cyprus	Nicosia
Czech Republic	Prague
Denmark	Copenhagen
Djibouti	Djibouti
Dominica	Roseau
Dominican Republic	Santo Domingo
Ecuador	Quito
Egypt	Cairo
El Salvador	San Salvador
England	London
Equatorial Guinea	Malabo
Eritrea	Asmara
Estonia	Tallinn
Ethiopia	Addis Ababa
Fiji	Suva
Finland	Helsinki
France	Paris
French Guiana	Cayenne
French Polynesia	Papeete, Tahiti
Gabon	Libreville
Gambia	Banjul
Georgia	Tbilisi
Germany	Berlin & Bonn
Ghana	Accra
Gibraltar	Gibraltar
Greece	Athens
Greenland	Nuuk
Grenada	St. George's
Guadeloupe	Basse-Terre (administrative) Pointe-a-Pitre (commercial)
Guam	Agana
Guatemala	Guatemala City
Guernsey	St. Peter Port
Guinea	Conakry
Guinea-Bissau	Bissau
Guyana	Georgetown
Haiti	Port-au-Prince
Honduras	Tegucigalpa
Hong Kong	Victoria
Hungary	Budapest
Iceland	Reykjavik
India	New Delhi
Indonesia	Jakarta
Iran	Tehran
Iraq	Baghdad
Ireland	Dublin
Israel	Jerusalem
Italy	Rome
Ivory Coast (see Cote d'Ivoire)	
Jamaica	Kingston
Japan	Tokyo
Jersey	St. Helier
Jordan	Amman
Kazakhstan	Alma-Alta
Kenya	Nairobi
Kiribati	Bairiki
Korea (Dem. Rep.)	Pyongyang
Korea (Rep.)	Seoul
Kuwait	Al Kuwait
Kyrgyzstan	Bishkek
Laos	Vientiane
Latvia	Riga
Lebanon	Beirut
Lesotho	Maseru
Liberia	Monrovia
Libya	Tripoli
Liechtenstein	Vaduz
Lithuania	Vilnius
Luxembourg	Luxembourg
Macau	Macau
Macedonia	Skopje
Madagascar	Antananarivo
Malawi	Lilongwe
Malaysia	Kuala Lumpur
Maldives	Male
Mali	Bamako
Malta	Valletta
Marshall Is.	Majuro
Martinique	Fort-de-France
Mauritania	Nouakchott
Mauritius	Port Louis
Mexico	Mexico City
Micronesia	Kolonia
Moldova	Kishinev
Monaco	Monaco-Ville
Mongolia	Ulaanbaatar
Montserrat	Plymouth
Morocco	Rabat
Mozambique	Maputo
Myanmar	Yangon
Namibia	Windhoek

Nauru	Yaren District
Nepal	Kathmandu
Netherlands	The Hague Amsterdam
Netherlands Antilles	Willemstad
New Caledonia	Noumea
New Zealand	Wellington
Nicaragua	Managua
Niger	Niamey
Nigeria	Abuja
Niue	Alofi
Northern Ireland	Belfast
Norway	Oslo
Oman	Muscat
Pakistan	Islamabad
Palau	Koror
Panama	Panama City
Papua New Guinea	Port Moresby
Paraguay	Asuncion
Peru	Lima
Philippines	Manila
Poland	Warsaw
Portugal	Lisbon
Puerto Rico	San Juan
Qatar	Doha
Romania	Bucharest
Russia	Moscow
Rwanda	Kigali
St. Kitts & Nevis	Basseterre
St. Lucia	Castries
St. Vincent & the Grenadines	Kingstown
San Marino	San Marino
Sao Tome & Principe	Sao Tome
Saudi Arabia	Riyadh
Scotland	Edinburgh
Senegal	Dakar
Seychelles	Victoria
Sierra Leone	Freetown
Singapore	Singapore
Slovak Republic	Bratislava
Slovenia	Ljubljana
Solomon Islands	Honiara
Somalia	Mogadishu
South Africa	Cape Town (legislative) Pretoria (administrative) Bloemfontein (judicial)
Spain	Madrid
Sri Lanka	Colombo
Sudan	Khartoum
Suriname	Paramaribo
Swaziland	Mbabane
Sweden	Stockholm
Switzerland	Bern
Syria	Damascus
Taiwan	Taipei
Tajikistan	Dushanbe
Tanzania	Dodoma (administraive) Dar es Salaam (commercial)
Thailand	Bangkok
Togo	Lome
Tonga	Nuku'alofa
Trinidad & Tobago	Port of Spain
Tunisia	Tunis
Turkey	Ankara
Turkmenistan	Ashkhabad
Turks & Caicos Islands	Cockburn Town, Gran Turk
Tuvalu	Funafuti
Uganda	Kampala
Ukraine	Kiev
United Arab Emirates	Abu Dhabi
United Kingdom	London
U.S.A.	Washington, DC
U.S. Virgin Islands	Charlotte Amalie, St. Thomas
Uruguay	Montevideo
Uzbekistan	Tashkent
Vanuatu	Vila
Venezuela	Caracas
Vietnam	Hanoi
Wales	Cardiff
Western Samoa	Apia
Yemen	San'a
Yugoslavia	Belgrade
Zaire	Kinshasa
Zambia	Lusaka
Zimbabwe	Harare

YOU MAY NEED TO REFER TO THIS LIST WHEN COMPLETING THE REVIEWS ON WORLD AREAS.

NOTES

CHAPTER 3

United States of America

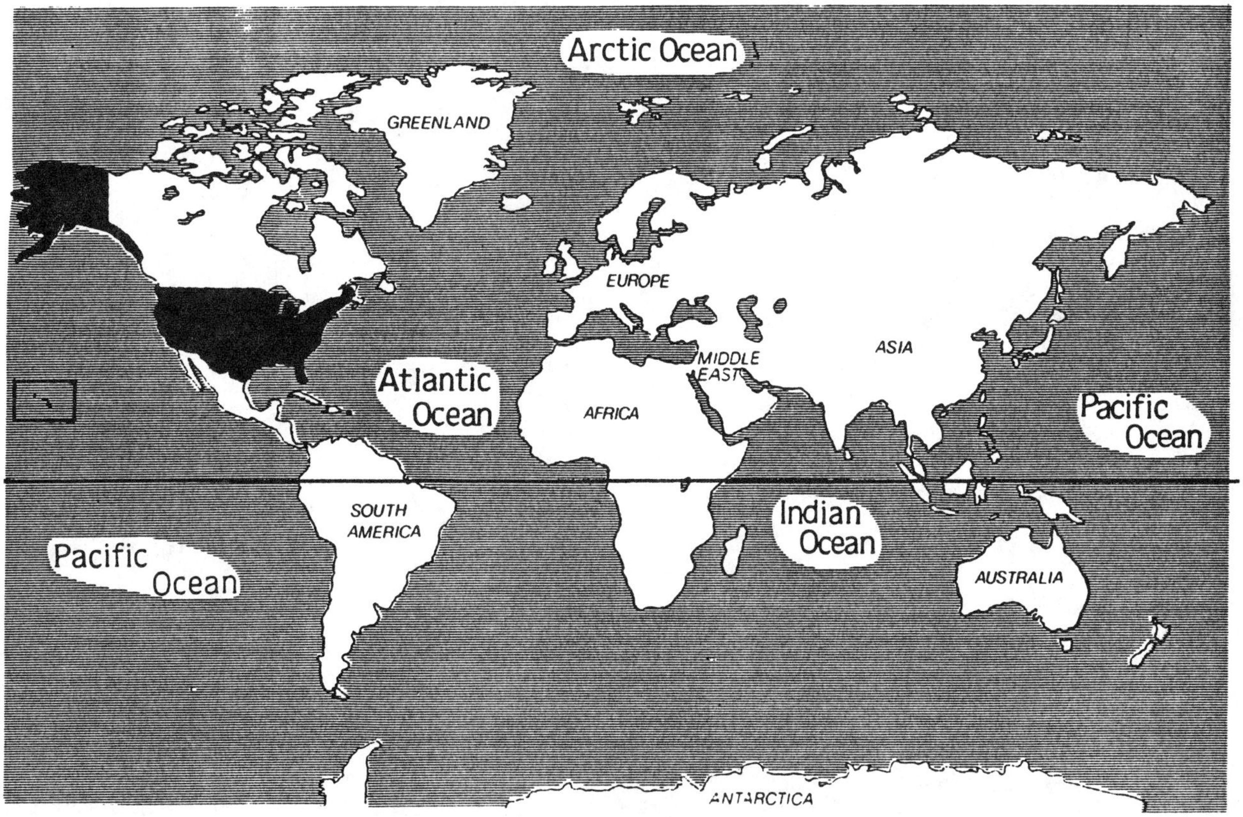

NOTES

U.S. STATES, TWO-LETTER ABBREVIATIONS, AND CAPITAL CITIES

ALABAMA = AL = MONTGOMERY
ALASKA = AK = JUNEAU
ARIZONA = AZ = PHOENIX
ARKANSAS = AR = LITTLE ROCK
CALIFORNIA = CA = SACRAMENTO
COLORADO = CO = DENVER
CONNECTICUT = CT = HARTFORD
DELAWARE = DE = DOVER
FLORIDA = FL = TALLAHASSEE
GEORGIA = GA = ATLANTA
HAWAII = HI = HONOLULU
IDAHO = ID = BOISE
ILLINOIS = IL = SPRINGFIELD
INDIANA = IN = INDIANAPOLIS
IOWA = IA = DES MOINES
KANSAS = KS = TOPEKA
KENTUCKY = KY = FRANKFORT
LOUISIANA = LA = BATON ROUGE
MAINE = ME = AUGUSTA
MARYLAND = MD = ANNAPOLIS
MASSACHUSETTS = MA = BOSTON
MICHIGAN = MI = LANSING
MINNESOTA = MN = ST. PAUL
MISSISSIPPI = MS = JACKSON
MISSOURI = MO = JEFFERSON CITY
MONTANA = MT = HELENA
NEBRASKA = NE = LINCOLN
NEVADA = NV = CARSON CITY
NEW HAMPSHIRE = NH = CONCORD
NEW JERSEY = NJ = TRENTON
NEW MEXICO = NM = SANTA FE
NEW YORK = NY = ALBANY
NORTH CAROLINA = NC = RALEIGH
NORTH DAKOTA = ND = BISMARCK
OHIO = OH = COLUMBUS
OKLAHOMA = OK = OKLAHOMA CITY
OREGON = OR = SALEM
PENNSYLVANIA = PA = HARRISBURG
RHODE ISLAND = RI = PROVIDENCE
SOUTH CAROLINA = SC = COLUMBIA
SOUTH DAKOTA = SD = PIERRE
TENNESSEE = TN = NASHVILLE
TEXAS = TX = AUSTIN
UTAH = UT = SALT LAKE CITY
VERMONT = VT = MONTPELIER
VIRGINIA = VA = RICHMOND
WASHINGTON = WA = OLYMPIA
WEST VIRGINIA = WV = CHARLESTON
WISCONSIN = WI = MADISON
WYOMING = WY = CHEYENNE

Capital of the U.S. is WASHINGTON, DC = DC

U.S. TIME ZONES MAP

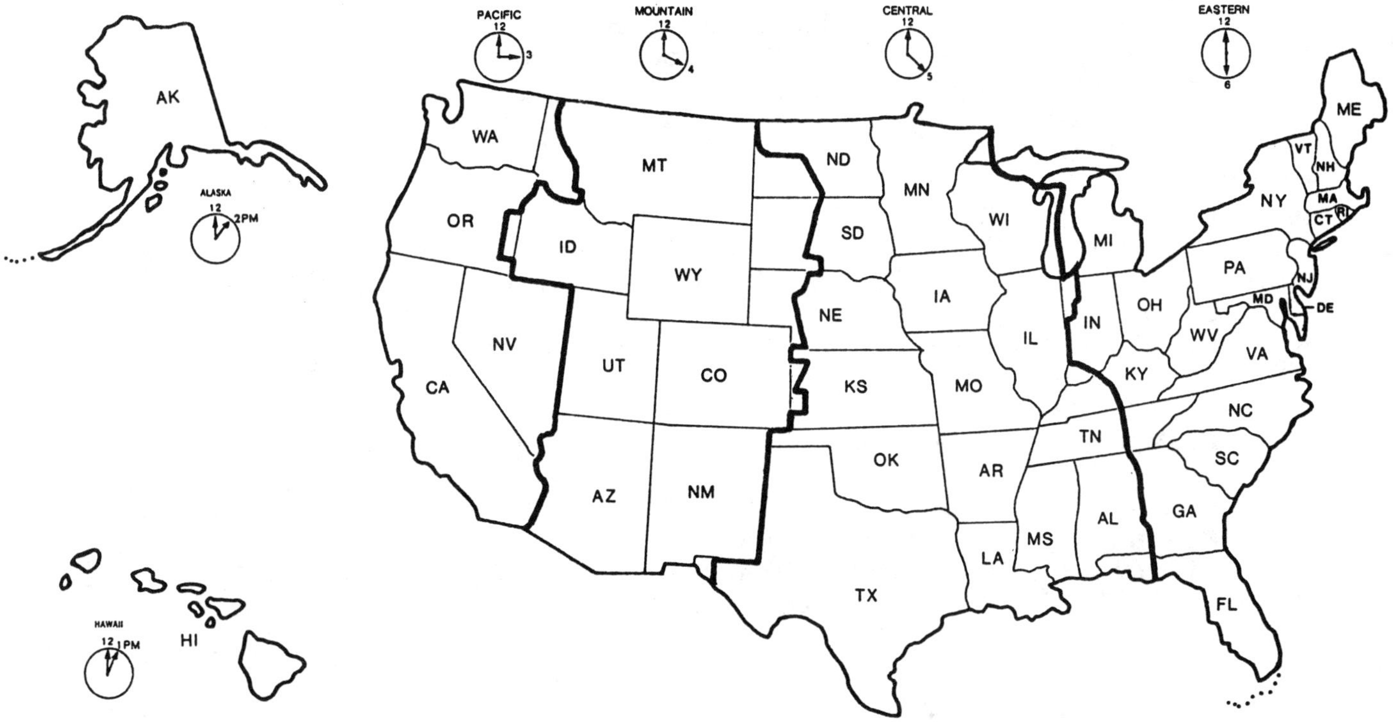

MAJOR CITIES AND THEIR CITY/AIRPORT CODES - BY STATE

AK - Fairbanks - FAI, Anchorage - ANC, Juneau - JNU, Nome - OME, Kodiak - ADQ, Homer - HOM, Barrow - BRW, Ketchikan - KTN, Valdez - VDZ, Sitka - SIT
AL - Montgomery - MGM, Birmingham - BHM, Mobile - MOB, Huntsville - HSV, Gadsden - GAD
AR - Little Rock - LIT, Hot Springs - HOT, Ft. Smith - FSM
AZ - Phoenix - PHX, Tucson - TUS, Flagstaff - FLG
CA - Los Angeles - LAX, Burbank - BUR, Ontario - ONT, Long Beach - LGB, San Francisco - SFO, Oakland - OAK, San Diego - SAN, Sacramento - SMF, Fresno - FAT, San Jose - SJC
CO - Denver - DEN, Aspen - ASE, Colorado Springs - COS, Pueblo - PUB, Grand Junction - GJT
CT - Hartford - BDL, Bridgeport - BDR, New Haven - HVN
DC - Washington - WAS, Washington (Dulles) - IAD, Washington (National) - DCA, Baltimore MD/Washington DC - BWI
DE - Wilmington - ILG
FL - Miami - MIA, Tampa - TPA, Jacksonville - JAX, Tallahassee - TLH, Daytona Beach - DAB, Key West - EYW, Orlando (McCoy) - MCO, Pensacola - PNS, Panama City - PFN, Ft. Myers - RSW, Marathon - MTH, West Palm Beach - PBI, Ft. Lauderdale - FLL, Sarasota/Bradenton - SRQ, Melbourne - MLB, Naples - APF
GA - Atlanta - ATL, Macon - MCN, Savannah - SAV, Albany - ABY, Augusta - AGS, Columbus - CSG
HI - Honolulu - HNL, Kahului - OGG, Molokai - MKK, Hilo - ITO, Kona - KOA, Lihue - LIH
IA - Des Moines - DSM, Cedar Rapids - CID, Sioux City - SUX, Waterloo - ALO, Dubuque - DBQ
ID - Boise - BOI
IL - Chicago - CHI, Chicago (O'Hare) - ORD, Chicago (Midway) - MDW, Peoria - PIA, Springfield - SPI
IN - Indianapolis - IND, Terre Haute - HUF, Fort Wayne - FWA, Evansville - EVV, South Bend - SBN
KS - Kansas City (Int'l) - MCI, Topeka - TOP, Wichita - ICT
KY - Louisville - SDF, Lexington - LEX
LA - New Orleans - MSY, Baton Rouge - BTR, Shreveport - SHV, Lake Charles - LCH
MA - Boston - BOS
MD - Baltimore - BWI
ME - Augusta - AUG, Bangor - BGR, Portland - PWM
MI - Detroit - DTT, Detroit (Metro) - DTW, Grand Rapids - GRR, Flint - FNT
MN - Duluth - DLH, Minneapolis/St. Paul - MSP
MO - St. Louis - STL, Kansas City, MO (Downtown) - MKC
MS - Jackson - JAN, Meridian - MEI
MT - Bozeman - BZN, Butte - BTM, Billings - BIL, Helena - HLN, Great Falls - GTF
NC - Asheville - AVL, Charlotte - CLT, Raleigh/Durham - RDU
ND - Bismarck - BIS, Fargo - FAR
NE - Lincoln - LNK, Omaha - OMA
NH - Concord - CON, Manchester - MHT

NJ - Newark - EWR, Atlantic City (Bader) - AIY, Atlantic City (Pomona) - ACY, Trenton - TTN
NM - Albuquerque - ABQ, Roswell - ROW, Sante Fe - SAF
NV - Las Vegas - LAS, Reno - RNO
NY - New York (Kennedy) - JFK, New York (La Guardia) - LGA, Albany - ALB, Syracuse - SYR, Buffalo - BUF, Rochester - ROC
OH - Columbus - CMH, Cincinnati - CVG, Cleveland - CLE, Dayton - DAY, Toledo - TOL
OK - Tulsa - TUL, Oklahoma City - OKC
OR - Portland - PDX, Salem - SLE, Eugene - EUG
PA - Philadelphia - PHL, Pittsburgh - PIT, Harrisburg/Int'l - MDT Wilkes-Barre - AVP
RI - Providence - PVD
SC - Charleston - CHS, Columbia - CAE
SD - Rapid City - RAP, Pierre - PIR, Sioux Falls - FSD
TN - Knoxville - TYS, Nashville - BNA, Memphis - MEM Chattanooga - CHA
TX - Dallas (Love) - DAL, Dallas/Ft. Worth (Int'l) - DFW, Houston (Hobby) - HOU, Houston (Int'l) - IAH, Amarillo - AMA, San Antonio - SAT, Austin - AUS, Lubbock - LBB, Wichita Falls - SPS, Corpus Christi - CRP
UT - Salt Lake City - SLC
VA - Richmond - RIC, Roanoke - ROA, Newport News/ Williamsburg - PHF
VT - Burlington - BTV, Montpelier - MPV
WA - Seattle/Tacoma - SEA, Spokane - GEG
WI - Milwaukee - MKE, Madison - MSN, Green Bay - GRB
WV - Charleston - CRW, Clarksburg - CKB
WY - Cheyenne - CYS, Jackson Hole - JAC

OTHER RESOURCES:

The OAG(Official Airline Guide) - North American Edition has a complete list of city/airport codes for the U.S., Canada, Mexico and the Caribbean.

The Travel Dictionary has lists of worldwide city/airport codes in both a "decoding" and an "encoding" format.

SPECIAL NOTE

Try to learn as many codes as you can so that you can handle travel planning and requests in an expedient and professional manner.

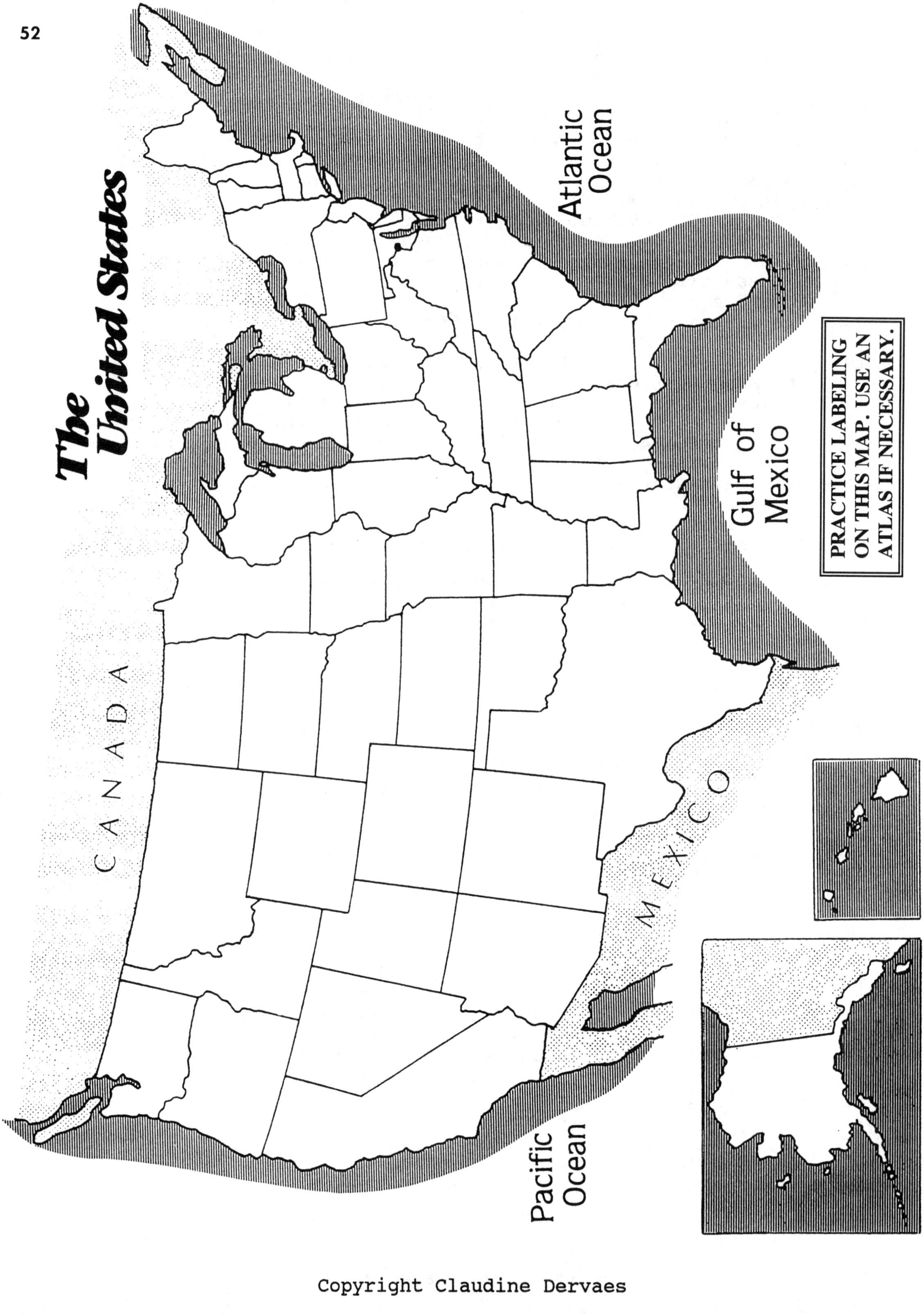
The United States
Atlantic Ocean
Gulf of Mexico
PRACTICE LABELING ON THIS MAP. USE AN ATLAS IF NECESSARY.
CANADA
MEXICO
Pacific Ocean

SOME NATIONAL PARKS OF THE U.S.

For the traveler, the sights and destinations of the U.S. include many state and national parks, monuments, major cities, natural and man-made attractions, and scenic areas. Use an atlas or detailed state maps to locate landmarks, parks, major cities, ports, etc.

ACADIA in MAINE --Includes Mt. Desert Island, half of Isle au Haut, and the highest point on the east coast of the U.S.

ARCHES in UTAH --Contains giant red sandstone arches and other products from erosion.

BIG BEND in TEXAS --Contains the Rio Grande River and Chisos Mts.

BRYCE CANYON in UTAH --Spectacular displays of the colorful and unusual effects of erosion.

CANYONLANDS in UTAH --At the junction of the Green and Colorado Rivers, the park includes evidence of prehistoric Indians.

CAPITOL REEF in UTAH --A 70 mile uplift of sandstone cliffs cut in pieces by high walled gorges.

CARLSBAD CAVERNS in NEW MEXICO --Largest known underground caverns.

CRATER LAKE in OREGON --Breathtakingly blue lake in the crater of an extinct volcano, encircled by walls of lava from 500 to 2,000 feet high.

DENALI NATIONAL PARK AND PRESERVE in ALASKA --The highest point in North America, Mt. McKinley. The park contains glaciers and wildlife, but transportation is mostly restricted to park vehicles and organized trips.

EVERGLADES NATIONAL PARK in FLORIDA --The largest remaining sub-tropical wilderness in the continental U.S., a marshland of alligators and other wildlife, with airboat trips to the interior available.

GLACIER NATIONAL PARK in MONTANA --Rocky Mountain scenery, glaciers, and glacier lakes.

GRAND CANYON in ARIZONA --Spectacular views, and the Colorado River.

GRAND TETON in WYOMING --The Teton Mts. at their most impressive part.

GREAT SMOKY MOUNTAINS in NORTH CAROLINA AND TENNESSEE --Largest eastern mountain range of the U.S. and the beginning of the 2,000 mile Appalachian Trail.

GUADALUPE MOUNTAINS in TEXAS --A tremendous earth fault, containing an extensive Permian limestone fossil reef.

HALEAKALA in HAWAII --Dormant volcano, 10,023 feet high, located on the island of MAUI.

HAWAII VOLCANOES NATIONAL PARK in HAWAII --Contains Kilauea and Mauna Loa (active volcanoes); located on the island of Hawaii.

HOT SPRINGS in ARKANSAS --Government supervised bath houses, using the natural hot springs water.

ISLE ROYALE in MICHIGAN --The largest island in Lake Superior.

KINGS CANYON in CALIFORNIA --Mountain wilderness with giant sequoias.

LASSEN VOLCANIC NATIONAL PARK in CALIFORNIA --Containing Lassen Peak, one of the recently active volcanoes in the contiguous U.S.

MAMMOTH CAVE in KENTUCKY --144 miles of underground passages.

MESA VERDE in COLORADO --Well preserved prehistoric cliff dwellings.

MOUNT RAINIER in WASHINGTON --From this dormant volcano comes the greatest single peak glacier system in the U.S.

NORTH CASCADES in WASHINGTON --Mountainous region with many glaciers and lakes.

OLYMPIC in WASHINGTON --Active glaciers and scenic mountain views.

PETRIFIED FOREST in ARIZONA --Indian artifacts and an extensive petrified forest; contains part of the Painted Desert.

REDWOOD NATIONAL PARK in CALIFORNIA --Ancient redwoods and 40 miles of the Pacific coastline scenery.

ROCKY MOUNTAINS in COLORADO --Contains 107 named peaks that rise over 11,000 feet.

SEQUOIA in CALIFORNIA --Giant sequoia trees.

SHENANDOAH NATIONAL PARK in VIRGINIA --The Blue Ridge Mountains and the Skyline Drive scenic road.

VIRGIN ISLANDS NATIONAL PARK in the U.S. VIRGIN ISLANDS --One of the U.S. territories, the island of St. John, U.S.V.I., offers this park of scenic beauty and beaches.

VOYAGEURS in MINNESOTA --Abundant lakes, forests, and wildlife.

WIND CAVE in SOUTH DAKOTA --Limestone caverns in the Black Hills.

YELLOWSTONE in WYOMING, IDAHO, AND MONTANA (MOSTLY WYOMING) --Oldest and largest National Park, one of the largest geyser areas in the world, containing about 3,000 geysers and hot springs. Home of the geyser called "Old Faithful."

YOSEMITE in CALIFORNIA --Yosemite Valley, the highest waterfall in the U.S., and an area containing giant sequoias.

ZION in UTAH --Unusual shapes and landscapes, resulting from erosion and faulting activity, areas with sheer walls rising to 2,500 feet.

NOW SEE IF YOU CAN IDENTIFY THE NATIONAL PARKS PICTURED BELOW:

Give the name of the park and the state where it is located.

1. ________________________________

2. ________________________________

3. ________________________________

4. ________________________________

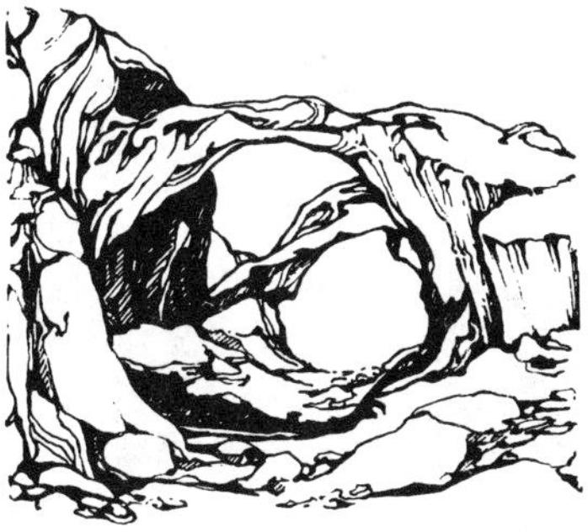

5. ________________________________

THE UNITED STATES OF AMERICA

The United States is a country of great diversity in landscape, climate, attractions, and cultural traditions. The U.S. will be covered in sections or regions, highlighting the states in those regions and their major cities and attractions.

We will begin with **THE REGION OF NEW ENGLAND**

Maine, New Hampshire, Vermont, Connecticut, Massachusetts, and Rhode Island make up the area known as New England. History and scenery describe this area - known particularly for fall foliage tours, quaint towns and villages, numerous covered bridges, and skiing in mountain resorts, such as Stowe and Smuggler's Notch. There's the scenic, rugged coastline of Maine, where puffin-watching has become a popular pastime (especially during June and July at their breeding grounds). Travelers can easily spend two weeks in the region - starting in Boston and going through New Hampshire and Vermont or up to Maine and Acadia National Park. In Boston see Paul Revere's House, the Old North Church, Bunker Hill, the U.S.S. Constitution, and more. Rest at the Boston Common/ Public Garden, and shop at the Faneuil Hall Market or famous Filene's department store - known for its bargain basement.

We will now go into detail on the states that make up the area known as New England:

MAINE - Maine offers unspoiled beauty and appeals to the visitor seeking a quieter and slower lifestyle than big cities and the hustle and bustle. Acadia National Park is a magnificent preserve of spruce forests, rocky cliffs, little islands, and placid bays. Major cities include Bangor, Portland, and Bar Harbor, and Augusta. This largest of the northeast states is almost entirely a recreation area (particularly in summer). Enjoy famous Maine lobster and blueberry pie.

NEW HAMPSHIRE - New Hampshire features the scenic White Mountains area, a region of waterfalls, hiking trails, wildlife and fishing streams. The towering granite summit of Mt. Washington (6,288 ft. high) is in the highest range - the Presidential Range, and several other peaks exceed 5,000 ft. elevation (Mt. Adams, Mt. Jefferson, Mt. Monroe, and Mt. Madison). Passes known as "notches" contain some of the state's most scenic features. Franconia, Crawford, Dixville, Kinsman and Pinkham are popular "notches" to tour.

VERMONT - While New Hampshire has the White Mountains, Vermont has Green Mountains and one of New England's most extensive ski resorts is located in the Green Mountains of Vermont - Killington ski resort. Stowe, Sugarbush, Smuggler's Notch are other quality ski resorts in Vermont. The winters are cold and summer is temperate. Burlington is the state's largest city, overlooking Lake Champlain. Montpelier is the capital and headquarters of the state's vast granite-quarrying interests. Maple sugar products are popular best buys of the state.

CONNECTICUT - Connecticut is a small and yet diverse state. Major cities and attractions are Hartford (major center of the insurance industry), New Haven (home of Yale University), and Mystic (where the Mystic Seaport Museum, Aquarium, and other museums and attractions are found).

MASSACHUSETTS - The city of Boston is not all there is to see in the state of Massachusetts, but Boston has so many sights that your visit to the other state attractions may be limited by time constraints. The city (and its suburbs) is home to many leading colleges and universities, including Harvard and MIT. Walk the Freedom Trail for the sights of the Old State House, Paul Revere's House, the Old North Church, and much more. The Faneuil Hall Marketplace is famous for shopping and dining. Bunker Hill Monument and the U.S.S. Constitution are other attractions to visit. If time permits, venture out to see Plymouth Rock, the Cape Cod National Seashore, the town of Salem (famous for the witch trials), the two islands off the coast of the state - Nantucket and Martha's Vineyard, and the tranquil beauty of the Berkshires - hills, forests, ponds, and lakes located in the far west region.

RHODE ISLAND - One of the most popular destinations in Rhode Island is Block Island - an island off the coast reached by ferry. Walk around or rent a bicycle to take in the island's charm. Besides the typical New England villages, Rhode Island has the beautiful seaport city of Newport - notable for the summer homes (mansions!) along the oceanfront.

NEW YORK - New York state has it all - from the "Big Apple" (New York City) to Niagara Falls near Buffalo. The state has an abundance of vacation areas: Catskill, Adirondack, and Allegheny Mountains, the Finger Lakes region, the Hudson River Valley, and the Thousand Islands area in the St. Lawrence River.

New York City is divided into five parts - known as boroughs. Most tourists visit Manhattan - an island 13 miles long - that features the sights of Central Park, Times Square, Fifth Avenue, Wall Street, the World Trade Center, the Empire State Building, Greenwich Village, United Nations headquarters, Broadway district, Rockefeller Center, and famous museums (Guggenheim, Museum of Natural History, Metropolitan Museum of Art, etc.). The Statue of Liberty is reached by ferry from lower Manhattan. The borough of Brooklyn is known for its ethnic neighborhoods and Coney Island (a seaside amusement park). Queens is the borough that has La Guardia and Kennedy airports. The Bronx is known for its zoo. Staten Island is mostly a residential borough. Brooklyn and Queens are located on Long Island, separated from Manhattan by the East River. The southshore beaches - Jones Beach and Fire Island are popular sights of Long Island. North and west of New York City is the area known as Upstate New York. The Hudson Valley is just north of the city and farther north is the capital of the state, Albany. The Adirondack Mountains run north of Albany and reach to the border of Canada. At the far north of the state are the Thousand Islands in the St. Lawrence River between New York and Canada. The area west of Albany is called the Finger Lakes Region - featuring eleven long, narrow lakes that stretch southward from Lake Ontario. Cooperstown is home to the Baseball Hall of Fame Museum. Niagara Falls is one of the greatest natural wonders and it is worthwhile to see the falls from both the U.S. and the Canadian sides, as the views are different. Although there is a lot of commercialism and many tourist shops (and now a casino), the falls stand alone in their powerful impression.

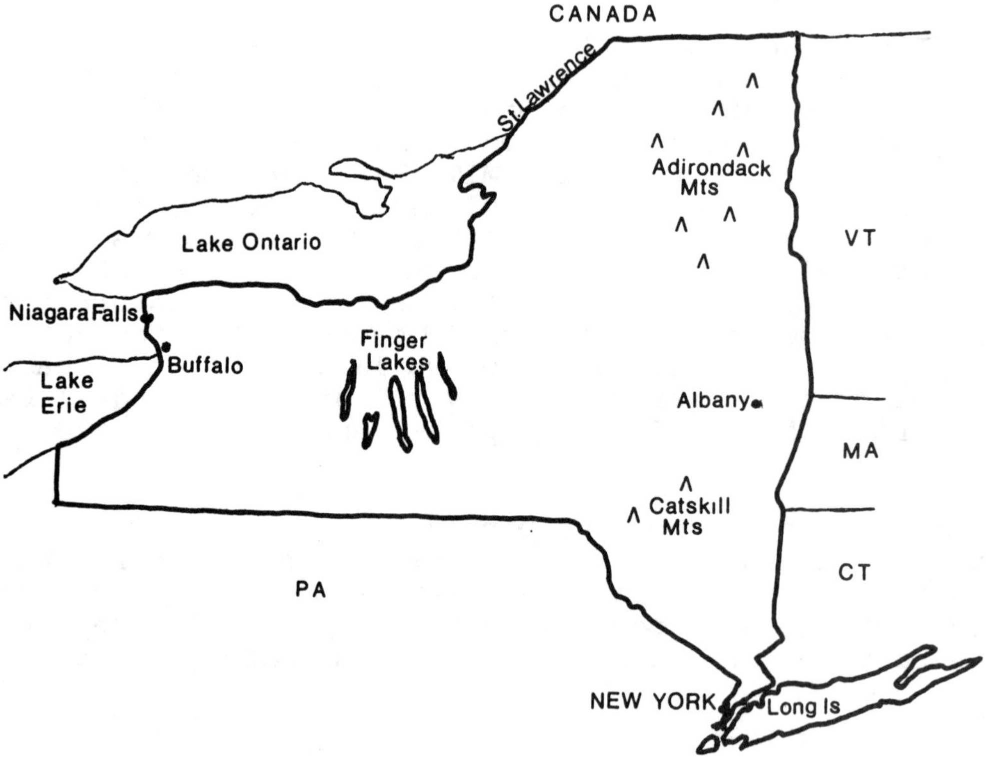

REVIEW - NEW ENGLAND AND NEW YORK

1. The well-known ski resort of Killington is in the state of ___________________.
2. ______________________________ and ______________________________ are two islands off the coast of Massachusetts to visit.
3. Franconia Notch is in the ____________________ Mountains area of New Hampshire.
4. Home of Yale University is ____________________, Connecticut.
5. Block Island is a wonderful recreation area in the state of ___________________.
6. Acadia National Park is off the coast of the state of _________________.
7. The walking trail in Boston to see sights such as Paul Revere's House is called the ______________________________.
8. Salem (famous for witch trials) is in Connecticut. True or False ____________
9. The five boroughs of New York City are ______________, ______________, ____________________, ____________________, ____________________.
10. Home to the Baseball Hall of Fame is ______________________, New York.
11. Jones Beach and Fire Island are southshore beaches on Long Island. True or False ___________________
12. La Guardia and Kennedy Airports are in the borough of the Bronx. True or False ______________
13. If you are in the state of ____________________, you can tour the seaside cottages (mansions!) of the city of Newport.
14. The Berkshires are in the far west region of the state of ___________________.
15. Montpelier is the capital of ____________________.

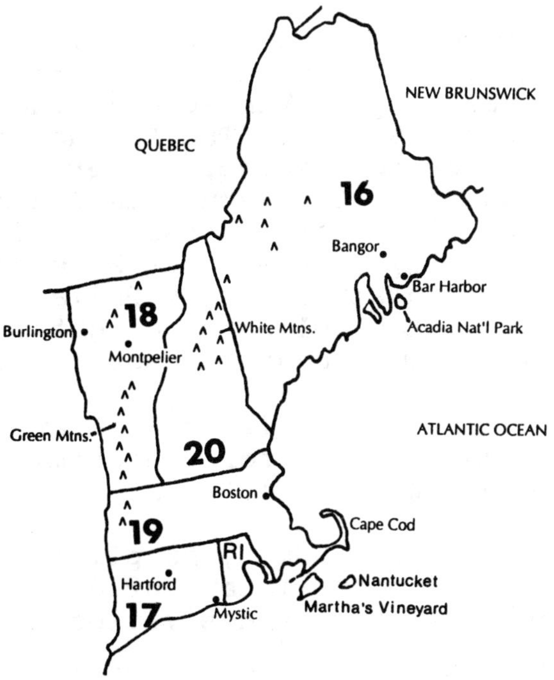

IDENTIFY THESE NEW ENGLAND STATES

16. ______________________________
17. ______________________________
18. ______________________________
19. ______________________________
20. ______________________________

We continue with the **MID-ATLANTIC REGION OF THE U.S.**

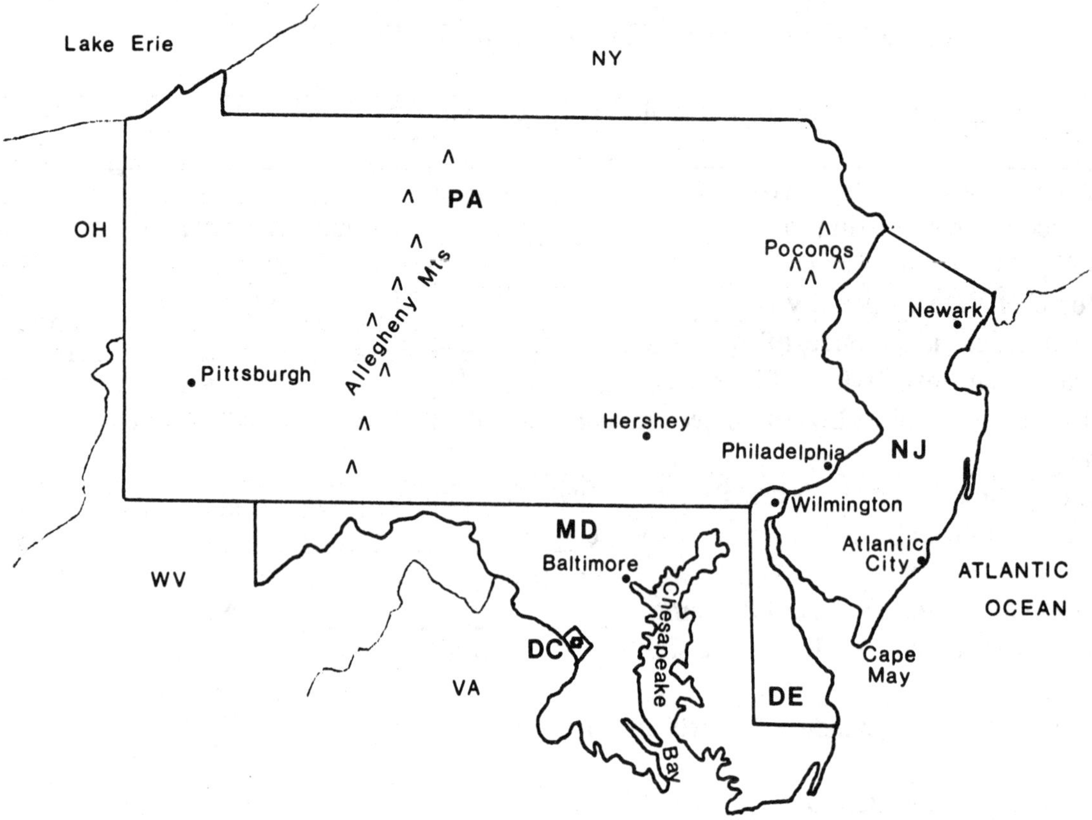

NEW JERSEY - Known as "The Garden State," New Jersey features Atlantic City for gambling and entertainment and Cape May is popular for its quaint bed and breakfast inns. The Newark airport serves as a gateway to New York City.

PENNSYLVANIA - There's historic Philadelphia (known as the "City of Brotherly Love"), where you can see the Liberty Bell and Independence Hall. Visit the Amish country (around the city of Lancaster), the city of chocolate - Hershey, and the Allegheny Mountains. The Pocono Mountains in the northeast are very popular for honeymooners. There is also skiing, hiking, fishing, hunting, and boating. Gettysburg is the site of one of the most famous battles of the Civil War. Pittsburgh offers a dazzling skyline and the center of the city is where the Allegheny and Monongahela Rivers meet to form the Ohio River. Enjoy Philadelphia cheese steak sandwiches and Pennsylvania Dutch culinary delights, such as pretzels, cheeses, and "Shoofly pie" (brown sugar/molasses pie).

DELAWARE - Brandywine Valley is a scenic area of this small state that has many historic sights. Wilmington is known for the chemical industry as the DuPont Company began production here.

MARYLAND - Sailing, yachting, visiting historic homes, sampling crab cakes, and spending time in Baltimore to see Inner Harbor and the National Aquarium - these are just a few of the activities the state of Maryland has to offer.

WASHINGTON, DC - The nation's capital is a sophisticated, diverse city with attractions such as the Smithsonian Institute (a large group of museums), the various memorials (Washington, Jefferson, Lincoln, etc.), and historic Georgetown. There is an excellent subway system.

We finish off the **MID-ATLANTIC** area with Virginia and West Virginia, then continue with the **SOUTHEAST REGION.** The state of Florida is featured separately for emphasis.

VIRGINIA - Just across the Potomac River from the nation's capital are the cities of Alexandria and Arlington (suburbs of Washington, DC). Arlington features Arlington National Cemetery and the Pentagon, and Alexandria features museums, restaurants, and shops along its seaport setting and is popular for its nightlife. Richmond is the capital and sixty miles from the city are the historic triangle cities - Williamsburg, Jamestown, and Yorktown. Virginia Beach on the Atlantic coast is a popular summer recreation area. The Shenandoah and Blue Ridge Mountains start at Front Royal in the northwest and run southwest to the border of North Carolina. The Skyline Drive through Shenandoah National Park runs for 100 miles. Luray Caverns is also in this area.

WEST VIRGINIA - The Allegheny Mountains, white-water rivers, forests and lakes typify West Virginia. The state has several top resorts and spas, and offers some great downhill skiing in winter. The prestigious Greenbrier Resort (AAA rated five diamond) is in White Sulphur Springs.

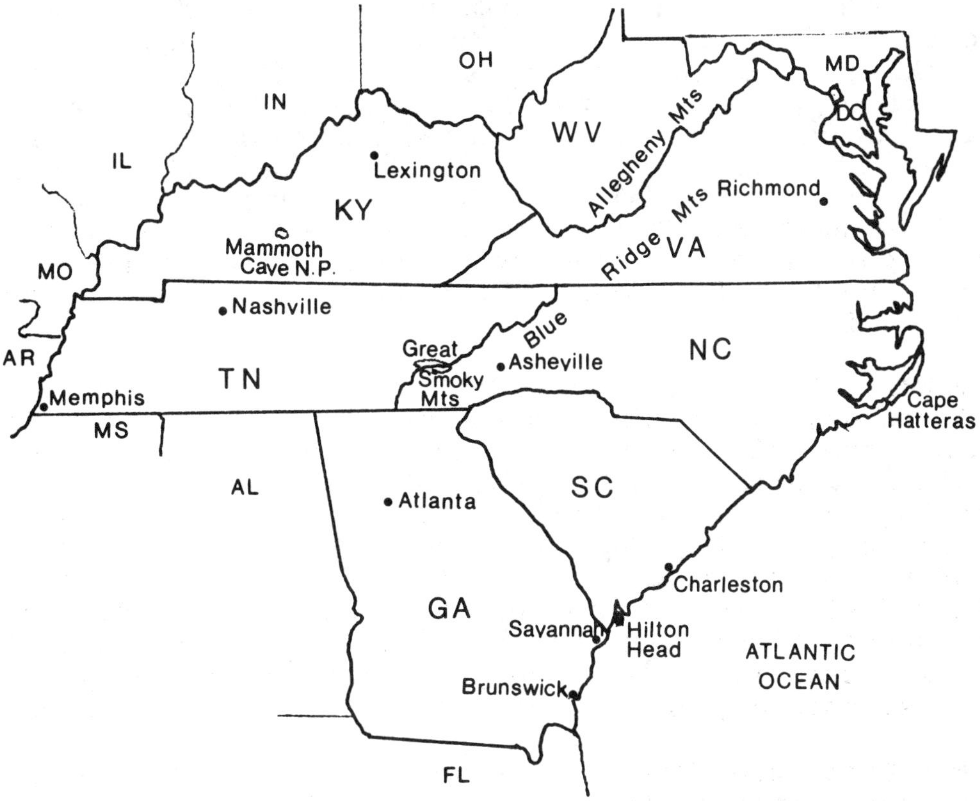

KENTUCKY - Mammoth Cave National Park is the world's longest cave system. Horse farms, bourbon distilleries, and southern cooking are some of this state's attractions. Local favorites in the heart of the "Bluegrass Region" include fried banana peppers, spoon bread, Mint Juleps, and hot browns (sandwiches with the bread fried/grilled). Major cities are Louisville and Lexington. Frankfort is the capital.

TENNESSEE - From Nashville (home of country music, the Grand Ole Opry and Opryland) to the city of Memphis and Graceland, Tennessee offers popular music, theme parks, and scenery. Enjoy southern hospitality and "down home" southern cooking. Breakfast menus here will feature grits, sausage gravy and hash browns.

NORTH CAROLINA - One of the most popular national parks of the U.S. is located here (and partly in Tennessee) - the Great Smoky Mountains National Park. Mt. Mitchell in the Pisgah National Forest is the highest point in the eastern U.S. The Outer Banks and the Cape Hatteras National Seashore are popular coastal areas. Asheville is a good base city to work from to sightsee in North Carolina, and the Biltmore Estate (built by George W. Vanderbilt in the 1890's) is a popular attraction.

SOUTH CAROLINA - Charleston is a well-preserved historic city - ideal for a walking tour. Hilton Head Island is a year-round, well-developed resort area.

GEORGIA - Atlanta is a major city with a wide variety of attractions. Shop at Lenox Square Mall and dine and be entertained in Underground Atlanta. See Stone Mountain - a park with a huge dome of granite that rises 825 feet above the surrounding plain. Three gigantic figures are sculpted on the mountain's north side - Jefferson Davis, General Thomas "Stonewall" Jackson, and General Robert E. Lee. There's also Six Flags Over Georgia (a 331-acre amusement park), many museums, shopping plazas, and numerous events and festivals. Savannah, Georgia is another city to visit. It offers a quaint and historic downtown laid out in squares, with beautiful landscaping, statues, and fountains and a restored riverfront walking area. The "Golden Isles" of Georgia generally refer to St. Simon's Island, Jekyll Island, and Sea Island - all near the city of Brunswick. Other attractions of the state include Callaway Gardens, the Okefenokee National Wildlife Refuge,, and the North Georgia Mountains. Pecans, peaches, and Vidalia onions are featured at roadside stands.

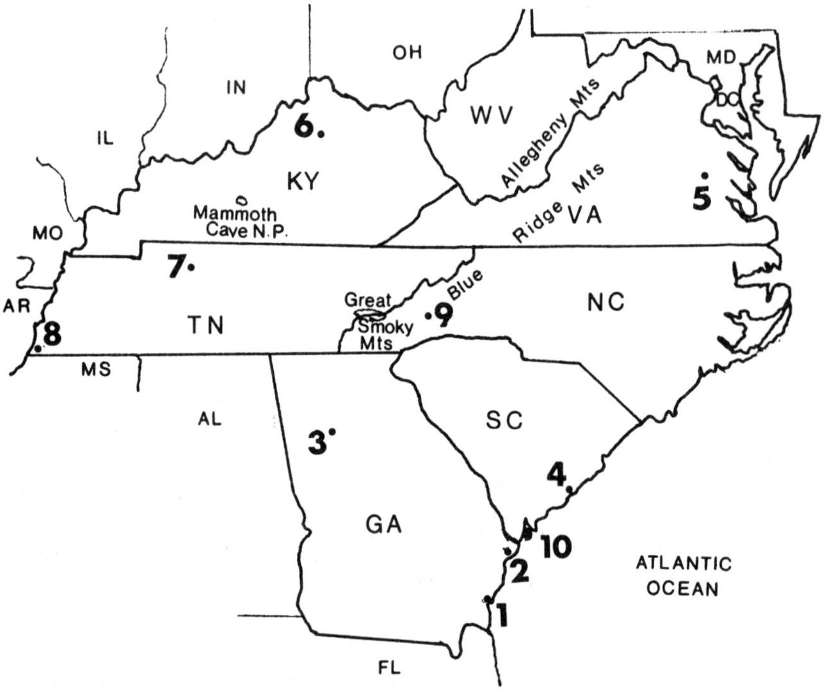

IDENTIFY THESE CITIES/PLACES

1. ____________
2. ____________
3. ____________
4. ____________
5. ____________
6. ____________
7. ____________
8. ____________
9. ____________
10. ____________

REVIEW - MID-ATLANTIC AND SOUTHEAST U.S.

1. The Allegheny and Monongahela Rivers meet to form the ___________ River in Pittsburgh.
2. Inner Harbor and the National Aquarium are sights in the city of _____________, Maryland.
3. Mt. Mitchell (the highest point in the eastern U.S.) is in the _________________ National Forest.
4. Hilton Head Island is a year-round resort area in the state of ________________.
5. Delaware's scenic beauty is found in an area called __________________ Valley.
6. St. Simon's, Jekyll, and _________________ are together called the Golden Isles of Georgia. They are all located near the city of ___________________.
7. In what state are the Outer Banks and Cape Hatteras National Seashore?

   ____
8. The three gigantic figures on Stone Mountain in Georgia are of Jefferson Davis, ___________________________, and ______________________________.
9. Mammoth Cave National Park is in the state of ______________________.
10. Two of the suburbs of Washington, DC are Alexandria, VA and ___________ _____________, Virginia.
11. The "Bluegrass Region" is an area of Kentucky. True or False ____________
12. If you visit the city of Asheville, you should try to tour the _________________ Estate.
13. The city of ________________________, Georgia features a quaint and historic downtown that is laid out in squares, with beautiful landscaping, statues, and fountains.
14. The Great Smoky Mountains National Park is in the states of ________________ and ________________________.
15. Richmond is the capital of _____________________.
16. The Skyline Drive in Virginia runs for ________ miles.
17. The historic triangle cities sixty miles from Richmond are the cities of Jamestown, ___________________, and _____________________
18. The Shenandoah and Blue Ridge Mountains start at Front Royal in northern Virginia and run southwest to the border of South Carolina. True or False ______
19. Historic Georgetown is a suburb of Asheville. True or False _______
20. Luray Caverns is in West Virginia. True or False _________

FLORIDA - The sunshine state is one of the most popular tourist destinations, with attractions such as Disney World, Busch Gardens, Cypress Gardens, the Kennedy Space Center, Everglades National Park, historic St. Augustine (oldest city in the U.S.), the art-deco district of Miami and trendy Coconut Grove, greek-influenced Tarpon Springs, and tropical Key West. There are beaches, beaches, beaches. The Gulf of Mexico is generally calmer and warmer than the Atlantic. Sanibel and Captiva on the west coast offer lovely beaches. The Panhandle beaches feature sand dunes on the crystal white, powdery shoreline (visit Destin, Ft. Walton, and Panama City). Key Biscayne is a lovely beach area of Miami, and the surfers frequent Cocoa Beach on the Atlantic. Tourism is everywhere in Florida, and some visitors don't even leave Orlando because of all the attractions (EPCOT, Disney World, Sea World, Wet 'n Wild, Universal Studios, Arabian Nights, the Church Street Station complex, the International Drive shops, and nearby Winter Park). More natural settings are found in the state's many national and state parks, wildlife preserves, river areas and springs. Enjoy Key Lime Pie, orange marmalade, fresh seafood (grouper sandwiches, shrimp, red snapper), and Cuban cuisine in areas of Miami and Ybor City (a district of Tampa). A map with detailed information on areas is provided below.

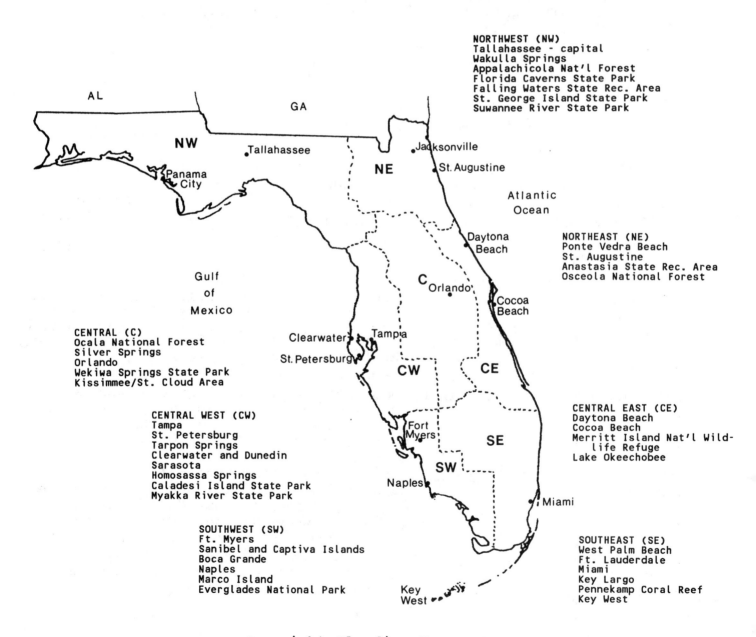

NORTHWEST (NW)
Tallahassee - capital
Wakulla Springs
Appalachicola Nat'l Forest
Florida Caverns State Park
Falling Waters State Rec. Area
St. George Island State Park
Suwannee River State Park

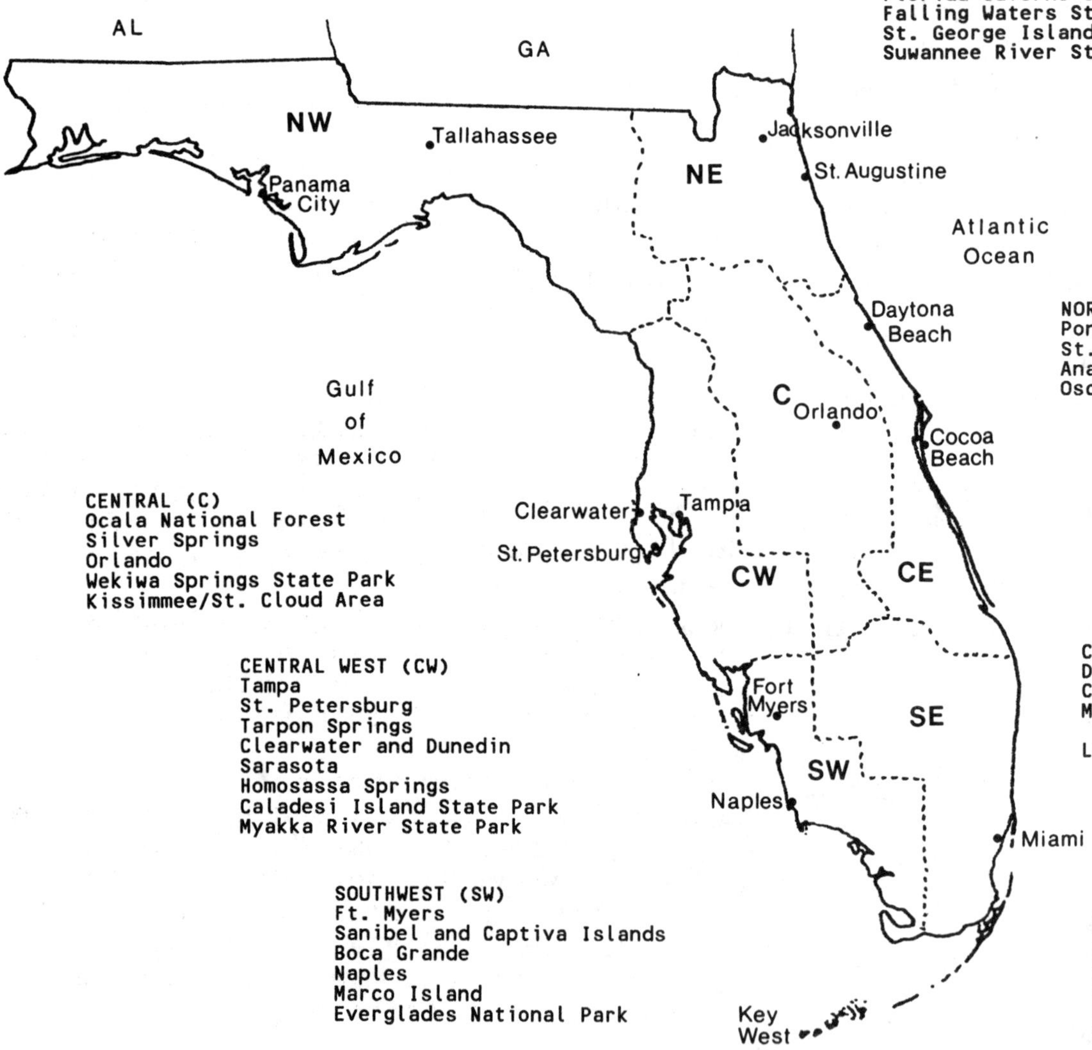

NORTHEAST (NE)
Ponte Vedra Beach
St. Augustine
Anastasia State Rec. Area
Osceola National Forest

CENTRAL (C)
Ocala National Forest
Silver Springs
Orlando
Wekiwa Springs State Park
Kissimmee/St. Cloud Area

CENTRAL WEST (CW)
Tampa
St. Petersburg
Tarpon Springs
Clearwater and Dunedin
Sarasota
Homosassa Springs
Caladesi Island State Park
Myakka River State Park

CENTRAL EAST (CE)
Daytona Beach
Cocoa Beach
Merritt Island Nat'l Wild-life Refuge
Lake Okeechobee

SOUTHWEST (SW)
Ft. Myers
Sanibel and Captiva Islands
Boca Grande
Naples
Marco Island
Everglades National Park

SOUTHEAST (SE)
West Palm Beach
Ft. Lauderdale
Miami
Key Largo
Pennekamp Coral Reef
Key West

The **SOUTHEAST** states of Alabama, Mississippi, Louisiana, and Arkansas are next. We will also include Texas.

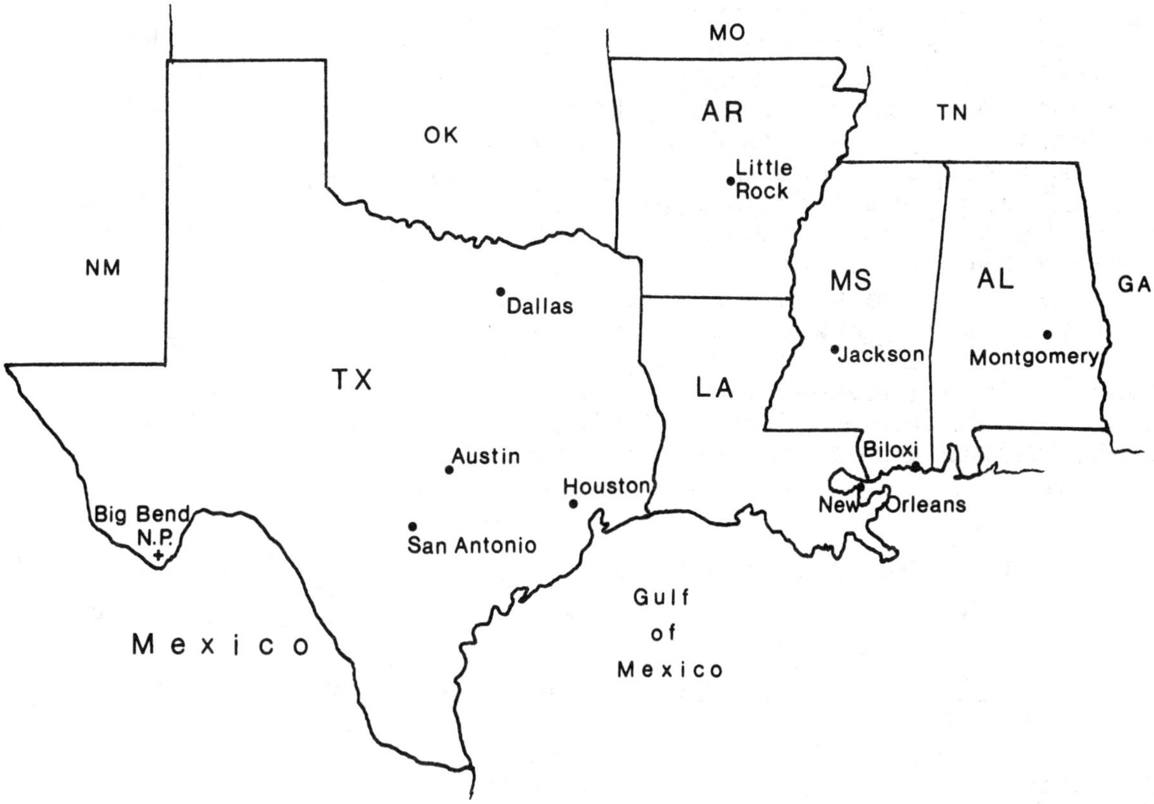

ALABAMA and MISSISSIPPI - Antibellum homes, gulf beaches, and the history and culture of the south are some of the highlights of Alabama and Mississippi. More than 30 casinos welcome tourists in the cities of Biloxi and Gulfport, Mississippi (nicknamed the "Magnolia State").

LOUISIANA - The most popular city for tourism in Louisiana is New Orleans, legendary for Dixieland Jazz, the French Quarter (Vieux Carre) area, and the ultimate party of Mardi Gras in February. Enjoy po-boy sandwiches, crawfish, and gumbo at some of the many restaurants. Watch the artists in Jackson Square, have beignets at the Cafe du Monde, take the Canal Street trolley to visit Audubon Zoo and see the Superdome.

ARKANSAS - Famous for its natural springs (Hot Springs and Eureka Springs) and the Ouachita and Ozark Mountains, Arkansas is ideal for outdoor recreation and vacations. Little Rock is the capital - a city that combines big city sophistication with small town ways.

TEXAS - Dallas/Ft. Worth is a sprawling metropolitan area (the Cotton Bowl and Reunion Tower are famous landmarks) and Houston - one of the largest cities in the U.S. - features the Astrodome and the NASA Space Center. In west Texas is Big Bend National Park and the Guadalupe Mountains. The city of San Antonio is where you can see the Alamo and walk along the Riverwalk. This is the "Lone Star State," and rivers that flow into the coastal plain region of Texas include the Trinity, Brazos, Colorado, Guadalupe, and San Antonio.

REVIEW - FLORIDA, SOUTHEAST AND TEXAS

1. Cities on the west coast of Florida include Ft. Lauderdale and West Palm Beach. True or False ______________
2. Key Biscayne is part of Key West. True or False ____________
3. Naples is in the Panhandle region of Florida. True or False ___________
4. The Everglades National Park is in the center of Florida. True or False _______
5. Surfers flock to ______________ Beach on the Atlantic Ocean side of Florida.
6. The capital of Texas is Dallas. True or False _____________
7. The Ouachita and Ozark Mountains are in the state of _________________
8. Visit the Astrodome and NASA Space Center in New Orleans. True or False ___________________
9. Casinos abound in the cities of Gulfport and ____________, Mississippi.
10. The Alamo and the Riverwalk are sights in what city?___________________
11. Tourists can visit the historic city of St. Augustine when touring Alabama. True or False ________________
12. Mardi Gras takes place in the month of _____________________.
13. The Vieux Carre is another name for the _________________ in New Orleans.
14. Big Bend National Park is in Florida. True or False _____________
15. The state of ________________ is famous for its natural springs (Hot Springs and Eureka Springs).

A MIXED-UP MAP

The numbered cities are in the wrong place. Give the number of the correct city.

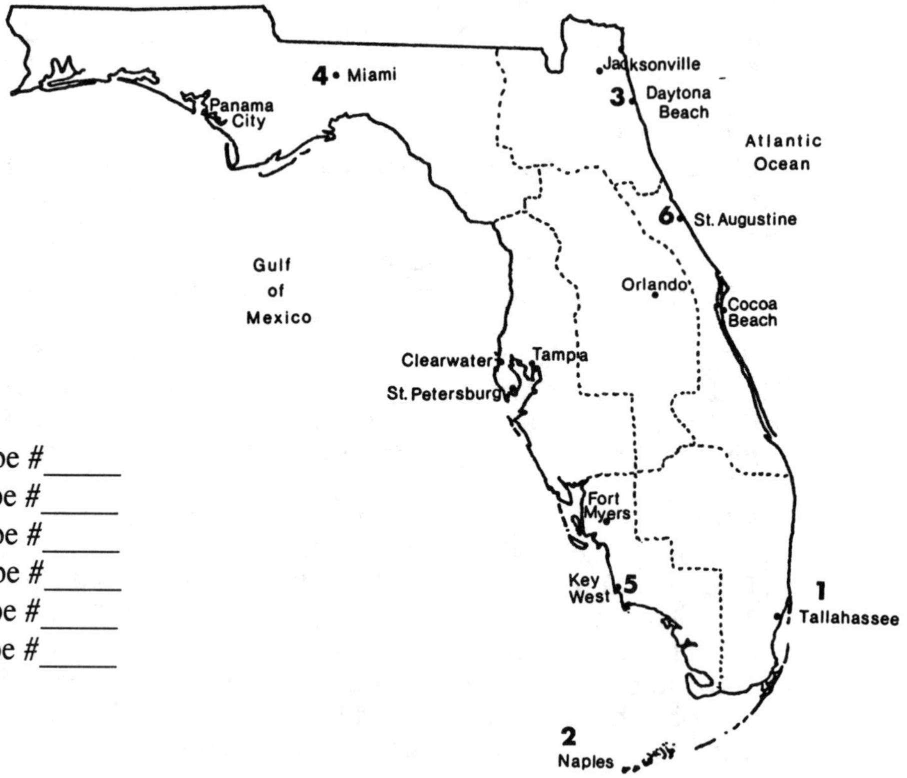

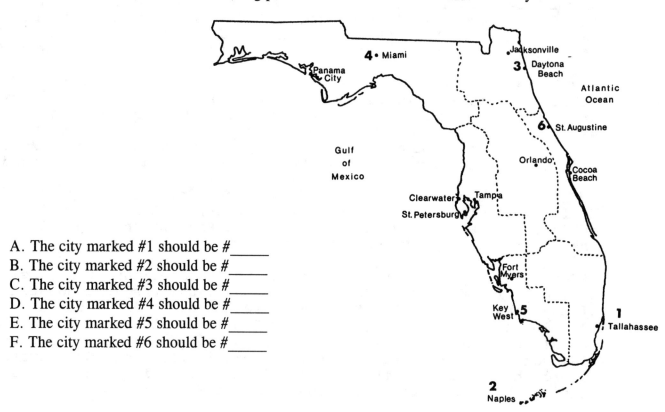

A. The city marked #1 should be #_____
B. The city marked #2 should be #_____
C. The city marked #3 should be #_____
D. The city marked #4 should be #_____
E. The city marked #5 should be #_____
F. The city marked #6 should be #_____

On to the **GREAT LAKES, MIDWEST AND PLAINS REGIONS**, to cover Ohio, Michigan, Indiana, Illinois, Wisconsin, Minnesota, Iowa, Missouri, North Dakota, South Dakota, Nebraska, Kansas, and Oklahoma.

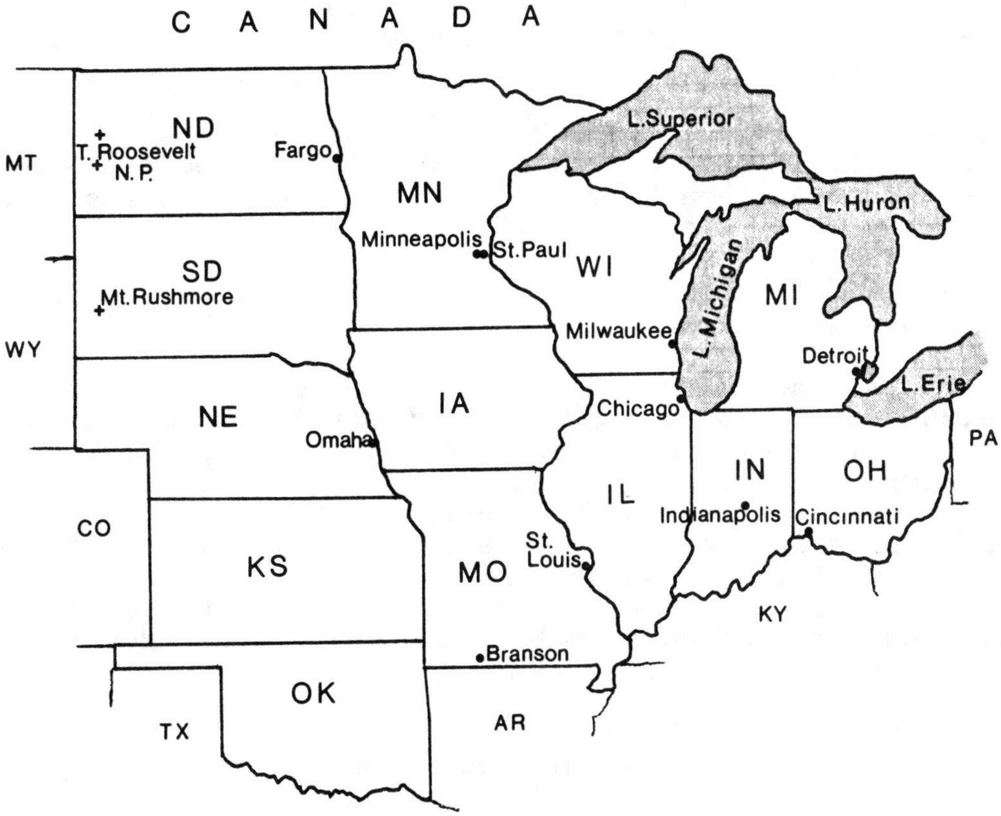

OHIO AND MICHIGAN - Ohio's major cities include Dayton, Akron, Cleveland, Cincinnati, and Toledo. Michigan boasts more than 11,000 lakes and Detroit is its major city. Detroit is home to automobile production - see the Henry Ford Museum there - and shop and dine at the Renaissance Center.

ILLINOIS - Chicago is the "Windy City" and features famous museums, and an extensive network of parks and beaches along Lake Michigan (but the water stays pretty cold). Chicago's theater/club scene is very popular, and the Chicago Symphony Orchestra is world renowned. Chicago is divided into two areas: the Loop, south of the Chicago River, which is the financial district and home to State Street's retail giants; and Michigan Avenue, north of the river - called the "Magnificent Mile" because of the exclusive retailers there. The John G. Shedd Aquarium, the Field Museum of Natural History, and the Art Institute of Chicago are all worth a visit. Nightclubs are concentrated in the Loop area - especially on Rush Street. Chicago's O'Hare airport is one of the world's busiest.

INDIANA - Racing fans will appreciate the Indianapolis 500 in May, and the state offers good hunting, fishing, cross-country skiing, bicycling and lakefront beaches.

WISCONSIN AND MINNESOTA - Wisconsin is the dairy state - and is also known for the production of beer. Minnesota has a great deal of pristine wilderness and the bustling twin cities of Minneapolis and St. Paul.

IOWA - Iowa is mostly farmland and is known as the "Hawkeye State." Major cities include Dubuque, Cedar Rapids, and Davenport.

MISSOURI - Missouri's major cities for tourism are St. Louis, Kansas City, and the new hot spot, Branson. Branson is popular for music and variety shows (especially country-western singers/shows). St. Louis is known as the "Gateway to the Western U.S." and has a landmark arch that rises 630 feet.

NORTH DAKOTA - Visit North Dakota to experience native American culture. There is also some legalized gambling. Theodore Roosevelt National Park is a popular area to visit. The most populous region - the Red River Valley - has two major cities, Fargo and Grand Forks. The world's largest buffalo - a 60-ton giant sculpture - is clearly visible from Interstate 94 at Jamestown, and is accompanied by a pioneer village with museums and shops.

SOUTH DAKOTA - Mount Rushmore is located here in the Black Hills. This 6,200 foot high rock carving depicts the heads of Washington, Jefferson, Lincoln, and Theodore Roosevelt. Impressive caves are another feature of this state. You can also see the huge monument being carved of Crazy Horse. Enjoy a buffalo burger (supposedly healthier than regular ground beef). The Badlands National Park features spires, pinnacles, buttes, and gorges throughout its 244,000 acres of eerie topography. The Corn palace in Mitchell is a man-made attraction that is both stunning and whimsical - it's a structure decorated with 3,000 bushels of corn.

NEBRASKA, KANSAS, OKLAHOMA - These states offer a taste of the Old West and a more leisurely, uncrowded atmosphere.

REVIEW - GREAT LAKES, MIDWEST, AND PLAINS REGIONS OF THE U.S.

1. Michigan boasts more than ________________ lakes.
2. ________________________ is the dairy state.
3. Name three cities in Iowa. ____
4. The Black Hills are in North Dakota. True or False ____________
5. The landmark arch in St. Louis rises ______ feet high.
6. Mt. Rushmore depicts the heads of Washington, __________________, ______ ___________________ , and ______________________________.
7. Branson is the new hot spot in the state of __________________.
8. The "twin city" of Minneapolis is ____________________.
9. There is some legalized gambling in North Dakota. True or False ___________
10. The Indianapolis 500 takes place in the month of ___________.
11. Nightclubs are concentrated in Chicago's Loop area, especially on ____________ Street.
12. The _________________________ Aquarium is a popular attraction of Chicago.
13. ________________________ National Park in South Dakota features an eerie topography of spires, pinnacles, buttes, and gorges.
14. The world's largest buffalo can be seen in the city of ___________________, North Dakota.
15. Chicago's ___________ airport is one of the world's busiest.

Now on to the **MOUNTAIN STATES AND PACIFIC COAST REGION OF THE U.S.**

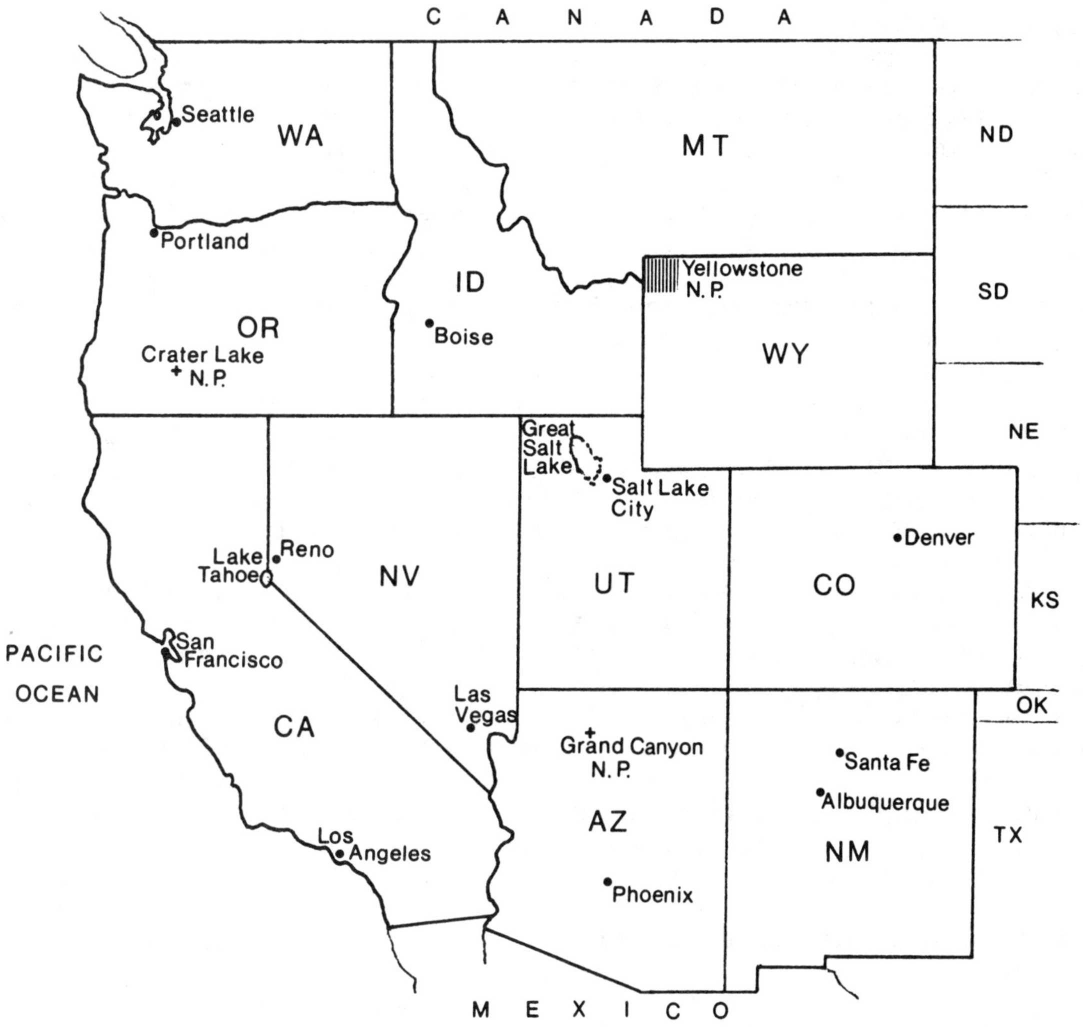

COLORADO - Denver is the "Mile High City" and it's where most people fly to for traveling to the state's many ski resorts. The city is clean and attractions include the U.S. Mint and Larimer Square. Visit the U.S. Air Force Academy or explore the nearby Garden of the Gods and Cave of the Winds. Northwest of Denver is Rocky Mountain National Park - an area of magnificent peaks, valleys, and nature trails. Beautiful Pike's Peak is near Colorado Springs. Mesa Verde National Park is in the "Four Corners" area of the state (the corner shared with the borders of Utah, New Mexico, and Arizona). A breathtaking journey can be taken on the Durango-Silverton Narrow Gauge Railroad through the San Juan Mountains. Colorado has a lot to offer in outdoor activities and great scenery.

WYOMING - Here you will find Yellowstone National Park and Grand Teton National Park - with some of the most impressive scenery in America. More than 200 geysers are found in Yellowstone, with "Old Faithful" being the most famous. Witness geology in action at Mammoth Hot Springs in Yellowstone. The Grand Tetons are "purple mountains of majesty" and the Snake River in this area is popular for white-water rafting trips. Jackson is a ski resort and the town retains the atmosphere of the Old West (visit the Million Dollar Cowboy Bar where the seats are saddles!). In addition to the Rocky Mountains, Wyoming also has the Bighorn and Laramie Mountains. Devil's Tower National Monument is also here.

IDAHO - The Snake and Salmon Rivers run through this state and they offer popular recreational activities. There is one of the best ski areas here - Sun Valley. The Hells Canyon National Recreation Area (along the border of Oregon) has the deepest gorge in North America - with walls rising almost 8,000 feet/2,500 meters from the canyon base. And there's only one way to see it - board a jetboat to speed you through its pristine wilderness, and skim over miles of whitewater rapids between sheer granite walls. Craters of the Moon National Monument offers excellent views of vast lava fields covered by cinder cones of hardened lava. Boise is the capital of the state, and other major cities are Twin Falls, Pocatello, and Coeur d'Alene.

MONTANA - Visitors to Montana find quiet, scenic areas with little commercialism. On the border with Canada is the impressive Glacier National Park. The Rocky Mountains are part of Montana's topography, and the Bitterroot Mountain Range borders Montana with Idaho. While the eastern part of the state is farmland and good grazing land, the western part drew people for mining, especially to the areas around Missoula, Helena, and Butte. Ski resorts in the state include Big Sky, Big Mountain, the Great Divide, and Bridger Bowl.

UTAH - Salt Lake City is the center of "Mormon Country" and it is a unique experience to see the Great Salt Lake - the largest lake west of the Mississippi. Only the Dead Sea has a higher salt content than the Great Salt Lake. Visit Temple Square - world headquarters for the Church of Jesus Christ Latter-day Saints (Mormon), and hear the Mormon Tabernacle Choir accompanied by the massive pipe organ. Other attractions in the city include Brigham Young University, Joseph Smith Memorial Building, and the "This is the Place" monument. The state's awesome natural attractions include: Bryce and Zion National Parks, Monument Valley, Arches National Park, Canyonlands, Capitol Reef National Park, Flaming Gorge Recreational Area, Natural Bridges, Rainbow Bridge, and Dinosaur National Monument. The renowned Wasatch Mountains conveniently cluster the majority of ski areas (Park City, Deer Valley, Alta, and Snowbird). There is a popular myth that it's hard to get an alcoholic drink in Utah. Alcoholic beverages may be bought in several ways. There are state-owned liquor stores that offer most major brands. They are open every day, with varying hours, except on Sunday. Most fine restaurants in Utah have liquor licenses. Many other restaurants provide set-ups (mixers) for "brown-bag" liquor (alcohol that the customers bring in).

ARIZONA - This state is home to the Grand Canyon, Oak Creek Canyon, Sycamore Canyon, Walnut Canyon and Canyon de Chelly National Monuments, and more. There is the Painted Desert, the Petrified Forest, Sedona and the Red Rock Country, cactus-studded deserts, scenic Lake Powell, and the living history town of Tombstone. There are ghost towns and mining camps, rivers for white-water rafting, Lake Havasu (the site of the London Bridge), Indian reservations (Navajo, Hopi, Apache, and many others), dude ranches, and world-class resorts. Tucson is a good base for exploring the Sonora Desert. Phoenix is the major gateway city and the capital. South Mountain Park, eight miles south, contains more than 14,000 acres of canyons, peaks, rock formations, and other landscapes. Phoenix and approximately 20 other surrounding communities are often collectively referred to as the "Valley of the Sun," because of the warm, dry desert climate that all the Salt River Valley communities share. Grand Canyon National Park is about four hours' drive from Phoenix. This product of 10 million years of erosion from the Colorado

River and elements of nature is a spectacular sight. The South Rim is open year round. The North Rim is open from mid-May to mid-October.

NEW MEXICO - Santa Fe is both the capital and one of the most popular cities to visit. Known as the "Land of Enchantment," New Mexico is a great combination of rolling hills, mountains, valleys, rivers, deserts, plains, and farmland. Albuquerque is a big city with a "small town" feel. Walk through Old Town, the city's historic district, see the museums, shop the shops, and dine in some of the quaint or the sophisticated restaurants. Tour outside the city to Sandia Peak for the views or go to the Puye Cliff Dwellings and see the petrogylphs (inscriptions in the rock). Visit Taos Pueblo and learn some of the special features in the culture and lifestyle of these Indians. Taos, at the foothills of the Sangre de Christo Mountains, is a well-known art center and a popular ski resort in winter. Carlsbad Caverns is located near the Texas border. The caverns and the huge underground rooms are estimated to be the oldest in the world. Self-guiding tours will take you nearly 830 feet down for an inspection of three miles of chambers.

NEVADA - Las Vegas and Reno are famous gambling and entertainment centers. There's lots of neon and noise in Las Vegas and the architecture of some of the lavish hotels is really stunning. The new Stratosphere Tower is probably the most visible attraction at 1,149 feet high - and there's a roller coaster ride at the top! Visit the magnificent Hoover Dam (southwest of the city) which creates Lake Mead. Lake Tahoe (near Reno) offers a year-round resort area and lush natural scenery. Ski resorts are dotted around the lake that is shared with the state of California - Diamond Peak on the Nevada side; Squaw Valley, Heavenly, Homewood, and Northstar-at-Tahoe are all on the California side.

CALIFORNIA - California is such a large state with so many different places to visit, it would be hard to see it all in one trip. LA - Los Angeles is home to the Queen Mary, Disneyland, Knotts Berry Farm, Little Tokyo, Hollywood, and the beaches of Malibu, Redondo, Venice, and Santa Monica - to name a few. Visit Mann's Chinese Theater to see the footprints, handprints, pawprints, and hoofprints of the stars. The studios for CBS and NBC offer tours. The colorful Farmer's Market is best visited mid-day - enjoy an outdoor lunch there. San Diego has one of the world's finest zoos. You can also make a quick trip down to Tijuana, Mexico from here. The Spanish missions and rugged coastline are worth touring. San Francisco - a multi-cultural city that boasts sights such as Fisherman's Wharf, the Embarcadero, Chinatown, Ghirardelli Square, Nob Hill, The Cannery, the Golden Gate Bridge - is one of the best cities to visit. Chinatown souvenirs, miniature cable cars, sourdough bread starter, and Ghirardelli chocolate are all popular souvenirs. Don't miss a trip to the island of Alcatraz, to see the famous prison closed since 1963. Tours are available from the Wharf. A day out to Sausalito is worthwhile, as well as trips to Mt. Tamalpais and Point Reyes National Seashore. Wine producing areas (Sonoma and Napa Valley in particular), the giant Redwoods, Yosemite and Sequoia National Parks, Lassen Volcanic National Park, Death Valley National Monument - these are other state attractions. Fly into Los Angeles and out of San Francisco so you can drive up the Pacific Coast Highway and visit Hearst Castle (it's less dangerous than driving down - in the lane on the cliff's edge!). The northern Sierra Nevada Range is a wonderful ski region.

CALIFORNIA

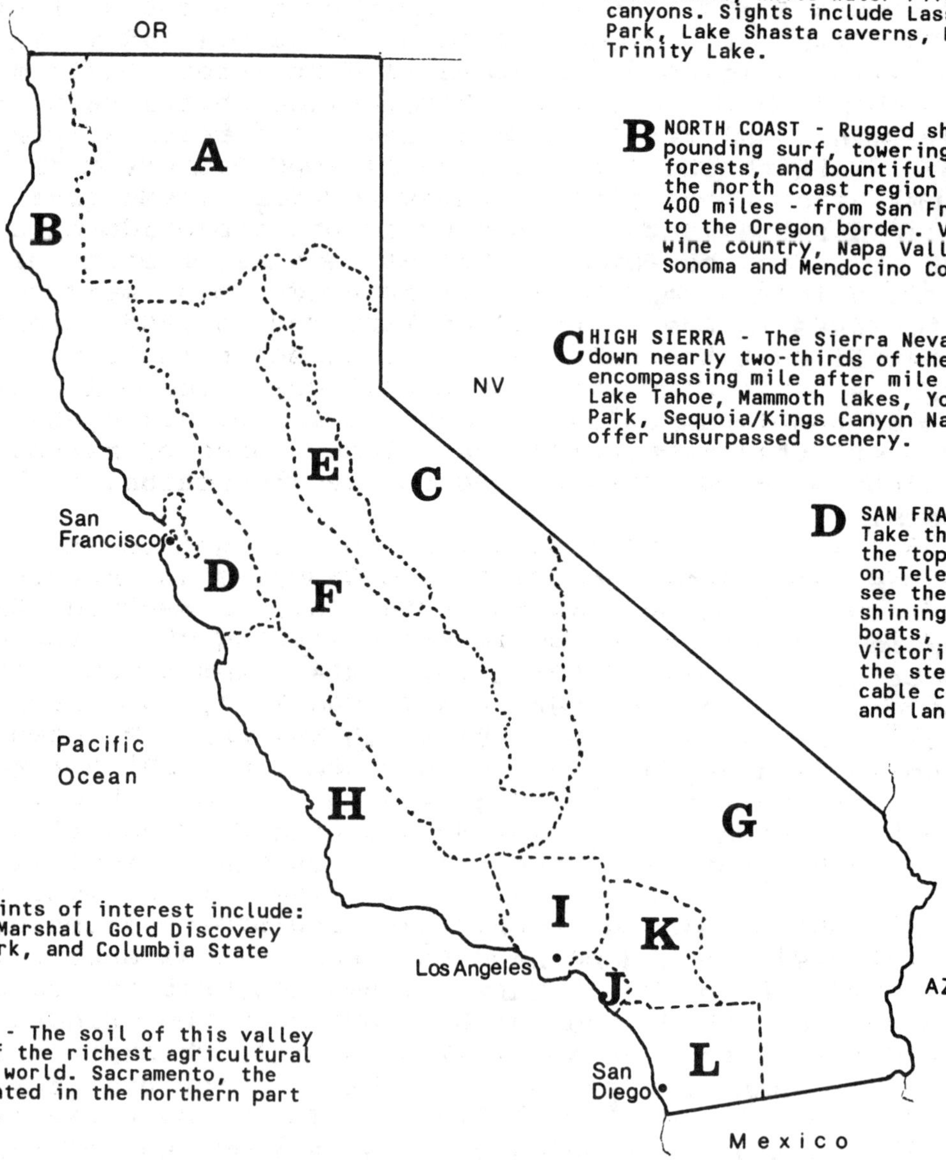

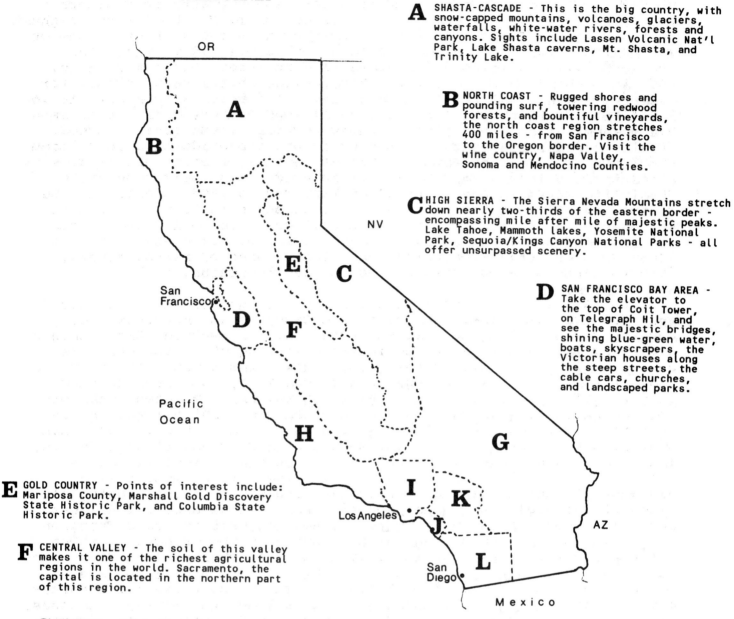

A SHASTA-CASCADE - This is the big country, with snow-capped mountains, volcanoes, glaciers, waterfalls, white-water rivers, forests and canyons. Sights include Lassen Volcanic Nat'l Park, Lake Shasta caverns, Mt. Shasta, and Trinity Lake.

B NORTH COAST - Rugged shores and pounding surf, towering redwood forests, and bountiful vineyards, the north coast region stretches 400 miles - from San Francisco to the Oregon border. Visit the wine country, Napa Valley, Sonoma and Mendocino Counties.

C HIGH SIERRA - The Sierra Nevada Mountains stretch down nearly two-thirds of the eastern border - encompassing mile after mile of majestic peaks. Lake Tahoe, Mammoth lakes, Yosemite National Park, Sequoia/Kings Canyon National Parks - all offer unsurpassed scenery.

D SAN FRANCISCO BAY AREA - Take the elevator to the top of Coit Tower, on Telegraph Hil, and see the majestic bridges, shining blue-green water, boats, skyscrapers, the Victorian houses along the steep streets, the cable cars, churches, and landscaped parks.

E GOLD COUNTRY - Points of interest include: Mariposa County, Marshall Gold Discovery State Historic Park, and Columbia State Historic Park.

F CENTRAL VALLEY - The soil of this valley makes it one of the richest agricultural regions in the world. Sacramento, the capital is located in the northern part of this region.

G DESERTS - Miles of sand and cactus, combined with a wide variety of flora and fauna cover this area - along with world-class resorts and spas. Palm Springs, Cathedral City, Desert Hot Springs, Coachella Valley - these are a few communities.

H CENTRAL COAST - Here you will find enchanting Hearst Castle and Mediterranean-like market-places - an area that includes the cities of Ventura, San Luis Obispo, and Oxnard, the Channel Islands, the Monterrey Peninsula, and Ojai Valley. Visit the many missions.

I GREATER LOS ANGELES - This is the "Entertainment Capital of the World," and a huge metropolitan area.

J ORANGE COUNTY - Theme parks and beaches dominate this region.

K INLAND EMPIRE - Lakes for warm weather sports are just a short trip from snow-covered mountains - so you can water ski and snow ski in the same day.

L SAN DIEGO COUNTY - This area epitomizes the California lifestyle, with elegant shopping malls, ranches and estates, farms and golf-courses, forested mountains and historical sites.

OREGON - Outdoor activities and beautiful scenery attract visitors to Oregon. Portland is the state's largest city. Mt. Hood - the highest mountain in the state - is a ski resort area, along with Mt. Bachelor, Timberline, and others in the Cascade Mountains. Visit Crater Lake National Park, tour the Columbia River Gorge area, Multnomah Falls, and the Bonneville Dam and Lock. The Pacific shoreline stretches for 400 miles and features beautiful sandy, broad beaches from Astoria to Brookings. At Coos Bay, visit the Myrtlewood Factory to see craftsmen at work carving dishes, jewelry and decorative items from hardwood. Resort villages, small cities and campgrounds provide excellent accommodations for those seeking activities such as crabbing, fishing, sunbathing and surfing. Fort Clasop National Monument marks the spot where the explorers Lewis and Clark wintered in 1805. Seaside is the state's oldest resort and there is a monument here to mark the spot where Lewis and Clark constructed a salt cairn to boil down the sea water to obtain needed salt. The capital of the state, Salem, is located in the Williamette Valley, a lush region of farms, rivers, forests, and parks bordered by snow-capped mountains.

WASHINGTON - The state of Washington has a jagged coastline of lush rain forests, beautiful mountains (the Cascades and Mount Rainier), and the cosmopolitan and multi-cultural city of Seattle. Hint: When traveling to Seattle, bring comfortable walking shoes as there are quite a few steep hills in the city. Seattle was first settled in 1851 at Alki Point. It was then called New York, but later renamed in honor of a friendly Indian, Chief Sealth. The city grew considerably as a lumber town and later as a departure point for gold prospectors. Start your visit to Seattle with the Space Needle, and then tour Pike Place Marketplace, the Seattle Aquarium and Pioneer Square. The Puget Sound area is said to be one of the prettiest places in the world and one of the most satisfying to live in. The metropolitan district of Seattle-Tacoma-Everett has fine stores, restaurants, all kinds of cultural activities, and nice residential suburbs. Bridges and ferries provide scenic waterway views, as well as transportation to the islands. In north central Washington is the Grand Coolee Dam - the world's largest concrete gravity dam (a "coolee" is a deep valley gouged out by glacial waters). Olympic National Park is west of Seattle and North Cascades National Park is about 125 miles northeast of the city. Other places to visit include: the San Juan Islands, Mt. Baker, Spirit Lake at Mt. St. Helens, and Deception Pass. Grand Ronde Canyon and Paulouse Falls (north of the city of Walla Walla) are other remarkable sights in this state. The Blue Mountains offer hunting for deer and elk and the valleys teem with wild duck, geese, and other game birds. There is also skiing in the Blue Ridge area.

ALASKA AND HAWAII are covered separately - as they are such popular destinations.

REVIEW - MOUNTAIN AND PACIFIC STATES

1. The U.S. Mint and Larimer Square are sights of the city of _______________.
2. Squaw Valley is a ski resort of the Lake Tahoe area and is located on the California side. True or False ___________
3. ____________________ is the capital of New Mexico.
4. The living history town of Tombstone is in the state of _______________.
5. "This is the Place" monument can be seen when visiting __________________, Utah.
6. Hell's Canyon National Recreation Area has walls rising 8,000 ft. True or False ______
7. Park City, Deer Valley, and Alta ski resorts are in the _______________ Mountains.
8. The Stratosphere Tower in Las Vegas is most visible, with its __________ ft. height.
9. The Rocky Mountains are part of Montana's topography, and the ____________ Mountains border Montana and Idaho.
10. In the state of _________________ you can see the Painted Desert, the Petrified Forest, Sedona and Red Rock Country.
11. Rocky Mountain National Park is in Arizona. True or False __________
12. The "Four Corners" area refers to the region where the border of Colorado meets the borders of the states of __________________, _________________, and ____________________.
13. The Million Dollar Cowboy Bar where the seats are saddles is in ______________, Wyoming.
14. More than ______ geysers are found in Yellowstone National Park.
15. The Bighorn and Laramie Mountain Ranges are in Montana. True or False _________
16. Hoover Dam in Nevada creates Lake Tahoe. True or False ______________
17. Mt. Hood is the highest mountain in the state of _______________.
18. Name the four beaches mentioned in the Los Angeles area. ____________________, ______________, _________________, and ______________________________
19. What is the capital of California? ____________________
20. Death Valley is in Nevada. True or False __________
21. The state of ____________________ is known as the "Land of Enchantment."
22. Taos is at the foothills of the _________________________ Mountains.
23. The ______________ Rim of the Grand Canyon is open year round.
24. Footprints, handprints, and pawprints of the stars can be seen at _________________ ______________________ in Los Angeles.
25. The famous prison closed since 1963 off the coast of San Francisco on the island of ______________________.
26. Big Sky and Big Mountain are ski resorts of Lake Tahoe. True or False ___________
27. Flaming Gorge National Recreation Area is in New Mexico. True or False __________
28. Devil's Tower National Monument is in California. True or False ___________
29. The city of ___________________ and its surrounding communities are often collectively referred to as the "Valley of the Sun."
30. Mesa Verde National Park is in the state of ___________________.

U.S. - MAJOR CITIES AND STATES FOR TRAVELERS

The traveler in the U.S. can enjoy a variety of activities and sights. Major areas that travelers visit include New York, Florida, Texas, Arizona, Washington-DC, California, Alaska, Hawaii - just to name a few. It is worthwhile to know a little about every state, particularly if you intend to work as a travel agent.

Major cities of the U.S. include New York, Los Angeles, San Francisco, Dallas/Ft. Worth, Seattle, Boston, Philadelphia, Orlando, Miami, New Orleans, Chicago, Atlanta, San Diego, Phoenix, and Washington-DC.

Because the states of Hawaii and Alaska are major tourist destinations of their own, they will be studied separately with profiles to complete, marked, blank and test maps and exercises.

To complete your study of the U.S., fill out profiles on states. Use guide books, maps, magazines and other resources to research the areas. If you are a member of AAA, the tour books and maps available can be very helpful. Do major states first, then continue with other states.

A good idea is to create a file of index cards on states, cities, and country destinations, using the profile format. You may also want to start a library of information on states. Contact the state tourist offices to receive information and brochures.

Below is a sample profile form completed for MAINE:

STATE: Maine CAPITAL: Augusta

ABBREVIATION: ME MAJOR CITY/ AIRPORT CODES: AUG, BGR, PWM

MAJOR CITIES AND PLACES OF INTEREST: Augusta, Bangor, Portland. Acadia Nat'l Park - enter from Bar Harbor. Many lakes and ponds, scenic seashore areas, historic homes, nautical history. Kittery - oldest town, famous for shipbuilding. Ski areas & outdoor activities. Other cities to visit: Kennebunkport, Wiscasset, York, York Harbor, Bethel, Boothbay Harbor, Camden, Freeport

SPECIAL INFORMATION (NICKNAME, RESTRICTIONS, EVENTS, TAXES, WEATHER, ETC.): Pine Tree State, cold winters, scenic, horseracing at Presque Isle, etc.

ECONOMY (PRODUCTS, ETC.): lumber, paper, potatoes, cement, lobster, ship-building

Note: A limited number of forms is provided. Use index cards for extra study. A similar format can be used for detailing cities, provinces or territories of other countries.

STATE:______________________________ CAPITAL:______________________________

MAJOR CITY/

ABBREVIATION:______ AIRPORT CODES:____

MAJOR CITIES AND PLACES OF INTEREST:____

____

____

____

____

____

SPECIAL INFORMATION (NICKNAME, RESTRICTIONS, EVENTS, TAXES, WEATHER, ETC.):

____

ECONOMY (PRODUCTS, ETC.):____

STATE:______________________________ CAPITAL:______________________________

MAJOR CITY/

ABBREVIATION:______ AIRPORT CODES:____

MAJOR CITIES AND PLACES OF INTEREST:____

____

____

____

____

____

SPECIAL INFORMATION (NICKNAME, RESTRICTIONS, EVENTS, TAXES, WEATHER, ETC.):

____

ECONOMY (PRODUCTS, ETC.):____

STATE:______________________________ CAPITAL:______________________________

MAJOR CITY/

ABBREVIATION:______ AIRPORT CODES:____

MAJOR CITIES AND PLACES OF INTEREST:____

____

____

____

____

____

SPECIAL INFORMATION (NICKNAME, RESTRICTIONS, EVENTS, TAXES, WEATHER, ETC.):

____

ECONOMY (PRODUCTS, ETC.):____

STATE:______________________________ CAPITAL:______________________________

MAJOR CITY/

ABBREVIATION:______ AIRPORT CODES:____

MAJOR CITIES AND PLACES OF INTEREST:_____________________________________

____

____

____

____

____

SPECIAL INFORMATION (NICKNAME, RESTRICTIONS, EVENTS, TAXES, WEATHER, ETC.):

____

ECONOMY (PRODUCTS, ETC.):____

STATE:______________________________ CAPITAL:______________________________

MAJOR CITY/

ABBREVIATION:______ AIRPORT CODES:____

MAJOR CITIES AND PLACES OF INTEREST:_____________________________________

____

____

____

____

____

SPECIAL INFORMATION (NICKNAME, RESTRICTIONS, EVENTS, TAXES, WEATHER, ETC.):

____

ECONOMY (PRODUCTS, ETC.):____

STATE:______________________________ CAPITAL:______________________________

MAJOR CITY/

ABBREVIATION:______ AIRPORT CODES:____

MAJOR CITIES AND PLACES OF INTEREST:_____________________________________

____

____

____

____

____

SPECIAL INFORMATION (NICKNAME, RESTRICTIONS, EVENTS, TAXES, WEATHER, ETC.):

____

ECONOMY (PRODUCTS, ETC.):____

STATE:______________________________ CAPITAL:______________________________

MAJOR CITY/

ABBREVIATION:______ AIRPORT CODES:____

MAJOR CITIES AND PLACES OF INTEREST:____

____

____

____

____

____

SPECIAL INFORMATION (NICKNAME, RESTRICTIONS, EVENTS, TAXES, WEATHER, ETC.):

____

ECONOMY (PRODUCTS, ETC.):____

STATE:______________________________ CAPITAL:______________________________

MAJOR CITY/

ABBREVIATION:______ AIRPORT CODES:____

MAJOR CITIES AND PLACES OF INTEREST:____

____

____

____

____

____

SPECIAL INFORMATION (NICKNAME, RESTRICTIONS, EVENTS, TAXES, WEATHER, ETC.):

____

ECONOMY (PRODUCTS, ETC.):____

STATE:______________________________ CAPITAL:______________________________

MAJOR CITY/

ABBREVIATION:______ AIRPORT CODES:____

MAJOR CITIES AND PLACES OF INTEREST:____

____

____

____

____

____

SPECIAL INFORMATION (NICKNAME, RESTRICTIONS, EVENTS, TAXES, WEATHER, ETC.):

____

ECONOMY (PRODUCTS, ETC.):____

STATE:________________________________ CAPITAL:________________________________
MAJOR CITY/
ABBREVIATION:______ AIRPORT CODES:____

MAJOR CITIES AND PLACES OF INTEREST:____

____

____

____

____

____

SPECIAL INFORMATION (NICKNAME, RESTRICTIONS, EVENTS, TAXES, WEATHER, ETC.):

____

ECONOMY (PRODUCTS, ETC.):____

STATE:________________________________ CAPITAL:________________________________
MAJOR CITY/
ABBREVIATION:______ AIRPORT CODES:____

MAJOR CITIES AND PLACES OF INTEREST:____

____

____

____

____

____

SPECIAL INFORMATION (NICKNAME, RESTRICTIONS, EVENTS, TAXES, WEATHER, ETC.):

____

ECONOMY (PRODUCTS, ETC.):____

STATE:________________________________ CAPITAL:________________________________
MAJOR CITY/
ABBREVIATION:______ AIRPORT CODES:____

MAJOR CITIES AND PLACES OF INTEREST:____

____

____

____

____

____

SPECIAL INFORMATION (NICKNAME, RESTRICTIONS, EVENTS, TAXES, WEATHER, ETC.):

____

ECONOMY (PRODUCTS, ETC.):____

The United States

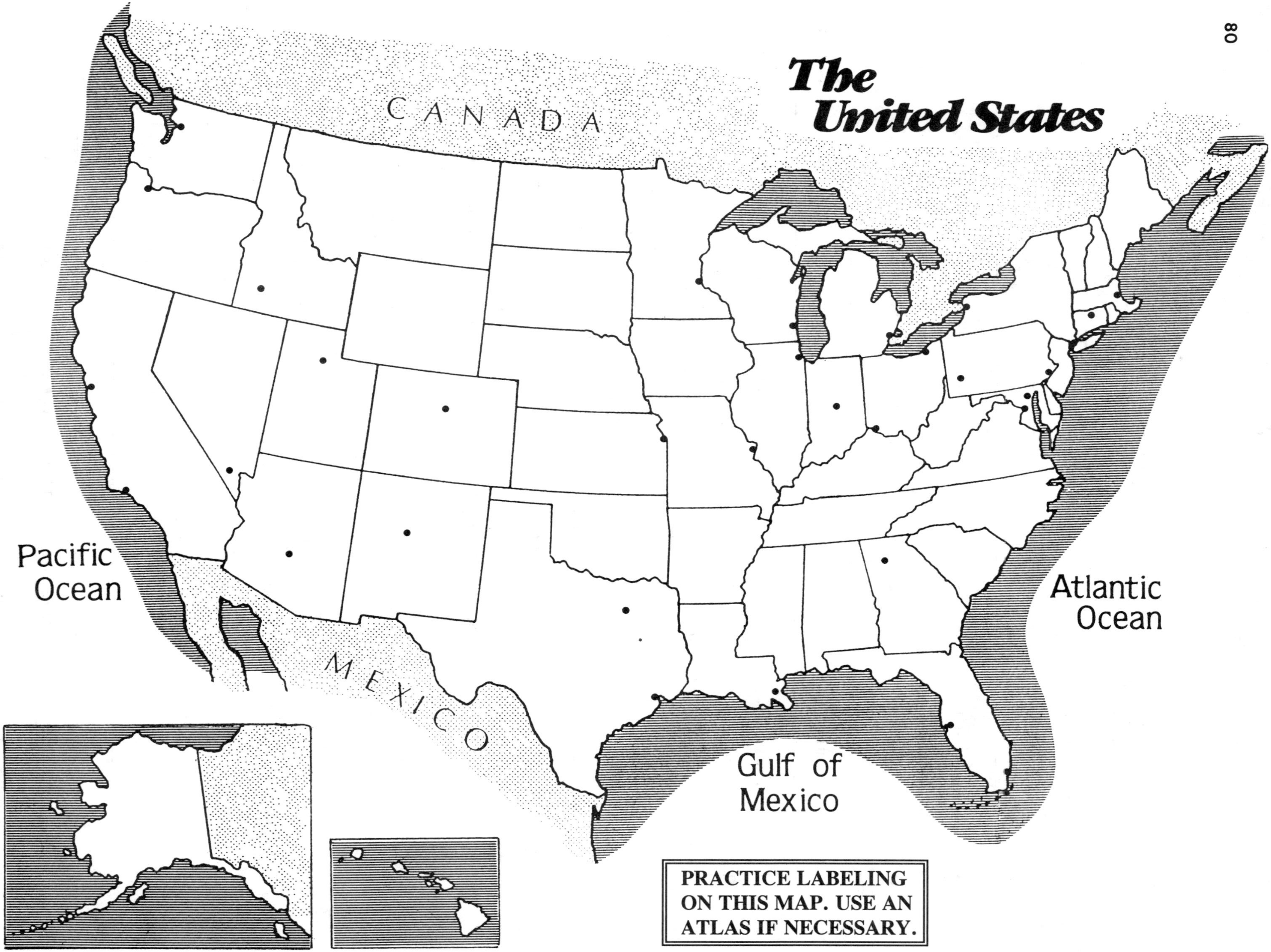

PRACTICE LABELING ON THIS MAP. USE AN ATLAS IF NECESSARY.

REVIEW

MATCH THE FOLLOWING NATIONAL PARKS TO THEIR STATES:

1. ______GRAND CANYON	A.	CALIFORNIA
2. ______YELLOWSTONE	B.	UTAH
3. ______YOSEMITE	C.	TEXAS
4. ______BIG BEND	D.	ARIZONA
5. ______EVERGLADES	E.	NORTH CAROLINA/TENNESSEE
6. ______GREAT SMOKY MTS.	F.	FLORIDA
7. ______MT. MCKINLEY/DENALI	G.	WYOMING (MOSTLY)
8. ______ZION	H.	ALASKA
9. ______CARLSBAD CAVERNS	I.	NEW MEXICO
10. ______SHENANDOAH	J.	VIRGINIA

MATCH THE CITIES WITH PLACES/ITEMS OF INTEREST:

11. ______SAN FRANCISCO	K.	BROADWAY, CENTRAL PARK, TIMES SQUARE
12. ______NEW ORLEANS	L.	MONUMENTS, GEORGETOWN
13. ______ORLANDO	M.	DISNEY WORLD, SEA WORLD
14. ______NEW YORK CITY	N.	FRENCH QUARTER, MISSISSIPPI RIVER
15. ______PHILADELPHIA	O.	LIBERTY BELL, HISTORIC SIGHTS
16. ______WASHINGTON, DC	P.	CABLE CARS, FISHERMAN'S WHARF
17. ______MIAMI	Q.	ART DECO, KEY BISCAYNE, BEACHES
18. ______LOS ANGELES	R.	STARS' HOMES, HOLLYWOOD, DISNEYLAND
19. ______ATLANTA	S.	SPACE NEEDLE, NEARBY MT. RAINIER
20. ______SEATTLE	T.	PEACHTREE ST., NEARBY STONE MTN.

REVIEW

1. In what state is Mt. Rushmore? ______________________
2. The state known as the "Lone Star State" is ____________________.
3. City of the Henry Ford Museum, automobile production, and the complex called the Renaissance Center is ______________________.
4. Situated on Lake Michigan, called the "Windy City" and a city that has one of the world's busiest airports is ____________________.
5. Name three places of interest in Washington, DC. ______________ ____
6. City called the "Gateway to the Western U.S." and that has a stainless steel arch 630 feet high is ________________________.
7. City of the Freedom Trail, the Bunker Hill Monument, and home to numerous colleges (MIT, Northeastern University, nearby Harvard) is the city of ______________ in ______________________ (state).
8. Name three places of interest in Los Angeles, CA. ______________ ____
9. City of country music fame, the Grand Ole Opry and Opryland is ____________________ in the state of ______________________.
10. Popular for the night club shows and gambling casinos, near to Lake Mead and the Hoover Dam is the city of ____________________.

U.S. REVIEW

1. Name the states that make up the area of New England. ____________
____
____

2. The city featuring cajun cuisine, jazz music, and the French Quarter is ______________________________.

3. Name three places of interest in San Francisco. ____________________
____

4. What is the highest point in North America and in what state is it located? Hint: Research National Parks List ____________________
____

5. What city is known as the "City of Brotherly Love" and has the historic Liberty Bell? ________________________________

6. Name three places of interest in New York City. ____________________
____

7. What state is the largest in size? ______________________________

8. What city has the Space Needle and nearby Mt. Rainier? ___________

9. The city called the "Mile High City" is ________________________.

10. The state containing the Painted Desert, several Indian reservations, and the old west town of Tombstone is _______________.

11. What state has Yosemite National Park, the Hearst Castle, and a scenic Pacific coast highway? ______________________________

12. The state having the major cities of Augusta, Bangor, and Portland is _________________________.

13. Known as the "Garden State," with Atlantic City as a destination for gambling and its famous boardwalk is ______________________.

14. The Great Salt Lake, Brigham Young University, and the Mormon Tabernacle Choir can be seen in ______________________________(city).

15. What is the <u>major</u> U.S. city near Niagara Falls? ____________________

16. Cleveland, Cincinnati, and Columbus are main cities in ___________.

17. Known as the "Hawkeye State," with cities such as Cedar Rapids, Dubuque, Des Moines, and Davenport is the state of ______________.

18. Cities such as Pocatello and Twin Falls, the Salmon River and Salmon Mountains, the Snake River and Mountains are all located in the state of ___________________________.

19. The state of ______________________________ has the "twin cities" of St. Paul and Minneapolis.

20. What state has cities such as Gulfport and Biloxi, and is nicknamed the "Magnolia State?" ______________________________

21. The city in Nevada known for casinos and located near Lake Tahoe is __________________.

22. Memphis, Tennessee is located in western Tennessee. True or False _________________.

23. Name three major rivers in Texas. _______________________________

____

USING AN ATLAS IF NECESSARY, MATCH THE FOLLOWING:
Note: Some answers may be used more than once.

24. _______WHITE MOUNTAINS		A. PENNSYLVANIA
25. _______GREEN MOUNTAINS		B. WEST VIRGINIA
26. _______ADIRONDACK MTNS.		C. UTAH
27. _______WASATCH MTNS.		D. CALIFORNIA
28. _______SIERRA NEVADA MTNS.		E. NEW HAMPSHIRE
29. _______ALLEGHENY MTNS.		F. VERMONT
30. _______POCONO MTNS.		G. NEW YORK
31. _______CATSKILL MTNS.		H. WYOMING
32. _______BITTERROOT MTS.		I. MONTANA
33. _______BIGHORN MTNS.		

CULINARY DELIGHTS

Can you match these specialties/foods with the most appropriate states or cities? Put the letter of the corresponding answer in the space.

_____ 1. Pecans, Vidalia onions, peaches	A. Florida
_____ 2. Po-boys, crawfish, gumbo	B. Vermont
_____ 3. Shoofly pie, pretzels, cheeses	C. Maryland
_____ 4. Sourdough bread, Ghirardelli chocolate	D. Kentucky
_____ 5. Lobster, blueberry pie	E. Louisiana
_____ 6. Sausage gravy, grits, corn bread	F. Pennsylvania
_____ 7. Maple sugar products	G. Tennessee
_____ 8. Crab cakes	H. Georgia
_____ 9. Orange marmalade, Key Lime Pie	I. San Francisco
_____10. Hot Browns, fried banana peppers	K. Maine

ARE YOU HUNGRY YET?

MATCH U.S. CITIES TO THEIR ATTRACTIONS/PLACES OF INTEREST

1. ________ATLANTA
2. ________BOSTON
3. ________DALLAS
4. ________NEW ORLEANS
5. ________SAN FRANCISCO
6. ________CHICAGO
7. ________NEW YORK
8. ________ORLANDO
9. ________ST. LOUIS
10. ________INDIANAPOLIS
11. ________DENVER
12. ________SAN DEIGO
13. ________HOUSTON
14. ________BALTIMORE
15. ________BUFFALO
16. ________PHILADELPHIA
17. ________PHOENIX
18. ________WASHINGTON, DC
19. ________SALT LAKE CITY
20. ________LOS ANGELES

A. HOLLYWOOD, KNOTTS BERRY FARM
B. WORLD TRADE CENTER, UNITED NATIONS BLDG.
C. TEMPLE SQUARE, "THIS IS THE PLACE"
D. NOB HILL, CHINATOWN, EMBARCADERO
E. LAKE MICHIGAN, MUSEUMS
F. THE ZOO, CLOSE TO TIJUANA
G. LENOX SQUARE, THE OMNI, UNDERGROUND
H. "GATEWAY TO THE WESTERN U.S."
I. DISNEY WORLD, EPCOT CENTER, SEA WORLD
J. ASTRODOME, NASA SPACE CENTER
K. COTTON BOWL, REUNION TOWER
L. JEFFERSON MEMORIAL, THE WHITE HOUSE
M. MONUMENT CIRCLE, "500" RACE & FESTIVAL
N. INNER HARBOR, HARBOR PLACE, AQUARIUM
O. NEAR NIAGARA FALLS, ON LAKE ERIE
P. LIBERTY BELL, INDEPENDENCE HALL
Q. FREEDOM TRAIL, FANEUIL HALL, THE COMMON
R. U.S. MINT, ROCKY MTNS., MINING TOWNS
S. GATEWAY CITY FOR VISITING SEDONA AND THE GRAND CANYON
T. JACKSON SQUARE, CANAL ST., SUPERDOME

SEE IF YOU CAN IDENTIFY THE CITIES BY THE PICTURES BELOW

1.________________________

2.________________________

3.________________________

The United States

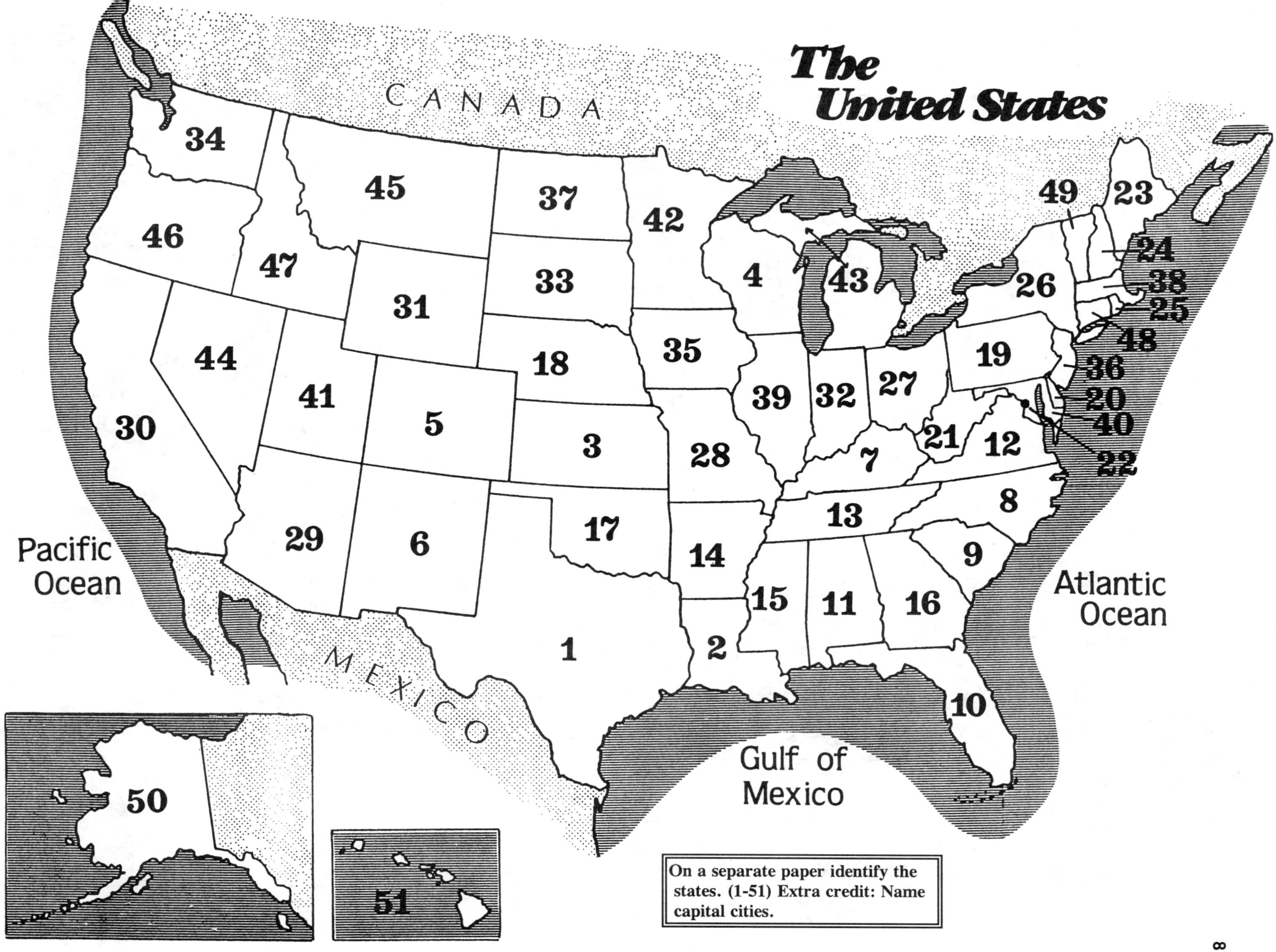

On a separate paper identify the states. (1-51) Extra credit: Name capital cities.

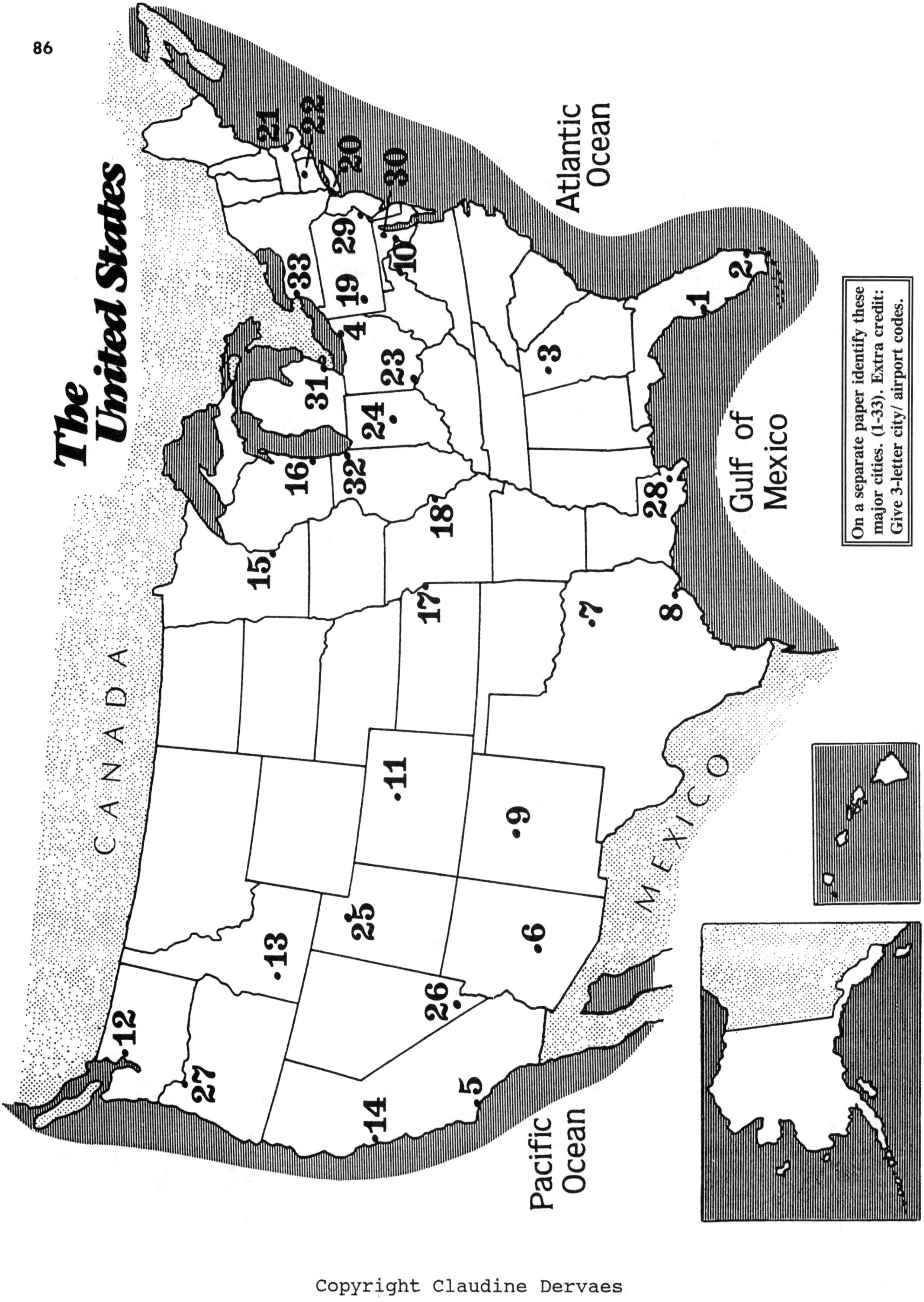
The United States
CANADA
Atlantic Ocean
Gulf of Mexico
MEXICO
Pacific Ocean
On a separate paper identify these major cities. (1-33). Extra credit: Give 3-letter city/ airport codes.

U.S. DESTINATIONS - FURTHER ACTIVITIES

If this manual is being used in a school or college curriculum, your instructor may assign some additional projects and activities.

Here are some assignments to enhance your knowledge of U.S. travel. These can be done in conjunction with a structured course or if you are pursuing a self-study of destination geography.

1. Plan a seven day tour of New England for a couple who will fly into Boston, MA and out of Providence, RI. They will be renting a car. Give a day-by-day sample itinerary and include any other information or helpful details.

2. List the sights and activities you would recommend for a young couple going for the first time to New York City. They will spend a weekend (Friday to Monday). Provide any special information and hints about travel to this destination.

3. A family of four (2 adults and 2 children, aged 10 and 8) are going to Washington, DC for four days in July. Suggest activities and sightseeing and provide any other useful information.

4. A couple in their late 40's is planning a trip to see the Grand Canyon. They are renting a car and would like to tour other areas of Arizona on their five day trip. What possible day-by-day itinerary can you suggest if they do not want to drive more than three hours a day?

5. Your clients are interested in a ski vacation in Colorado. List at least five major ski resorts and provide a little information about them.

FOR USE IN A COURSE OR SCHOOL CURRICULUM:

Do a project on a state. You may wish to acquire maps, brochures and information from the state tourist office. Addresses are in tour books, the <u>Travel Industry Personnel Directory</u> and other references. Present pictures, slides, or make a poster and present 10 minutes of information, a sample tour itinerary, etc.

NOTES

CHAPTER 4

Hawaii in more detail

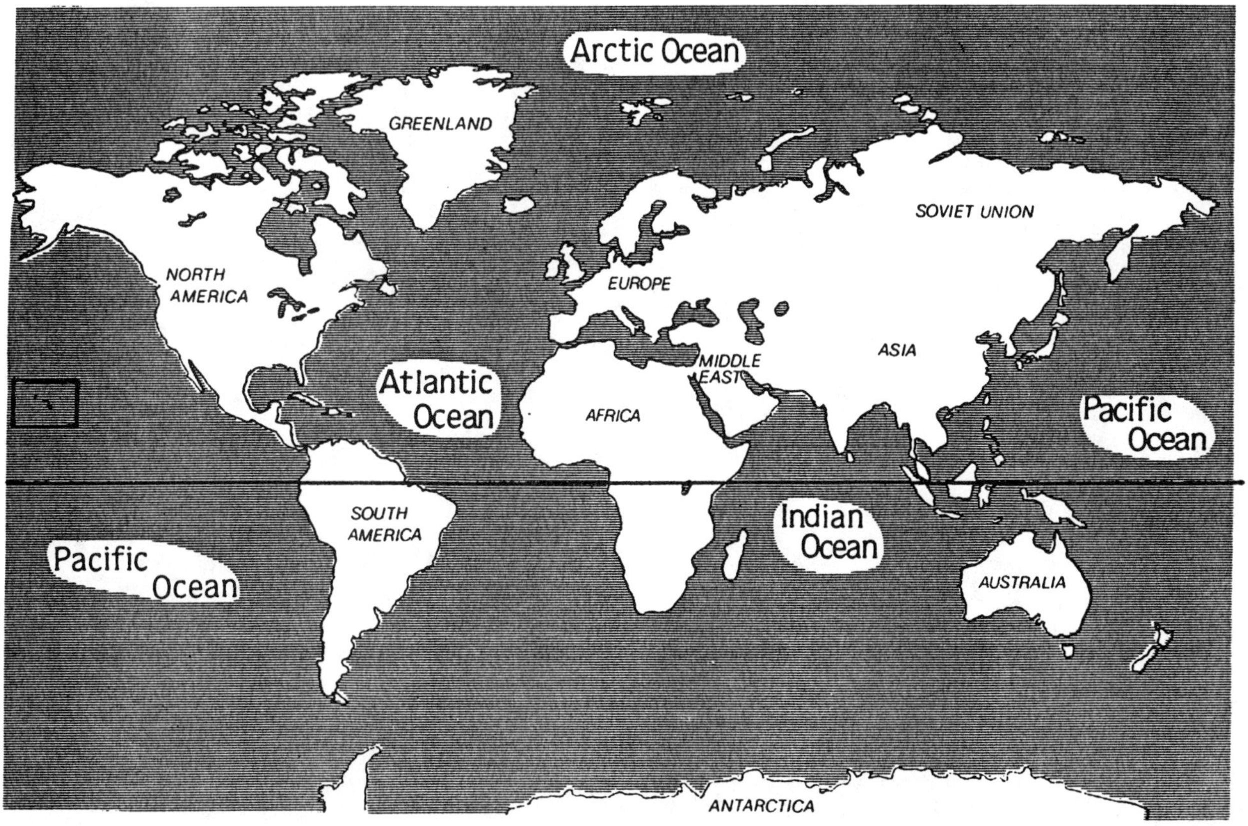

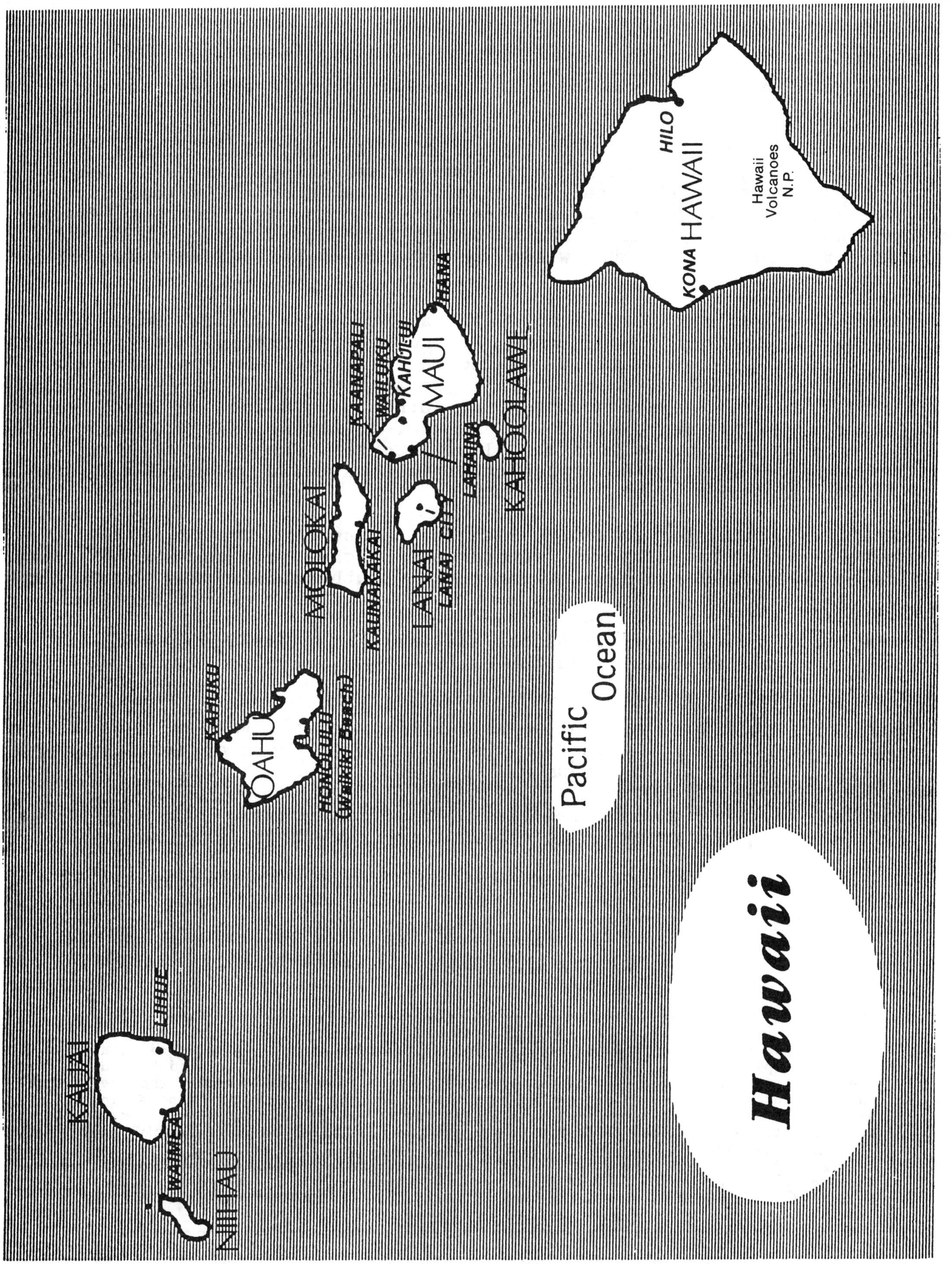
Hawaii
Pacific Ocean
KAUAI
LIHUE
WAIMEA
NIIHAU
OAHU
KAHUKU
HONOLULU
(Waikiki Beach)
MOLOKAI
KAUNAKAKAI
LANAI
LANAI CITY
MAUI
KAANAPALI
WAILUKU
KAHULUI
LAHAINA
HANA
KAHOOLAWE
HAWAII
HILO
KONA
Hawaii
Volcanoes
N.P.

HAWAII

The Hawaiian Islands are each distinctive in their natural beauty and charm.

Hawaii, the "Big Island," is larger than all the other islands combined. Active volcanoes (Mauna Loa and Kilauea) and a national park, the longest waterway in the state (Wailuku River), a waterfall with a drop of 442 feet (Akaka Falls), popular hotels, resorts, golf courses - these are what the "Big Island" has to offer. Tourists often start at Hilo, the orchid capital of the world, and end up at Kona, the other major city.

Oahu is called the "Gathering Place" and the busy Waikiki Beach area helps substantiate the nickname. At the peak of Diamond Head, the landmark extinct volcano, the panoramic Pacific views are both simple and stunning. Honolulu, the capital, is located on Oahu, the island that is home to most of Hawaii's population. Other sights include Pearl Harbor and the Arizona Memorial, Iolani Palace, Chinatown, Makapuu Point, Sea Life Park, and the Polynesian Cultural Center. Combine your visit to Oahu with a stay on one of the other islands to get a glimpse of the variety of areas.

The "Garden Island" is Kauai, with the famous Fern Grotto, Waimea Canyon, the Coco Palms resort, sundrenched beaches, and the wettest spot on earth - at Mt. Waialeale. The movie "South Pacific" was filmed here, and the North Shore Drive has beautiful views that cannot be described.

The "Valley Isle" of Maui offers the well-known Kaanapali Beach and Kapalaua resort areas, plus the strange lava formation - the Iao Needle in Iao Valley.

Lanai is known as the "Pineapple Isle," since it is almost wholly owned by the Dole Company. Jeeps are the most popular form of transportation here since many of the roads are unpaved.

Molokai, the "Friendly Isle," is quiet and unassuming - in many ways untouched by the frenzied development and growth of the other islands.

Kahoolawe is owned by the U.S. Navy and Niihau is privately owned.

MAJOR CITY AIRPORT CODES: HNL - Honolulu, Oahu; ITO - Hilo, Hawaii; KOA - Kona, Hawaii; MKK - Molokai; OGG - Kahului, Maui; LIH - Lihue, Kauai

> Aloha! Welcome to Hawaii... Greeted with a flower necklace - a lei - you begin your stay at this well-known paradise. Tonight you will attend a luau - the classic feast of a roast pig which has been steamed for hours in an underground oven. Drinks made from local fruits are just delicious - you are tempted to try guava nectar and the passion fruit juice. The Hula Dancers' performance and the other Polynesian dancing and singing seem to get everyone involved. The sports are so numerous that you may have trouble deciding what to do tomorrow - golf, tennis, sailing, surfing, diving, fishing, swimming, hiking, hunting, horse-back riding, and even skiing! You're sure to come across the name Kamehameha - for King Kamehameha or "King Kam" for short - whose story is surrounded by legend and romance. Hawaii offers a true "melting pot of peoples," each having contributed to the mosaic culture and richness that can be experienced by the visitor.

HAWAII - Q. AND A.

WHEN SHOULD YOU GO TO HAWAII?

Hawaii's climate is generally mild year round, with temperatures ranging from the mid-70's to the mid-80's most of the year. It can dip down to the mid-60's in winter and up to the mid-90's in the summer. Hawaii's rainy season (usually just passing showers) is during the months of December, January, and February.

WHAT TYPE OF CLOTHING SHOULD YOU BRING?

Casual resort wear is appropriate for the islands. Dress for comfort - shorts, jeans, sundresses, comfortable walking shoes, beach shoes, cotton shirts, etc. Sunglasses and a hat/visor are recommended. A sweater or jacket may come in handy for the evenings, which sometimes get a bit chilly. Travelers to high-elevation landmarks such as Haleakala on Maui should wear sweaters, coats, socks, and knitted hats or scarves. Some gourmet restaurants may require a jacket and tie.

ARE MOST OF THE BEACHES SAFE FOR SWIMMING?

Always observe posted warning signs regarding hazardous water conditions. During the winter months, waves on the North Shore often reach heights of 20 feet, and novice surfers and swimmers are advised to stay out of the water. Also, you should be aware that man-of-wars (stinging jellyfish) periodically find their way to the islands' shores.

WHAT ABOUT CRIME?

Like any popular tourist destination crime does exist. Use common sense when traveling. Keep expensive jewelry and valuables, passports and tickets in your hotel's safe. Avoid walking through alleys and side streets. Travel in groups after dark. Don't carry large amounts of cash.

DO THE PEOPLE SPEAK HAWAIIAN?

Although the Hawaiians have their own language and many words and expressions are incorporated into daily speech, English is the primary language. You may also hear other languages being spoken (Chinese, Japanese, Vietnamese, Filipino, etc.). Most people are bilingual in English and their native language.

WHAT TIME ZONE IS HAWAII IN?

Hawaii is on Hawaiian Standard Time and does not change to daylight savings time. Locals set their watches to "Hawaiian Time," which means the pace is slower and there's no need to rush. Take time to enjoy sunrises and sunsets, to splash in the waves, walk along the beaches, shop in the shops.

TRAVEL TO HAWAII - TIPS AND TIDBITS

Flying times from Honolulu, Oahu to	Maui --- 35 minutes Kauai --- 35 minutes Kona --- 41 minutes Hilo --- 50 minutes Lanai --- 30 minutes Molokai --- 30 minutes

COMMONLY USED WORDS

ae - yes
aloha - a greeting, meaning hello, goodbye, love.
ewa - heading westerly (used when giving directions)
hale - house
hana - work
haole - formerly any foreigner, now refers primarily to those of Caucasian ancestry
ia - fish
kahuna - priest, minister, expert in any field
kai - sea
kamaaina - native-born, local
kamalii - children
kane - man
kapu - forbidden, taboo
kauka - doctor
kokua - cooperation
kupuna - grandparent
lanai - porch, veranda
lei - wreath or garland of flowers, leaves, feathers, shells
luau - Hawaiian feast
mahalo - thank you
makai - heading towards the sea (used when giving directions)
malihini - newcomer, visitor
malo - loincloth
mana - spiritual power
mauka - inland, towards the mountains (used when giving directions)
Me ke aloha pumehana - With Warm Regards
mele - a song, chant or poem
muumuu - a loose-fitting gown
ohana - family
ono - tasty, delicious, savory
pahu - drum
pali - cliff, precipice
paniolo - cowboy
pau - finished
puaa - pig
puka - hole
pule - prayer
pupu - hors d'oeuvre
shaka - a hand gesture made with a closed fist except for the thumb and pinkie fingers. Used as a slang expression meaning "hang loose" or simply "hello."
tutu - grandmother
wahine - woman
wela - hot

WHAT TO BUY?
Look for perfume, native jams and jellies, shell jewelry and crafts, macadamia nuts, Kona coffees, Asian goods, silks and linens, Hawaiian shirts, quilts, handmade ukeleles, carved wooden items, and imported teak items.

DRIVING LIKE A KAMAAINA (LOCAL)

Many visitors will choose to rent a car and explore the Hawaiian islands on their own. Here are some tips to help:

Wear seat belts - they are required and the law is strictly enforced.

If distracted by the island's beauty or scenery, pull off the road.

Locals will use topographical references rather than geographic directions - on Oahu, for example, you'll be advised to drive "Diamond Head" or "Koko Head" for EAST.

Hawaii has rush hours too, so plan ahead to avoid morning and evening traffic congestion.

Some of Hawaii's highest altitude destinations are off limits for standard passenger vehicles and all but the most experienced drivers.

Be advised that rented vehicles may not be used on unpaved roads and private areas.

Hawaii's weather is changeable and can affect driving conditions considerably, particularly in wilderness areas. Even if it's a sunny day, a heavy rainfall can result in muddy roads.

Stock the vehicle with such necessary items as suntan lotion, sunblock and sunglasses, a bathing suit, rubber sandals/beach shoes, spare towels, bottled water, and anything else that might come in handy for a spontaneous swim on a quiet beach.

Bring or buy maps that are detailed for the highways, smaller roads, one-way streets, and cities.

LET'S GO ON A SAMPLE ESCORTED TOUR OF HAWAII

12 NIGHTS/13 DAYS VISITING 5 ISLANDS

DAY 1 - Arrive Honolulu.
Hawaiians with flower leis greet you on arrival - ALOHA! A limousine driver takes you to your hotel where your tour director will contact you. Your baggage will be claimed and delivered to your hotel by courier. Relax in your oceanfront room with a spectacular view of the Pacific.

DAY 2 - Pearl Harbor Cruise.
After breakfast on the terrace of your room, you'll depart your hotel and board a 110 ft. motor launch for a cruise to the historic sight of Pearl Harbor. The afternoon is free to shop or walk around the International Marketplace. Tonight is a private dinner party to get better acquainted with the other tour members and your Hawaii hosts.

DAY 3 - Oahu Sightseeing.
This special tour will take you through the Kahala residential district, past the rugged lava shoreline of Hanauma Bay, Koko Head, and Makapuu Point. You'll travel through Waimanalo, an old sugar plantation, then a stop for lunch. The drive will ascend the windy cliffs for a magnificent view of the Kailua and Kaneohe coasts, then wind through the Mount Tantalus Rain Forest. The remaining tour will cover downtown Honolulu. You have a choice of wonderful restaurants for dinner tonight.

DAY 4 - Molokai.
Leaving the fast pace of Oahu behind, this morning's flight takes you to Molokai. Upon arrival, you'll tour Palaau - a peaceful park with a view of the craggy cliffs that plummet 2,000 feet. This island is where Father Damien devoted the rest of his life to caring for the lepers. Back to the hotel you have the remainder of the day for relaxing, swimming, golf, tennis, or whatever you would like to do.

DAY 5 - Maui.
After arrival in Maui, you'll sightsee the verdant Iao Valley. Then on to the old capital of Lahaina for lunch. Tonight enjoy dinner and a show at your luxurious hotel on Kaanapali Beach.

DAY 6 - Maui.
This is your day to relax, go snorkeling, shop, play golf, tennis, or swim in the pool. The evening will feature the torch-lighting ceremony, followed by cocktails and a special private dinner.

DAY 7 - Hawaii - the Big Island.
You'll fly to the Kona coast and enjoy a morning glass-bottom boat sightseeing trip. Later you'll tour part of the island before reaching tonight's hotel.

DAY 8 - Hawaii.
The entire day is at leisure for you to enjoy the facilities of this extensive resort hotel. Dinner and a show will top off the evening.

DAY 9 - Hawaii and Kauai.
After a drive through Parker Ranch and along the Hamakua coast to Hilo, you'll tour the Hawaii Volcanoes National Park before taking the flight to Kauai. You'll spend the next two nights on Kauai.

DAY 10 - Kauai.
This is paradise and the helicopter sightseeing trip is going to be exciting and unforgettable. Waimea Canyon, the beaches, cliffs, and valleys will astound you with their beauty. A sumptuous dinner will be included.

DAY 11 - Kauai.
Today you'll visit the Fern Grotto and have lunch at Coco Palms. A short flight will take you back to Honolulu. Tonight is a wonderful dinner party to talk about the fantastic sights.

DAY 12 - Oahu.
The day is for you to enjoy Honolulu at your own pace and pick up those last minute souvenirs. Tonight is the farewell dinner party and show.

DAY 13 - Journey Home
Aloha again - only this time it's "good-bye" to these beautiful islands and a wonderful vacation. You'll already be thinking of when you can come back!

HAWAII

Now review the information you have read and perhaps do further research in order to complete the profile below

STATE:______________________________ CAPITAL:______________________________

MAJOR CITY/
ABBREVIATION:______ AIRPORT CODES:_______________________________________

____

MAJOR CITIES AND PLACES OF INTEREST:

OAHU____

____

____

HAWAII____

____

____

KAUAI____

____

____

MAUI____

____

____

MOLOKAI____

____

____

LANAI____

____

OTHER ISLANDS____

____

SPECIAL INFORMATION (NICKNAMES, RESTRICTIONS, EVENTS, TAXES, WEATHER, ETC.):

____

____

____

ECONOMY (PRODUCTS, ETC.):____

____

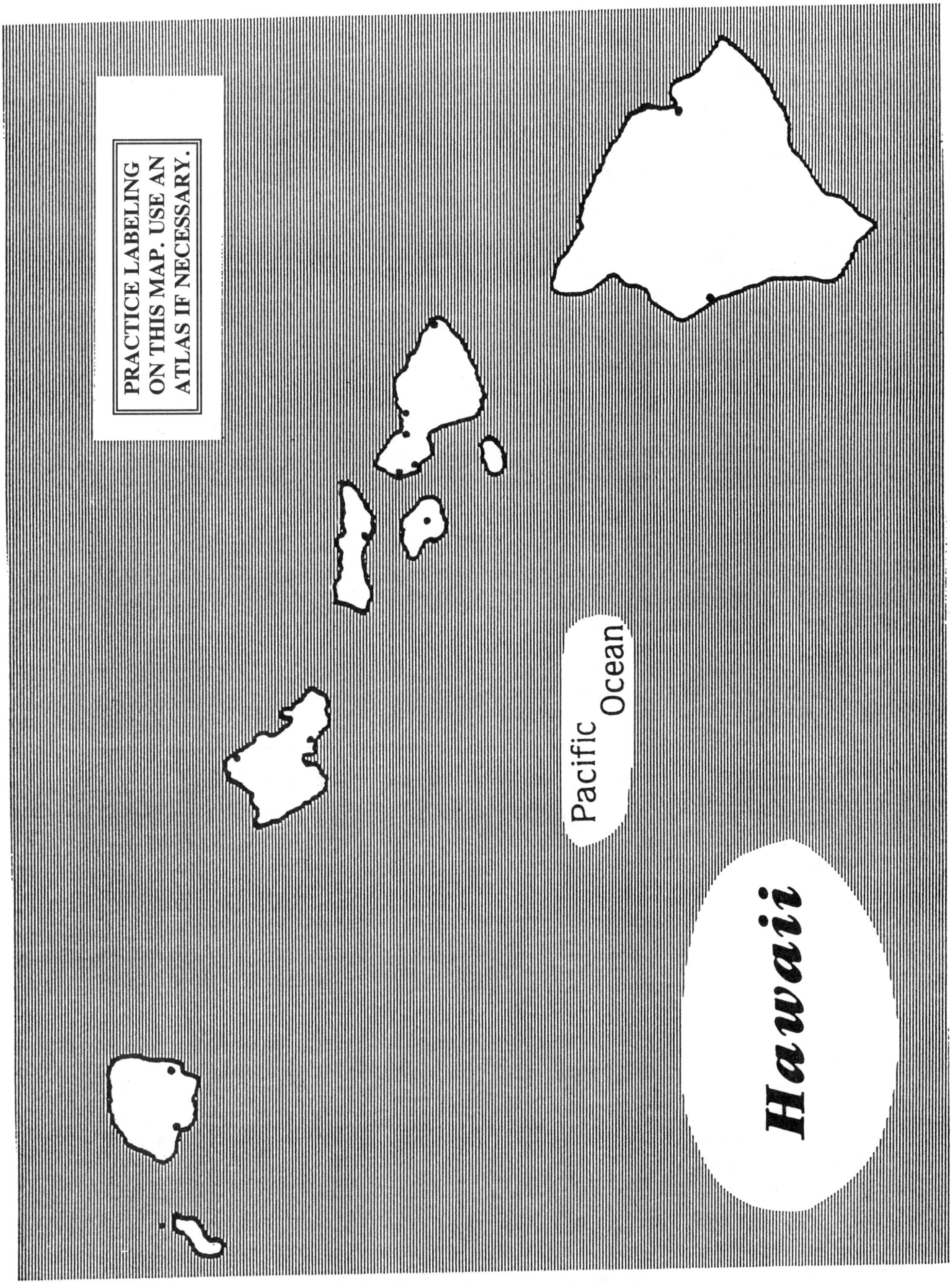
PRACTICE LABELING ON THIS MAP. USE AN ATLAS IF NECESSARY.
Pacific Ocean
Hawaii

HAWAII REVIEW

MATCH THE FOLLOWING CITIES/SIGHTS/NICKNAMES WITH THEIR ISLANDS:

Note: Some answers may be used more than once and some may not apply.

1. ________WAIKIKI BEACH
2. ________KAHULUI
3. ________HILO
4. ________LIHUE
5. ________KONA
6. ________HONOLULU
7. ________KAANAPALI
8. ________WAILUKU RIVER AND AKAKA FALLS
9. ________U.S.S. ARIZONA MEMORIAL
10. ________WAIMEA CANYON
11. ________DIAMOND HEAD
12. ________HAWAII VOLCANOES NAT'L PARK
13. ________LAHAINA
14. ________"GATHERING PLACE"
15. ________"FRIENDLY ISLE"
16. ________"GARDEN ISLAND"
17. ________"THE BIG ISLAND"
18. ________POLYNESIAN CULTURAL CENTER
19. ________FERN GROTTO
20. ________IAO VALLEY AND PARK
21. ________"PINEAPPLE ISLE"
22. ________COCO PALMS RESORT
23. ________"SOUTH PACIFIC" FILMED HERE
24. ________IOLANI PALACE
25. ________PRIVATELY OWNED

A. HAWAII
B. MOLOKAI
C. KAUAI
D. MAUI
E. LANAI
F. KAHOOLAWE
G. NIIHAU
H. OAHU

26. Name five best buys of Hawaii. ______________________________
____
27. What word will commonly be used to say "thank you"?__________
28. What is a lanai? ____
29. A muumuu is a song or chant. True or False ____________
30. The word used for man is ____________ and the word used for woman is ____________________.

Diamond Head

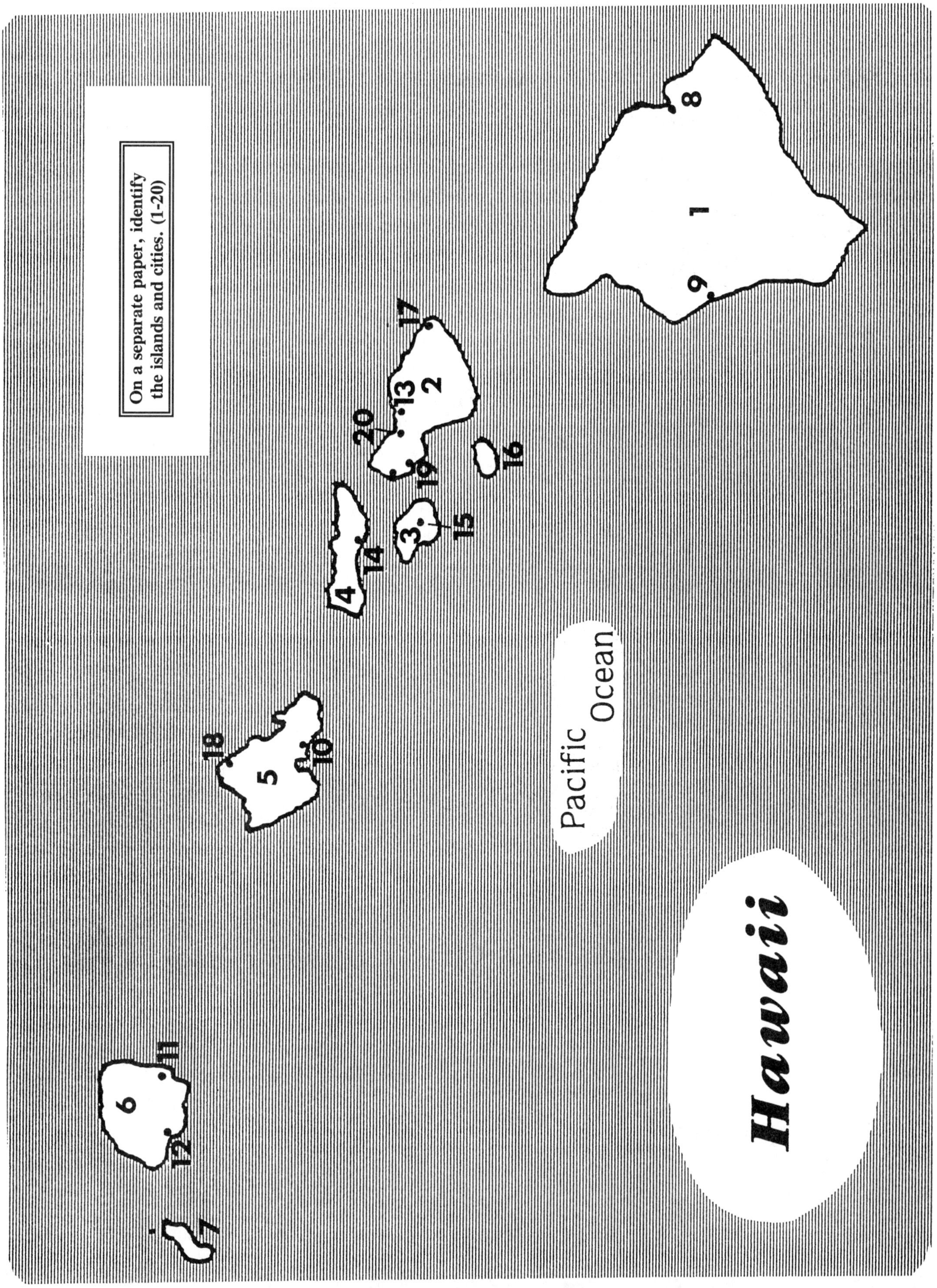
On a separate paper, identify the islands and cities. (1-20)
Pacific Ocean
Hawaii
1
2
3
4
5
6
7
8
9
10
11
12
13
14
15
16
17
18
19
20

NOTES

CHAPTER 5

Alaska in more detail

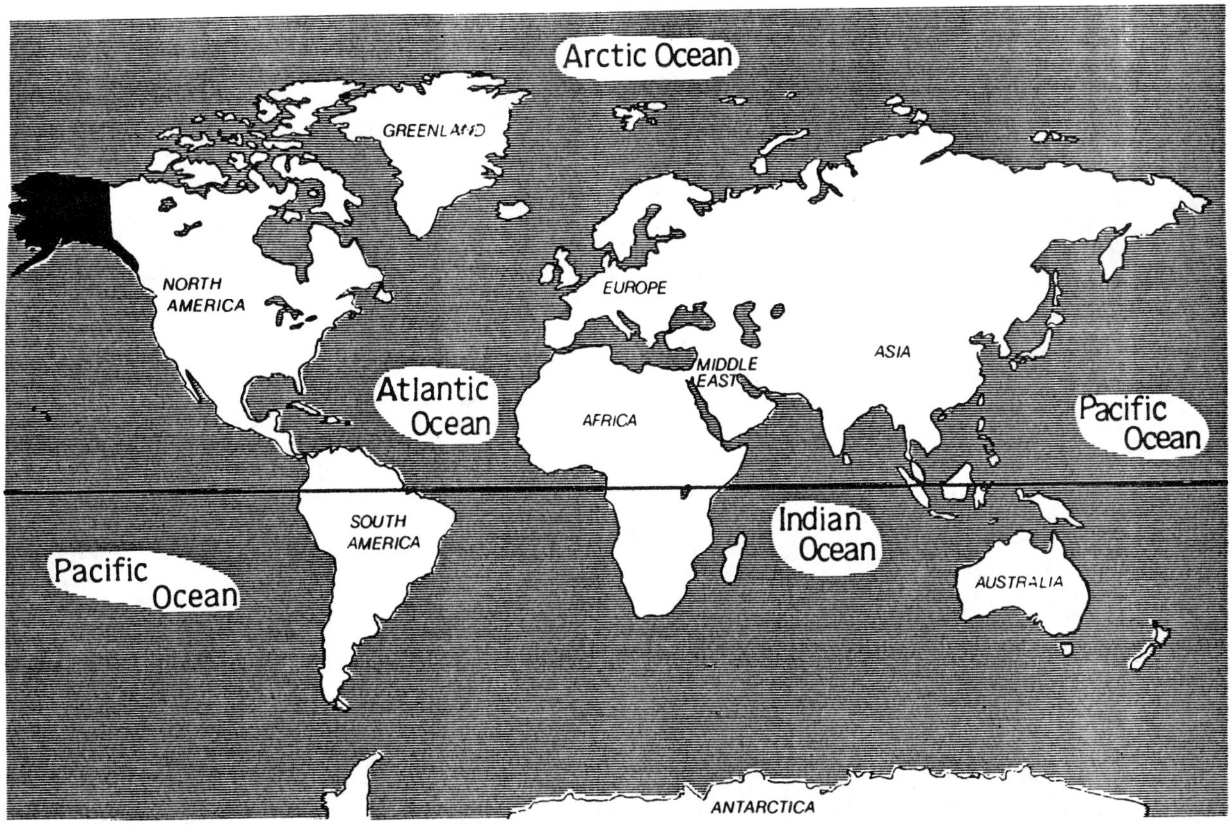

NOTES

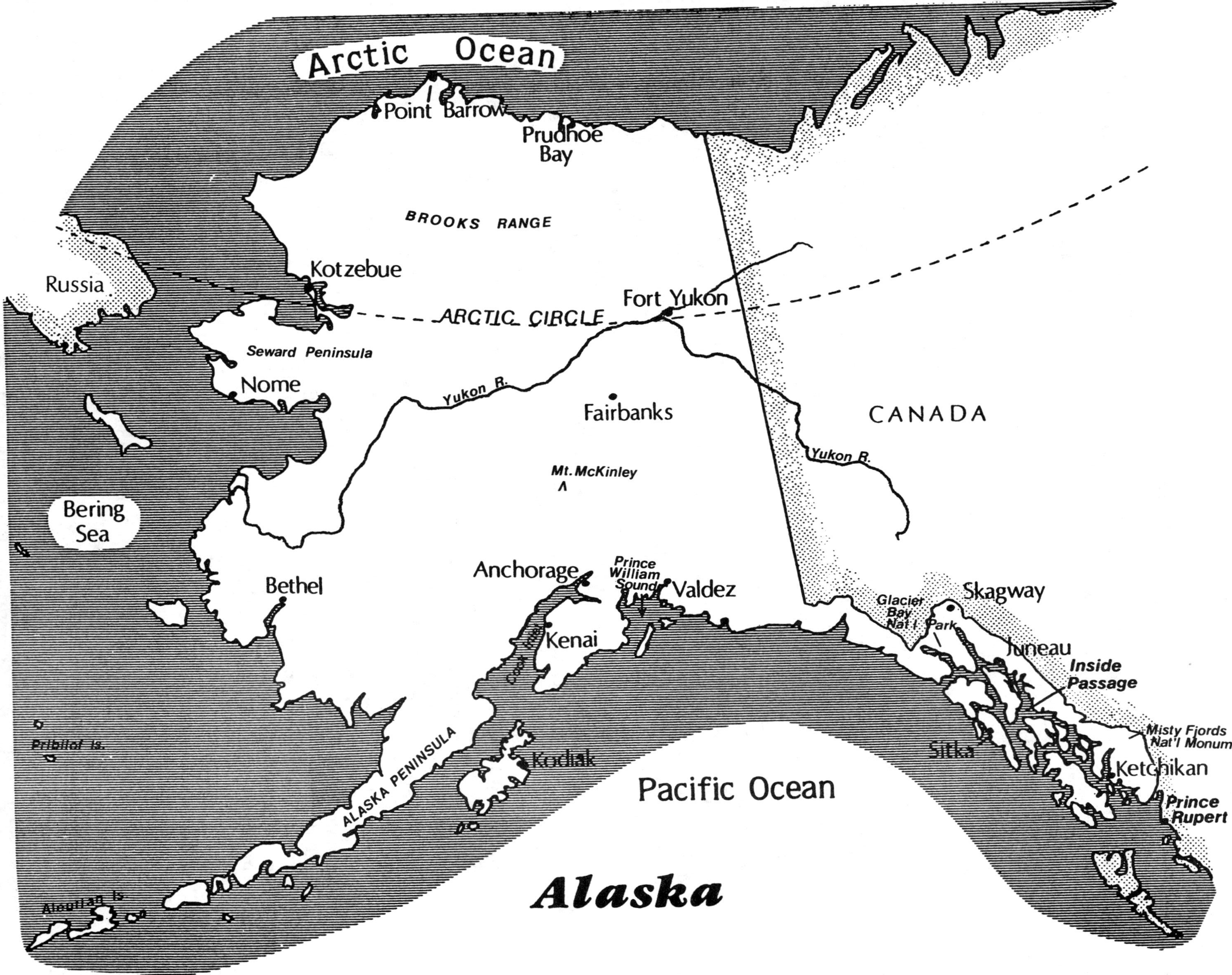
Arctic Ocean
Point Barrow
Prudhoe Bay
BROOKS RANGE
Russia
Kotzebue
Fort Yukon
ARCTIC CIRCLE
Seward Peninsula
Nome
Yukon R.
Fairbanks
CANADA
Yukon R.
Mt. McKinley
Bering Sea
Anchorage
Prince William Sound
Valdez
Bethel
Skagway
Glacier Bay Nat'l Park
Kenai
Cook Inlet
Juneau
Inside Passage
Pribilof Is.
Misty Fjords Nat'l Monument
Kodiak
Sitka
Ketchikan
ALASKA PENINSULA
Pacific Ocean
Prince Rupert
Aleutian Is.
Alaska

ALASKA

The largest U.S. state, Alaska, requires a good bit of time to visit and flying is a most important means of getting around - many Alaskans have a pilot's license and most communities have an airport, a seaplane base, or both. Alaska has a wide range of climates from a moderate weather pattern along the coastal areas to extreme cold in the winter in the far north and remote interior areas.

Popular trips to Alaska include an Inside Passage cruise combined with some motorcoach or train travel. The Inside Passage, located in the southeastern part of Alaska, is carved by glaciers and forested with spruce and hemlock trees - offering some of Alaska's most beautiful scenery. Misty Fjords National Monument, Ketchikan, Wrangell, Sitka, Juneau, and Skagway are some of the stops along cruise itineraries. From Skagway, some tours begin a land portion, traveling through the Yukon Territory of Canada and on to the interior of Alaska to visit Fairbanks and Denali National Park. Then, you can take a train to Anchorage - Alaska's "Big Apple."

No one is credited with discovering Alaska. Before the arrival of the Europeans, the Aleuts, Eskimos, and Indians lived there. In the early 18th century, the Russian Czar Peter the Great commissioned Dane Vitus Bering to find out if North America and Asia were connected by land. By 1787, Russians had a three-year-old settlement on Kodiak Island. In 1824 and 1825 Russia signed separate treaties with Great Britain and the U.S. In 1867, the U.S. bought Alaska from Russia for about 7 million dollars (about 2 cents an acre). A few years later the Gold Rush brought a flood of prospectors. In 1959, Alaska became the 49th state of the U.S. Alaska suffered a tremendous earthquake in 1964 which hit hard in the Anchorage-Valdez area where many Alaskans live. Earthquake Park in Anchorage marks the site where huge tracts of land slid into Cook Inlet. The Tony Knowles Coastal Trail is a 12-mile paved trail offering panoramic views of the city and its surroundings. Chugach State Park offers nearly a half-million acres of wilderness for year-round recreation. Visitors can drive to the slopes of the Chugach Mountains for views of Anchorage, Turnagain Arm, and Knik Arm. Not too far from Anchorage is Portage Glacier, and there is also Beluga Point - where you can look for Beluga and other whales. Alyeska is a popular ski resort in this area. Sailing, fishing, glacier-viewing, hiking and camping are just some of the opportunities to be enjoyed in the Prince William Sound area. The ice-carved valleys of Matanuska and Susitna offer diverse scenery and recreational activities. The Matanuska Valley is called Alaska's breadbasket. The growing season isn't long, but the long days of sunlight during the summer easily produce 20 pound cabbages and zucchinis that are a yard long. In the town of Wasilla you can visit the Iditarod Trail Sled Dog Race Headquarters and see memorabilia of this internationally famous race. The Kenai Peninsula is an outdoor vacation land, with campgrounds, canoe trails, and opportunities for hiking, boating, and fishing and more. Kodiak is Alaska's crab capital and is also famous for its population of brown bears. Katmai National Monument is a volcanic tribute covering 100 miles of ocean bays, fjords and lagoons against a backdrop of glacier-covered peaks and volcanic crater lakes. This area is also called the Valley of Ten Thousand Smokes. Valdez, on the Gulf of Alaska, is home to the terminus of the 800-mile trans-Alaska pipeline (which starts at Prudhoe Bay in the far north).

Fairbanks is a base city for exploring Denali National Park - in the interior of the state. Mt. McKinley, the tallest mountain in North America at 20,320 ft., is the focal point of the park and preserve.

If you have more time (and money) - take a flight to Nome or Barrow, above the Arctic Circle. If you wish to learn about the Eskimo people, visit Kotzebue. Juneau is the state's capital.

You may find things expensive - the cost of living in Alaska is high, when compared with some other U.S. states. Best buys include soapstone items, Alaska coral items and jewelry, clothing, baskets, gold nuggets, jade articles, hematite (a semi-precious black mineral known as black diamond) jewelry, furs, local handicrafts and pottery, Eskimo art, miniature totem poles, and novelties.

Many people really enjoy visiting Alaska because of its wildlife: it is where you can see whales, seals, otters, sea lions, eagles, dall sheep, mountain goats, moose, bears, foxes, partridges and many other birds and mammals. The ptarmigan, Alaska's state bird, is characterized by completely feathered feet, and plumage that is brown/black in the summer and almost completely white in winter (great camouflage!). If you travel to the remote Pribilof Islands in summer, you can see northern fur seals and millions of shore birds, some quite rare. The Aleutian Islands stretch for 1,100 miles from the southwest tip of the state.

The aurora borealis or "Northern Lights" can be seen throughout Alaska in autumn and winter. This colorful glow visible at night has the appearance of a fan of ascending luminous streamers near the northern horizon and is supposed to be of electrical origin.

Dog mushing is Alaska's official sport and short trips are available - from half an hour to half a day.

The people are Eskimos, Indians, and a mixture of many other immigrants. The Russian Orthodox religion is practiced widely in some areas.

This is the last frontier of the U.S., and a visit to Alaska means you will have experiences and see sights on your trip that you'll always treasure as unique.

WHAT'S ALL THIS ABOUT GLACIERS....

There's no way you can go to Alaska and fail to observe glaciers. How do glaciers form? As more snow falls than melts over a number of years it becomes ice, which packs together and fuses into a solid mass that begins flowing, impelled by gravity, its weight, and its volume. How many glaciers are there in Alaska? Probably some 100,000 if you count the tiny glaciers high in the mountains to the valley glaciers that you are most likely to see. Are the glaciers advancing or retreating? Some are advancing and others are retreating. What is "calving"? Calving is the birth of an iceberg, when a mass of ice breaks away from a glacier. What is the best glacier to see in Alaska? The top glaciers for tourists to visit in Alaska are: Mendenhall (near Juneau), Portage (near Anchorage), and the Columbia and Hubbard glaciers.

ALASKA

Now recap your study and reading by completing the profile below. If possible, use tour brochures and other resources to expand your knowledge of this popular destination.

STATE:______________________________ CAPITAL:____________________________

ABBREVIATION:______ MAJOR CITY/ AIRPORT CODES:____

____

SIZE:_______________________________ POPULATION:_________________________

MAJOR CITIES, SIGHTS, AND NEARBY PLACES OF INTEREST:

ANCHORAGE____

____

FAIRBANKS____

____

NOME____

____

KOTZEBUE____

____

KODIAK____

____

KENAI____

____

OTHER CITIES OR PLACES OF INTEREST____

____

INSIDE PASSAGE CITIES INCLUDE:____

____

WILDLIFE YOU MIGHT SEE IN ALASKA:____

____

SPECIAL INFORMATION (NICKNAME, RESTRICTIONS, EVENTS, TAXES, WEATHER, ETC.):

____

____

____

ECONOMY (PRODUCTS, ETC.):____

____

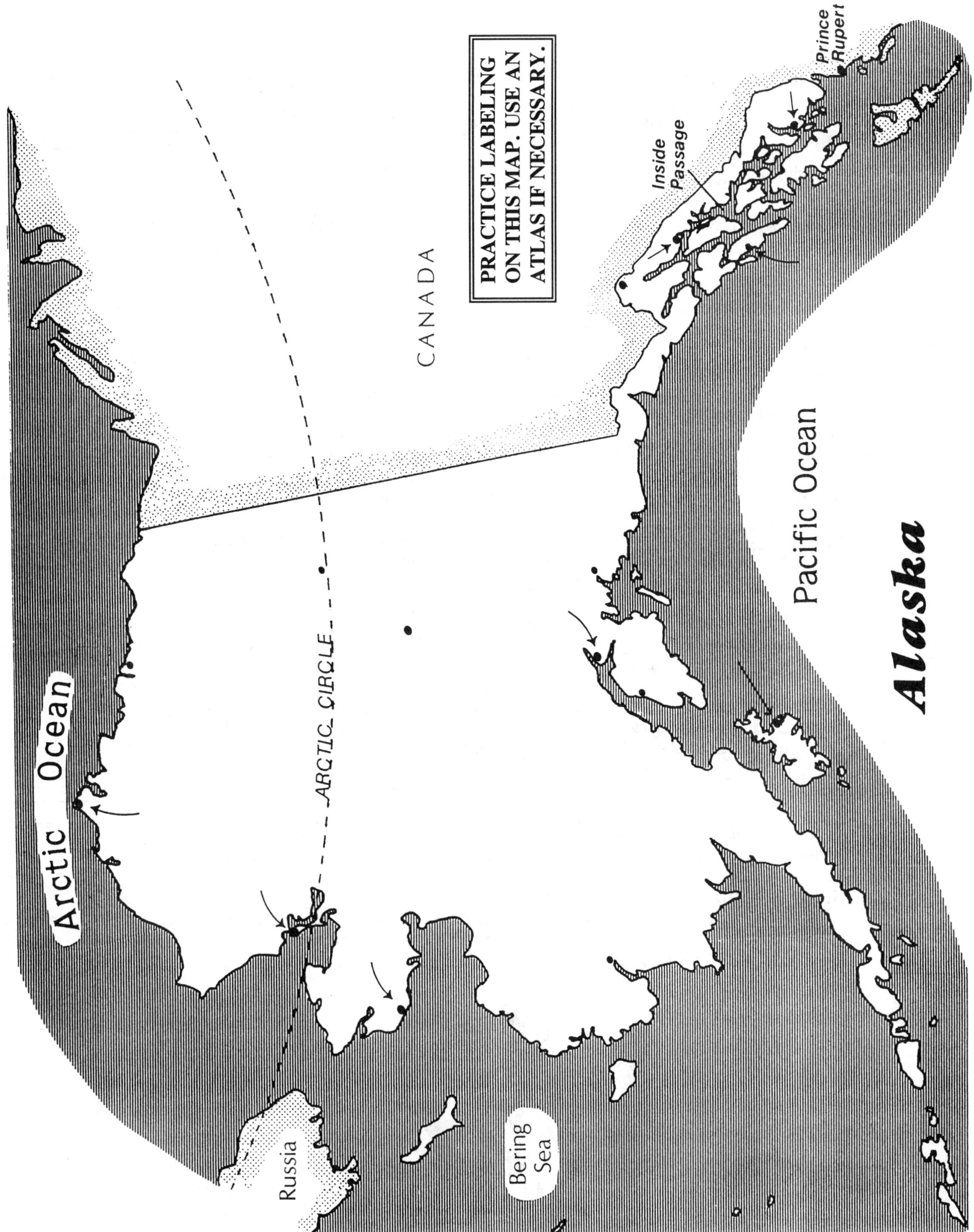
Alaska
PRACTICE LABELING ON THIS MAP. USE AN ATLAS IF NECESSARY.
Arctic Ocean
ARCTIC CIRCLE
CANADA
Inside Passage
Prince Rupert
Pacific Ocean
Bering Sea
Russia

ALASKA REVIEW

1. Name four major cities in Alaska. ______________________________
____
2. Alaska is the largest U.S. state. True or False ______
3. The Alaskan oil pipeline runs from _________________ to the port city of ________________ on the Gulf of Alaska.
4. Name three popular activities for tourists in Alaska. __________
____
5. Name a city in Alaska above the Arctic Circle. ____________
6. The capital of Alaska is ________________________.
7. Shown on the marked map is a mountain range located within the Arctic Circle. What is the name of the range? __________
8. Also shown on the Alaska map is the main river that flows through the middle of the state, the _______________ River.
9. The ________________________ Islands stretch for 1,100 miles from the southwest tip of Alaska.
10. _____________ island, is Alaska's crab capital and is also famous for its brown bear population.
11. The _____________________ Valley is called Alaska's breadbasket.
12. Which religion is practiced widely in some areas? ____________
____
13. What is the name of the ski resort located near Anchorage? _______
____
14. _______________ National Park and Preserve is where the highest mountain in North America is located.
15. Name three of the best buys in Alaska. ______________________
____
16. Alaska became the 49th state in 19___.
17. In the town of _________________ you can see the Iditarod Trail Sled Dog race headquarters.
18. _________________ is a volcanic tribute covering 100 miles of ocean bays, fjords, and lagoons against a backdrop of glacier-covered peaks and crater lakes.
19. The aurora borealis can be seen in the winter. True or False _____________
20. What does it mean when a glacier is calving? ________________
____
21. Portage Glacier is near Juneau. True or False __________
22. The tremendous earthquake that hit the Anchorage area was in 19___.
23. A drive up to the slopes of the _______________ Mountains will provide you with views of Anchorage, Turnagain Arm, and Knik Arm.
24. The ________________ is Alaska's state bird.
25. Prince William Sound is in the Inside Passage. True or False _____

Alaska

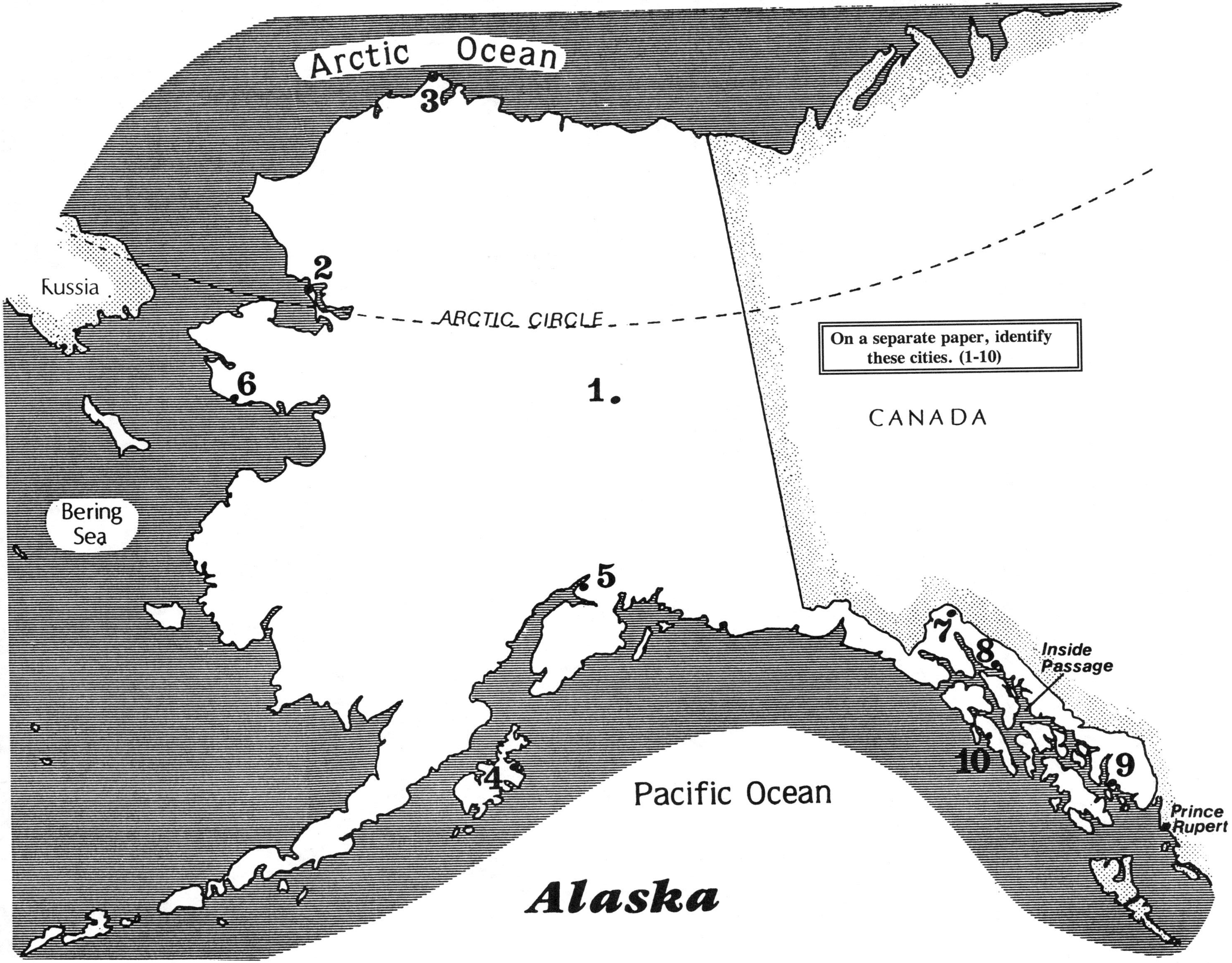

On a separate paper, identify these cities. (1-10)

NOTES

CHAPTER 6

International Travel and Selling Travel

PLUS SOME GENERAL INFORMATION ON GREENLAND

NOTES

INTERNATIONAL TRAVEL

Before beginning a study of destinations outside the U.S., here is a list of important particulars concerning the U.S. traveler going to another country.

The documentary requirements (for U.S. citizens) can be obtained from most travel agency computers. If the traveler is not a U.S. citizen, the airlines, cruise, and tour companies and current reference books may have the information. If ever in doubt, check with the consulate or government tourist office of the destination country. The addresses and phone numbers for many government offices are listed in various tour guides, the Travel Industry Personnel Directory, and other resources. Be sure to use up-to-date information, as requirements may change. In addition, always check for travel advisories that may exist.

U.S. PASSPORTS - For adults (over 18) a passport costs $55.00 plus a $10.00 fee - for first time applicants (if renewing, just $55.00); the passport is valid for 10 years. For those under 18, a passport costs $40.00 ($30.00 if renewing) and the validity is 5 years. The general requirements are: 2 passport photos, a birth certificate (with seal), application and monies. The processing takes about 2 weeks but may take longer during busy travel times. When traveling, take a photocopy of your passport along and put it in a separate place; also leave a copy of your itinerary and your documents with a relative at home. If your passport gets lost or stolen, report immediately. Having a copy may make the replacement process easier.

VISAS - A visa is a stamp or endorsement issued by a consulate or government official allowing a person to enter the country, for a limited time. A visa may require photos, itinerary details, prepaid arrangements, etc. Some types of visas are: tourist or visitor, work, transit, student, and immigrant.

TOURIST CARDS - Some countries require or issue tourist cards as a document for entry and exit. A passport or proof of citizenship is usually necessary; sometimes a photo and a fee. Tourist cards are issued by the consulate or sometimes by an airline or tour company.

VACCINATIONS - Proof of immunization against certain diseases is required for entry to some countries. The shots are usually obtained from local health departments and an "International Certificate" pamphlet documents the shots given.

MEDICAL ASSISTANCE ABROAD - Buy medical/sickness insurance and contact organizations that can provide assistance (IAMAT, Intermedic, etc.).

INSURANCE - Clients can purchase flight, baggage, medical/sickness and trip cancellation insurance. In addition, some agencies offer "airline default protection" and weather insurance.

CURRENCIES - Major banks and agencies such as Thomas Cook provide "currency packets," foreign bank drafts and travelers checks. Generally the best place to exchange money is at a bank.

CUSTOMS - U.S. Customs require persons leaving the country with more than $10,000 in cash or monetary items to fill out a form. Cameras, electronic equipment and fine jewelry should be "registered" with customs at the major airports so they are not confused with purchases made abroad. U.S. Citizens/residents can bring back $400.00 of duty-free purchases ($600.00 from many Caribbean islands) and 1 liter of alcoholic beverages (if of legal age) from an international journey. If returning from U.S. territories, $1200.00 and 4 liters are allowed duty-free.

CUSTOMS - Other countries' customs may limit the amount of gifts, film, cameras, liquor, cigarettes, electronic equipment, literature, money, etc., that a traveler can bring into the country. Again the government tourist offices or current travel guides can provide this information. "Customs," as in socially acceptable behavior and social practices, are also very different from country to country. Practical hints are sometimes given in travel guides. In addition, the book Do's and Taboos Around the World lists many local customs and practices. One of the most important practices is to be a "good" traveler.

THE "GOOD TRAVELER" COMMANDMENTS

D DO not expect things to be "like home" - you are not at home. Be patient if there are delays or problems - some are bound to happen and some cannot be controlled, such as bad weather, strikes, etc. Try not to get angry or upset unnecessarily.

B BE considerate of local customs, practices, and the lifestyle of the people. Don't make demands or be critical of local procedures.

A ADJUST to the local lifestyle and make every effort to follow the saying "When in Rome, do as the Romans do."

G GOOD MANNERS and COMMON SENSE go a long way in making travel enjoyable. Don't remark that things are "bigger, better, easier, etc." at home. Guard valuables or leave them at home, don't flash jewelry or money, don't buy currency on the black market, etc.

T TRY to get to know the country and its people. Appreciate the differences and benefit from the sharing and exchange of ideas and ways.

DO BE A GOOD TRAVELER

GSP - The U.S. offers a "Generalized System of Preferences" - which exempts some items from duty if purchased in the origin country.

VAT - Value Added Tax is an added tax on goods and services (in Canada there is a GST) primarily levied on local residents. Tourists can sometimes obtain a form for a "rebate" of the taxes paid.

SELLING TRAVEL

Before we continue in presenting and studying world areas, it is important to realize the aspects of geography that are important in **selling** travel.

It is not enough to know the sights of Paris, the food specialties of Greece, and the best buys in Japan. Travel agents must also spend the time getting to know the customers and making sure the selection of a destination is appropriate. Qualifying the clients is done by asking many questions and taking into consideration the answers to those questions. Clients have usually chosen a travel agency to assist them with their plans because they are unsure about where to go and what to do.

Forms can be useful in noting the clients' preferences, past experiences, budget, and so on. In other manuals of this training series, a "Traveler's Profile Form" is presented, along with types of forms for reservations and evaluations.

Factors or aspects of what clients may desire in a vacation or trip include:

BARGAINS

EXOTIC CULTURES

PEACE AND QUIET

SCENERY

WARM CLIMATE

FAMILY ACTIVITIES

HISTORICAL ATTRACTIONS

BEACHES

SPORTS

NIGHTLIFE

RELIGIOUS SIGHTS/EXPERIENCES

NATURE AND WILDLIFE

GENEALOGY

HEALTH

You can already imagine that certain destinations are particularly geared towards some of the factors above.

As a travel professional you can appreciate what every area of the world has to offer. Your work includes providing information to clients, giving practical tips and hints, realistic evaluations, and also recommending ways to overcome negative attitudes, fears, or psychological barriers.

SELLING TRAVEL EXERCISE

At times clients may voice concerns and comments that require the travel agent to respond. To practice professional communication skills, provide factors and alternatives or positive reassuring comments for each of the following statements below.

1. "New Yorkers are rude and the city is dangerous and expensive."

2. "Mexico is dirty and poverty stricken."

3. "There's nothing to do on a Caribbean island."

4. "It isn't safe to go to South America with all the disease there."

5. "The French dislike Americans and are rude."

6. "There's nothing but museums and churches to see in Europe."

7. "It rains all the time in England."

8. "It's too expensive in Scandinavia."

9. "The health conditions are deplorable in Africa."

10. "The climate in Africa is hot and there are too many insects."

11. "The countries are so unstable in Africa, I would be afraid of political and social unrest."

12. "I've heard that flights get cancelled and luggage gets lost or damaged when people travel to Africa."

GREENLAND

Before we begin detailed studies of Canada, Mexico, the Caribbean and other western hemisphere destinations, some brief information on Greenland will be presented.

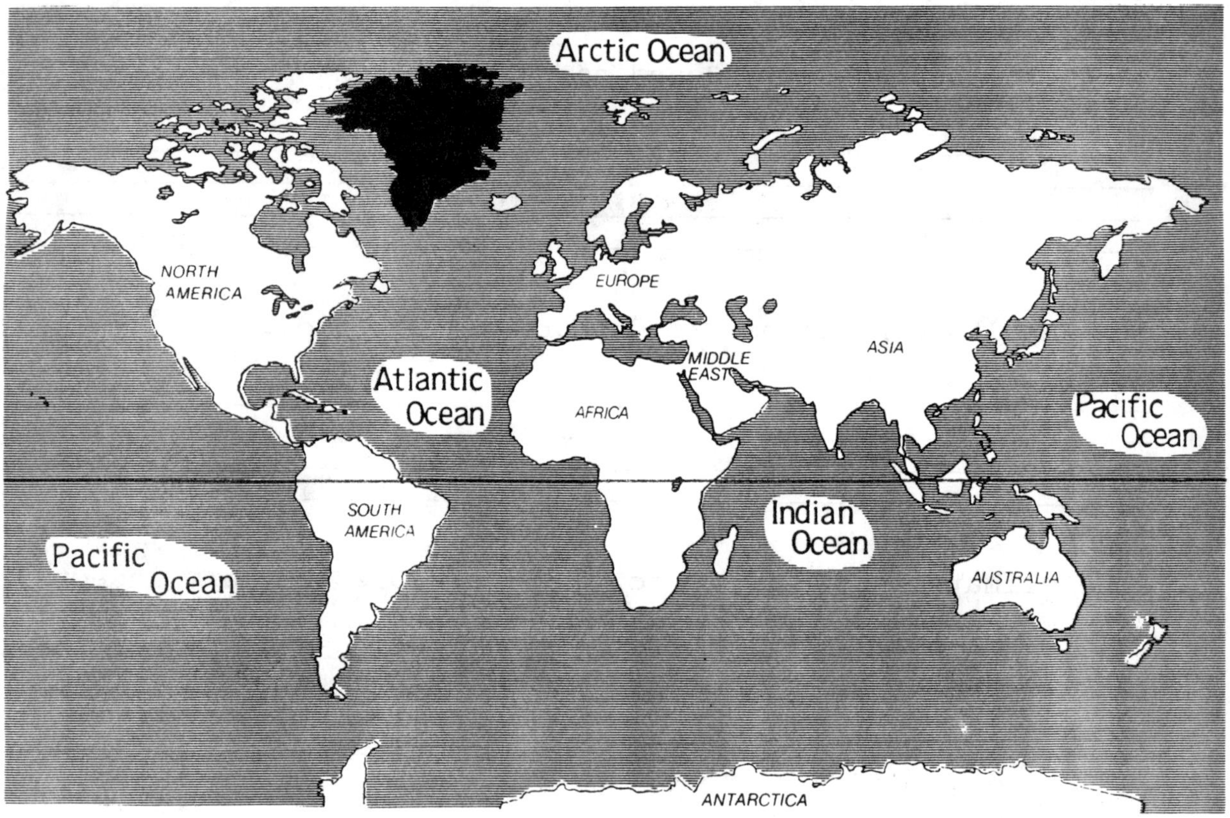

Greenland is the world's largest island (if Australia is counted as a continent) and is now an overseas territory in association with the European Community, while remaining heavily dependent on subsidies from Denmark. The surrounding seas are either permanently frozen or very chilled by the cold currents of the Arctic and North Atlantic Ocean. With an arctic climate and mostly covered by ice (in the center the ice can be up to two miles thick!), the country does not appeal to the ordinary traveler. The ice-free coastal region is where all the population is found. This region is intersected by deep fjords. There are hotels in the major towns, but there are no rail or road networks, making air and seacraft the only practical means of getting from place to place. The Arctic weather conditions can cause delays and interruptions in transport services or changes to planned itineraries. It is strongly recommended that travelers take extra monies to cover expenses that may be incurred by such delays. No further study on Greenland is provided here, so let's move on to the areas of Canada, Mexico, etc.

CHAPTER 7

Canada

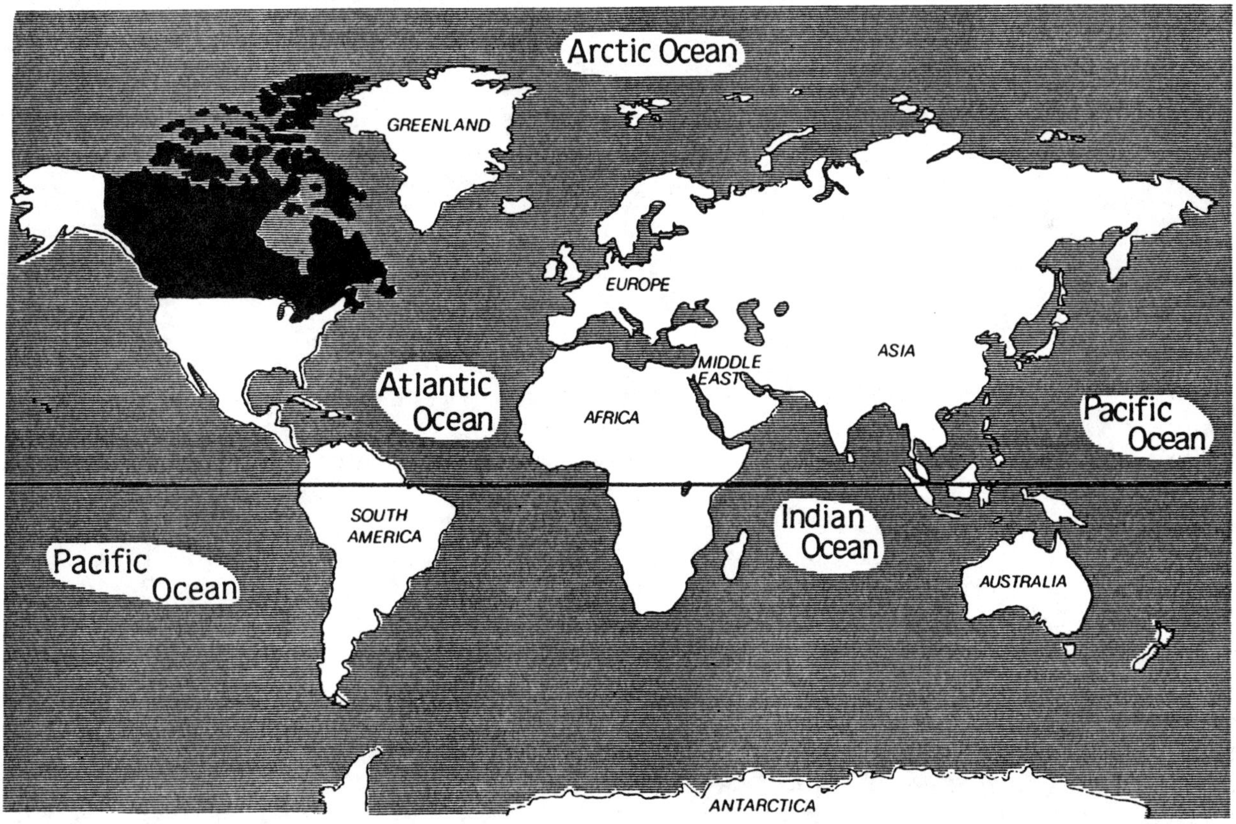

NOTES

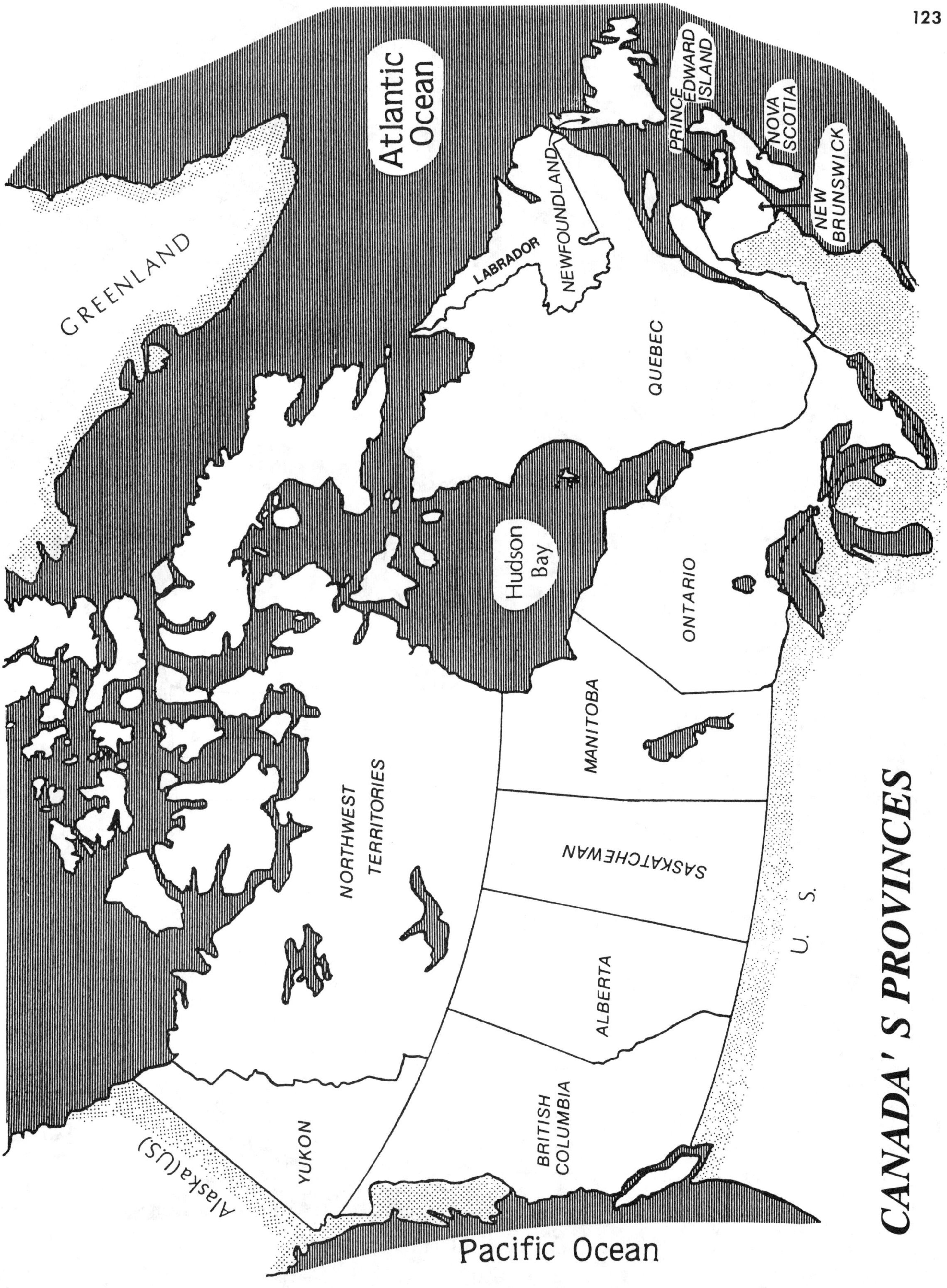

CANADA'S PROVINCES

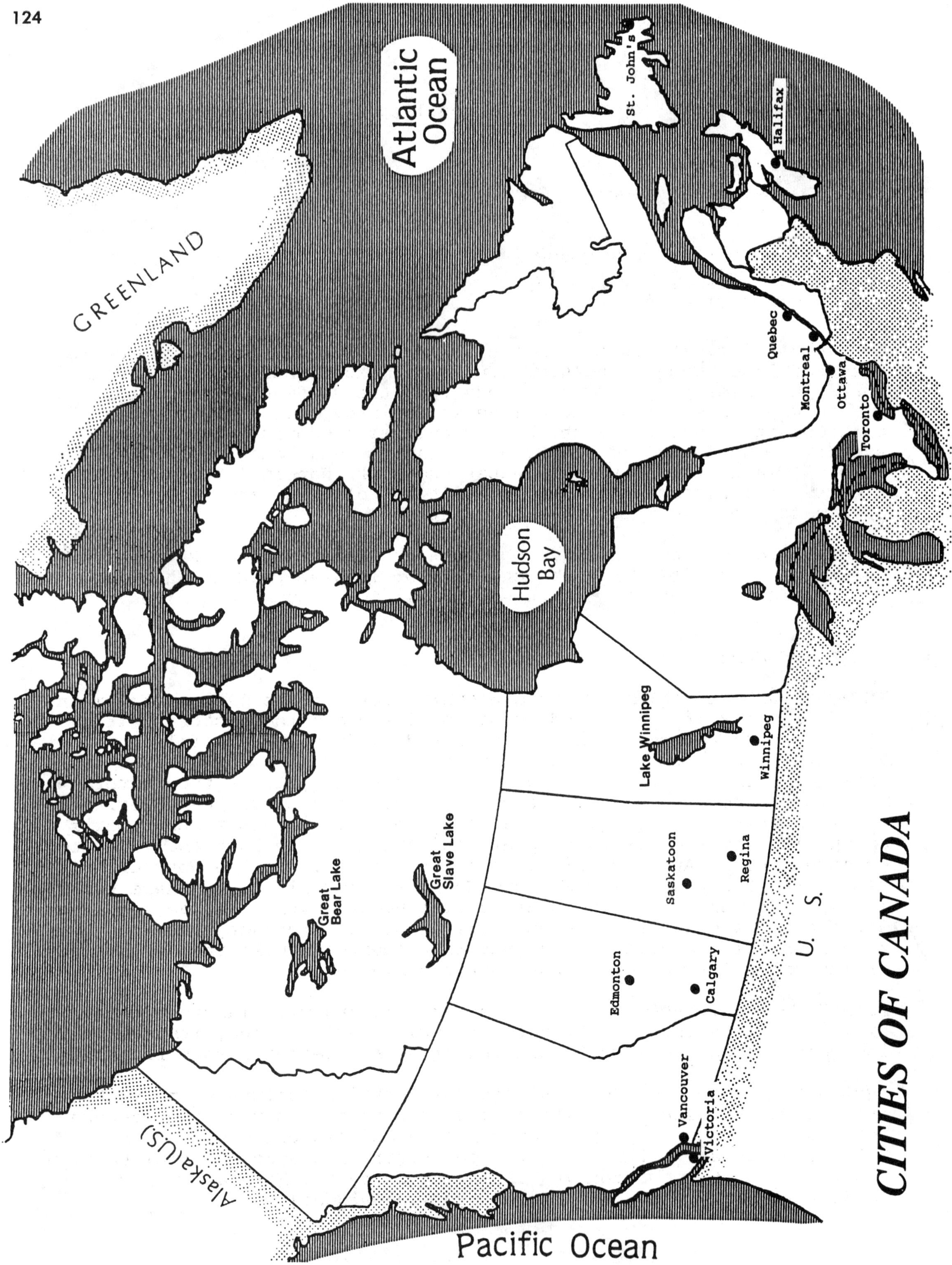
Atlantic Ocean
GREENLAND
St. John's
Halifax
Quebec
Montreal
Ottawa
Toronto
Hudson Bay
Lake Winnipeg
Winnipeg
Saskatoon
Regina
Great Bear Lake
Great Slave Lake
Edmonton
Calgary
U. S.
Vancouver
Victoria
Alaska (U.S.)
Pacific Ocean

CITIES OF CANADA

CANADA

MAJOR CITY/AIRPORT CODES (alphabetically by province, city):

YYC - Calgary, Alberta
YEG - Edmonton, Alberta
YVR - Vancouver, British Columbia
YWG - Winnipeg, Manitoba
YOW - Ottawa, Ontario
YTO - Toronto, Ontario
YYZ - Toronto, Ontario (Pearson International)
YMQ - Montreal, Quebec
YUL - Montreal, Quebec (Dorval Airport)
YQR - Regina, Saskatchewan

The second largest country in the world with almost 4 million square miles of land, Canada includes twelve political entities (although Quebec has been proposing to secede from the unified government). Since two-thirds of Canadians live in the provinces of Quebec and Ontario, study and research these provinces predominantly. But the scenery of Newfoundland and Nova Scotia, the quaintness of Prince Edward Island, the beauty of Jasper and Banff National Parks in Alberta, the fjords and inlets of British Columbia, and other areas of Canada are also worthwhile destinations.

Canada's borders are on three oceans - the Atlantic, the Pacific, and the Arctic, and it is a vast country. The longest road is the Trans-Canada Highway, running from west to east for about 5,000 miles.

EASTERN CANADA

NEWFOUNDLAND and LABRADOR. This eastern province consists of the main-land territory of the Island of Newfoundland and the eastern half of the Ungava Peninsula, known as Labrador. This area is filled with beautiful seascapes and landscapes, history and lore. Visit Gros Morne National Park for its dramatic fjord-like scenery. Tour the Victorian streets of the capital, St. John's. The city surrounds the waterfront and is simply enchanting. It's also a good base to visit other parts of the island, such as Cape Spear National Historic Park and the Ocean Science Center. Another main town is St. Anthony (on the northern tip), famous for the L'Anse Aux Meadows National Historic Park, where you'll see an 11th century Viking area consisting of several houses, cooking pits, and a sauna. The mainland portion of the province, Labrador, has rich iron ore deposits and was virgin wilderness until the exploration of its natural resources began in the early 1950's.

PRINCE EDWARD ISLAND (P.E.I.) is a small island with luscious green hills, white beaches and bright blue sky. Charlottetown, its capital, is a commercial and educational center with a restored waterfront area.

NOVA SCOTIA means New Scotland and the Scottish influence and culture are everywhere. The Cabot Trail, a scenic circle tour of the eastern and western shores of Cape Breton Island and picturesque Margaree Valley, winds along the edge of Cape Breton Highlands National Park. Visit the Maritime Museum in Halifax or enjoy the Halifax Public Gardens (one of Canada's finest Victorian gardens).

NEW BRUNSWICK's capital, Fredericton, features riverside mansions and is a city of grace and charm. St. John, a major port, has a fashionable area of hotels, restaurants, nightclubs, and shops - Market Square. Don't miss the Reversing Falls here, which occur when the tide comes into the St. John River from the Bay of Fundy, causing the river to literally flow backwards.

QUEBEC, a province that is seeking to be independent, is predominantly French speaking (Montreal is the second largest French speaking city in the world). From dining out in one of the over 3,000 restaurants in Montreal, to skiing in the Laurentian Mountains, to sightseeing in the Old Town of Quebec City, this part of Canada is "magnifique!" The St. Lawrence River region of this province offers lovely scenery, splendid driving tours, quaint fishing villages, and beaches.

ONTARIO is "yours to discover" according to some car license plates. Toronto is a modern, clean, friendly city, and has the tallest free-standing structure in the world - the CN Tower. Visit the castle called Casa Loma, the Royal Ontario Museum, the Ontario Science Centre, and the Art Gallery of Ontario. For shopping try the Harbourfront or Ontario Place (a huge complex with a marina, children's villages, an IMAX theater, restaurants, and shops). Stroll down Bloor Street and dine in one of the ethnic restaurants (Greek, Italian, Indian, Ethiopian - you name it!). About an hour's drive away is Niagara Falls - a place that has to be seen because postcards cannot do it justice. Niagara-on-the-Lake and St. Catherine's are also cities to visit. Ottawa, Canada's capital, is home to museums, the old world charm of Canada, and government buildings and events. The Rideau Canal has some scenic walking and jogging paths and in winter it becomes the world's longest ice skating rink. The impressive Parliament Buildings, the Byward Market, the National Gallery, the Rideau Mall - this city is a wonderful combination of open-air markets, indoor shops, and loads of restaurants, pubs, and nightclubs.

SPOTLIGHT ON ONTARIO AND QUEBEC

WESTERN CANADA

MANITOBA's capital, Winnipeg, has become an international center and its famous Folklorama Festival in August showcases the many ethnic groups and cultures. Save an evening for cruising the Red and Assiniboine Rivers aboard one of the riverboats, complete with dinner, a glowing sunset, and prairie stars. Churchill is the province's northernmost city, on the shores of Hudson Bay. It's a train or plane trip from Manitoba, but the reasons to visit include: beautiful scenery, whale-watching, the annual polar bear migration in late fall, and the heaviest concentration of the aurora borealis (Northern Lights).

SASKATCHEWAN is the breadbasket province of Canada - filled with parks, forests, lakes, farms, and wheat fields. Major cities are Regina (the capital) and Saskatoon. Visit the Headquarters of the Royal Canadian Mounted Police in Regina.

ALBERTA is famous for Jasper and Banff National Parks, Lake Louise, the world's largest mall at Edmonton, the annual Calgary Stampede, and much more. On Alberta's southwestern border with the U.S. is Waterton Lakes National Park - once joined to Glacier National Park in Montana and the world's first International Peace Park.

BRITISH COLUMBIA's beauty spreads from the Queen Charlotte Islands, to cities such as Victoria and Vancouver, to the rugged mountain interior. Vancouver is a major port city with large German, Ukranian, and Chinese populations. Popular to visit are the museums in Vancouver as well as Stanley Park, the Vancouver Aquarium, and the Grouse Mountain Skyride. A scenic drive from Vancouver will take you to the interior of the province to see the Caribou-Chilcotin Mountains, the Fraser River, the mountains called the Seven Sisters, and several Indian villages with their totems. Just north of Vancouver is Whistler, a popular ski resort. The city of Victoria is located on Vancouver Island and it is a most English of Canadian towns. Just north of Victoria is famous Butchart Gardens - with its English, Japanese, and Italian themed gardens.

Most of the **NORTHWEST TERRITORIES'** population and commercial activity is centered in Yellowknife and around the Great Slave Lake. In the northern expanse, the Inuit (Eskimos) live by age old methods of fishing, hunting, and trapping.

YUKON TERRITORY is Canada's "last frontier" and is largely a forested and mountainous wilderness. Mt. Logan is situated in the southwest corner. At 19,524 feet it is Canada's highest point.

Niagara Falls (viewed from the U.S. side)

CANADA

Complete profile forms on provinces, practice labeling the maps, and complete the reviews and tests on Canada.

PROVINCE/TERRITORY:________________________ CAPITAL:________________________

ABBREVIATION:______ MAJOR CITY/ AIRPORT CODES:____

MAJOR CITIES AND PLACES OF INTEREST:____

____

____

____

____

____

____

SPECIAL INFORMATION (NICKNAME, RESTRICTIONS, EVENTS, TAXES, WEATHER, ETC.):

____

____

ECONOMY (PRODUCTS, ETC.):____

____

PROVINCE/TERRITORY:________________________ CAPITAL:________________________

ABBREVIATION:______ MAJOR CITY/ AIRPORT CODES:____

MAJOR CITIES AND PLACES OF INTEREST:____

____

____

____

____

____

____

SPECIAL INFORMATION (NICKNAME, RESTRICTIONS, EVENTS, TAXES, WEATHER, ETC.):

____

____

ECONOMY (PRODUCTS, ETC.):____

____

PROVINCE/TERRITORY:________________________ CAPITAL:______________________

MAJOR CITY/
ABBREVIATION:______ AIRPORT CODES:____

MAJOR CITIES AND PLACES OF INTEREST:______________________________________

____

____

____

SPECIAL INFORMATION (NICKNAME, RESTRICTIONS, EVENTS, TAXES, WEATHER, ETC.):

____

____

ECONOMY (PRODUCTS, ETC.):____

____

PROVINCE/TERRITORY:________________________ CAPITAL:______________________

MAJOR CITY/
ABBREVIATION:______ AIRPORT CODES:____

MAJOR CITIES AND PLACES OF INTEREST:______________________________________

____

____

____

SPECIAL INFORMATION (NICKNAME, RESTRICTIONS, EVENTS, TAXES, WEATHER, ETC.):

____

____

ECONOMY (PRODUCTS, ETC.):____

____

PROVINCE/TERRITORY:________________________ CAPITAL:______________________

MAJOR CITY/
ABBREVIATION:______ AIRPORT CODES:____

MAJOR CITIES AND PLACES OF INTEREST:______________________________________

____

____

____

SPECIAL INFORMATION (NICKNAME, RESTRICTIONS, EVENTS, TAXES, WEATHER, ETC.):

____

____

ECONOMY (PRODUCTS, ETC.):____

____

PROVINCE/TERRITORY:________________________ CAPITAL:_______________________

MAJOR CITY/
ABBREVIATION:______ AIRPORT CODES:____

MAJOR CITIES AND PLACES OF INTEREST:_______________________________________

SPECIAL INFORMATION (NICKNAME, RESTRICTIONS, EVENTS, TAXES, WEATHER, ETC.):

ECONOMY (PRODUCTS, ETC.):____

PROVINCE/TERRITORY:________________________ CAPITAL:_______________________

MAJOR CITY/
ABBREVIATION:______ AIRPORT CODES:____

MAJOR CITIES AND PLACES OF INTEREST:_______________________________________

SPECIAL INFORMATION (NICKNAME, RESTRICTIONS, EVENTS, TAXES, WEATHER, ETC.):

ECONOMY (PRODUCTS, ETC.):____

PROVINCE/TERRITORY:________________________ CAPITAL:_______________________

MAJOR CITY/
ABBREVIATION:______ AIRPORT CODES:____

MAJOR CITIES AND PLACES OF INTEREST:_______________________________________

SPECIAL INFORMATION (NICKNAME, RESTRICTIONS, EVENTS, TAXES, WEATHER, ETC.):

ECONOMY (PRODUCTS, ETC.):____

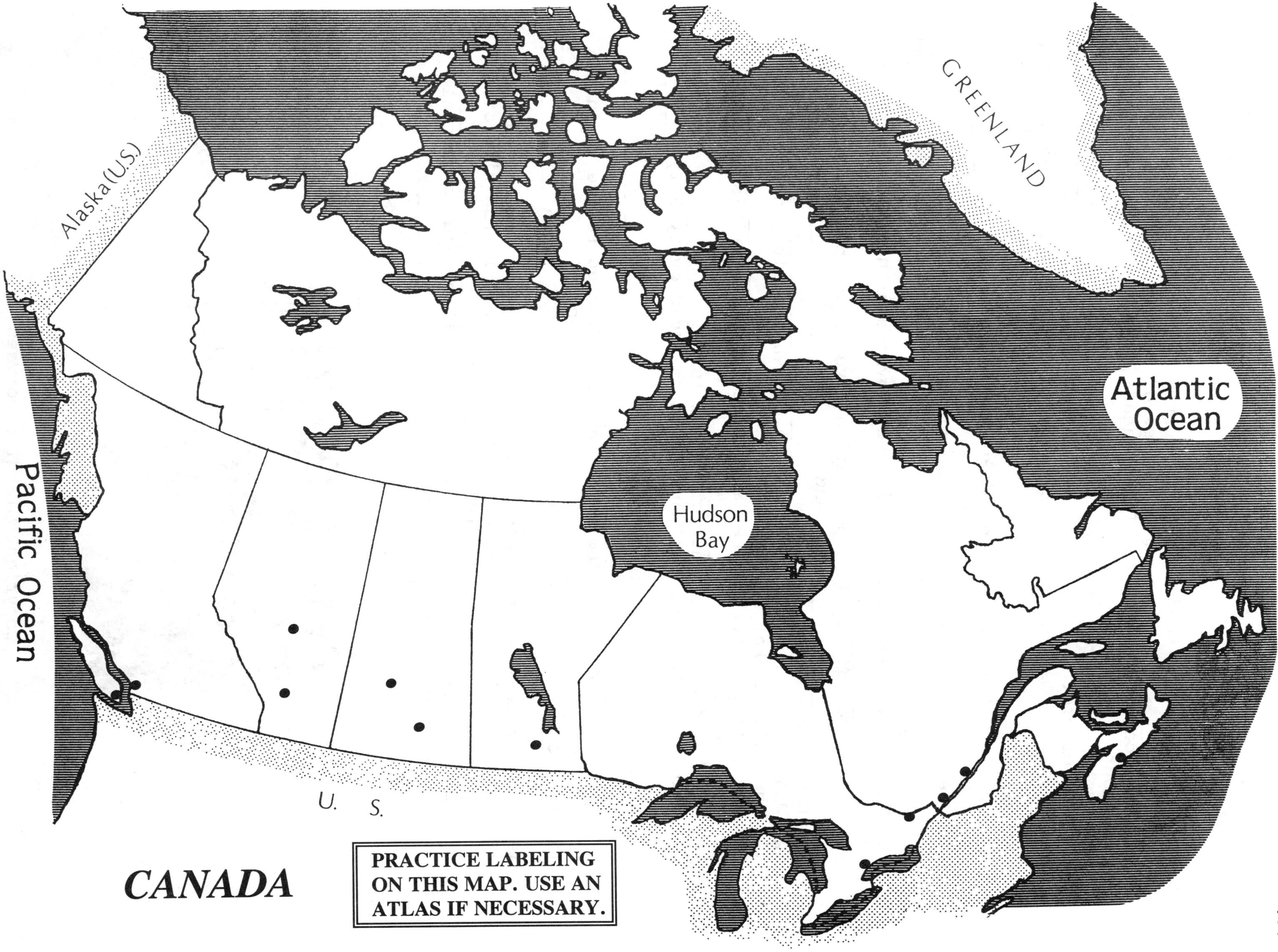

CANADA

PRACTICE LABELING ON THIS MAP. USE AN ATLAS IF NECESSARY.

CANADA REVIEW

1. Canada is the second largest country in the world with almost ____________ million square miles of land.
2. The longest road is the Trans-Canada Highway, which runs for about _______________ miles.
3. The tallest free standing structure is the ______________________ in Toronto.
4. Niagara Falls is about 4 hours drive from Toronto. True or False ______________.
5. Canada's capital is _________________.
6. Charlottetown is the capital of the province of _________________ ____________________________.
7. The province that means New Scotland is _________________________.
8. __________________ is the second largest French speaking city in the world.
9. The scenic Cabot Trail is in the province of Nova Scotia. True or False _______________
10. Two-thirds of Canada's population live in the provinces of ________________________ and ________________________.
11. New Brunswick's capital is ___________________________.
12. What is the name of the canal in Ottawa that in winter becomes the longest skating rink? ________________________
13. The mountains called the Seven Sisters are in British Columbia. True or False ____________
14. The breadbasket province of Canada is _____________________________.
15. Which city features a famous stampede, held every July? _________ _______________________.
16. Name two national parks located in Alberta. _____________________ __________________________________
17. The headquarters of the Royal Canadian Mounted Police is in the city of ___________________ in the province of _________________.
18. A famous gardens located just north of Victoria is ______________ Gardens.
19. The Reversing Falls, which occur when the tide comes into the St. John River from the Bay of Fundy can be seen in the city of ____________________ in the province of ________________________.
20. Most of the Northwest Territories' population and commercial activity is centered in the city of _____________________ and around Great Slave Lake.

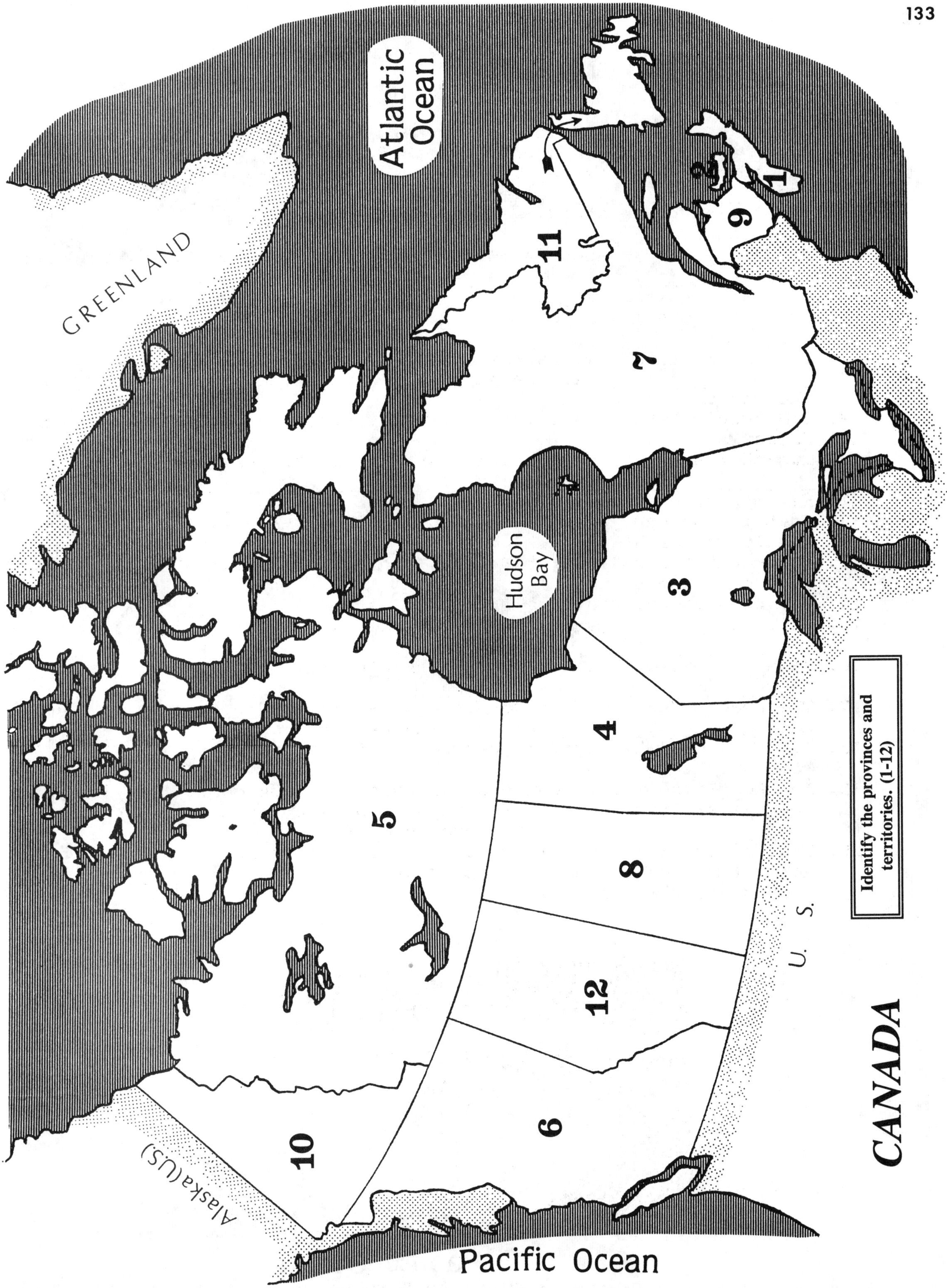

Identify the provinces and territories. (1-12)

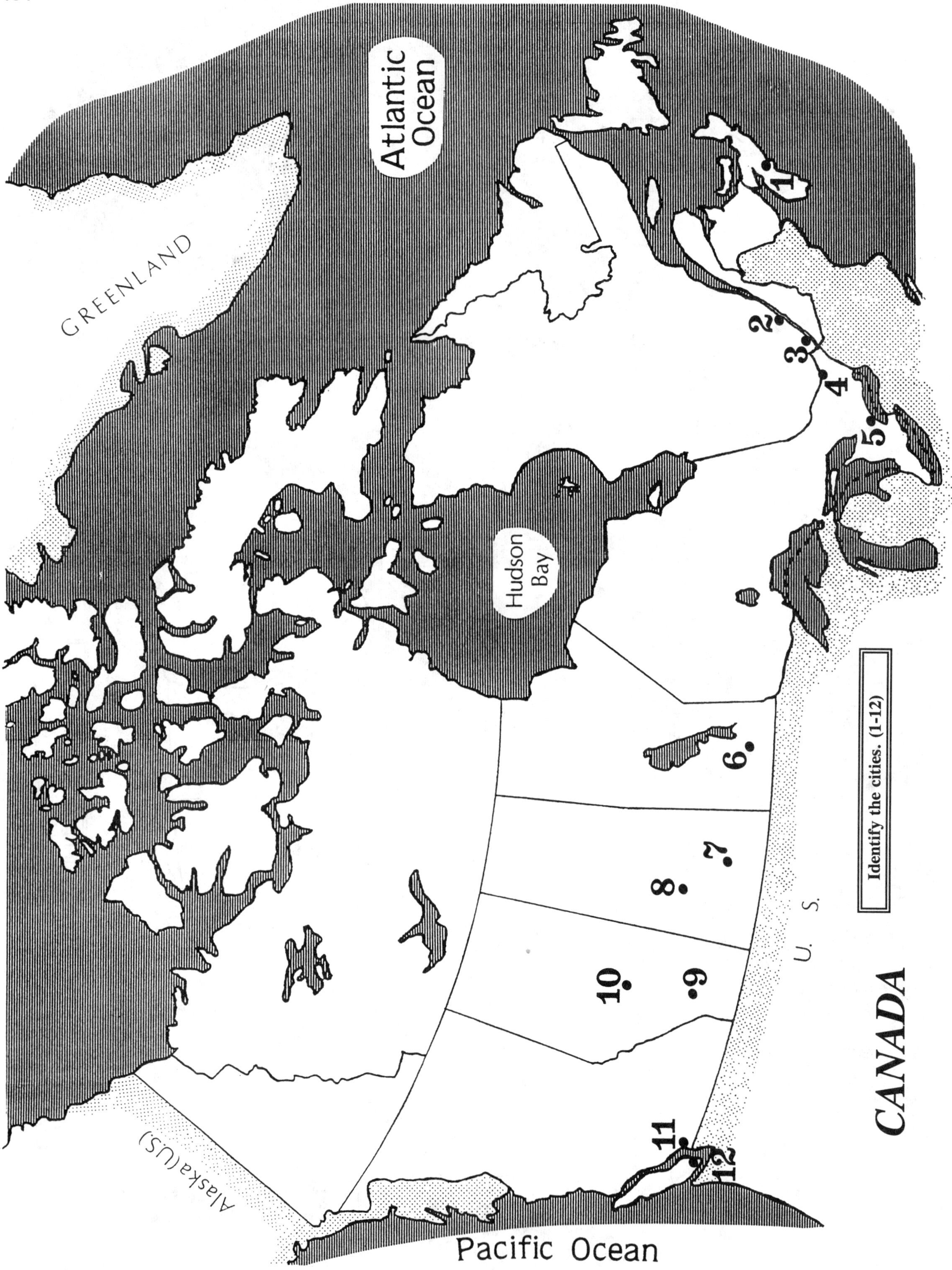

CANADA

Identify the cities. (1-12)

CHAPTER 8

Mexico

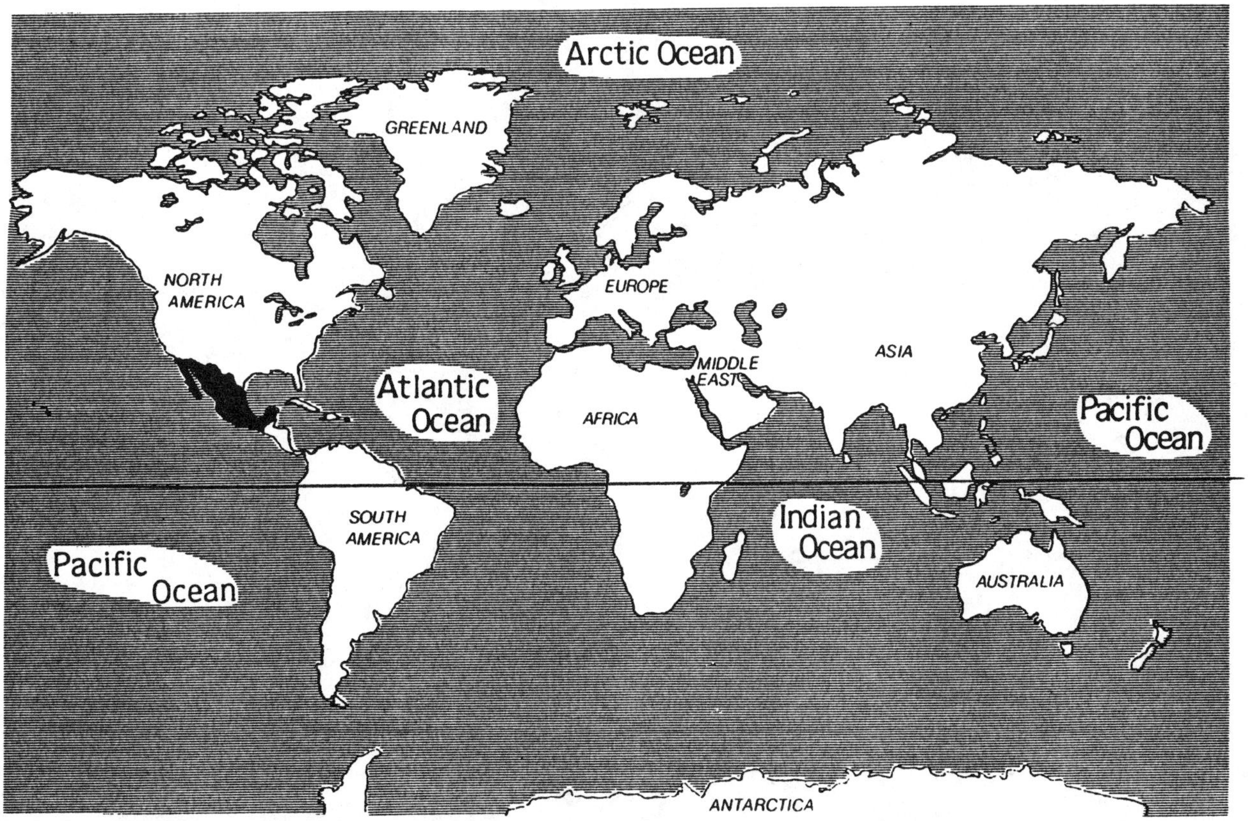

NOTES

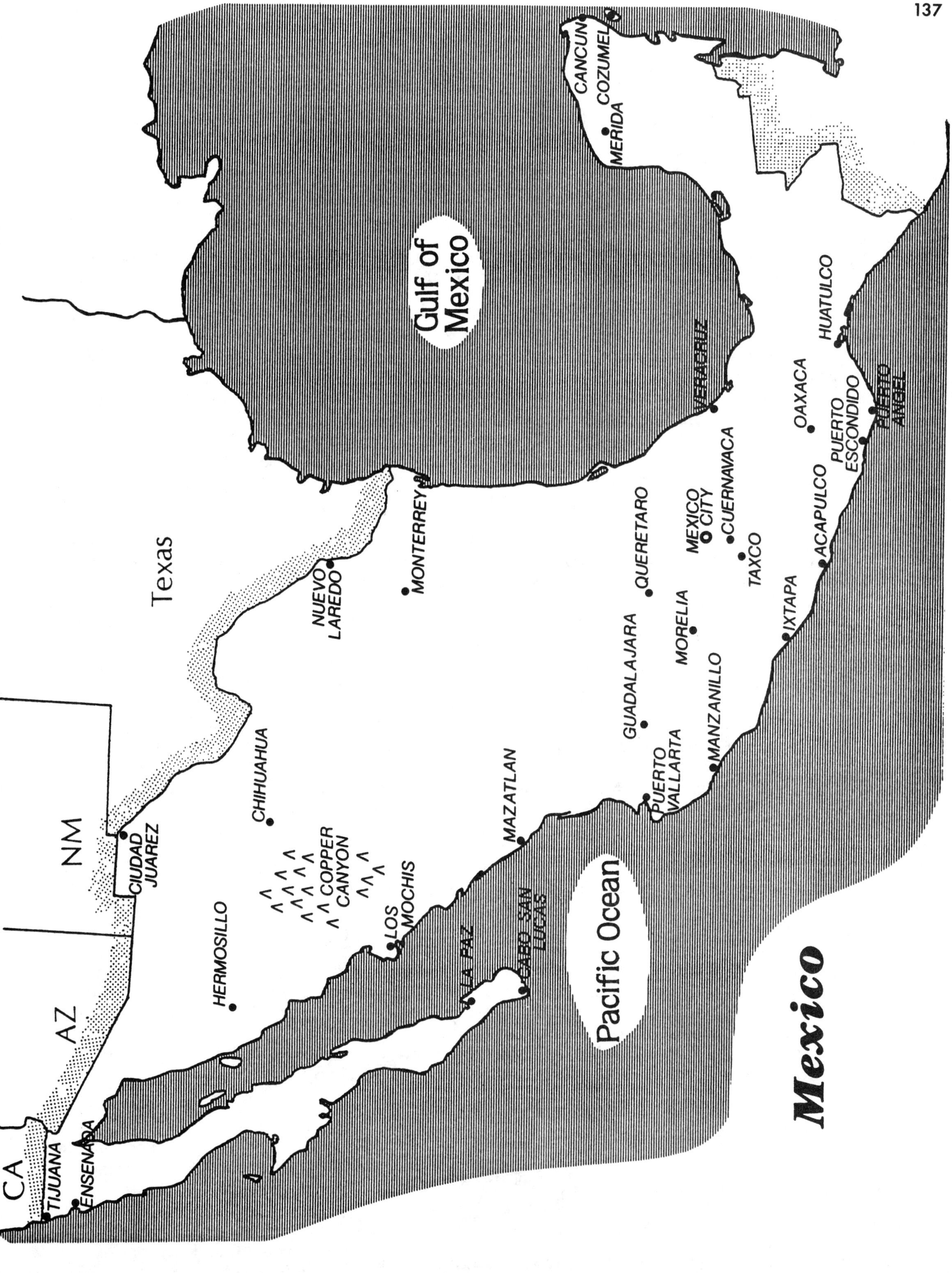
Mexico
Gulf of Mexico
Pacific Ocean
Texas
NM
AZ
CA
TIJUANA
ENSENADA
HERMOSILLO
CIUDAD JUAREZ
CHIHUAHUA
COPPER CANYON
LOS MOCHIS
LA PAZ
CABO SAN LUCAS
MAZATLAN
NUEVO LAREDO
MONTERREY
PUERTO VALLARTA
GUADALAJARA
MANZANILLO
MORELIA
QUERETARO
IXTAPA
MEXICO CITY
CUERNAVACA
TAXCO
ACAPULCO
VERACRUZ
PUERTO ESCONDIDO
OAXACA
PUERTO ANGEL
HUATULCO
MERIDA
CANCUN
COZUMEL

MEXICO

MAJOR CITY/AIRPORT CODES

ACA - Acapulco
CUN - Cancun
CZM - Cozumel
GDL - Guadalajara
MEX - Mexico City
MID - Merida
MZT - Mazatlan
OAX - Oaxaca
PVR - Puerto Vallarta
SJD - Los Cabos
ZIH - Zihuatanejo/Ixtapa
ZLO - Manzanillo

Mexico is a country of very distinct regions, offering a variety of experiences to travelers. The narrow Baja Peninsula is rugged and arid, dotted with fishing towns and offering resorts such as Cabo San Lucas, located at the tip. Enjoy the rustic adventure of the Copper Canyon rail trip through the Sierra Madre Mountains and venture into the domain of the Tarahumara Indians. Visit archaeological zones in the Yucatan Peninsula, or relax at posh resorts in Cancun, Acapulco, Ixtapa, Manzanillo, Puerto Vallarta, and Mazatlan. Snorkel in the clear waters and reefs of Cozumel. Go to colonial cities such as Morelia, Puebla, San Miguel de Allende, Guadalajara, etc., and visit the capital, Mexico City - all in all Mexico's destinations are numerous. The currency is the nuevo peso. Here's a brief list of the major cities, resort areas, and tourist activities:

MEXICO CITY - Visit the National Museum of Anthropology, Chapultepec Castle and Park, the National Palace, the Zocalo, the Shrine of Guadalupe, Alameda Park, the markets, etc. Shop, dine, and enjoy the nightlife in the Zona Rosa district. Walk down the Paseo de la Reforma and see the Angel (or Independence) Monument, enjoy the famous Ballet Folklorico at the Palacio de Belles Artes, or take the subway to various areas of this large, sprawling metropolis. This bustling capital, where people dress mostly in conservative or business attire, does have some problems with traffic congestion and noise. And the city's air pollution can present a health threat. Teotihuacan - 30 miles north of Mexico City - is one of the most important archaelogical sites in the country.

CUERNAVACA - On the way to Taxco many tours take in some sightseeing of this clean, friendly city, overflowing with lush vegetation and flowers.

TAXCO - This is called the "Silver City" and is nestled in the hills on the route between Mexico City and Acapulco.

ACAPULCO - Acapulco is a very developed and populated international resort with a long string of high rise hotels and exclusive resorts. From Las Brisas - with hillside villas having their own pools - to the Acapulco Princess and the Pierre Marques extensive resorts, to the Condesa Acapulco in the middle of the strip, there is a variety of accommodations. The cliff divers perform at La Quebrada near here. The restaurants and nightlife have to be experienced - the discos here are extravagant in their decoration and sophistication.

A popular itinerary for some first time travelers to Mexico is to stay three nights in Mexico City, one night in Taxco, and three nights in Acapulco - combining a cosmopolitan city, a more colonial city, and a sophisticated beach resort.

PUERTO ESCONDIDO - Located south of Acapulco, this hideaway offers uncrowded beaches, a few hotels and resorts, and a surfing beach at Zikatela.

HUATULCO - One of Mexico's newest master-planned resorts, this city located south of Acapulco has the ideal beauty and isolation for the atmosphere desired in totally self-contained resorts.

IXTAPA/ZIHUATANEJO - About 150 miles north of Acapulco is another resort area. Zihuatanejo is the fishing village, Ixtapa is the row of hotels and resorts on a pristine beach setting.

MANZANILLO - Continuing along the Pacific coast are other destinations for enjoying beaches, fishing, golf, and other sports. Las Hadas ("the Fairies") is one of the most striking hotels - with its white Moorish architecture in a 250-acre paradise.

PUERTO VALLARTA - Called "PV" for short, this resort has a quaint charm along with its highly developed resorts and condominium developments. A day trip on a yacht to Yelapa for lunch, swimming and relaxing is a popular option.

MAZATLAN - The resort of Mazatlan has a more carefree and informal atmosphere, and is a paradise for a variety of sports - waterskiing, sailing, diving, windsurfing, fishing, golf, tennis, surfing, horseback riding, and more.

TIJUANA - Claiming to receive more than 20 million visitors a year, Tijuana is a popular day trip from San Diego, California.

BAJA CALIFORNIA - This peninsula comprises two states, Baja California Norte and Baja California Sur. The enclosed gulf is rich in marine life.

MEXICALI - The capital of Baja California Norte, Mexicali provides a base for exploring the surrounding mountains and countryside.

LOS CABOS - Los Cabos is a destination that includes the colonial city of San Jose del Cabo and the city at the tip of the Baja - Cabo San Lucas. "Cabo" is a place to get away from it all and enjoy the panoramic natural beauty and topography.

LA PAZ - Capital of Baja California Sur, this city is known for low prices, duty-free shopping, and great fishing.

VERACRUZ - A lively seaport city on the Gulf of Mexico, Veracruz offers excellent seafood and a particularly well-known carnival time.

The COPPER CANYON of Mexico is explored by train. The trip stretches from Chihuahua to Los Mochis and takes up to 14 hours. Overnight stays in the canyon are popular - there are rustic lodges at Creel or at the Divisadero. The Tarahumara Indians live here - a reserved tribe - whose men are known for their running ability and whose women will often be encountered selling their beautiful baskets and crafts.

COLONIAL MEXICO includes cities such as Morelia, Queretaro, San Miguel de Allende, Patzcuaro, Tonala, Guanajuato, Tlaquepaque, and Guadalajara. Here you will find the old world charm of Mexico and its people, plazas and churches, open air markets, local festivals and fiesta days. These are cities to admire the architecture, to speak Spanish, to watch the craftspeople and to bargain for beautiful ceramics, embroidered clothes, handmade jewelry, blankets, tiles, leather and straw goods, glassware, and many other handicrafts. You may also want to buy tequila and kahlua, as they are liquors made in Mexico. Vanilla and a number of spices are other buys.

The YUCATAN PENINSULA features a number of archaeological ruins. MERIDA is often used as a starting point for visiting Kabah, Uxmal, Coba, and Chichen Itza. The Yucatan Peninsula is divided into three states: Campeche, Yucatan, and Quintana Roo.

CANCUN, a well-known resort, has beautiful white powdery sand beaches, gorgeous turquoise water, and the island of Isla Mujeres is nearby to spend a day snorkeling. Cancun is a very developed resort and the hotel standards (water, plumbing, cleanliness) and services are very good. It is a good destination for those travelers who are not interested in trying to speak Spanish (almost all the staff will speak English) and those who do not want to experience the "real" local culture of Mexico.

COZUMEL, an island off the coast of the Yucatan, is a diver's dream, with reefs surrounding the island. There's Palancar Reef, Chancanab Lagoon and Park, a sunken plane wreck 100 yards from the La Ceiba Hotel, and reefs right beside the shore in front of many of the beach hotels.

Not necessarily typical of the rest of Mexico are the border towns, which include Tijuana, Nogales, Nuevo Laredo, and Ciudad Juarez. Health insurance is recommended for travel to Mexico. Medicines are often available without prescriptions and pharmacists are permitted to diagnose and treat minor ailments. General advice for travelers to Mexico (as well as most of Latin America) includes: drink only bottled water and drinks without ice, avoid street vendors' foods, peel fruits and make sure all vegetables are cooked. Check for current advisories. The country is a Republic with 31 states and one Federal District (City and state examples: Guadalajara, Jal.- the state is Jalisco, Cancun, Q.Roo. - the state is Quintana Roo. There has been some unrest in the southern state of Chiapas).

A NIGHT OUT IN MEXICO

Dining out in Mexico can be a real treat - there are many specialties containing a score of ingredients. Of course there are tacos, enchilades and tamales. But there are also excellent seafood dishes and every area has its own unique recipes. Chicken mole is an intriguing blend of chicken in a sauce of chilis, tomatoes, peanuts, chocolate, almonds, onions and garlic. A Yucatan specialty is chicken baked in a banana leaf (chicken pebil). Sopa de tortilla (tortilla soup) is a great start and can be a meal in itself. Refried beans, rice, and guacamole often accompany the entree. Mexican beers are numerous: Corona, Bohemia, Dos Equis, Carta Blanca, Tecate, and more. Tequila and kahlua are popular liquors. At resorts and deluxe hotels, there may be a mariachi band or folkloric dance/show, and discos and nightclubs may also be a choice for entertainment.

MEXICO - SPOTLIGHT ON ARCHAEOLOGY

The mystique of Mexico's ancient past is exciting to many travelers and tours to the ruins and sites are included on many visitors' itineraries. There are over 11,000 documented archaeological sites throughout Mexico and new discoveries continue. The civilizations that occupied this vast area include the Aztecs, the Olmecs, the Toltecs, and the Mayans.

As a starting point, the capital, Mexico City, is actually built on the remnants of the capital of the Aztec empire, Tenochitlan. A spectacular collection of artifacts and treasures can be seen at the Museum of Anthropology, in Chapultepec Park. Outside Mexico City are the pyramids of Teotihuacan. The Pyramid of the Sun is magnificent - actually larger in volume than the pyramid of Cheops in Egypt. The smaller Pyramid of the Moon and other excavated areas add to the site's impressiveness. There is a sound and light show performed every evening from October through May.

Cholula offers the Tepanapa Pyramid, with tunnels through its hillside location that are open to visitors.

Tula is another site located about 90 miles northwest of Mexico City.

Near Toluca is an Aztec ceremonial center with temples carved directly from the rock. The site is called Malinalco.

Xochicalco has a main temple that has a variety of reliefs and hieroglyphics in the place that was once a crossroads city for the Aztec, Toltec, and Mayan peoples.

About 120 miles northwest of Veracruz, near the village of Papantla, is El Tajin. Known for its unique architecture and design, the Pyramid of the Niches here is believed to have been built by the Huastecs, relatives of the Mayans.

Zempoala is thought to have the same origins as El Tajin and the site features the Great Pyramid and the Temple of the Little Faces.

In Southern Mexico, the ruins of Monte Alban are very intriguing in their mixture of styles and influences. They are located in a beautiful setting about six miles from Oaxaca. Also in this area are the ruins of Mitla - located in the midst of a village. In the lush jungle area of the state of Chiapas is Palenque, believed to have been the ceremonial center for a great Mayan dynasty. Plan to spend the day at this area - located about 95 miles southeast of Villahermosa.

The Yucatan is probably the best known archeaological area because some sights are very accessible and are located near developed resorts. 70 miles south of the popular resort of Cancun is Tulum, a walled city thought to have still been occupied at the time of the Spanish conquest. Set amid several lakes and located 60 miles southwest of Cancun is Coba, a relatively unspoiled site. South of Merida (about 60 miles) are the sites of Kabah and Uxmal. And perhaps the most famous of all Mayan cities is Chichen Itza, which includes temples, ball courts, pyramids, an observatory, and a sacred well.

MEXICO

Now complete a profile on the country of Mexico, practice labeling the map, and then work through the written and map identification tests.

COUNTRY:______________________________ CAPITAL:____________________________

DOCUMENTARY REQUIREMENTS FOR U.S. CITIZENS:

____

OTHER PARTICULARS (SHOTS, ETC.):____

CURRENCY:___________________ CURRENCY CODE:_________ EXCHANGE RATE:_________

LANGUAGE(S):____

SIZE:_______________________________ POPULATION:___________________________

CLIMATE:____

BEST TIME TO VISIT:____

MAJOR CITIES AND PLACES OF INTEREST:

____

____

____

____

____

____

____

____

____

____

____

____

____

SPORTS:____

RELIGION(S):_____________________________ GOVERNMENT:______________________

FOOD SPECIALTIES:____

BEST BUYS:____

SPECIAL INFORMATION (SAMPLE ITINERARIES, RESTRICTIONS, EVENTS, TAXES, ETC.):

____

____

____

MAJOR AIRLINES:____

MAJOR CITY/AIRPORT CODES:____

TRANSPORTATION PARTICULARS:____

____

____

SPECIAL HOTELS/RESORTS/MISCELLANEOUS INFO___________________________________

____

____

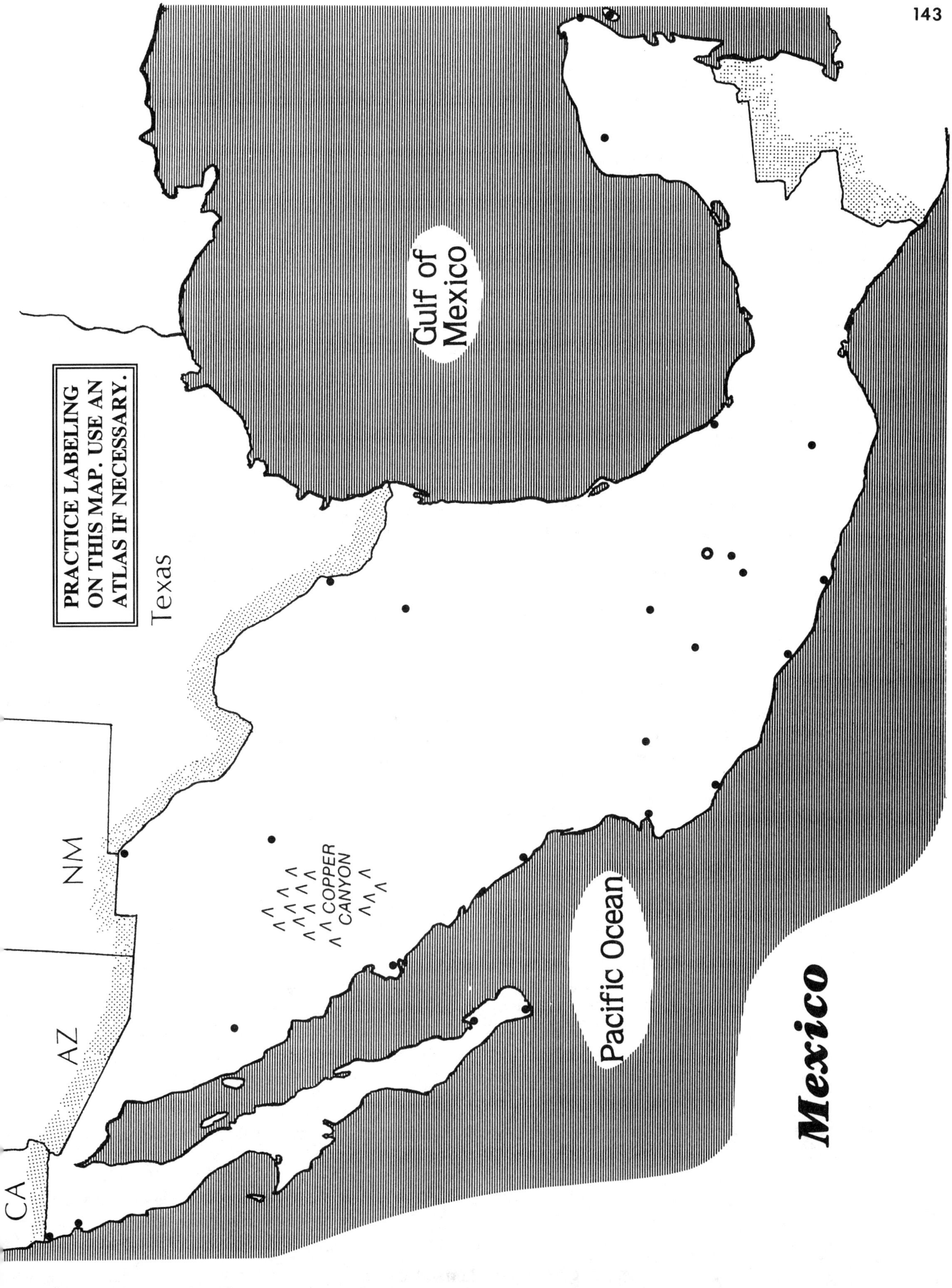
PRACTICE LABELING ON THIS MAP. USE AN ATLAS IF NECESSARY.
Texas
NM
AZ
CA
COPPER CANYON
Gulf of Mexico
Pacific Ocean
Mexico

MEXICO REVIEW

Using the descriptions provided on Mexico's cities and destinations, answer the following:

1. Name three colonial cities. ______________________________

2. ____________________ is a city of lush vegetation and flowers and often included as a stop on the way from Mexico City to Taxco.

3. A possible itinerary for some first time travelers to Mexico is to stay three nights in ________________________, one night in __________, and three nights in ____________________.

4. Las Brisas is a resort hotel of

   A. Manzanillo B. Ixtapa C. Cancun D. Acapulco

   ANSWER: __________________

5. "Cabo" is short for ______________________________.

6. Claiming to receive more than 20 million visitors a year, the city of ___________ is a popular day trip from San Diego, California.

7. Which of the following is not a dive area off Cozumel?

   A. Plane wreck B. Palancar Reef C. The Wall D. Chancanab

   ANSWER: _________

8. A young couple who have never been to Mexico would like to go for a weekend. They do not speak Spanish and would prefer first class and modern accommodations. They especially like beaches and want to be near restaurants and shops. The best destination to suggest would be

   A. La Paz B. Cholula C. Taxco D. Cancun

   ANSWER: _________

9. The Copper Canyon rail trip would most likely appeal to which **two** of the following types of clients:

   A. A couple on their honeymoon who have never been to Mexico
   B. Active senior couple who like the outdoors
   C. Two single college students on spring break
   D. A couple in the 40's who have traveled several times to Mexico

   ANSWER: ________ & ________

10. The country of Mexico is divided into _____ states and one Federal District.

MEXICO REVIEW

1. The currency of Mexico is the _______________.
2. Name two food specialties of Mexico. ____________________________
3. Two of the best buys of Mexico are __________________________ and ____________________________.
4. Name three border towns of Mexico. ______________________________ ____
5. What city in Mexico is known as the "Silver City?" ______________
6. Name three places of interest in Mexico City. _________________ ____
7. Which of the following is not a resort city in Mexico?
   A. Puerto Vallarta   C. Belize
   B. Acapulco   D. Cancun

   ANSWER___________
8. The famous cliff divers can be seen near the resort city of ____________________.
9. The Copper Canyon rail trip travels from Chihuahua to the city of ____________________ on the Pacific Coast.
10. Two popular liquors of Mexico are ___________ and _______________.
11. Next to the fishing village of Zihuatanejo is the resort area of _______________________.
12. Puerto Vallarta is called _________ for short.
13. The ________________________ Indians live in the Copper Canyon area of Mexico.
14. Isla Mujeres is a nearby island to the resort area of ___________ _____________.
15. The city of ____________ is a good starting point for seeing the Chichen Itza, Uxmal and Kabah ruins in the Yucatan Peninsula.
16. Colonial Mexico includes cities such as Acapulco and Cancun. True or False _______________
17. Visitors to Cancun can see the ruins at ___________, located 70 miles south.
18. Palancar Reef and Chancanab Lagoon and Park are diving areas off the coast of _________________.
19. There are over __________ documented archaeological sites throughout Mexico.
20. The city of __________________ offers the Tepanapa Pyramid, with tunnels through its hillside location.

Briefly provide some particulars and hints about travel to Mexico.

____
____
____
____
____

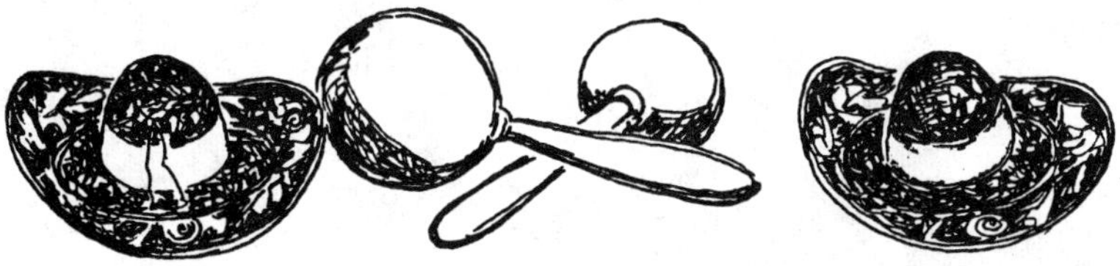

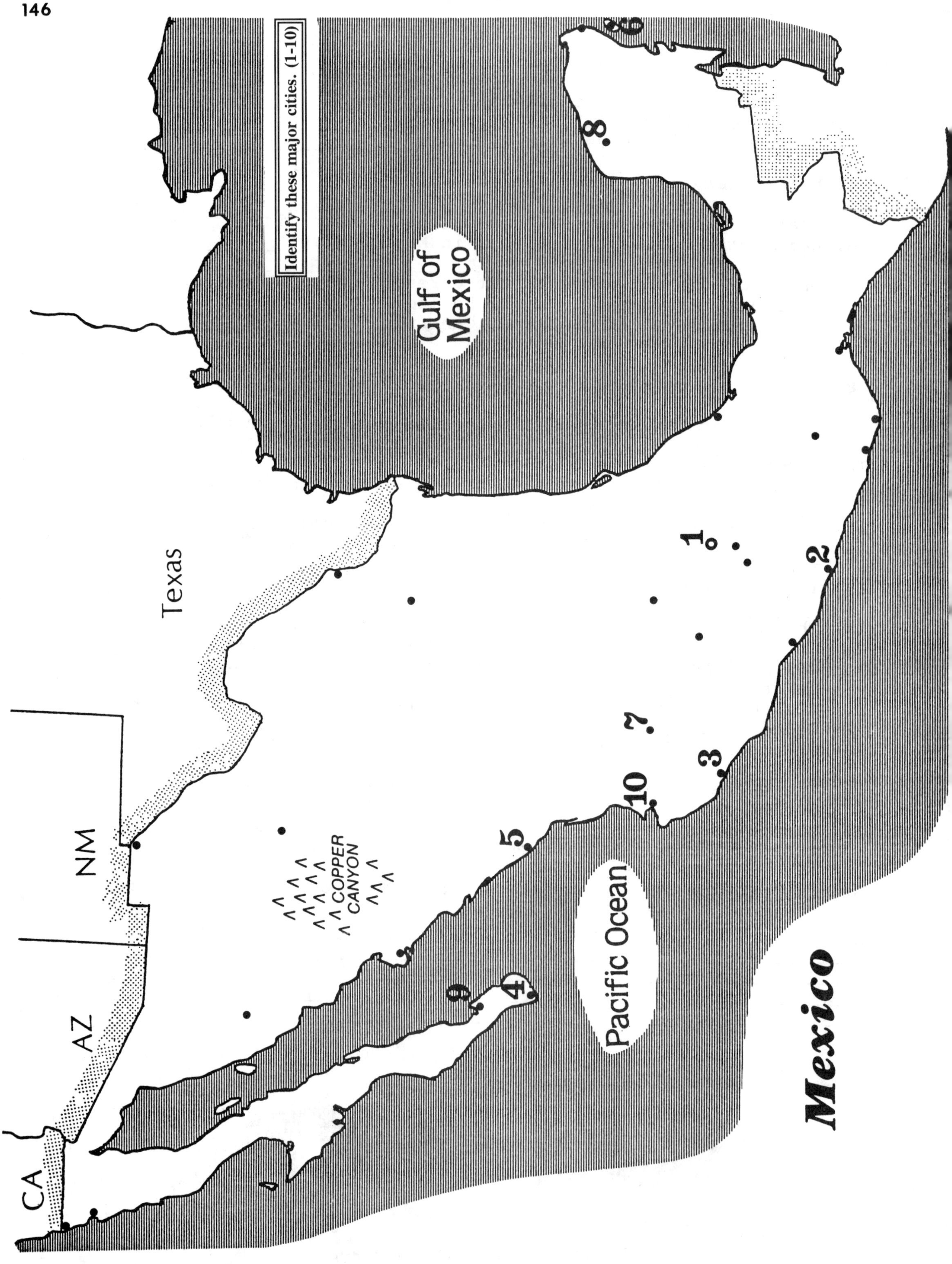
Identify these major cities. (1-10)
Gulf of Mexico
Texas
NM
AZ
CA
COPPER CANYON
Pacific Ocean
Mexico
1
2
3
4
5
6
7
8
9
10

CHAPTER 9

Central America

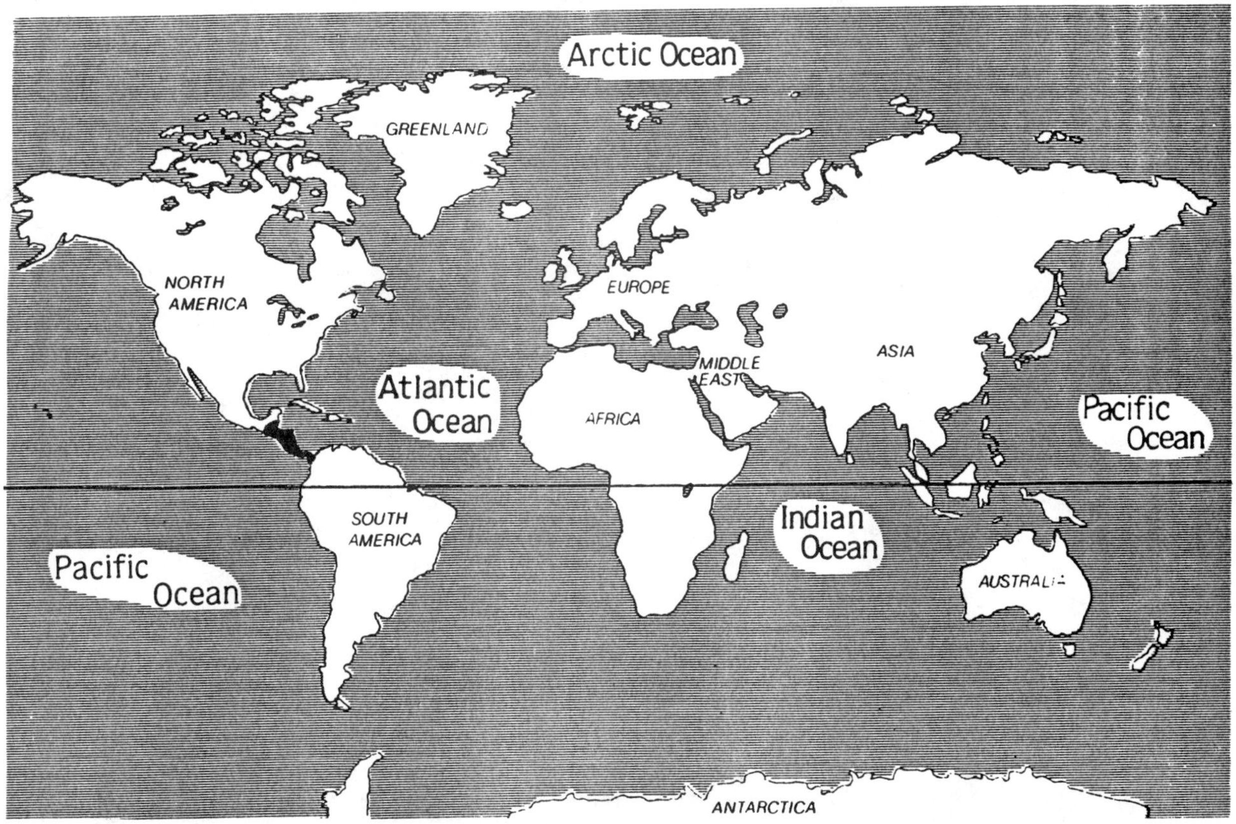

NOTES

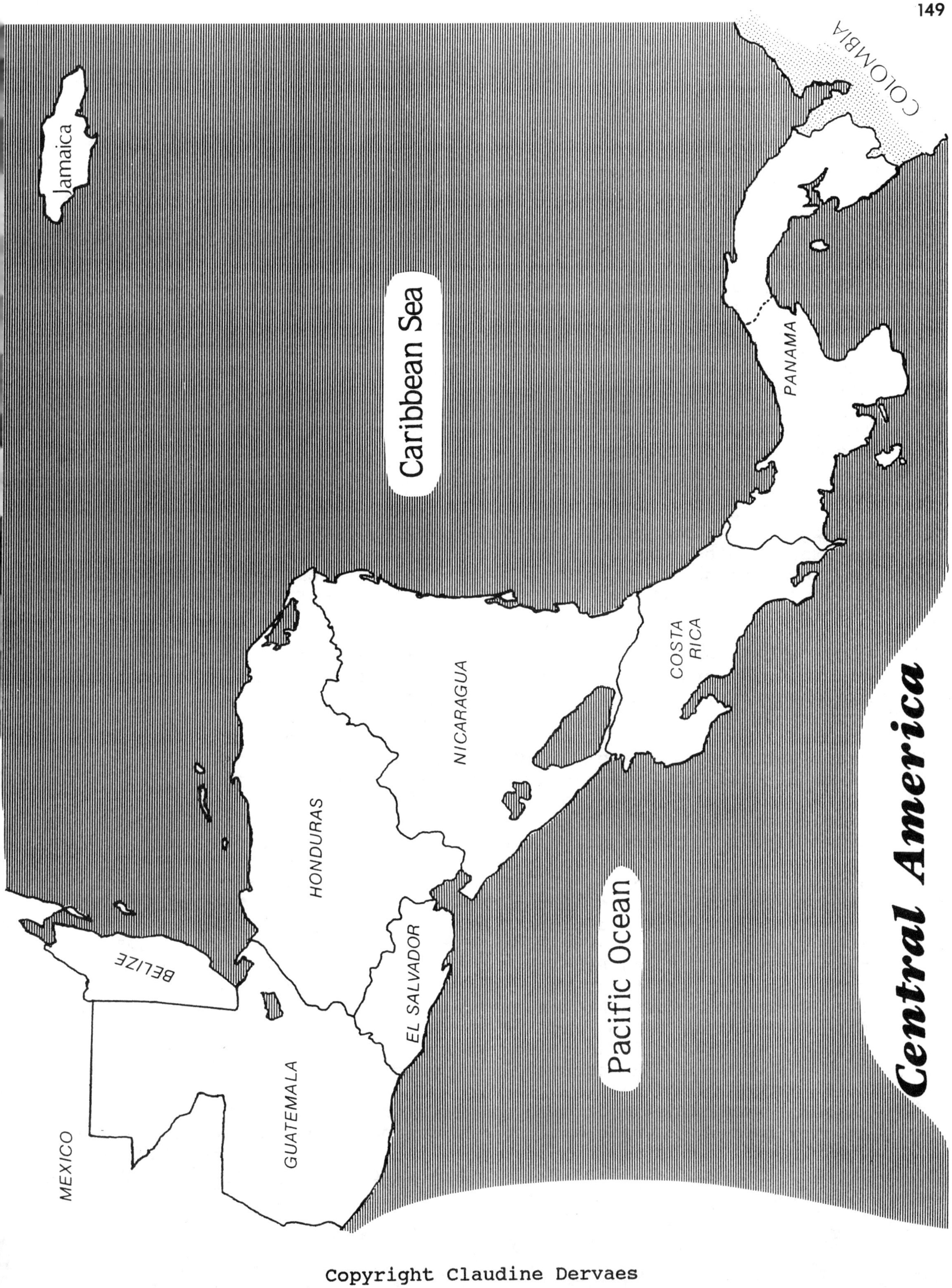
Central America
Caribbean Sea
Pacific Ocean
Jamaica
COLOMBIA
PANAMA
COSTA RICA
NICARAGUA
HONDURAS
EL SALVADOR
BELIZE
GUATEMALA
MEXICO

CENTRAL AMERICA

MAJOR CITY/AIRPORT CODES:

BZE - Belize City
GUA - Guatemala City
PTY - Panama City
SAP - San Pedro Sula, Honduras
SJO - San Jose, Costa Rica

GUATEMALA is a beautiful country with spectacular scenery and features the famous Mayan ruins of Tikal. The recent history of Guatemala is one of political unrest so that travel outside of major commercial and tourist centers is not recommended. Places to visit include the capital Guatemala City, Antigua - the former capital until largely destroyed by earthquakes in 1773, Lake Atitlan - one of the most beautiful lakes in the world, Chichicastenango - town of markets and the Church of Santo Tomas, and of course Tikal for the ruins. The currency of Guatemala is the quetzal, divided into 100 centavos.

HONDURAS - Resorts and excursions in Honduras include the Bay Islands (Roatan, Guanaja, Utila, and several smaller islands) for fishing and diving/snorkeling, the beach resorts of La Ceiba and Trujillo, Copan for Mayan ruins, the major city on the north coast - San Pedro Sula, and the capital city of Tegucigalpa. This country's lush rain forests have some rare and fascinating wildlife. The currency here is called the lempira.

COSTA RICA - As the most stable and democratic of Central American countries, Costa Rica is unlike some of its neighbors. The country has become very popular for the interest in ecotourism (travel that focuses on nature, the preservation of the environment, and the controlled management of resources). San Jose is the capital and shops are plentiful here. The Gold Museum features an extensive collection of artifacts. San Jose's population is over 400,000 people, so it is not a small town. Guard your purse and wallet and leave valuables at home as petty theft is a big problem in San Jose. Poas and Irazu volcanoes are both short drives from San Jose. Other attractions of the country include the town of Sarchi (famous for crafts and colorful oxcarts), the national parks of Tortuguero, Corcovado, Santa Rosen, Braulio Carrillo, Manuel Antonio, and Chirripo, and the many beach resorts. White-water rafting trips are very popular. Beginners usually tackle the Reventazon River first, because its water level is dam-controlled. Costa Rica has some of the best sportfishing in the world (marlin, sailfish, tuna, wahoo, kingfish, reef snapper, etc.). The "Ticos," as Costa Ricans are called are quite friendly and helpful. The climate can be cool at the higher altitudes and the rainy season runs from mid-May to December (the wettest months are September to November). The currency is the Costa Rican colon.

PANAMA - Worldwide importance is given to the Panama Canal and this country's other attractions include casinos, jungles, shopping, and visiting the San Blas Islands - home to the Cuna Indians. Panama City is the capital. U.S. Dollars are widely accepted, although its equivalent, the balboa, is also in circulation in coins only. The cities of Colon and Cristobal are on the Atlantic end of the Panama Canal, and the city of Balboa is at the Pacific Ocean side.

BELIZE - This country used to be called British Honduras and most of the people speak English. The country has been politically stable and free from civil war. Ambergris Cay is the most popular destination in Belize. It is at the northern end of a barrier reef and is a very informal island. There isn't a lot to do except relax and enjoy the water sports. Cay Caulker is also becoming popular; it is much smaller than Ambergris. Other than snorkeling, diving and reef exploring, this country offers tropical jungles and nature reserves, archaeological ruins, and wildlife. Belmopan is the capital. As in most developing countries, the roads are often unpaved and services poor - making travel somewhat difficult and uncomfortable. Placentia, a southern town located on a peninsula, has lovely beaches and lots of water sports. The city is not easy to get to (flights are recommended), but it is a good place to spend several nights to enjoy the variety of activities available.

EL SALVADOR AND NICARAGUA - Extreme political unrest and instability make travel to anywhere other than commercial centers in these countries not recommended. San Salvador is the capital of El Salvador and the currency is the colon. Managua is the capital of Nicaragua and the currency is the cordoba. Nicaragua is the country in Central America with the largest area.

Because of some countries' possible political and economic instability, always check with the U.S. Department of State about travel advisories. Complete profiles on the countries of Costa Rica and Belize, and maybe Guatemala and Panama. Research countries, practice labeling the map, and complete the review tests.

THE MUNDO MAYA - THE MAYAN WORLD

Five centuries before the birth of Christ, the civilization of the Maya began to emerge. It grew into a network of powerful Maya city-states, mostly between A.D. 250 and 900. The Maya introduced a complex writing system, measured time by a calendar as precise as ours, and built sprawling cities in the tropical lowlands and jungles of Guatemala, Belize, Honduras, El Salvador, and in the Mexican states of Quintana Roo, Yucatan, Tabasco, Campeche, and Chiapas. Tours of the Mundo Maya - Mayan World combine the visiting of pyramids and temples with touring the colonial towns and villages, churches, museums, and enjoying the beaches and wildlife in the variety of ecosystems.

CENTRAL AMERICA

COUNTRY: ____________________ CAPITAL: ____________________

DOCUMENTARY REQUIREMENTS FOR U.S. CITIZENS:

____

OTHER PARTICULARS (SHOTS, ETC.): ____________________

CURRENCY: ____________ CURRENCY CODE: ________ EXCHANGE RATE: ________

LANGUAGE(S): ____________________

SIZE: ____________________ POPULATION: ____________________

CLIMATE: ____________________

BEST TIME TO VISIT: ____________________

MAJOR CITIES AND PLACES OF INTEREST:

____

____

____

SPORTS: ____________________

RELIGION(S): ____________________ GOVERNMENT: ____________________

FOOD SPECIALTIES: ____________________

BEST BUYS: ____________________

SPECIAL INFORMATION (SAMPLE ITINERARIES, RESTRICTIONS, EVENTS, TAXES, ETC.):

____

MAJOR AIRLINES: ____________________

MAJOR CITY/AIRPORT CODES: ____________________

TRANSPORTATION PARTICULARS: ____________________

____

SPECIAL HOTELS/RESORTS/MISCELLANEOUS INFO ____________________

____

COUNTRY: ____________________ CAPITAL: ____________________

DOCUMENTARY REQUIREMENTS FOR U.S. CITIZENS:

____

OTHER PARTICULARS (SHOTS, ETC.): ____________________

CURRENCY: ____________ CURRENCY CODE: ________ EXCHANGE RATE: ________

LANGUAGE(S): ____________________

SIZE: ____________________ POPULATION: ____________________

CLIMATE: ____________________

BEST TIME TO VISIT: ____________________

MAJOR CITIES AND PLACES OF INTEREST:

____

____

____

SPORTS: ____________________

RELIGION(S): ____________________ GOVERNMENT: ____________________

FOOD SPECIALTIES: ____________________

BEST BUYS: ____________________

SPECIAL INFORMATION (SAMPLE ITINERARIES, RESTRICTIONS, EVENTS, TAXES, ETC.):

____

MAJOR AIRLINES: ____________________

MAJOR CITY/AIRPORT CODES: ____________________

TRANSPORTATION PARTICULARS: ____________________

____

SPECIAL HOTELS/RESORTS/MISCELLANEOUS INFO ____________________

____

COUNTRY:______________________________ CAPITAL:____________________________
DOCUMENTARY REQUIREMENTS FOR U.S. CITIZENS:

____
OTHER PARTICULARS (SHOTS, ETC.):____
CURRENCY:___________________ CURRENCY CODE:_________ EXCHANGE RATE:________
LANGUAGE(S):____
SIZE:________________________________ POPULATION:_________________________
CLIMATE:____
BEST TIME TO VISIT:____
MAJOR CITIES AND PLACES OF INTEREST:
____
____
____
SPORTS:____
RELIGION(S):______________________________ GOVERNMENT:_____________________
FOOD SPECIALTIES:____
BEST BUYS:____
SPECIAL INFORMATION (SAMPLE ITINERARIES, RESTRICTIONS, EVENTS, TAXES, ETC.):
____
MAJOR AIRLINES:____
MAJOR CITY/AIRPORT CODES:____
TRANSPORTATION PARTICULARS:____
____
SPECIAL HOTELS/RESORTS/MISCELLANEOUS INFO_________________________________
____

COUNTRY:______________________________ CAPITAL:____________________________
DOCUMENTARY REQUIREMENTS FOR U.S. CITIZENS:

____
OTHER PARTICULARS (SHOTS, ETC.):____
CURRENCY:___________________ CURRENCY CODE:_________ EXCHANGE RATE:________
LANGUAGE(S):____
SIZE:________________________________ POPULATION:_________________________
CLIMATE:____
BEST TIME TO VISIT:____
MAJOR CITIES AND PLACES OF INTEREST:
____
____
____
SPORTS:____
RELIGION(S):______________________________ GOVERNMENT:_____________________
FOOD SPECIALTIES:____
BEST BUYS:____
SPECIAL INFORMATION (SAMPLE ITINERARIES, RESTRICTIONS, EVENTS, TAXES, ETC.):
____
MAJOR AIRLINES:____
MAJOR CITY/AIRPORT CODES:____
TRANSPORTATION PARTICULARS:____
____
SPECIAL HOTELS/RESORTS/MISCELLANEOUS INFO_________________________________
____

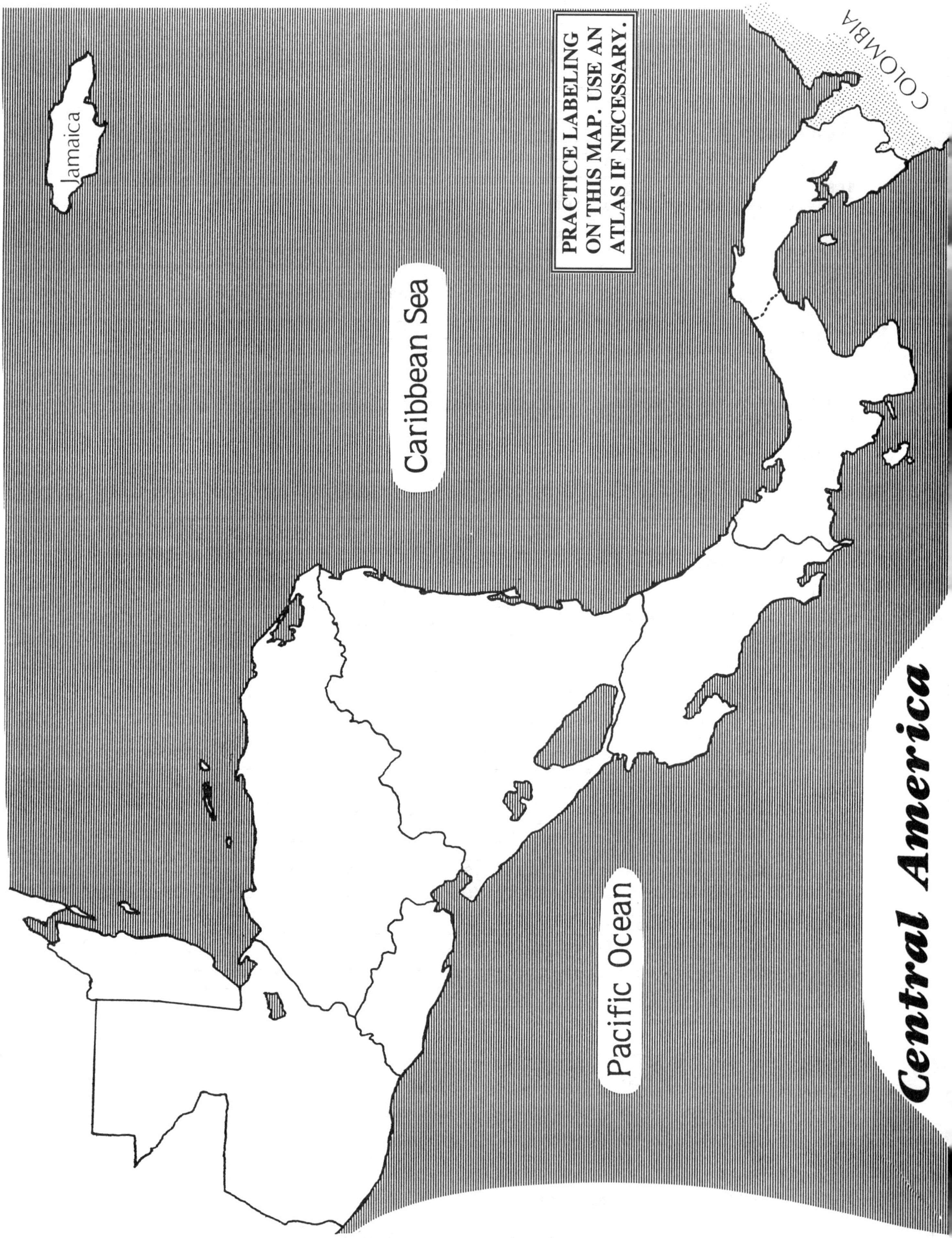
Jamaica
Caribbean Sea
PRACTICE LABELING ON THIS MAP. USE AN ATLAS IF NECESSARY.
COLOMBIA
Pacific Ocean
Central America

CENTRAL AMERICA REVIEW

MATCH THE FOLLOWING COUNTRIES TO THEIR CAPITALS:

1. ______Guatemala
2. ______Belize
3. ______Honduras
4. ______Costa Rica
5. ______Panama
6. ______Nicaragua
7. ______El Salvador

A. Tegucigalpa
B. San Salvador
C. Guatemala City
D. Panama City
E. Belmopan
F. Managua
G. San Jose

MATCH THE FOLLOWING CURRENCIES TO THEIR COUNTRIES:

8. ______Lempira
9. ______Balboa
10. ______Cordoba
11. ______Quetzal

H. Panama
I. Guatemala
J. Honduras
K. Nicaragua

12. The country of ________________ used to be called British Honduras.
13. The Irazu and Poas volcanoes are in ______________________.
14. At the Atlantic end of the Panama Canal are the cities of Colon and Cristobal. On the Pacific Ocean side is the city of ______________ and nearby is Panama City.
15. The ruins of Tikal are in the country of ____________________.
16. Ambergris Cay is a resort island off the coast of ________________.
17. Lake Atitlan and the market city of Chichicastenango are in the country of ______________________.
18. The San Blas Islands, home of the Cuna Indians, are off the coast of _________________________.
19. The Mayan ruins of Copan, the Bay Islands of Roatan and Utila, and the cities of San Pedro Sula and La Ceiba are in _________________.
20. The Central American country with the largest area is _________________________.

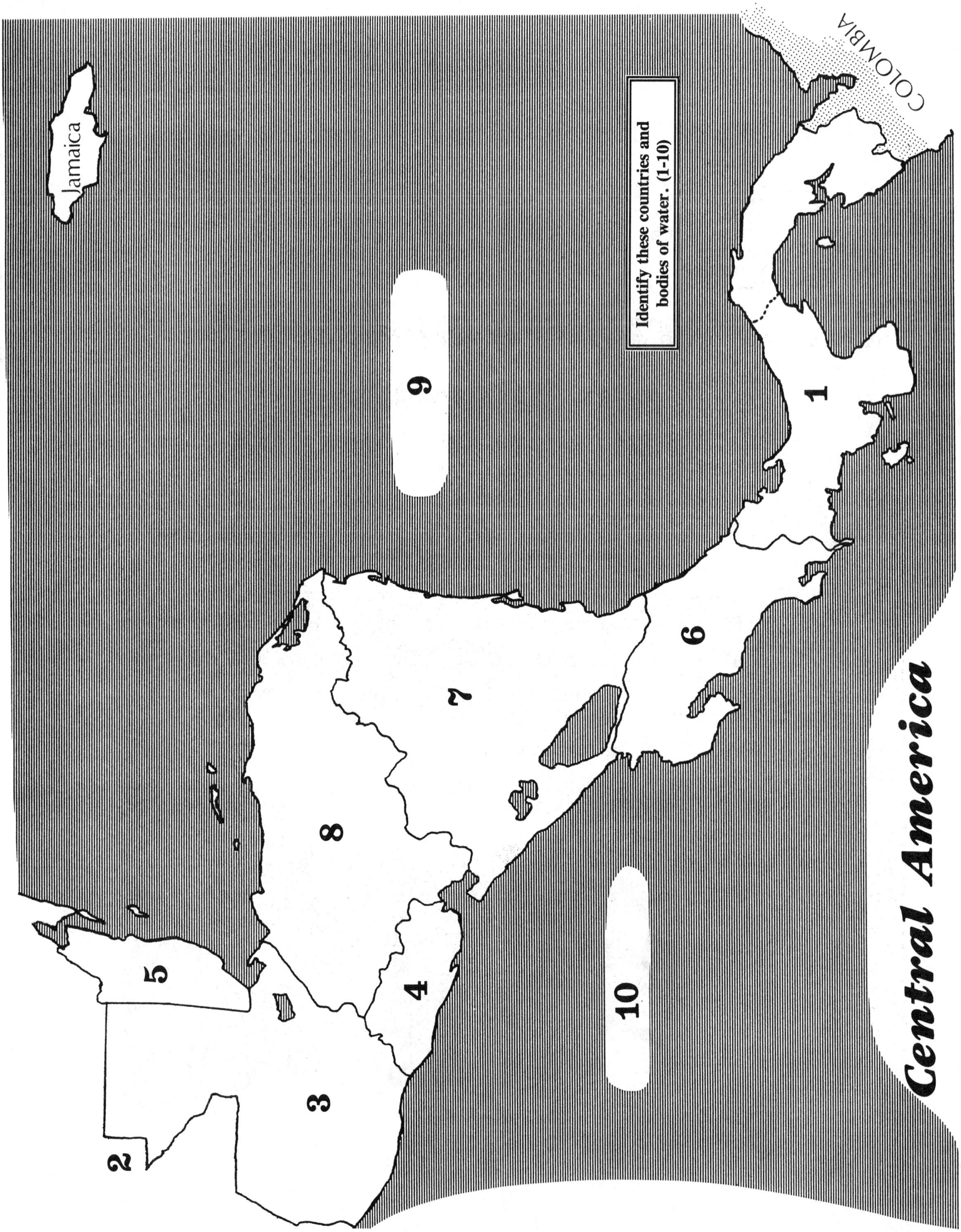
Central America
Identify these countries and bodies of water. (1-10)
Jamaica
COLOMBIA
1
2
3
4
5
6
7
8
9
10

CHAPTER 10

The Caribbean and Bermuda

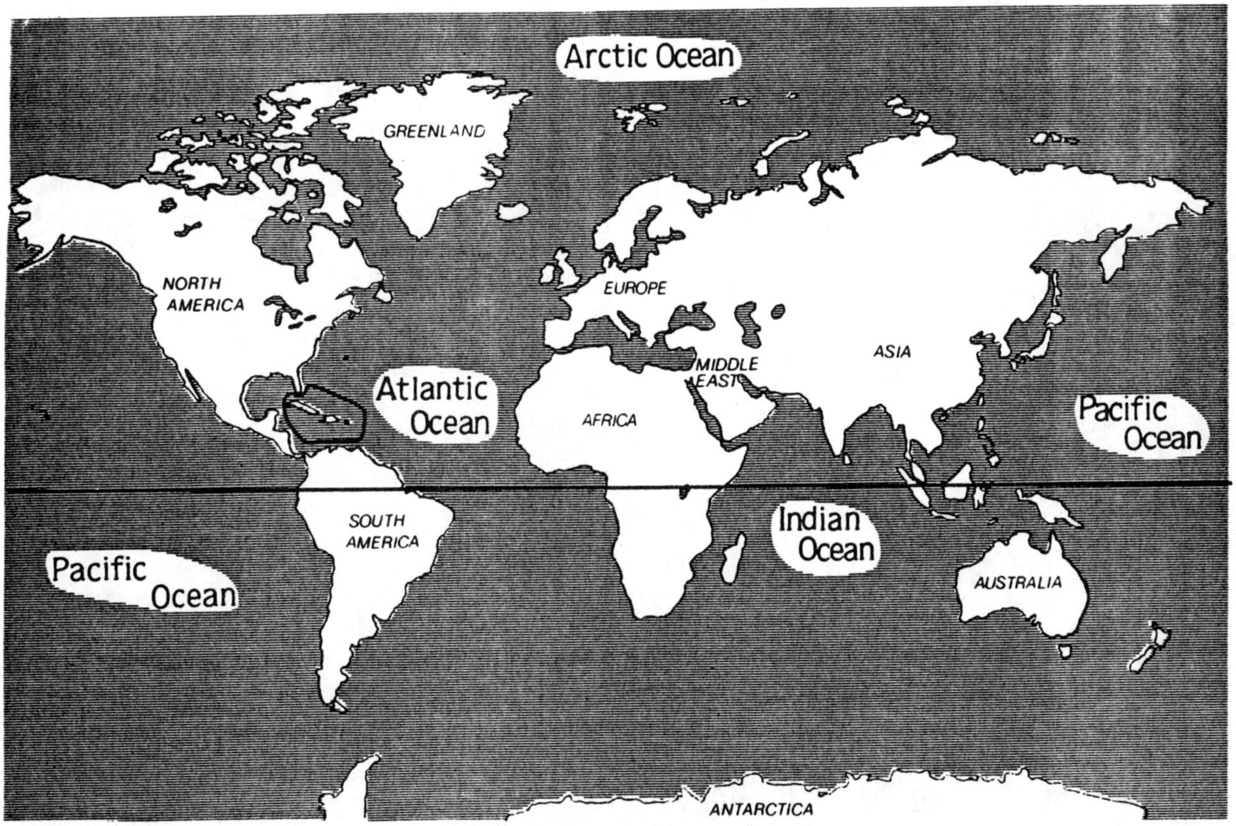

NOTES

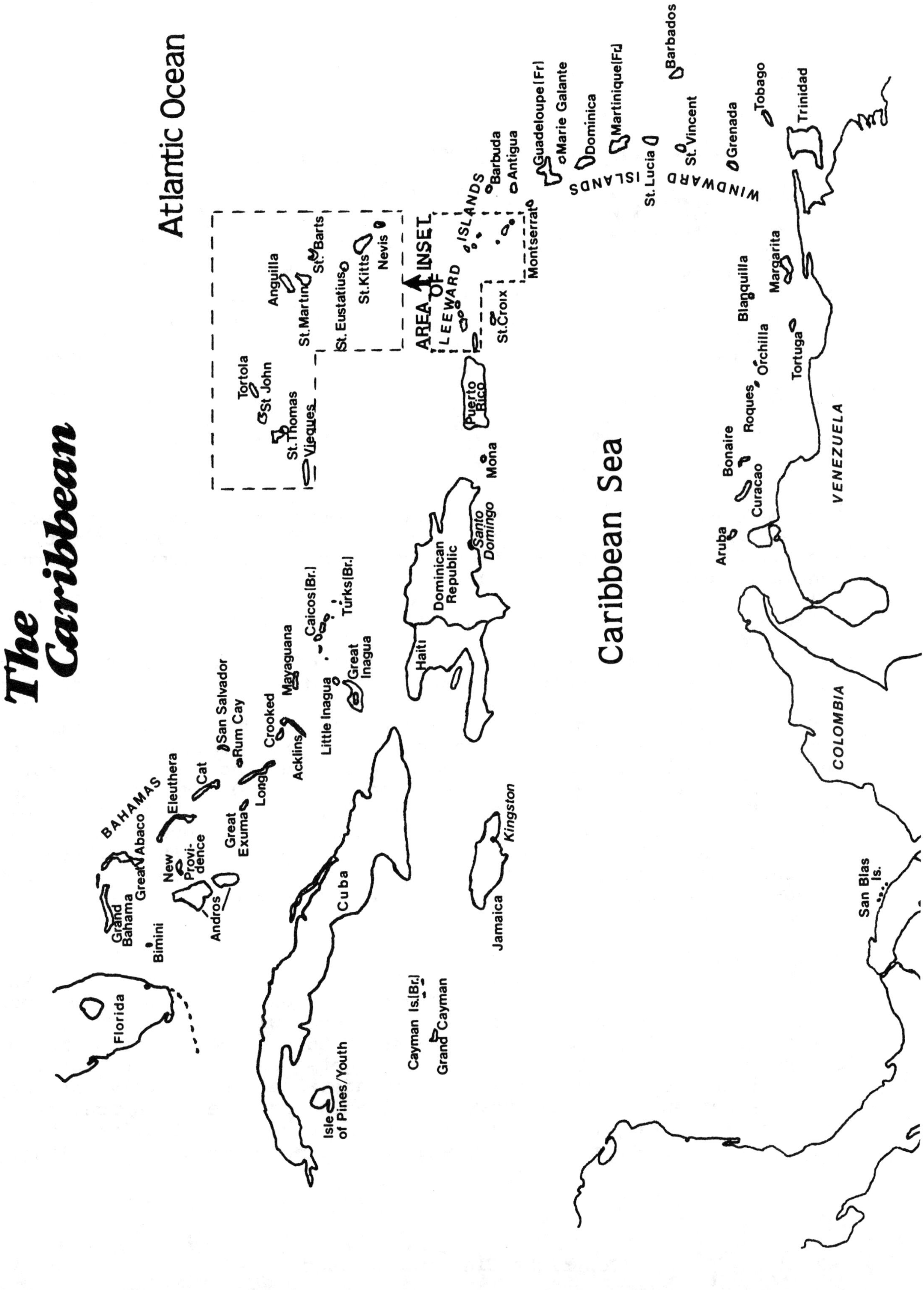

The Caribbean
Atlantic Ocean
Caribbean Sea
Florida
Bimini
Grand Bahama
Great Abaco
BAHAMAS
New Providence
Andros
Eleuthera
Cat
Great Exuma
Long
San Salvador
Rum Cay
Crooked
Acklins
Mayaguana
Little Inagua
Great Inagua
Caicos [Br.]
Turks [Br.]
Cuba
Isle of Pines/Youth
Cayman Is. [Br.]
Grand Cayman
Jamaica
Kingston
Haiti
Dominican Republic
Santo Domingo
Mona
Puerto Rico
Vieques
St. Thomas
St John
Tortola
Anguilla
St. Martin
St. Barts
St. Eustatius
St. Kitts
Nevis
AREA OF INSET
LEEWARD ISLANDS
St. Croix
Montserrat
Barbuda
Antigua
Guadeloupe [Fr]
Marie Galante
Dominica
Martinique [Fr.]
St. Lucia
St. Vincent
Barbados
Grenada
Tobago
Trinidad
WINDWARD ISLANDS
Margarita
Blanquilla
Tortuga
Orchilla
Roques
Bonaire
Curacao
Aruba
VENEZUELA
COLOMBIA
San Blas Is.

THE BAHAMAS

MAJOR CITY/AIRPORT CODES
(alphabetically by code)

ASD - Andros Town, Andros
AXP - Spring Point, Acklins
BIM - Bimini, Bahamas
ELH - North Eleuthera, Eleuthera
FPO - Freeport, Grand Bahama Is.
GGT - George Town, Exuma
GHB - Governor's Harbour, Eleuthera
IGA - Inagua, Bahamas
LGI - Deadmans Cay, Long. Is.
MHH - Marsh Harbour, Great Abaco
MYG - Mayaguana, Bahamas
NAS - Nassau, New Providence Is.
RSD - Rock Sound, Eleuthera,
SAQ - San Andros, Andros
SML - Stella Maris, Long. Is.
TCB - Treasure Cay, Abaco
TZN - South Andros, Bahamas
ZSA - San Salvador, Bahamas

Off the coast of Florida is the group of over 700 islands that make up the **BAHAMAS**. Our study will be divided into three sections: first, Nassau, the capital, on New Providence Island, then Freeport on Grand Bahama Island, and then the many islands that are called the Family Islands of the Bahamas, such as Eleuthera, Abaco, Andros, the Berry Islands, Exuma, Cat Island, Long Island, Mayaguana, and Inagua.

Banking and tourism form the economic base of the Bahamas. The reputation as a tax haven and banking privacy laws make the country an international financial center. The Bahamian Dollar is on a par with the U.S. Dollar, but it is not necessary to change monies into Bahamian currency. There are two significant and colorful festivals held each year in the Bahamas - Junkanoo and Goombay. Junkanoo celebrates the new year and there are two parades - one on Boxing Day (Dec. 26) and one on New Year's Day. The Goombay Festival is held during the summer (June, July, and August). It includes beach parties, sporting events, carnivals, and folkloric shows. Rum drinks are very popular throughout the Bahamas and conch chowder, conch fritters and conch salad are on most local menus. Nassau and Freeport are the two main cities that tourists visit.

NASSAU, New Providence Island
As the nation's capital, it boasts some fine government buildings and gardens. Prince George's Wharf is where many of the cruise ships dock - so the area (Bay Street particularly) teems with shops, shops, shops! Not to be missed is the huge Straw Market to see local crafts and local color. Bargaining is a must! Historic sights include Ft. Charlotte and Ft. Montague. Coral World features an underwater observatory. At the Ardastra Gardens & Zoo the "marching flamingoes" are an unusual treat. This island is very developed and so there's a lot of tourist activity. Many U.S. chain restaurants are here: McDonald's, Burger King,

Kentucky Fried Chicken, Tony Roma's, and much more. But there are also the British pubs, Bahamian cuisine, and many seafood restaurants. Cable Beach - an expansive resort area with luxurious hotels, casinos, and restaurants - is located about 8 miles from downtown Nassau. **PARADISE ISLAND** - just across a bridge from downtown Nassau - is another area featuring extensive hotels (the Atlantis Resort has a 14-acre water-scape, six exhibit lagoons, five swimming pools, a 30,000 sq. ft. casino, 12 remarkable gourmet and specialty restaurants, and more!). Nassau and Freeport are the two main international gateway cities of the Bahamas.

FREEPORT, Grand Bahama Island
Championship golf courses, international shopping, casino gambling, and a variety of water sports all welcome the visitor to Freeport. The International Bazaar showcases architecture and shops from 25 countries. Five miles from downtown Freeport is the Port Lucaya area, offering waterfront entertainment, and white sandy beaches. West End is the oldest settlement on the island and offers a more relaxing change of pace.

****

LEGAL AGE - You must be 18 or older in order to gamble in the casinos of the Bahamas. Although there is no legal drinking age, club owners will prefer that patrons be at least 18 or older.

****

THE FAMILY ISLANDS

In this group, each island offers its own charm and local color, and the experience is quite different from the extremely developed areas of Nassau and Freeport. Little or no nightlife, no casinos (as yet), small intimate, family-owned hotel properties, and an extremely casual, relaxed, and informal atmosphere - this is what the visitor will experience in the Family Islands. Snorkeling, diving, sailing, bicycling, and fishing are the focal points of activity.

GREAT ABACO
Known as a sailing capital, this island features charming 18th century fishing villages where the art of shipbuilding continues as it has for centuries. Marsh Harbour and Treasure Cay are the two airports. It's a boomerang shaped chain of islands, with Walker's Cay in the north, then Little Abaco connected to Great Abaco, then many smaller cays (reached by water ferries).

BIMINI
Bimini is the game fishing capital of the world and the waters teem with marlin, sailfish, bluefin tuna, and more.

ELEUTHERA
110 miles long but only about a mile wide, Eleuthera has wonderful beaches, some cave exploring opportunities, great snorkeling and diving, steep cliffs and dramatic scenery (particularly the Glass Window - a narrow strip of rock that separates the Atlantic from the Caribbean), plus the nearby islands of Spanish Wells and Harbour Island to enjoy (reached by water ferries). Everyone seems to know everyone on these islands, and nearly everyone waves when you pass each other in cars. Take time and relax - this is no place to hurry.

CAT ISLAND
Ancient Indian caves, gently rolling hills, and beautiful white beaches - this is the scenery of Cat Island. The highest point in the Bahamas, Mt. Alvernia (206 ft.) is located here.

ANDROS
Andros is the largest and least developed of the Bahamas Islands. Off its coast is one of the largest barrier reefs in the world.

EXUMA
There is Great Exuma and Little Exuma and 365 cays that make up this island chain. Georgetown is the capital of Exuma.

SAN SALVADOR
Originally known as Guanahani, this island retains much of its natural beauty and charm. Four sites on the island mark the spot where it is thought that Columbus set foot in the New World.

RUM CAY
Snorkeling and diving are the main attractions of this island.

LONG ISLAND
The interesting contrast of the two coastlines of Long Island make it one of the most scenic in the Bahamas. The northeastern beaches have a rocky shoreline and the northwestern shore is white, powdery sand.

CROOKED ISLAND and **ACKLINS**
These islands are remote and tranquil vacation spots.

MAYAGUANA
Enjoying unspoiled beaches and great fishing dominate a visit to Mayaguana.

INAGUA
There's Little Inagua and Great Inagua, and this area is home to one of the world's largest flamingo colonies, with a bird population that can number 50,000.

WANT TO GET MARRIED IN THE BAHAMAS? (1) A two-week residency in the Bahamas by at least one party is required (although this can be waived if the couple sends a request in advance to the Registrar General's Office), (2) Apply for a license from the Office (by mail or in person). Documentation of citizenship and proof of marital status are required (blood tests are not), (3) With the waiver, the marriage can take place the day after the license is issued. Contact the Registrar's General Office, POB N-532, Nassau, Bahamas.

THE TURKS AND CAICOS ISLANDS
This British Crown Colony is a group of low lying islands completely surrounded by coral reefs. The islands are basically flat, salty deserts (except for Providenciales, which is a bit greener and hilly). The Caicos group consists of six main islands: Providenciales, South Caicos, East Caicos, Middle Caicos, North Caicos, and West Caicos. The Turks consist of two main islands - Grand Turk and Salt Cay. English is the official language and some creole is spoken.

- -

The country of **CUBA**, the largest Caribbean island, includes the Isle of Pines/Youth and hundreds of small coral cays. At this time U.S. citizens are permitted to travel to Cuba for official business, news reporting, or research. Other possibilities include originating travel in another country, such as the Bahamas, Canada, Mexico, etc. Visa procedures can be somewhat complicated.

- -

The **CAYMAN ISLANDS** (Grand Cayman, Little Cayman, and Cayman Brac) are a British Crown Colony and are most noted for diving and snorkeling. A ring of coral reefs surrounds the Caymans; hundreds of shipwrecks in waters with up to 200 feet visibility and "The Wall" - a natural cliff formation that drops from about 80 feet to 1,200 feet - can provide the diver or snorkeler with breathtaking experiences. **GRAND CAYMAN** offers sights such as Seven Mile Beach, the Cayman Turtle Farm, and Pedro's Castle. Send a postcard from Hell, Grand Cayman - that's the name of the place just past West Bay on Grand Cayman. Play golf with the unique "Cayman Ball" which is specially designed to react like a normal golf ball but used in shorter distances. The Atlantis submarine takes 28 passengers to a depth of 150 feet along the Cayman Wall and for more adventure, the Research Submersibles Ltd. submarines take dives of 800 and 3,000 feet! Deep-sea fishing is popular and don't miss the chance to hold and feed sting rays at Sting Ray City (you are taken by boat to an area where the sting rays come to feed). **LITTLE CAYMAN** is less developed and **CAYMAN BRAC** offers cave exploring, a tropical wilderness with unique birds, and of course incredible diving. The Caymans are very appealing because they have a safe, clean, atmosphere, there's not a lot of poverty, and the people are educated and sincere. Note: Unlike most of the Caribbean, bargaining for pur-purchases isn't customary. Georgetown is the capital of the Caymans.

MAJOR CITY AIRPORT CODES
GCM - Grand Cayman
CYB - Cayman Brac
LYB - Little Cayman

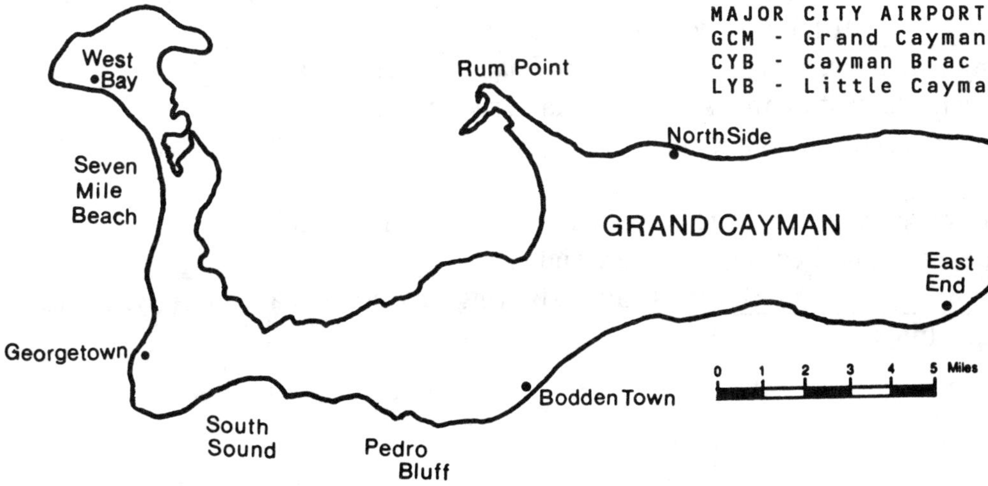

REVIEW - THE BAHAMAS

1. Over ______ islands make up the Bahamas.
2. Junkanoo is celebrated with two parades, one on Dec. ___, and one on Jan. ___.
3. Five miles from Freeport is the Port ____________ area for entertainment and beaches.
4. The capital of Exuma is ____________________.
5. One of the largest barrier reefs in the world is located off the island of ___________.
6. The island of ___________________ is known for the four sites which mark the spot where Columbus is said to have set foot.
7. The highest point in the Bahamas is Mt.________________ located on __________ island.
8. Spanish Wells and Harbour Island can be reached by water ferries from the island of ________________________.
9. ______________________ is a boomerang shaped chain of islands, with Walker's Cay in the north.
10. ____________________ Island is located across a bridge from Nassau.
11. The "marching flamingoes" can be seen at the __________________ Gardens and Zoo in Nassau.
12. Goombay is held during the months of ______________, ________________, and ____________.
13. MHH is the city airport code for ____________________, __________________.
14. The city airport code for Nassau is _______.
15. What island was originally known as Guanahani? ______________________

REVIEW - TURKS AND CAICOS, CUBA, AND CAYMAN ISLANDS

1. What are the two main islands of the Turks? _________________________________
2. Travel to Cuba is restricted. Name two countries that can be used to originate travel to Cuba (if other restrictions have been met and visas processed). __________________ ________________________
3. The Turks and Caicos Islands are basically flat, salty deserts except for the island of ___________________________.
4. The Research Submersibles submarines take passengers down 7,000 feet. True or False ______________ If false, how far down can they go? ___________ feet.
5. Bargaining is not customary in the Cayman Islands. True or False ___________
6. Hell is a place to visit on the island of Cuba. True or False ___________
7. Both the Turks and Caicos and the Cayman Islands are British Crown Colonies. True or False __________
8. Besides English, what language is spoken in the Turks and Caicos? _____________
9. The Turtle Farm and Pedro's Castle are sights on ______________________.
10. ______________________ offers cave exploring, diving, and a tropical wilderness with unique birds.

JAMAICA, a fairly large island of the Caribbean, has resorts in Negril, Ocho Rios, Runaway Bay, and Montego Bay ("Mo-Bay"); rafting trips on the Martha Brae and Rio Grand Rivers; tours of plantations such as Good Hope, Greenwood, Tryall, Prospect; and sights such as Dunn's River Falls (near Ocho Rios), and the Rose Hall Great House (where Annie Palmer, the "White Witch," is said to have met with a violent death). Gardens, beaches, mountains, tropical scenery, reggae music, mysterious voodoo, Jamaican rum and coffee - the mixture of Jamaica's offerings can be delightful or "boonoonoonoos." Although you see people openly smoking marijuana ("ganja") and can be offered a variety of drugs to buy, do not think it is legal. The buying of even small quantities is forbidden and buyers risk large fines and/or jail. You drive on the left here (as on most British-influenced islands - like the Bahamas, Caymans, etc.). Tourists need to be careful of crime and only use the licensed taxis and buses in Jamaica (taxis display JUTA - Jamaican Union of Travellers Association stickers). There are gated shopping areas particularly for the tourists - which can make you feel uncomfortable, unwelcome, and unsafe if you venture outside the areas. Best buys include rum, coffee, jewelry, local handicrafts, straw goods, and carved mahogany items. Red Stripe is the local beer. All-inclusive resorts are one of the main draws to Jamaica. Some all-inclusives take couples only, some only singles, some mixed, some take families, etc. All-inclusive resorts feature a large variety of water and many other sports, and they usually include all meals and some snacks, planned activities, entertainment, and sometimes all drinks (or maybe just beer and wine). The capital of Jamaica is Kingston. Reggae music is played everywhere on the island, and Jamaica's main summer event is Reggae Sunsplash in August (top musicians/performers are featured).

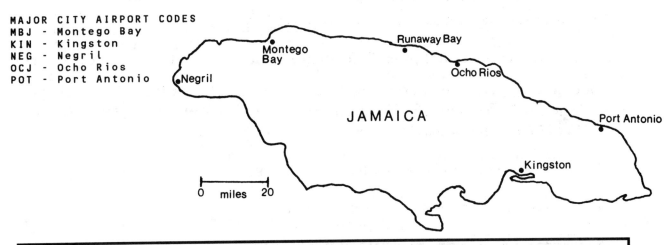

MAJOR CITY AIRPORT CODES
MBJ - Montego Bay
KIN - Kingston
NEG - Negril
OCJ - Ocho Rios
POT - Port Antonio

JAMAICAN CUISINE
Jamaica's most popular dish is called jerk. Pork, chicken, sausage, and fish are first marinated in a mixture of island-grown ingredients including Scotch bonnet peppers - one of the hottest chili peppers, and then cooked in an outdoor pit over a fire made with local pimento wood. Hot pepper sauces, roasted sweet potatoes, roasted bread-fruit (a mild potato-like fruit), festivals (fried dumplings made with cornmeal) are traditional accompaniments. Other fruits, vegetables, and dishes include:

ackee - a tree vegetable that is cooked and served for breakfast - such as "scrambled with dried salt cod.
bammy - a round flatbread made from grated cassava (which is like a yam and is also known as manioc).
callaloo - a vegetable that closely resembles spinach.
chocho - part of the squash family but resembling a large pear.
duckunoo - a pudding made from cornmeal, green bananas, coconut, sugar, and spices.
Johnny Cake - a fried dumpling often served at breakfast.
patty - a crescent-shaped meat pie made with seasoned ground beef, chicken, or seafood.
paw-paw/papaya - a yellow or orange fruit that is full of vitamin A.
pear - what we know as an avocado.
pimento - the Jamaican word for allspice (blend of cinnamon, mace, cloves, nutmeg).
soursop - a large, green-skinned fruit with a custard-like pulp.

The island of Hispaniola is comprised of **HAITI** and the **DOMINICAN REPUBLIC**. As these countries are not British, driving is on the right.

HAITI is French influenced, suffers from poverty, has a weak economy and unstable politics, but it is a land of friendly, warm, open, and resourceful people. Haiti is a mountainous country and the topography is dominated by five mountain ranges than run east-west. Jacmel, on the southern coast, has some of the best beaches on the island and some inexpensive hotels. There are resorts in the mountain village of Petionville, above Port-au-Prince, the capital. The city of Cap Haitien has sights such as the Palace of San Souci and La Citadelle. The stronghold of voodoo plays an important part in the lives of the Haitian people. Visitors should not try to attend an authentic voodoo service and should ask permission of people before taking photographs.

MAJOR CITY AIRPORT CODES: PAP - Port-au-Prince
CAP - Cap Haitien

- -

DOMINICAN REPUBLIC, Haiti's neighbor, is quite different. Travel between the two is restricted. Spanish is the official language and Santo Domingo, the capital, has the famous Cathedral of Santa Maria La Menor - with a Madonna painting by Murillo, a silver carillon by Cellini, the crown of Isabella of Spain, and the buried remains of Christopher Columbus. Visit Boca Chica's beautiful beach on the way to La Romana on the southeast coast and stay at the Casa de Campo resort. Nearby is the artists' village of Altos La Chavon. The area around Punta Cana also features hotels and resorts. Most of the activity along the northern coast is at Playa Dorada, next to Puerto Plata. There are some extensive resorts and all-inclusives. The best buys of the country are items made from amber and amber jewelry. Amber is a fossilized form of resin. It is yellowish in color and translucent. It is especially prized when insects, leaves, or other types of remains are embedded in it. Make sure you buy products from established shops as street vendors sometimes sell plastic imitations. Larimar, or Dominican turquoise, is also popular for jewelry and other souvenirs.

MAJOR CITY AIRPORT CODES: SDQ - Santo Domingo
POP - Puerto Plata
PUJ - Punta Cana

- -

HIGH/LOW SEASONS AND ALL-INCLUSIVES

The rates for hotels and packages in the Caribbean will be much higher during the winter months - that is the peak season for travelers vacationing in the islands to get a break from cold weather. The High/Peak Season can run from November to April or May. The Low/Off Season rates will run from April/May to October/November (it depends on the resort).

ALL-INCLUSIVES have become very popular in the Caribbean as well as Mexico and other areas. It is important to ask questions about what the rates actually include as resorts vary. Some include all drinks, some includes taxes and tips, some include transfers, etc. The meals may be served buffet-style or there may be a limited choice of entrees. All-inclusives may also cater to a certain type of client (single, families, active couples, Europeans and other nationals, etc.). Ask questions before making recommendations or choices.

PUERTO RICO, a commonwealth of the U.S., is a highly industrialized island. U.S. citizens can enter and depart freely, but visitors should take along proof of citizenship for re-entry into the U.S. Puerto Rico is warm and sunny year round. The wettest months are May to December and the summer is hurricane season. San Juan is a cruise hub of the Caribbean, and ships dock conveniently near Old San Juan. Old San Juan, a 62-acre area more than 450 years old, is defined by the forts of El Morro and San Cristobal. Casinos are found in the larger hotels and journeys to El Yunque, a tropical rain forest, are popular. El Yunque is located 35 miles east of San Juan, and the waterfalls, giant ferns, wild orchids, towering tabonuco trees and sierra palms make the forest a photographer's paradise. Visitor's can combine a morning trip to the rain forest with an afternoon swim at Luquillo Beach. The sugar and rum industry - common to many Caribbean islands - is particularly widespread here and tours of the Bacardi Rum Plant are available. On the south coast is Ponce, Puerto Rico's second largest city. The Ponce Art Museum, Hacienda Buena Vista (a restored 19th century hacienda), and the Tibes Indian Ceremonial Center are attractions. Local crafts include santos - which are small carved wooden figures representing a saint or religious scene. Puerto Rican coffee, rum, cigars, musical instruments, festival masks of papier mache, and mundillo (handmade bobbin lace made into bands, doilies, collars and tablecloths) are other good buys. On the southwest coast is La Parguera, a fishing village that has developed into a small resort center. The attraction is Phosphorescent Bay, where millions of luminescent dinoflagellates light up when disturbed by movement; moonless nights are best. The LeLoLai is a weeklong festival highlighting Puerto Rico's music, folklore, culture, and natural attractions. Pick up a copy of Que Pasa (What's Happening) to find out the events as well as other tourism details. Visitors should note that San Juan is a developed and populated city and the possibility of theft and crime calls for common-sense precautions. From the port of Fajardo, tourists can catch the ferry to the islands of Culebra and Vieques, known for their secluded white sand beaches, clear waters, coral reefs, and relaxing atmosphere. On Culebra there are no fancy shops, deluxe hotels, extensive resorts or gourmet restaurants - the place is unspoiled and the pace is slow. For budget-minded travelers, Puerto Rico's system of government approved inns and guest houses, the paradores, are perfect. Paradores Puertorriquenos are small properties (less than 50 rooms) located in scenic rural areas.

MAJOR CITY
AIRPORT CODES:
SJU - San Juan
MAZ - Mayaguez
PSE - Ponce

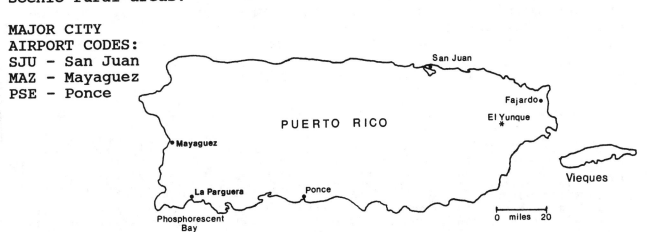

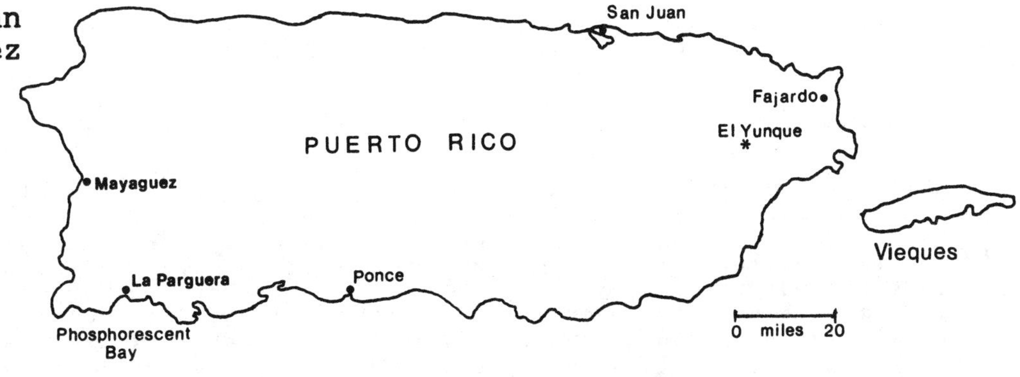

The **U.S. VIRGIN ISLANDS** are comprised of about 50 islands - some big, some small, some merely rocks jutting out of the clear blue sea. **ST. THOMAS, ST. CROIX, ST. JOHN** are the three principal islands. They are very popular for shopping, as duty-free imports from all over the world can be found in the many shops (particularly in the city of Charlotte Amalie on St. Thomas). Although a U.S. territory, driving is on the left-hand side of the road.

ST. THOMAS
St. Thomas is the most developed and most populated island. The major city of Charlotte Amalie is also the capital of the island group. Cruise ships dock here and the shops and streets can be packed with tourists on days the ships are in port. The oldest building is the 17th century Fort Christian and the most attractive is Crown House, an 18th century colonial residence at the top of 99 Steps on Blackbeard's Hill. Have a banana daiquiri at Blackbeard's Castle at the top of the hill. Other attractions include the marine park of Coral World and the tropical plants of the Orchidarium. Hotel resorts dot the sandy beaches and beautiful bays such as Magens Bay, Bolongo, Sapphire and Morningstar Bay.

ST. CROIX
On St. Croix, the two main towns are Christiansted and Fredericksted, both named after Danish kings. In Christiansted, the outdoor market on Company Street is a great place to sample local fruits and vegetables. The shopping here is less hectic than on St. Thomas. If visiting the city of Fredericksted, stroll down Strand Street to enjoy the shops and cafes. The harbor area is particularly scenic and the little St. Croix Aquarium is worth a visit. Outside the main towns are some great beaches - Cane Bay is good for snorkeling/diving, Davis Beach is good for bodysurfing, Reef Beach is good for windsurfing, and Rainbow Beach is good for shelling. A day trip from St. Croix is superb Buck Island - where you can enjoy unspoiled beaches and wonderful snorkeling and diving.

ST. JOHN
Most of St. John is a national park and it's an unspoiled island of deserted beaches and wooded mountains; popular beaches include Trunk Bay, Caneel Bay, Cinnamon Bay, Maho Bay, and Hurricane Hole. A colorful event found mostly on St. John is Fish Fry. It usually happens on the weekend around town, the food is prepared by the best local cooks. Try some maubi - a local drink made from ginger, herbs, sugar, and bark. The Fry is usually crowded, but friendly. Most visitors get to St. John by ferry service from St. Thomas (it takes about 30 minutes).

MAJOR CITY AIRPORT CODES: STT - St. Thomas
STX - St. Croix

SHOPPING IN THE SHOPPER'S PARADISE - Shopping in the U.S.V.I. means taking advantage of the duty-free goods and local handicrafts. Best buys include liquor, jewelry, electronic equipment, clothes (especially knits and sportswear), leather goods, china, crystal, swimsuits, Caribbean art, straw goods, candles, pottery, novelties and souvenirs. U.S. RESIDENTS can bring back up to $1200.00 duty-free from the U.S. Virgin Islands, as opposed to $600.00 from many other Caribbean islands and only $400.00 for other international destinations. Up to 4 liters of alcohol (per adult of age) is allowed - as opposed to only 1 liter of alcohol from most other destinations. As always, travelers should check prices at home for items before purchasing abroad - not everything will perhaps be such a bargain!

THE ISLANDS - DESTINATION CHECKLIST

He who has never seen himself surrounded on all sides by the sea can never possess an idea of the world, and of his relation to it.

- Goethe

Islands come in a variety of shapes and sizes. Some are new creations formed by ocean storms and movements of sand and silt. Others are formed of coral and fossils, compacted into limestone. Some are the remnants of volcanoes and volcanic eruptions. They are all under the domain of the sea and subject to the forces of nature.

The Caribbean is a huge beckoning region of islands - and each one is DIFFERENT. It is important to know the Caribbean, know the islands and their special features, their idiosyncrasies, the advantages and disadvantages to the traveler considering them.
ASK CLIENTS MANY QUESTIONS BEFORE RECOMMENDING AN ISLAND DESTINATION.

Are they looking for certain type of scenery?
___ Mountainous ___ Architecture
___ Flat ___ Bustling cities
___ Sandy beaches ___ Caves to explore
___ Cliffs to climb ___ Scenic coastline
___ Quiet, secluded ___ Parks and Reserves
___ Unusual wildlife ___ Lush vegetation
___ Clear water ___ Reefs

Do they prefer to get there easily, quickly?
___ Direct flights ___ Max. 4 hour travel
___ One change is O.K. ___ Max. 6 hrs.
___ Two changes O.K. ___ Max. 8 hrs.
___ Doesn't matter ___ Doesn't matter

Does the traveler mind small planes? ____ Yes
____ No If no --- ___ 12 seater O.K.
___ 8 seater O.K.
___ 4/2 seater O.K.

Is it all right to travel to the destination in a small boat? ____ Yes ____ No

What type of weather are you looking for? ____ Warm ____ Hot is O.K. ____ Dry
____ Some rain is O.K. ____ Breezy
____ Calm ____ Some breeze is O.K.

What type of accommodations are preferred? ____ Deluxe hotels ____ Standard hotels
____condos ____ First class hotels ____ Economy hotels
____apartments ____ Small hotels ____ Large hotels
____homes ____ Historic hotels ____ Convenient hotels
If convenient is selected, convenient to ___ beach ___ restaurants ___ docks
___ snorkeling ___ diving ___ golf ___ tennis ___ shops ___ activities ___ airport
If hotels are chosen, check here if you prefer accommodations with some kitchen facilities ___

What activities are enjoyed? ___ swimming ___sailing ___snorkeling ___ wind surfing ___ shelling
___ golf ____tennis ___sightseeing ___shopping ____sunning ___ relaxing ___seeing wildlife
___ visiting museums ___ experiencing cuisines ___experiencing languages ___spectator sports
___ local entertainment ___ gambling ___walking ___bicycling ___ hiking ___running ___ diving
___ driving around ___TV ___radio ___ lots of nightlife ___ some nightlife ___competitive sports
___ casual atmosphere ____more formal atmosphere ____ topless bathing, swimming

REVIEW - JAMAICA, HAITI, AND THE DOMINICAN REPUBLIC

1. Marijuana is legal in Jamaica. True or False ___________
2. Reggae Sunsplash in Jamaica is held in July. True or False ___________
3. The "White Witch" of the Rose Hall Great House was Annie Prospect. True or False ____________
4. Another word for delightful in Jamaica is _______________________.
5. Most of the activity along the northern coast of the Dominican Republic is at Playa ___________________, next to Puerto Plata.
6. PAP is the city airport code for _____________________, __________________.
7. Santo Domingo's city airport code is ______.
8. The Palace of San Souci and La Citadelle are sights of the city of _______________.
9. The capital of Haiti is ___________________________.
10. Licensed taxis in Jamaica display JTA. True or False ___________
11. Rafting trips are available on the Martha Brae and the ______________ Rivers in Jamaica.
12. Voodoo is practiced in both Haiti and Jamaica. True or False ___________
13. Montego Bay is the capital of Jamaica. True or False __________
14. Dominican turquoise is called ________________.
15. Haiti is a mountainous country and its topography is dominated by ____ mountain ranges.

REVIEW - PUERTO RICO AND THE U.S. VIRGIN ISLANDS

1. What is the name of the rain forest in Puerto Rico? __________________
2. Magens Bay, Bolongo Bay, Sapphire and Morningstar Bays are on the island of ________ ________________.
3. Most of this island is a national park and popular beaches include Trunk Bay and Caneel Bay. _____________________
4. Ferry service from St. Thomas to St. John takes about _____ minutes.
5. The magazine to pick up to find out current events in Puerto Rico is called __________ _________________.
6. Phosphorescent Bay can be seen when visiting St. Croix. True or False __________
7. The small government approved properties on Puerto Rico that are good for budget-minded travelers are called ________________________________.
8. From the port of Fajardo in Puerto Rico, tourists can catch ferry services to the islands of _____________________ and _____________________.
9. The two main towns of St. Croix are _______________ and ____________________.
10. Buck Island is a good day trip from St. Thomas. True or False ____________
11. Driving is on the left in the U. S. Virgin Islands. True or False ____________
12. Crown House, an 18th century colonial residence is at the top of 99 steps on ________ ______________ Hill on St. Thomas.
13. On St. Croix, Davis Beach is good for snorkeling/diving. True or False _________
14. _____ is the city airport code for San Juan, Puerto Rico.
15. STX is the city/airport code for St. Croix. True or False ___________

The **BRITISH VIRGIN ISLANDS** include Tortola, Virgin Gorda, Peter Island, Norman Island, Salt Island, Jost van Dyke, Anegada, Cooper Island and Mosquito Island. These islands are for yachting, fishing, relaxing, diving, and for nature lovers - not for gambling, lavish night clubs or extensive developments and shops. Of the 50 B.V.I. (British Virgin Islands), only about 16 are inhabited and only about 10 have tourist facilities.

VIRGIN GORDA
Virgin Gorda has beautiful reefs, several resorts, a copper mine, and main attraction of The Baths (a unique rock formation with dimly lit, ethereal caves). All around the coastline are superb restaurants and hotels, and over 20 beaches.

TORTOLA
This is the main island of the BVI and Road Town is the major city and capital of the island group. A variety of accommodations is available. Ferry boats connect Road Town and West End on Tortola with various docks on St. Thomas, St. Croix, and St. John. Most of the British Virgin Islands are accessible only by boat.

- -

ST. MARTIN/ST. MAARTEN is an island with two spellings, two cultures, and two currencies (although the U.S. Dollar is widely accepted). The French side (St. Martin) has the capital Marigot, and the capital of the Dutch side (St. Maarten) is Philipsburg. There is no customs or bureaucracy involved between the two sides and everyone is friendly on this unique destination of the Caribbean. Local legend proposes that the border was established by having a Dutchman and a Frenchman walk from a starting point in opposite directions until they met. It's assumed the Frenchman must have been a faster walker since the the French side is slighter larger than the Dutch side. The islands of **SABA** and **ST. BARTHELEMY** (called ST. BARTS for short) are reached by small planes from St. Maarten.

MAJOR CITY AIRPORT CODE: SXM - St. Maarten

- -

ST. BARTS (or ST. BARTHELEMY) has a distinct appeal with its small population of mostly Swedish or French descent.

- -

ST. EUSTATIUS, commonly called "Statia," has a capital city of the same name as the island of Aruba, Oranjestad. One of the group called the Netherlands Antilles (the islands of Bonaire, Curacao, St. Maarten, Saba, and St. Eustatius), "Statia" is not set up for mass tourism and offers the solitude and lack of commercialism some travelers seek.

- -

ST. KITTS and **NEVIS** are two more quiet islands for exploring. The capital of St. Kitts is Basseterre and Charlestown is the capital of Nevis (pronounced "NEE-vis").

- -

ANTIGUA and BARBUDA's main attractions are the beaches, and there are luxury resorts and casinos on Antigua. St. John's is Antigua's capital, and it is located in a sheltered cove on the northwestern tip of the island. Antigua (pronounced "an TEE ga") claims to have 365 beaches - one for every day of the year. At Nelson's Dockyard, examples of 18th century nautical life abound. A very scenic road on Antigua is Fig Tree Drive - lush with tropical vegetation, the road twists and turns through this old banana plantation and is a botanical marvel with breathtaking views of the island. Antigua's sister island, Barbuda (pronounced "Bar BEW da"), is a small, tranquil island about 25 miles north. The natural attractions of the island include the more than 200 underwater wrecks and the island's bird sanctuaries that are home to the rare frigate bird.

- -

GUADELOUPE

Shaped like a butterfly but actually two island masses connected by a bridge, Guadeloupe has quite extensive tourist facilities and roads, and is French influenced and governed. The eastern "wing," Grand-Terre, is actually flat and has the principal port city of Pointe-a-Pitre. The western "wing" is mountainous Basse-Terre, offering spectacular scenery and the possibility of hiking to the top of Mt. Soufriere (4,813 ft.). As an overseas region of France this island also includes the dependency islands of Iles des Saintes (eight tiny islands that are sometimes called Les Saintes), Marie Galante, and La Desirade (a tiny island of only eight square miles). The administrative capital is Basse-Terre (city) and the commercial capital is Pointe-a-Pitre.

MAJOR CITY AIRPORT CODE: PTP - Pointe-a-Pitre

- -

DOMINICA is a relatively unspoiled and natural island, with about 20,000 people living in the capital, Roseau. It's accessible only by small planes from islands such as Antigua, Guadeloupe, and Barbados. English and French patois (a local dialect of French) are spoken. The island is an independent nation within the British Commonwealth.

- -

The French-influenced island of **MARTINIQUE** is a land of unexpected contrasts, a mixture of black, white, and in between colored peoples of African, European, and Indian descent. The capital city of Fort-de-France reminds some people of the French Quarter in New Orleans, but it is much more quaint and quieter. Visit Mt. Pelee, a volcano that erupted in 1902 killing all but one of the 30,000 inhabitants (the sole survivor was a prisoner in a dungeon). Casual attire is customary, but women are encouraged not to wear shorts in the shopping district. The island is a shopper's mecca - especially for French goods (crystal, china, perfumes, scarves, French wine and champagne) and local handicrafts (shell figures, wood carvings, Creole dolls, bamboo and wicker items, straw goods, and appliqued wall hangings). Stores are generally closed in the middle of the day (from 12:30 to 2:30 pm) and reopen from 2:30 to 5:30 pm Monday through Friday. They are open Saturdays from 9:00 am to 1:00 pm and they are usually closed on Sundays/holidays.

MAJOR CITY AIRPORT CODES: FDF - Fort-de-France

ST. LUCIA (pronounced Saint "LOO sha") offers sights such as the twin peaks of Gros Piton and Petit Piton, a volcano called La Soufriere, sulphur springs and mineral baths dating back to the 1780s, and a national park named Pigeon Island that is connected to St. Lucia by a causeway. The history of the island includes a changeover of rule of at least 14 times. Though the island finally became British, the French influence is still evident in the island's place names, the local French Creole language, and in some of the laws. It has been under Carib control, European invasions, sugar cane dominance, slave emancipation, labor shortages, and economic depression - but there was always employment available in Castries, the capital. St. Lucia's large, deep sheltered harbor was used as the chief coaling station in the West Indies. Coal that was imported from the U.S. was stored on the wharf here and loaded onto ships that stopped for refueling on their voyages from Europe and North America to South America and the Pacific.

- -

Visiting **BARBADOS** means you have the chance to shop in the duty-free shops of Bridgetown, the capital; walk through the arts and crafts center of Pelican Village; drive through beach resort areas, sugar cane fields and along scenic coastal areas with cliffs, plunging headlands, and sometimes turbulent surf; visit Sam Lord's Castle; enjoy the view at Ragged Point; or take in the sights of Bathsheba, Cherry Tree Hill, St. Nicholas Abbey, Welchman Hall Gully, Animal Flower Cave, the city of Speightstown, and the more tranquil Platinum Coast. Barbados is the most easterly of the West Indian islands and the island's compact size - 22 miles long by 14 miles wide covers an area about the size of the city of San Antonio, Texas. On Barbados the terms windward and leeward have real meaning as the leeward side features fine, sandy beaches and the windward side has a rugged and dramatic coastline. Driving is on the left of the British influenced island. The island is independent and its history has been fairly free of strife - it has only lived under two flags: England and its own. There is some nightlife as most hotels feature a local floor show and dinner, dancing and dinner theaters can be enjoyed.

MAJOR CITY AIRPORT CODES: BGI - Barbados

- -

ST. VINCENT is linked to the Grenadines (a string of about 100 islands that lie between St. Vincent and Grenada). On St. Vincent is another La Soufriere, an active volcano (several peaks in the Caribbean are called "soufriere," meaning sulphurous). St. Vincent's volcanic origins have endowed the island with some black sand beaches, although light sandy beaches are found in the south. The capital of St. Vincent is Kingstown and the Botanic Gardens here have a breadfruit tree that is said to be descended from one that Captain Bligh of the Bounty brought in 1793.

GRENADA is called the "spice island," and the aroma of nutmeg, cocoa, and cinnamon is present as you tour the island's plantations area. The political events which led to the invasion by U.S. troops in 1983 have resulted in a stabilized and peaceful atmosphere. The southern third of the Grenadines is administered by Grenada and the other two-thirds are administered by St. Vincent. Grenada (pronounced "gre NAY da") is volcanic in origin and the central mountain range divides the island in half - with desert and cactus in the southwest, banana and spice plantations in the southeast and northwest area. Lake Antoine and Grand Etang are crater lakes formed in the extinct volcanos. Rain forest covers the center of the island and the island has excellent beaches. Grenada's capital, St. George's, is a picturesque seaport with 18th century buildings.

MAJOR CITY AIRPORT CODE: GDA - Grenada

- -

The sister islands of the independent republic of **TRINIDAD and TOBAGO** couldn't be more different. Trinidad is dynamic, vibrant, busy - home of calypso, steel bands, and one of the most spectacular Carnival celebrations. Tobago is tranquil, with small and special hotels and scattered fishing villages.

TRINIDAD
Rectangular in shape, this island is about 50 miles long and 36 miles wide. Tropical forests cover half the island - swamps are found along part of the east and west coasts. Pitch Lake on Trinidad's southwest coast is the world's largest asphalt bog. Port-of-Spain, the capital, is a busy, business-like city - except for one week in February - the week of Carnival. Like many Caribbean islands, Carnival is celebrated here - but on a grand scale. The celebration is a folk festival, art show, talent contest, theatrical spectacle, dance and music concert, a time for parades, and more. Trinidad has a wide range of flora and wildlife - the Caroni Bird Sanctuary is home to the scarlet ibis - Trinidad's national bird. The wildlife includes mongooses, bats, wild hogs, ocelots, armadillos, and agouti.

TOBAGO
Tobago is for birdwatching, fishing, snorkeling, diving, golfing, and just relaxing.

MAJOR CITY AIRPORT CODES: POS - Port-of-Spain
TAB - Tobago

- -

MONTSERRAT has the port and capital city of Plymouth. Unfortunately the island's recent volcanic eruptions have caused many residents to evacuate. Check with current news sources for updates.

- -

The ABC islands - ARUBA, BONAIRE, and CURACAO are each unique. Part of the Netherlands Antilles (except for Aruba - which is independent), the islands are Dutch influenced. Driving is on the right in these islands, and roads are in fairly good condition in most areas. Aruba and Curacao are pretty populated islands (Willemstad's population is about 85,000 people, 145,000 on the island of Curacao), so major cities can have traffic jams and be very busy. MAJOR CITY AIRPORT CODES: AUA - Aruba, BON - Bonaire, CUR - Curacao

ARUBA
Aruba is flat and arid and famous for the divi divi tree that grows horizontally because of the winds. Elegant hotels and casinos are along the beautiful beaches. Sophisticated shopping streets line Oranjestad, the capital. The southwest coast is fringed with white sandy beaches and the northeast coast is rugged and rocky with a rough surf. The wind conditions can be great for windsurfing, and an indication of the pounding sea is the Caribbean's highest and most dramatic natural bridge - carved by the sea out of coral cliffs into a high arch. Most of the islanders on Aruba (as well as Bonaire and Curacao) speak English, Dutch, and Spanish, as well as the local language, Papiamento (evolved from Spanish, Dutch, Portuguese and Arawak, with a sprinkling of African, English and French - quite unique!). Colorful pastel homes, surrounded by hibiscus, oleander and bouganvillea decorate the scenery. One thing you can see from almost anywhere on the island is Haystack Mountain (Hooiberg) that towers 500 ft. high. The trip up the concrete steps to the top is worth it - what a great view! Nassau Street in Oranjestad is the main shopping area. There are casinos, nightclubs, discos, and dance/music shows. Jackets are required for men, and dressy clothes for women are recommended for the casinos and nightclubs.

BONAIRE
Bonaire is a bird watcher's destination. The northern quarter is a 13,500 acre national park and a sanctuary for over 150 species of migratory birds, including flamingoes, Caribbean parakeets, and yellow orioles. Offshore coral reefs have made Bonaire one of the finest diving areas. South of the capital, Kralendijk, are salt pans or ponds. Salt was the major industry of the island hundreds of years ago and recent modernization has made it a big business. Huge snowy mountains of salt evaporated from the sea water stand out in haunting relief against the blue sky. Algae causes the shallow flats to change color - purple one moment, orange the next, then pink, or fuchsia, or red. Bonaire is an island for the escapist.

CURACAO
On Curacao in the capital of Willemstad, watch the Queen Emma Pontoon Bridge swing open to let ships pass, which it does at an average of thirty times a day. Downtown has the Floating Market - with fresh fruits and vegetables, lots of restaurants, shops, casinos, discos and nightclubs. Outside of town stop by the 17th century estate called "Chobo lobo" to sample the famous Curacao liqueur (usually orange or blue). Interesting architecture examples are here in the form of landhuizen (plantation houses) built on the hilltops over 300 years ago. The Jan Kock House, built in 1650 now serves as a restaurant/museum/private home and is said to be haunted! Linger in the charming villages on your way to Christoffel Park and the Botanical Gardens, eventually winding up at Boca Tabla - a natural grotto where the sea sprays powerfully above the rocks.

NOW COMPLETE PROFILE FORMS FOR MAJOR ISLANDS AND THE REVIEWS.

ISLAND NAME/GROUP:____________________ CAPITAL:____________________
DOCUMENTARY REQUIREMENTS (U.S. CITIZENS):____________________
CURRENCY:____________ CURRENCY CODE:________ EXCHANGE RATE:__________
LANGUAGE(S):____________________
SIZE:__________ POPULATION:__________CLIMATE:____________________
MAJOR CITIES/PLACES OF INTEREST:____________________
____
____
SPORTS:____________________
RELIGION(S):____________________ GOVERNMENT:____________________
FOOD SPECIALTIES:____________________
BEST BUYS:____________________
SPECIAL INFORMATION (EVENTS, TAXES, ETC.):____________________
____
AIRLINES:____________________CITY/AIRPORT CODES:____________________
TRANSPORTATION:____________________DRIVE ON________
SPECIAL HOTELS/RESORTS/MISCELLANEOUS INFO____________________
____

ISLAND NAME/GROUP:____________________ CAPITAL:____________________
DOCUMENTARY REQUIREMENTS (U.S. CITIZENS):____________________
CURRENCY:____________ CURRENCY CODE:________ EXCHANGE RATE:__________
LANGUAGE(S):____________________
SIZE:__________ POPULATION:__________CLIMATE:____________________
MAJOR CITIES/PLACES OF INTEREST:____________________
____
____
SPORTS:____________________
RELIGION(S):____________________ GOVERNMENT:____________________
FOOD SPECIALTIES:____________________
BEST BUYS:____________________
SPECIAL INFORMATION (EVENTS, TAXES, ETC.):____________________
____
AIRLINES:____________________CITY/AIRPORT CODES:____________________
TRANSPORTATION:____________________DRIVE ON________
SPECIAL HOTELS/RESORTS/MISCELLANEOUS INFO____________________
____

ISLAND NAME/GROUP:____________________ CAPITAL:____________________
DOCUMENTARY REQUIREMENTS (U.S. CITIZENS):____________________
CURRENCY:____________ CURRENCY CODE:________ EXCHANGE RATE:__________
LANGUAGE(S):____________________
SIZE:__________ POPULATION:__________CLIMATE:____________________
MAJOR CITIES/PLACES OF INTEREST:____________________
____
____
SPORTS:____________________
RELIGION(S):____________________ GOVERNMENT:____________________
FOOD SPECIALTIES:____________________
BEST BUYS:____________________
SPECIAL INFORMATION (EVENTS, TAXES, ETC.):____________________
____
AIRLINES:____________________CITY/AIRPORT CODES:____________________
TRANSPORTATION:____________________DRIVE ON________
SPECIAL HOTELS/RESORTS/MISCELLANEOUS INFO____________________
____

ISLAND NAME/GROUP:________________________ CAPITAL:________________
DOCUMENTARY REQUIREMENTS (U.S. CITIZENS):________________________
CURRENCY:______________ CURRENCY CODE:________ EXCHANGE RATE:__________
LANGUAGE(S):____
SIZE:__________ POPULATION:____________CLIMATE:____________________
MAJOR CITIES/PLACES OF INTEREST:________________________________
____
____
SPORTS:____
RELIGION(S):__________________________ GOVERNMENT:________________
FOOD SPECIALTIES:____
BEST BUYS:____
SPECIAL INFORMATION (EVENTS, TAXES, ETC.):_______________________
____
AIRLINES:_____________________CITY/AIRPORT CODES:________________
TRANSPORTATION:___________________________________DRIVE ON________
SPECIAL HOTELS/RESORTS/MISCELLANEOUS INFO_________________________
____

ISLAND NAME/GROUP:________________________ CAPITAL:________________
DOCUMENTARY REQUIREMENTS (U.S. CITIZENS):________________________
CURRENCY:______________ CURRENCY CODE:________ EXCHANGE RATE:__________
LANGUAGE(S):____
SIZE:__________ POPULATION:____________CLIMATE:____________________
MAJOR CITIES/PLACES OF INTEREST:________________________________
____
____
SPORTS:____
RELIGION(S):__________________________ GOVERNMENT:________________
FOOD SPECIALTIES:____
BEST BUYS:____
SPECIAL INFORMATION (EVENTS, TAXES, ETC.):_______________________
____
AIRLINES:_____________________CITY/AIRPORT CODES:________________
TRANSPORTATION:___________________________________DRIVE ON________
SPECIAL HOTELS/RESORTS/MISCELLANEOUS INFO_________________________
____

ISLAND NAME/GROUP:________________________ CAPITAL:________________
DOCUMENTARY REQUIREMENTS (U.S. CITIZENS):________________________
CURRENCY:______________ CURRENCY CODE:________ EXCHANGE RATE:__________
LANGUAGE(S):____
SIZE:__________ POPULATION:____________CLIMATE:____________________
MAJOR CITIES/PLACES OF INTEREST:________________________________
____
____
SPORTS:____
RELIGION(S):__________________________ GOVERNMENT:________________
FOOD SPECIALTIES:____
BEST BUYS:____
SPECIAL INFORMATION (EVENTS, TAXES, ETC.):_______________________
____
AIRLINES:_____________________CITY/AIRPORT CODES:________________
TRANSPORTATION:___________________________________DRIVE ON________
SPECIAL HOTELS/RESORTS/MISCELLANEOUS INFO_________________________
____

ISLAND NAME/GROUP:____________________ CAPITAL:____________
DOCUMENTARY REQUIREMENTS (U.S. CITIZENS):____________
CURRENCY:__________ CURRENCY CODE:______ EXCHANGE RATE:______
LANGUAGE(S):____________
SIZE:________ POPULATION:________CLIMATE:____________
MAJOR CITIES/PLACES OF INTEREST:____________
____
____
SPORTS:____________
RELIGION(S):____________ GOVERNMENT:____________
FOOD SPECIALTIES:____________
BEST BUYS:____________
SPECIAL INFORMATION (EVENTS, TAXES, ETC.):____________
____
AIRLINES:____________CITY/AIRPORT CODES:____________
TRANSPORTATION:____________DRIVE ON______
SPECIAL HOTELS/RESORTS/MISCELLANEOUS INFO____________
____

ISLAND NAME/GROUP:____________________ CAPITAL:____________
DOCUMENTARY REQUIREMENTS (U.S. CITIZENS):____________
CURRENCY:__________ CURRENCY CODE:______ EXCHANGE RATE:______
LANGUAGE(S):____________
SIZE:________ POPULATION:________CLIMATE:____________
MAJOR CITIES/PLACES OF INTEREST:____________
____
____
SPORTS:____________
RELIGION(S):____________ GOVERNMENT:____________
FOOD SPECIALTIES:____________
BEST BUYS:____________
SPECIAL INFORMATION (EVENTS, TAXES, ETC.):____________
____
AIRLINES:____________CITY/AIRPORT CODES:____________
TRANSPORTATION:____________DRIVE ON______
SPECIAL HOTELS/RESORTS/MISCELLANEOUS INFO____________
____

ISLAND NAME/GROUP:____________________ CAPITAL:____________
DOCUMENTARY REQUIREMENTS (U.S. CITIZENS):____________
CURRENCY:__________ CURRENCY CODE:______ EXCHANGE RATE:______
LANGUAGE(S):____________
SIZE:________ POPULATION:________CLIMATE:____________
MAJOR CITIES/PLACES OF INTEREST:____________
____
____
SPORTS:____________
RELIGION(S):____________ GOVERNMENT:____________
FOOD SPECIALTIES:____________
BEST BUYS:____________
SPECIAL INFORMATION (EVENTS, TAXES, ETC.):____________
____
AIRLINES:____________CITY/AIRPORT CODES:____________
TRANSPORTATION:____________DRIVE ON______
SPECIAL HOTELS/RESORTS/MISCELLANEOUS INFO____________
____

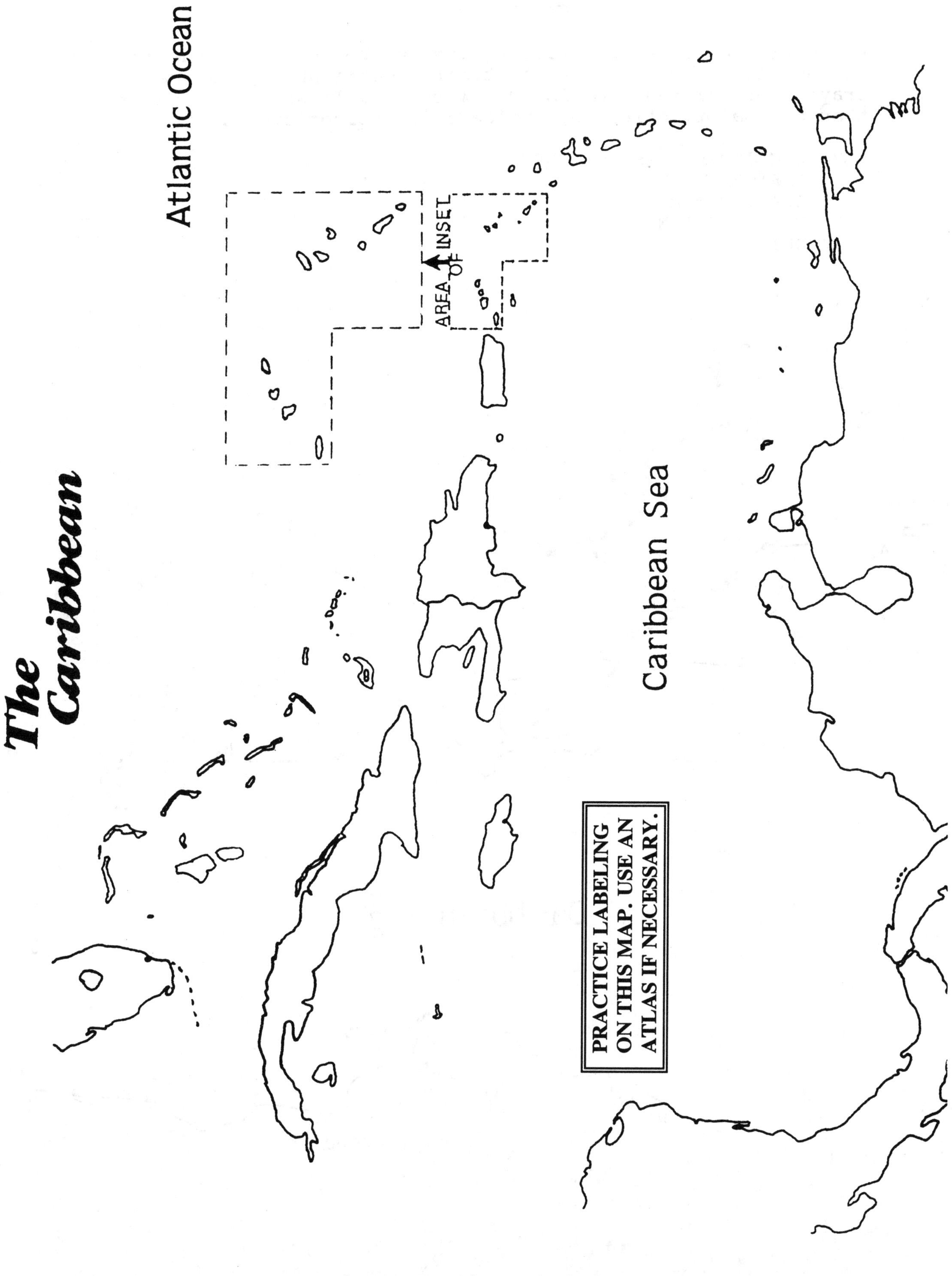
The Caribbean
Atlantic Ocean
AREA OF INSET
Caribbean Sea
PRACTICE LABELING ON THIS MAP. USE AN ATLAS IF NECESSARY.

CARIBBEAN

As another activity in studying the Caribbean, color the islands on the map below according to their predominant influence (use crayons or colored pencils, NOT markers). If an island has more than one major influence, indicate it appropriately.

KEY: ENGLISH/BRITISH = GREEN
FRENCH = BLUE
SPANISH = RED
U.S. = WHITE
DUTCH = YELLOW

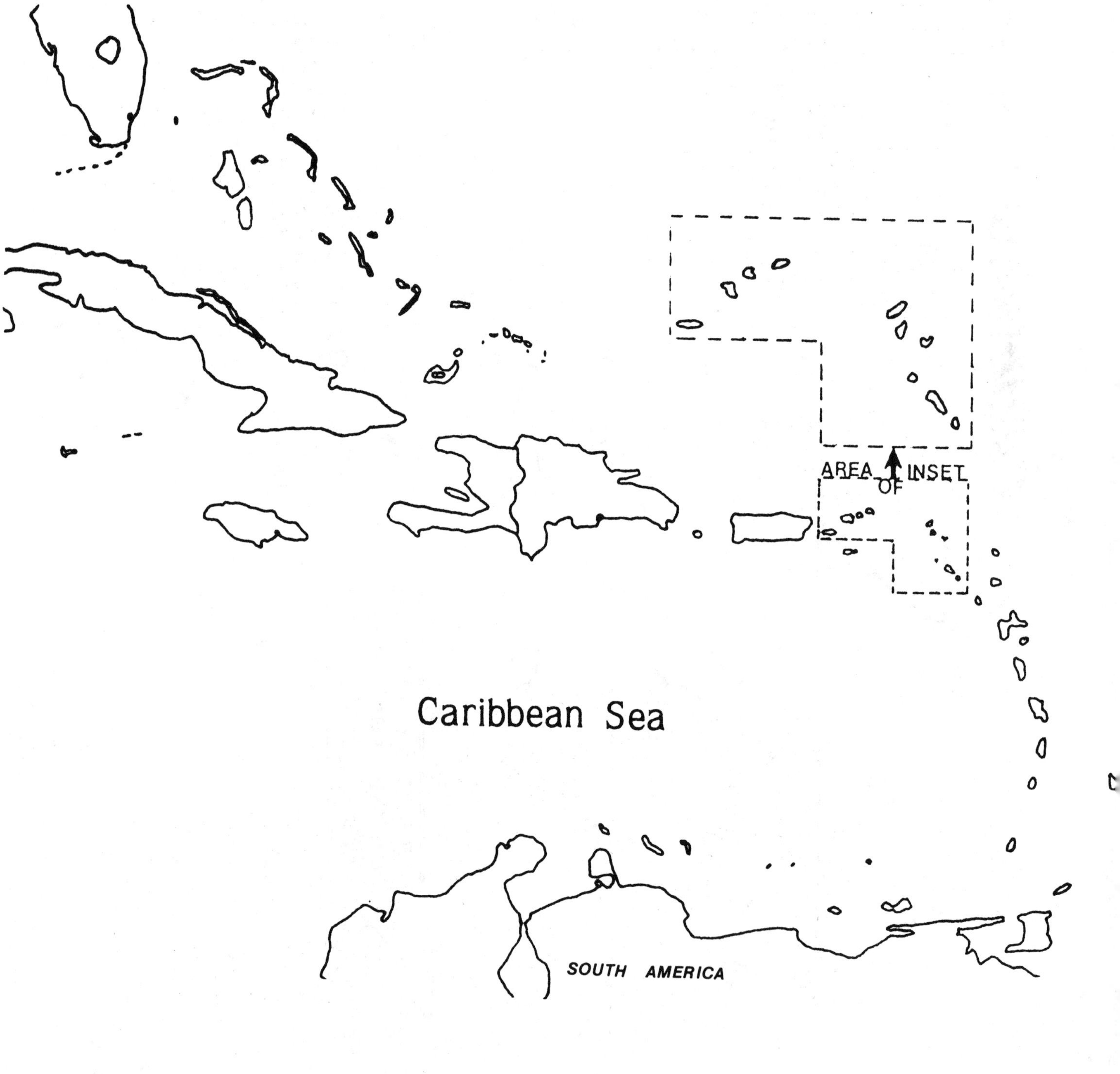

CARIBBEAN REVIEW

MATCH THE FOLLOWING CITIES TO ISLANDS (some answers may be used more than once):

1. ________Fort-de-France	A. Grand Bahama Island
2. ________Georgetown	B. Grand Cayman
3. ________San Juan	C. Puerto Rico
4. ________Willemstad	D. St. Martin
5. ________Oranjestad	E. Aruba
6. ________Port-au-Prince	F. St. Maarten
7. ________Santo Domingo	G. Barbados
8. ________Charlotte Amalie	H. Jamaica
9. ________Philipsburg	I. Haiti
10. ________Kingston	J. Dominican Republic
11. ________Roseau	K. Curacao
12. ________Montego Bay	L. St. Thomas
13. ________Bridgetown	M. New Providence Island
14. ________Marigot	N. Guadeloupe
15. ________Puerto Plata	O. Martinique
16. ________Freeport	P. Dominica
17. ________Pointe-a-Pitre	Q. St. Croix
18. ________Nassau	R. St. Lucia
19. ________Christiansted	S. Grenada
20. ________Ocho Rios	
21. ________Ponce	
22. ________Hell	
23. ________Runaway Bay	
24. ________Cap Haitien	
25. ________Port Antonio	
26. ________Port Lucaya	
27. ________Basse Terre	
28. ________Castries	
29. ________Fredericksted	
30. ________St. George's	

CARIBBEAN REVIEW

1. Two major cities tourists visit in the Bahamas are ______________ and ________________.
2. The three principal U.S. Virgin Islands are ______________________, ___________________________, and ______________________________.
3. It is customary to bargain on purchases made on all the Caribbean islands. True or False______________
4. The "ABC islands" are __________, ______________ & ______________.
5. On what island is the city of Montego Bay? ______________________
6. What are some of the best buys of the U.S. Virgin Islands? ______ ____
7. The capital of Cuba is ___________________.
8. In the Caribbean, the popular liquor used in drinks is _________.
9. What amount of duty-free purchases can a U.S. resident bring back from the U.S. Virgin Islands? _____________________________________
10. How much liquor can be brought back by a U.S. resident of legal age, if returning from visiting the U.S. Virgin Islands? ________
11. The capital of Puerto Rico is ________________________.
12. What islands are popular for scuba diving, one of which has a well-known turtle farm and famous Seven Mile Beach? ____________
13. The island that looks like a butterfly viewed from above is _____ ___________________________.
14. What island is divided into two cultures, one side is Dutch and one side is French? _____________________
15. Name two islands that have gambling casinos. ____________________ ____
16. What countries make up the island known as Hispaniola? _________ ____
17. Name five activities that tourists can enjoy when traveling to most of the Caribbean islands. ___________________________________ ____
18. What is the name of the tree particularly found on Aruba that grows horizontally due to the winds? _________________________
19. Two major British Virgin Islands that tourists visit are ________ _______________ & ____.
20. What are some of the best buys of Martinique? ___________________ ____
21. The capital of the Cayman Islands is ____________________________.
22. Driving is on the left in Haiti. True or False ____________
23. _________________________ is commonly called "Statia."
24. The "spice island" is __________________________.
25. ______ is the city airport code for Montego Bay.
26. Mt. Pelee erupted here and killed all but one of the 30,000 inhabitants. __________________
27. ___________________ features river rafting on the Martha Brae.
28. What is the population of Willemstad, Curacao? ________________
29. The Caroni Bird Sanctuary, home of the scarlet ibis, is on which island? _______________________
30. The capital of St. Maarten is __________________, and the capital of St. Martin is _________________________.
31. ______ is the city airport code for Aruba.

32. Eleuthera is ______________ miles long and about _________ mile wide.
33. The famous Cathedral of Santa Maria La Menor is in the capital city of ____________________, in the country of ______________________ _________________________.
34. El Yunque is about _______ miles east of San Juan.
35. The two islands off the coast of Puerto Rico that can be reached by ferry are ______________________ and ___________________.
36. Pitch Lake is on the island of ____________________________.
37. Sam Lord's Castle is a sight of ____________________.
38. A bird watcher's paradise, with the capital city of Kralendijk is the island of ______________________.
39. The Queen Emma Pontoon Bridge can be seen on the island of Aruba. True or False ___________
40. Tobago is a cosmopolitan island with lots of nightlife. True or False _______________
41. Callaloo is a fish. True or False ___________
42. Boonoonoonoos is a festival in Jamaica held every August. True or False ____________
43. The place where you can feed and hold sting rays off the coast of Grand Cayman is called Reef City. True or False ____________
44. Amber and larimar jewelry are best buys of Haiti. True or False ___________
45. Nelson's Dockyard is on the island of ___________________.
46. A special type of ball was designed to play golf on what island? _________________________
47. Phosphorescent Bay is on the northern coast of Puerto Rico. True or False ________________
48. French is the official language of the Turks and Caicos Islands. True or False _____________
49. Papiamento is spoken in Puerto Rico. True or False _____________
50. Roseau is the capital of __________________.

CARIBBEAN REVIEW

MATCH THE FOLLOWING (not every answer will be used):

1. ________Art, voodoo, crowded, poverty, La Citadelle
2. ________Duty-free, popular cruise port, Charlotte Amalie, Buck Island
3. ________Reggae music, Negril, river raft rides
4. ________French side, capital is Marigot
5. ________Turtle Farm, Seven Mile Beach, banks, "The Wall"
6. ________Very industrialized, El Yunque, El Morro Fortress
7. ________Dutch side, capital is Philipsburg
8. ________Divi divi tree, casinos, off the coast of Venezuela
9. ________Shaped like a butterfly, Grand-Terre and Basse-Terre
10. ________Part of the Netherlands Antilles, famous for a blue or orange liqueur of the same name
11. ________Christopher Columbus is buried here, La Romana resort area
12. ________Commonly called "Statia"
13. ________"Spice island"
14. ________Twin peaks of Gros Piton and Petit Piton
15. ________Mt. Pelee erupted and killed all but one of the 30,000 inhabitants

A. Puerto Rico
B. Haiti
C. U.S. Virgin Islands
D. St. Maarten
E. Dominica
F. Guadeloupe
G. St. Martin
H. Cayman Islands
I. Jamaica
J. Aruba
K. Curacao
L. Dominican Republic
M. Martinique
N. St. Lucia
O. Grenada
P. St. Eustatius

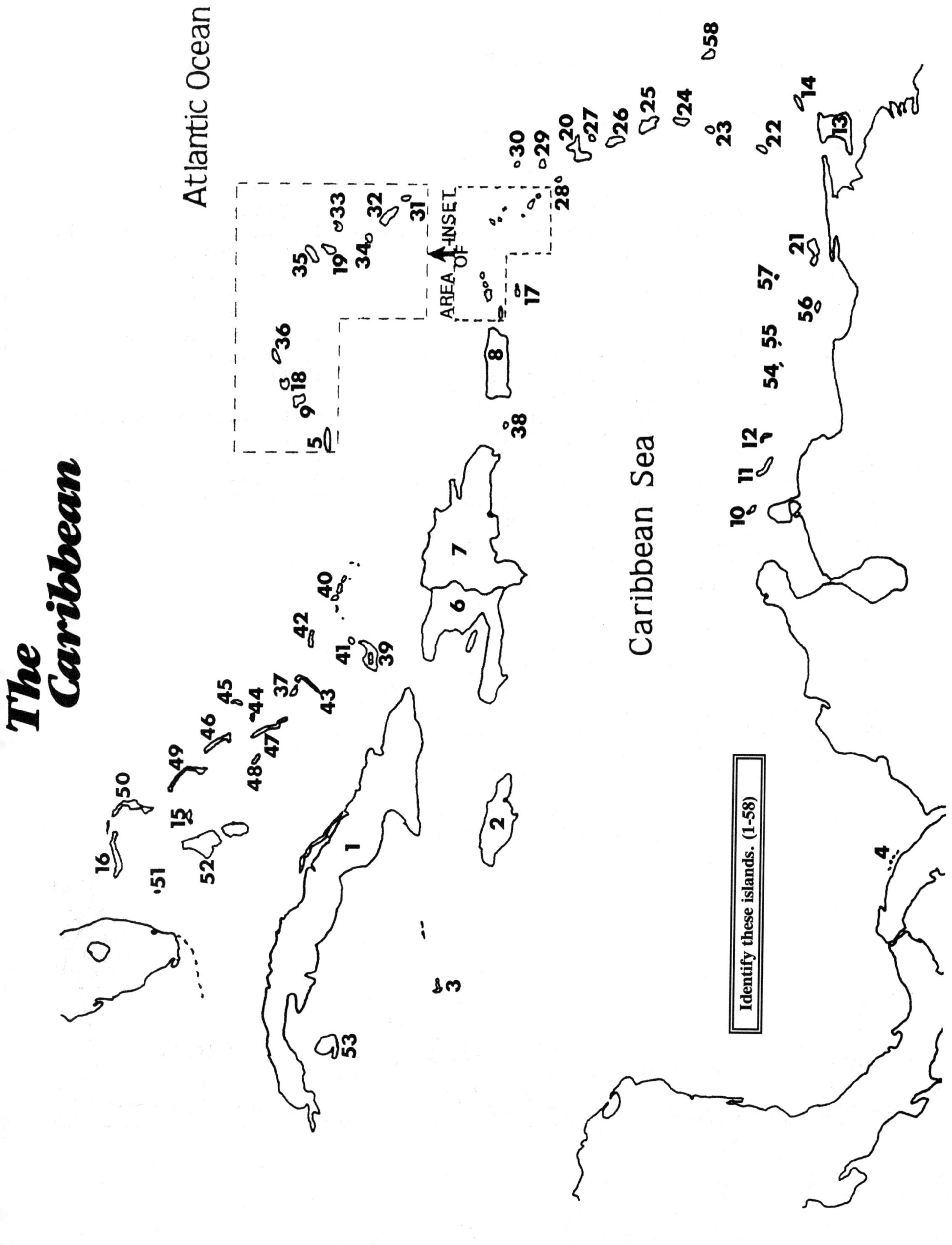
The Caribbean
Atlantic Ocean
Caribbean Sea
AREA OF INSET
Identify these islands. (1-58)

NOTES

BERMUDA

BERMUDA lies in the Atlantic Ocean about 600 miles east of the coast of North Carolina. This means it's closer to New York and Philadelphia than it is to the Caribbean islands. It also means that it is a more seasonal destination as the air and water temperature will be much cooler in winter than the Caribbean islands. Bermuda has no rainy season and very few hurricanes have passed its way. The capital city of Hamilton is near to the middle of the island. Front Street is the principal shopping area. Other sights in town include City Hall, the Bermuda Historial Society Museum, the Sessions House and Parliament Building, and the Cathedral of the Most Holy Trinity. A few minutes outside the town center is Fort Hamilton - with its massive ramparts and labyrinthine passages - offering a great view of the city and harbor. The West End is actually four islands connected not only by bridges but by history. When a visitor crosses over Somerset Bridge (the smallest drawbridge in the world), Bermudians will say he is "up the country." The main island of Somerset is a charming place of small farms, craggy coastlines, parks, preserves, and beaches. Three smaller islands stretch from Somerset to the northeast: Watford, Boaz, and Ireland Island. To explore West End, tourists can hop aboard a ferry from Hamilton. Sights of West End include Gibbs Hill Lighthouse, Scaur Lodge Property (with excellent views of Ely's Harbour), and the Bermuda Arts Centre at Dockyard. East End has St. George's, a most enchanting part of the island with the oldest Anglican church, St. Peter's, and the old rambling forts of St. Catherine and Gates Fort. In the Harrington Sound area visit the Leamington and Crystal Caves, the H.T. North Nature Reserve, and see the Blue Grotto Dolphin Show. Immaculate and very friendly, Bermuda has a wide variety of accommodations, excellent shopping, entertainment and fine restaurants. It is an upscale resort destination with a more formal atmosphere. Tourists cannot rent cars, but taxis, buses, hotel minivans, and ferry services provide public transportation, Visitors can rent mopeds - driving is on the left and caution is advised as traffic can be heavy and the roads are narrow (many are lined by rock walls). Bathing suits, bare feet, and bare chests are not permitted while riding mopeds or bicycles. Evening attire is more formal for both men and women (although men will wear coats and ties with their fashionable Bermuda shorts). It is best to check on dress codes when making dinner/nightclub reservations. Bermuda real estate is expensive and the costs of goods and services are high. The country is divided into administrative zones called parishes, and there is strict enforcement of the laws against buying/selling/importing/exporting drugs or carrying firearms, spearguns, or any weapons. Golf and tennis tournaments are frequent, as well as sailing and yachting regattas, cricket matches, fishing tournaments, cycling races and triathlons. Bermuda is actually a collection of about 150 islands, with the seven largest islands connected by bridges and causeways.

AND YES THE SAND IS PINK! STEP INTO ITS POWDERY SOFTNESS, ROSY WITH FLECKS OF SHELLS AND CORAL CHIPPED FROM THE REEFS OVER TIME. AND THERE ARE MORE COLORS TO ENJOY HERE - THE AQUAMARINE AND TURQUOISE WATER, THE GREEN GOLF COURSES, THE MULTI-COLORS OF THE FLOWERS (RED, YELLOW, PINK, WHITE, ORANGE), AND OF COURSE THE COLORS OF THE HOMES (LIME-GREEN, YELLOW, ROBIN'S EGG BLUE, AND ESPECIALLY PINK). THE "SNOW-CAPPED" ROOFS ARE BERMUDIAN TRADEMARKS AND UNLIKE ANY YOU'VE SEEN - PURE WHITE THEY SPARKLE IN THE SUN AND CAPTURE THE FRESH RAIN WATER SO PRECIOUS TO THE ISLAND.

BERMUDA

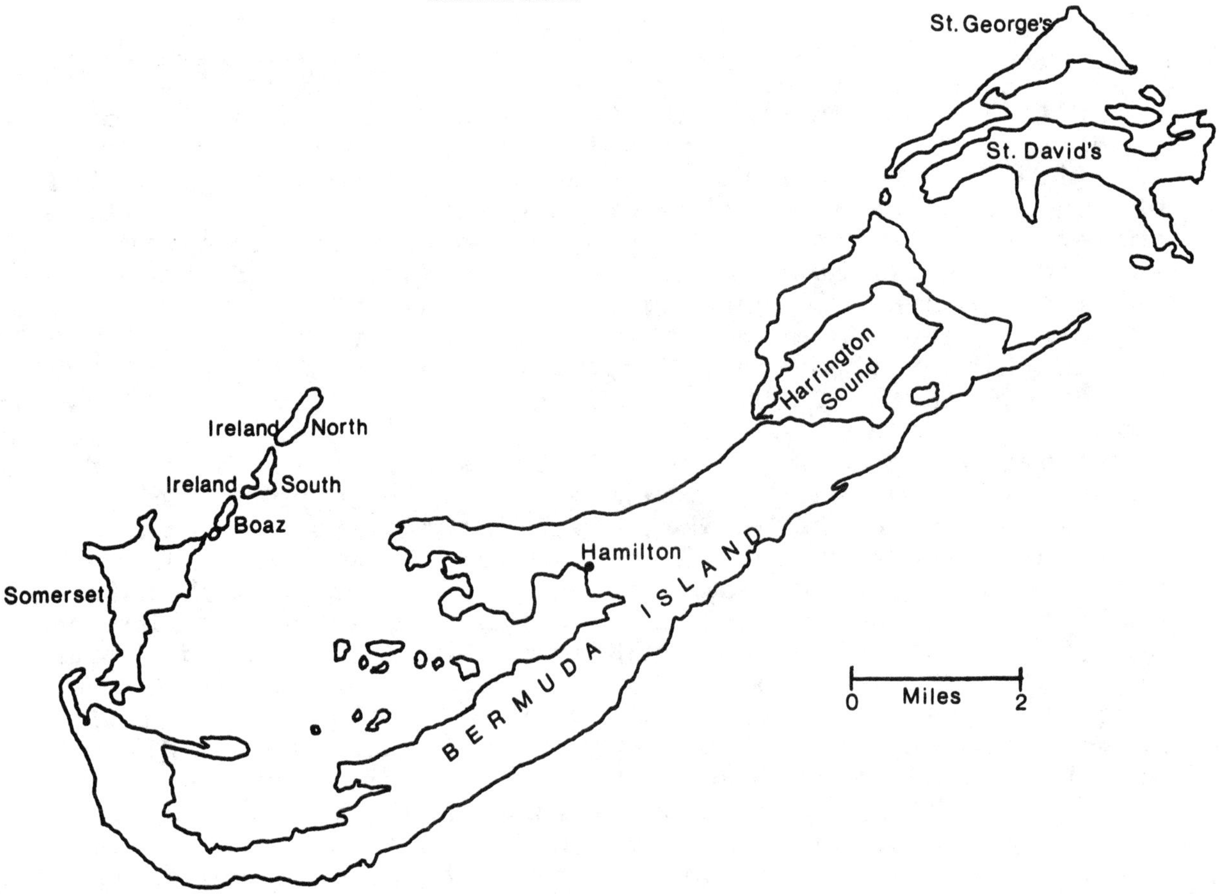

REVIEW ON BERMUDA

1. What is the capital of Bermuda? ____________________________
2. A few minutes outside of the capital is Fort ____________________, which offers a great view of the city and harbor.
3. Bermuda is actually a collection of about 150 islands, with the ________ largest islands connected by bridges and causeways.
4. The country is divided into administrative zones called ______________________.
5. The Leamington and Crystal Caves are in the ______________________ Sound area.
6. St. George's is at East End. True or False _______________
7. Bermuda is located about __________ miles off the coast of North Carolina
8. ___________________________ Bridge is the smallest drawbridge in the world.
9. The principal shopping street of Hamilton is ________________________.
10. What are some of the qualities/benefits of this destination? __________________
____
____

CHAPTER 11

South America

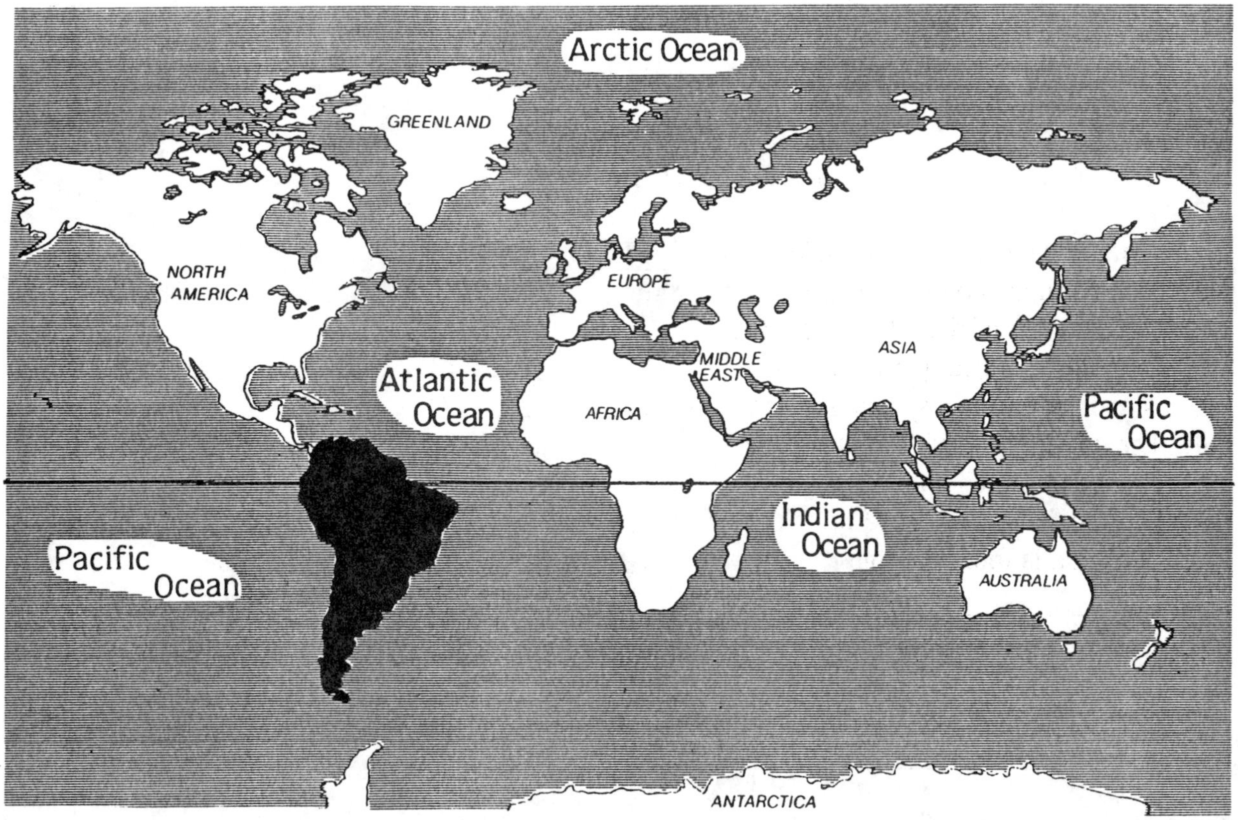

NOTES

COUNTRIES OF SOUTH AMERICA

SOME CAPITAL CITIES OF SOUTH AMERICA

SOUTH AMERICA - MAJOR CITY AIRPORT CODES

BRAZIL
RIO - Rio de Janeiro
GIG - Rio de Janeiro/Int'l Airport
BSB - Brasilia
SAO - Sao Paulo
FOR - Fortaleza

CHILE
SCL - Santiago
PUQ - Punta Arenas

PERU
LIM - Lima
CUZ - Cuzco
IQT - Iquitos
TRU - Trujillo
AQP - Arequipa

ECUADOR
UIO - Quito
GYE - Guayaquil

COLOMBIA
BOG - Bogota
MDE - Medellin
CTG - Cartagena
BAQ - Barranquilla

VENEZUELA
CCS - Caracas
CBL - Ciudad Bolivar

ARGENTINA
BUE - Buenos Aires
COR - Cordoba
ROS - Rosario

URUGUAY
MVD - Montevideo

BOLIVIA
LPB - La Paz
CBB - Cochabamba
SRE - Sucre

GUYANA
GEO - Georgetown

FRENCH GUIANA
CAY - Cayenne

SURINAME
PBM - Paramaribo

PARAGUAY
ASU - Asuncion

SOUTH AMERICA

South America has a wide range of geographic features: rain forests, jungles, glaciers, fjords, deserts, mountains, rivers, beaches, and lakes. Its mix of cultures, languages, history, and peoples is also fascinating for many travelers. The Andes mountains form the western coast's backbone - stretching from the northwest corner of Venezuela to the southern tip of the continent. Some countries are politically unstable and travelers should check with the U.S. Department of State for any current advisories. Health advisories may also be in effect - check with the CDC (Centers for Disease Control) for any advice/ precautions. The best time to travel to South America is during February and March (summer in the southern hemisphere) and air travel is the best way to get from country to country and between major cities in most countries.

BRAZIL - a country larger than the contiguous U.S. and varied in its regions and population, has a number of attractions. There is the massive Amazon River area, where the temperature stays around 80 degrees Fahrenheit, and the tropical rain forest, where broadleafed trees and plants grow to enormous proportions. As many as 3,000 different species of trees in a single square mile have been cataloged and thousands of types of insects can be found. Parrots, exotic birds, chattering monkeys, jungle cats, the up to 500-pound piracuru (the largest freshwater fish in the world) - these are just some of the wildlife of this amazing region. Swimming in the Amazon isn't advisable, because of the schools of piranha (small fish with razor-sharp teeth). Manaus is a base city for tourist excursions exploring the mid-Amazon region. The city is famous for its opera house, Teatro Amazonas, where world famous stars have performed. Belem is the port city on the Atlantic, where day trips can be arranged for those who are not going further up the Amazon. Unlike the deep interior is the city of Rio de Janeiro. Copacabana and Ipanema beaches are popular and can be extremely crowded. Make sure to leave valuables in a hotel safe (better yet, leave them home) and don't wear flashy or expensive jewelry. Sugar Loaf Mountain and the Corcovado statue of Christ provide views of the city known as one of the world's most beautiful. If weary from seeing the sights and visiting the many churches, gardens, shops, and museums, relax at a cafe or at one of many international restaurants. Nightlife includes discos, live music or Brazilian folklore shows, or watching/dancing the samba. Sao Paulo with its towering skyscrapers and fast pace is one of the world's most cosmopolitan cities. The capital, Brasilia, has some unusual and futuristic-looking architecture, and was designated the capital to help spur development of the country's vast interior. On the border with Argentina is the famous Iguassu* Falls, with water from some 30 rivers and streams rushing toward a 200 foot precipice. The country is composed of many different ethnic groups and a history filled with pirates, African slaves, native Indians, gold and rubber explorations, strange primitive religions, a rich supply of legends and folklore - so much so that nothing is really "typically Brazilian." Portuguese is the official language and the country is one of the largest producers of coffee in the world. Best buys are: fabrics, Papagaio kites, leather, gems, hammocks, crafts, and the figa (a clenched hand symbolizing good luck, fertility, passion). You'll see them made of almost anything (wood, plastic, gold, silver). However, to bring good luck a figa has to be given to you as a present. Brazil's currency is the real.

PERU is the sight of the "Lost City of the Incas," Machu Picchu. Situated high in the Andes, this city was built on a narrow area surrounded by mountains. The town, intact except for the straw roofs that have since rotted away, is a maze of empty plazas, chambers, and palaces connected by stairways all carved out of solid rock. The site is at an elevation of 8,000 feet so the effects of altitude (nausea, dizziness, headaches, insomnia, chest pains) are a consideration when visiting. Cuzco, the ancient capital of the Incas, can be used as a base for exploring the outlying archaeological regions. Travelers arriving in Cuzco may need to take it easy the first day or two - to get used to the 11,024 ft. altitude. A visit to the mysterious plains of Nazca means flying over ruins and figures that have been outlined on the ground for several miles - created drawings that can only be seen from the air. Excursions on the Amazon River are available from Iquitos in Peru and the tours can include visits to the villages of the Yagua Indians, who demonstrate their skillful use of blowguns. Peru's economy and politics are particularly unstable; there is at present an outbreak of cholera and some areas have been declared emergency zones and should be avoided. Visitors should avoid drinking tap water or drinks with ice and stay away from street vendors. There is also petty crime (pickpockets, etc.) so don't wear flashy jewelry, hide wallets and monies, and safeguard any valuables. The capital, Lima, features museums and churches and some first class hotels (other areas of the country have only adequate accommodations - not

*also spelled Iguazu and both are pronounced "ee-gwa-SUE"

up to the standards of upscale travelers). Best buys of the country are: alpaca and llama rugs and goods, gold, wooden carvings, straw goods, silver, linen and cotton fabrics and clothes, leather items, pottery, paintings, and local handicrafts. The national languages are Spanish and Quechua and the currency is the nuevo sol.

ECUADOR has three very distinct regions: the Amazon basin region, the high mountainous region, and the coastal lowlands region. Quito is the capital and Guayaquil is the major port city. A tourist center is built at the monument that marks the Equator and it is a novelty to have a picture taken of standing with one foot in the Northern and one foot in the Southern Hemisphere. The capital city has a beautiful natural setting - overshadowed by the volcano Pichina with its twin peaks of Ruca and Guagua. The architecture of the buildings is also quite nice as the city has retained much of its Spanish colonial character. Visit the cathedral in the Plaza Independencia, the Municipal Palace, Alameda Park, the Astronomical Observatory and the modern Legislative Palace. For many travelers, Ecuador's appeal lies in the colorful Indian markets. There are a dozen of these within a day's outing from Quito. Most lie south of the capital along the route called the Avenue of the Volcanoes (11 snow-capped peaks frame the Latacunga-Ambato Valley). The Ambato Market opens early on Mondays, the Pujili Market is on Wednesday and Sunday, Latacunga Market is on Tuesday, and Saquisili is on Thursday. Excellent crafts, embroideries, woven rugs, wood and metal work, gold and silver jewelry, wall hangings, weavings, carvings, highland musical instruments, trinkets, leather items, and imaginative colorful bread-dough figures are some of the many buys. The pisco sour cocktail is a favorite drink and there are many fine restaurants in Quito. After dinner, nightclub "penas" are popular (shows featuring Andean music). There are also casinos. About 45 minutes by air from Quito is the city of Cuenca. Isolated in a beautiful valley rimmed by the Andes, the city has four rivers to keep the land fertile. Visitors should wear heavy sweaters and good walking shoes when starting out for a day in the Cajas National Reserve, west of Cuenca. Within this area that starts at 10,000 ft. above sea level are dozens of lakes for trout fishing, hiking trails, flora, fauna, and birdlife that make this area a special treat. About 600 miles off the coast of Ecuador are the famed Galapagos Islands. It is a world of 13 major islands and scores of islets that became the living laboratory of Charles Darwin and his work on the theory of evolution. Now a National Park, these islands are volcanic in origin and are known for their rare reptiles and wildlife (giant tortoises, marine and land iguanas, red-footed and blue-footed boobies, penguins, flightless cormorants, frigate birds, etc.). The currency of Ecuador is the sucre.

ARGENTINA, the second largest country in South America, has varied scenery and climate, ranging from the freezing Southern tip to the tropical north. The pampas region is an area of treeless plains, where gauchos (South American cowboys) raise cattle. Buenos Aires, the capital, is an elegant shopper's paradise (check out Calle Florida and Calle Santa Fe). Shop for gems, leather, sheepskin products, wines, guitars, crafts, ponchos, rugs, and items made from vicuna wool (a vicuna is a llama-like animal). The district of La Boca (one of the older areas and home of the tango) is worth a nighttime visit. The city's host of parks and skyscrapers is at the heart of an extensive rail network reaching into the pampas. The resort area of Mar del Plata is full of luxury hotels and many other types of accommodations that line its five miles of clean, sandy beaches. New resorts and casinos are springing up along this developing area of coastline. Bariloche, an Alpine-like village and ski area, has a ski season that lasts from June to October. The currency of Argentina is the nuevo peso. Social conventions include a lot of handshaking on greeting or meeting someone and dinner is usually served around 9:00 or 10:00 pm (common in Latin American countries). Beef is of high quality and those inclined should dine at a parillada (grill room) where a large variety of barbeque-style dishes are served. Avoid casual discussion of the Falklands/Malvinas war (the Falkland Islands off the Argentine coast remain a British Crown Colony). Dress conservatively in cities.

VENEZUELA has tropical beaches, immense plains, rivers, forests, jungles, waterfalls and mountains. Off the coast is Margarita Island, a popular tourist resort. La Guaira is the main port for Caracas, the capital. Maracaibo and Lake Maracaibo are dominated by oil producing industries. The Guyana Highlands constitute half of the land area of the country and are known for their gold and diamond resources. One of the world's largest national parks, Canaima, is the setting for the world's highest waterfall, Angel Falls. The currency is the bolivar (Simon Bolivar was the Venezuelan statesman and soldier that liberated Venezuela, Ecuador, and other areas from Spanish rule). Many statues and plazas dedicated to Simon Bolivar are found in several South American countries.

COLOMBIA's capital is Bogota, which is also the largest city with a population of over 5 million people. Violence and kidnapping remain serious problems in Colombia, so travelers should check with the U.S. Department of State for current advisories. Other major cities of the country are Medellin, Cali, Barranquilla, and Cartagena. Besides oil, coffee, sugar, bananas, leather goods, and cotton, Colombia is a large producer of emeralds (they are known as some of the most perfect in the world). Visitors to Bogota should take a day or two to get used to the altitude. Tap water and drinks with ice should be avoided. Milk should be boiled, and avoid the foods from street vendors. Medical insurance is essential. The currency of Colombia is the peso.

URUGUAY enjoys an ideal climate, 300 miles of sandy beaches, and many other opportunities for sports and entertainment. Montevideo is the capital and Punta del Este is one of the most popular coastal resorts. Geographically, Punta del Este is a peninsula stretching out into the ocean like an open hand - with the spaces between the fingers filled with islets covered with seals, islands covered with cannons (witness to history), wild beaches, safe beaches and harbors. A big meat producing country, beef is a part of most meals.

CHILE is a ribbon of land with wide variations of soil and climate. The northern part of the country is mostly desert, the Atacama, which is the world's driest. The central zone is an agricultural region - an area for vineyards and orange groves. The south is forested and also has some agriculture, along with cattle and sheep grazing lands. The best known ski resort is Portillo and the skiing season runs from June to September. Portillo is a three hour bus ride from Santiago, the capital. Vina del Mar, about 85 miles from Santiago, is a delightful resort reminiscent of the French Riviera. Condominiums, hotels, motels, plush residences and shopping arcades stretch for miles along the coast. Across the bay is the port city of Valparaiso. About 570 miles south of Santiago is the town of Puerto Montt, western gateway to Patagonia, the superb Chilean-Argentine Lakes, and the unusual outpost city of Punta Arenas - beyond which lies a land of glaciers, icebergs, fjords and penguins. A Chilean possession in the Pacific is Easter Island (about 2300 miles from the mainland). It's most famous for the Moai - gigantic stone figures which are found all over the island.

BOLIVIA is one of the land locked countries (the other is Paraguay) and La Paz, its capital, is the world's highest, being situated at about 12,000 feet above sea level. Other major cities are Potosi, Tarija, Sucre, and Cochabamba. Lake Titicaca, the highest navigable lake in the world, is on the border of Bolivia and Peru. Passenger boats are operated between the various small islands on the lake, most of them leave from the city of Copacabana.

GUYANA was formerly known as British Guiana (independence was granted in 1966). Georgetown is the capital and Kaieteur Falls (about five times higher than Niagara Falls) is a notable attraction. Bauxite, sugar cane, rice, gold, and diamonds are the country's industries. The currency is the Guyana Dollar.

SURINAME used to be Dutch governed and is now independent. Paramaribo is the capital, Dutch is the official language (although Hindi, Javanese, Chinese, French, Spanish and English are spoken. "Taki-Taki" or "Sranan Tongo" - originating from Creole - is the popular language. The currency is the guilder and the climate is tropical, cooled by northeast tradewinds. There are no notable beaches but there are some nice wildlife reserves.

FRENCH GUIANA's economy is heavily dependent on France, especially for the imports of food and manufactured goods. The official language is French, though many speak a Creole patois and English is also spoken. The currency is the French Franc, Cayenne is the capital and the climate is tropical. Devil's Island, off the coast, was a former French penal colony.

PARAGUAY, a landlocked country surrounded by Argentina, Bolivia, and Brazil, has the capital, Asuncion. The currency is the guarani, and the climate is subtropical (with rapid temperature changes all year).

NOW RESEARCH AND FILL OUT PROFILE FORMS ON SOME COUNTRIES, THEN COMPLETE THE REVIEWS.

COUNTRY: ______ CAPITAL: ______
DOCUMENTARY REQUIREMENTS (U.S. CITIZENS): ______
SHOTS, OTHER INFO: ______
CURRENCY: ______ CURRENCY CODE: ______ EXCHANGE RATE: ______
LANGUAGE(S): ______
SIZE: ______ POPULATION: ______
CLIMATE: ______
BEST TIME TO VISIT: ______
MAJOR CITIES/PLACES OF INTEREST: ______
SPORTS: ______
RELIGION(S): ______ GOVERNMENT: ______
FOOD SPECIALTIES: ______
BEST BUYS: ______
SPECIAL INFORMATION: ______
AIRLINES: ______ CITY/AIRPORT CODES: ______
TRANSPORTATION: ______
SPECIAL HOTELS/RESORTS/MISCELLANEOUS INFO ______

COUNTRY: ______ CAPITAL: ______
DOCUMENTARY REQUIREMENTS (U.S. CITIZENS): ______
SHOTS, OTHER INFO: ______
CURRENCY: ______ CURRENCY CODE: ______ EXCHANGE RATE: ______
LANGUAGE(S): ______
SIZE: ______ POPULATION: ______
CLIMATE: ______
BEST TIME TO VISIT: ______
MAJOR CITIES/PLACES OF INTEREST: ______
SPORTS: ______
RELIGION(S): ______ GOVERNMENT: ______
FOOD SPECIALTIES: ______
BEST BUYS: ______
SPECIAL INFORMATION: ______
AIRLINES: ______ CITY/AIRPORT CODES: ______
TRANSPORTATION: ______
SPECIAL HOTELS/RESORTS/MISCELLANEOUS INFO ______

COUNTRY: ______ CAPITAL: ______
DOCUMENTARY REQUIREMENTS (U.S. CITIZENS): ______
SHOTS, OTHER INFO: ______
CURRENCY: ______ CURRENCY CODE: ______ EXCHANGE RATE: ______
LANGUAGE(S): ______
SIZE: ______ POPULATION: ______
CLIMATE: ______
BEST TIME TO VISIT: ______
MAJOR CITIES/PLACES OF INTEREST: ______
SPORTS: ______
RELIGION(S): ______ GOVERNMENT: ______
FOOD SPECIALTIES: ______
BEST BUYS: ______
SPECIAL INFORMATION: ______
AIRLINES: ______ CITY/AIRPORT CODES: ______
TRANSPORTATION: ______
SPECIAL HOTELS/RESORTS/MISCELLANEOUS INFO ______

COUNTRY: ____________ CAPITAL: ____________
DOCUMENTARY REQUIREMENTS (U.S. CITIZENS): ____________
SHOTS, OTHER INFO: ____________
CURRENCY: ____________ CURRENCY CODE: ____________ EXCHANGE RATE: ____________
LANGUAGE(S): ____________
SIZE: ____________ POPULATION: ____________
CLIMATE: ____________
BEST TIME TO VISIT: ____________
MAJOR CITIES/PLACES OF INTEREST: ____________
SPORTS: ____________
RELIGION(S): ____________ GOVERNMENT: ____________
FOOD SPECIALTIES: ____________
BEST BUYS: ____________
SPECIAL INFORMATION: ____________
AIRLINES: ____________ CITY/AIRPORT CODES: ____________
TRANSPORTATION: ____________
SPECIAL HOTELS/RESORTS/MISCELLANEOUS INFO ____________

COUNTRY: ____________ CAPITAL: ____________
DOCUMENTARY REQUIREMENTS (U.S. CITIZENS): ____________
SHOTS, OTHER INFO: ____________
CURRENCY: ____________ CURRENCY CODE: ____________ EXCHANGE RATE: ____________
LANGUAGE(S): ____________
SIZE: ____________ POPULATION: ____________
CLIMATE: ____________
BEST TIME TO VISIT: ____________
MAJOR CITIES/PLACES OF INTEREST: ____________
SPORTS: ____________
RELIGION(S): ____________ GOVERNMENT: ____________
FOOD SPECIALTIES: ____________
BEST BUYS: ____________
SPECIAL INFORMATION: ____________
AIRLINES: ____________ CITY/AIRPORT CODES: ____________
TRANSPORTATION: ____________
SPECIAL HOTELS/RESORTS/MISCELLANEOUS INFO ____________

COUNTRY: ____________ CAPITAL: ____________
DOCUMENTARY REQUIREMENTS (U.S. CITIZENS): ____________
SHOTS, OTHER INFO: ____________
CURRENCY: ____________ CURRENCY CODE: ____________ EXCHANGE RATE: ____________
LANGUAGE(S): ____________
SIZE: ____________ POPULATION: ____________
CLIMATE: ____________
BEST TIME TO VISIT: ____________
MAJOR CITIES/PLACES OF INTEREST: ____________
SPORTS: ____________
RELIGION(S): ____________ GOVERNMENT: ____________
FOOD SPECIALTIES: ____________
BEST BUYS: ____________
SPECIAL INFORMATION: ____________
AIRLINES: ____________ CITY/AIRPORT CODES: ____________
TRANSPORTATION: ____________
SPECIAL HOTELS/RESORTS/MISCELLANEOUS INFO ____________

SOUTH AMERICA

PRACTICE LABELING ON THIS MAP. USE AN ATLAS IF NECESSARY.

SOUTH AMERICA

WHO/WHAT AM I?

1. I am known as the Liberator of South America. ______________________________
2. I am a fish with razor-like teeth. ______________________________
3. I am a dance that is popular in the La Boca District of Buenos Aires. ______________
4. I am a clenched hand that symbolizes good luck. ______________________________
5. I am the official language of Brazil. ______________________________
6. I am the best known ski resort of Chile. ______________________________
7. I am the country whose currency is the guarani. ______________________________
8. I am the world's highest waterfalls. ______________________________
9. I am one of the most popular coastal resorts of Uruguay. ______________________
10. I am a llama-like animal whose products are best buys of Argentina. ______________
11. I am a South American cowboy. ______________________________
12. I am an Alpine-like ski resort in Argentina. ______________________________
13. I am the world's highest capital city. ______________________________
14. I am a notable attraction of Guyana and am five times higher than Niagara Falls. ______________________________
15. I am a Chilean possession in the Pacific. ______________________________
16. I am the base city for excursions into the Mid-Amazon region of Brazil. ____________
17. I am the famous islands off the coast of Ecuador that are popular for naturalists. ______________________________
18. I am the other national language of Peru besides Spanish. __________________
19. I am the currency of Brazil. ______________________________
20. I am the ancient capital city of the Incas. ______________________________

SOUTH AMERICA REVIEW

ANSWERS

1. Machu Picchu, the "Lost City of the Incas" is in
   A. Peru B. Argentina C. Brazil D. Ecuador — 1.______
2. The world's highest capital city is
   A. Lima B. La Paz C. Quito D. Santiago — 2.______
3. Venezuela's economy has a great deal of revenue from
   A. Bananas B. Coffee C. Steel D. Oil — 3.______
4. A country that exports a large amount of meat is
   A. Ecuador B. Uruguay C. Peru D. Colombia — 4.______
5. The city of __________ is located near the Equator.
   A. La Paz B. Bogota C. Caracas D. Quito — 5.______
6. Colombia is a large producer of
   A. Topaz B. Emeralds C. Diamonds D. Rubies — 6.______
7. What is the name of the famous falls located on the border of Brazil and Argentina?
   A. Angel B. Ignatius C. Victor D. Iguassu — 7.______
8. The most convenient way to travel around South America is by
   A. Car B. Rail C. Bus D. Air — 8.______
9. The official language of Brazil is
   A. English B. Portuguese C. Spanish D. French — 9.______
10. The currency of Suriname is the
    A. Franc B. Guilder C. Dollar D. Peso — 10.______
11. The capital of Guyana is
    A. Bogota B. Asuncion C. Cayenne D. Georgetown — 11.______
12. Located in Venezuela ________________ is one of the world's largest national parks.
    A. Amazonia B. Canaima C. Yagua D. Cajas — 12.______
13. Sugar Loaf Mountain and the Corcovado statue of Christ are sights of ______________________.
    A. Portillo B. Sao Paulo C. Brasilia D. Rio de Janeiro — 13.______
14. The Guyana Highlands are known for their resources of
    A. Gold B. Oil C. Coffee D. Coal — 14.______
15. The ________________ Islands off the coast of Argentina are a British Crown Colony.
    A. Falkland B. Galapagos C. Easter D. Margarita — 15.______

SOUTH AMERICA REVIEW

MATCH THE COUNTRIES TO THEIR CAPITALS:

1. ______Bolivia
2. ______Argentina
3. ______Brazil
4. ______Colombia
5. ______Chile
6. ______Paraguay
7. ______Ecuador
8. ______Venezuela
9. ______Suriname
10. ______Uruguay
11. ______French Guiana
12. ______Peru
13. ______Guyana

A. Quito
B. Lima
C. La Paz
D. Buenos Aires
E. Brasilia
F. Cayenne
G. Asuncion
H. Montevideo
I. Georgetown
J. Paramaribo
K. Caracas
L. Santiago
M. Bogota

MATCH THE FOLLOWING CURRENCIES TO THEIR COUNTRIES:

14. ______Nuevo Sol
15. ______Real
16. ______Sucre
17. ______Bolivanio
18. ______Guarani
19. ______Dollar
20. ______French Franc

N. Peru
O. Paraguay
P. Guyana
Q. French Guiana
R. Ecuador
S. Brazil
T. Venezuela

21. Why would it be important for travelers to take it easy the first day or two after arrival in Peru?
____
22. What is a figa? ____
____
23. What are some of the best buys of Ecuador? ____________________
____
24. If visiting Argentina, it's recommended to try dining at a ________________, which is a grill room that serves a variety of barbeque-style dishes.
25. What are some of the symptoms of altitude sickness? ____________
____

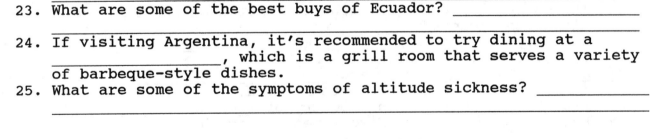

SOUTH AMERICA REVIEW

1. Name three major cities in Brazil. ____
____
2. What is a gaucho? ____
3. ___________________________ was formerly known as British Guiana.
4. What is the name of the island off the coast of French Guiana that was a former penal colony? ____________________________
5. ______________Falls are located on the Brazil and Argentina border.
6. The name of the mountain range that forms the "backbone" of South America is the ___________________________.
7. The major port city of Ecuador is ______________________________.
8. The name of the streets in Buenos Aires famous for shopping are ____________________________ and ______________________________.
9. The highest navigable lake located on the border of Peru and Bolivia is ______________________________.
10. Name the two famous beaches of Rio de Janeiro. _________________ and __________________________
11. What is the name of the island off the coast of Venezuela known as a popular tourist resort? ______________________________
12. The drawings of Nazca are in the country of ___________________.
13. A symbol of good luck called a "figa" is one of the popular gifts to buy in the country of _____________________________.
14. The city of __________________ is an Alpinelike village that is a popular ski resort in Argentina.
15. Name five species that are indigenous to the Galapagos Islands. ____
16. Who is the "Liberator of South America," to whom many statues and plazas are dedicated? _______________________________________
17. The base city on the Amazon River with a famous opera house is __________________.
18. The world's highest waterfall is Angel Falls, located in the country of ________________________.
19. Cartagena and Barranquilla are on the coast of __________________.
20. Two cities that begin with "V," located on the coast of Chile, west of Santiago are _________________________________ and __________________________________.
21. The country that has a beach resort area called Punta del Este along its riviera is ___________________________.
22. The busy port city of _______________________is just a few miles from Caracas, Venezuela.
23. _______________________ and _______________________ are the two landlocked countries of South America.
24. Lake Maracaibo is in the country of _________________________.
25. Kaieteur Falls, about five times higher than Niagara Falls, is located in ____________________.
26. A Chilean possession in the Pacific is __________________________.
27. West of Cuenca, Ecuador is a national reserve called _____________.
28. The ancient capital of the Incas is the city of ___________, Peru.
29. Home of the tango and an older area of Buenos Aires is the district of _________________.
30. The Galapagos Islands consist of ______ major islands.

SOUTH AMERICA

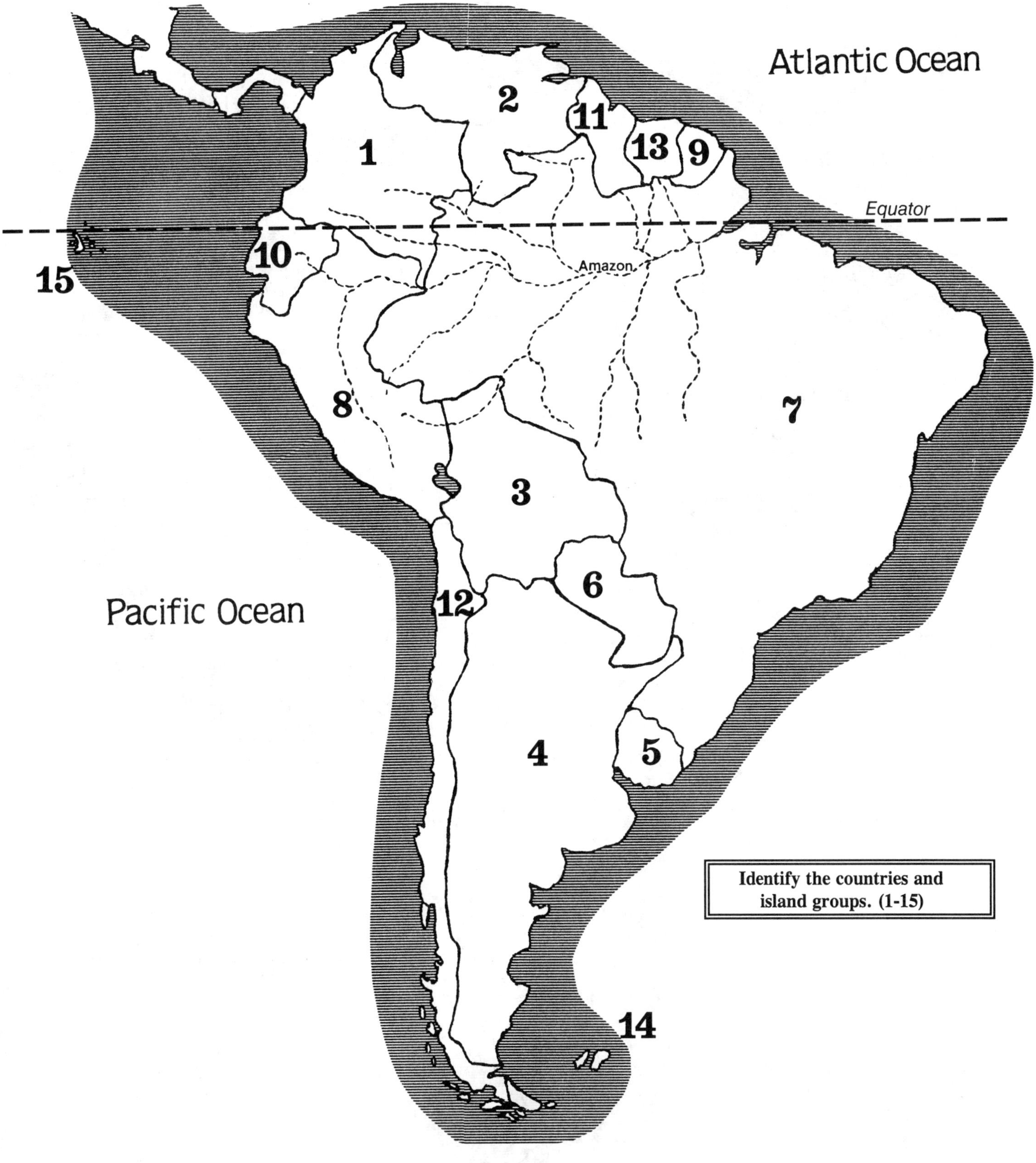

Identify the countries and island groups. (1-15)

SOUTH AMERICA

Identify these capital cities. (1-10)

CHAPTER 12

Europe

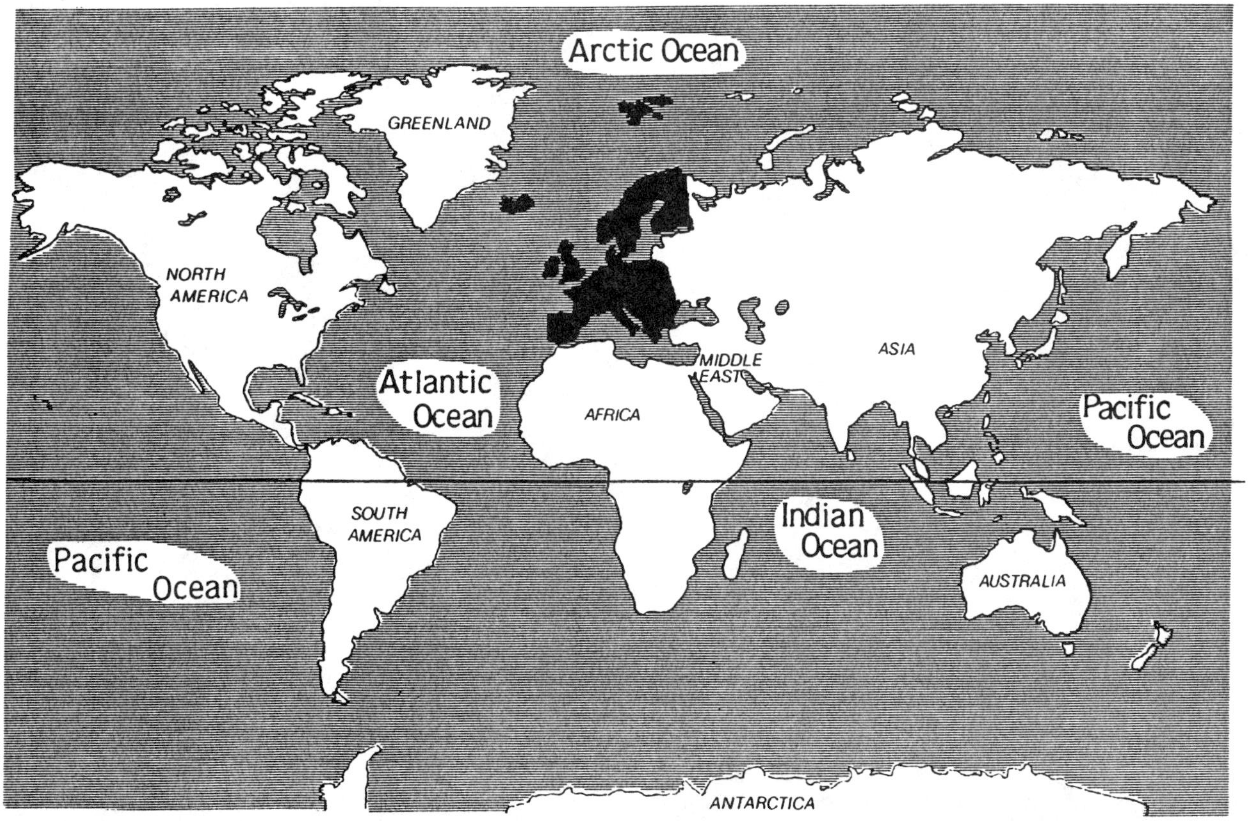

NOTES

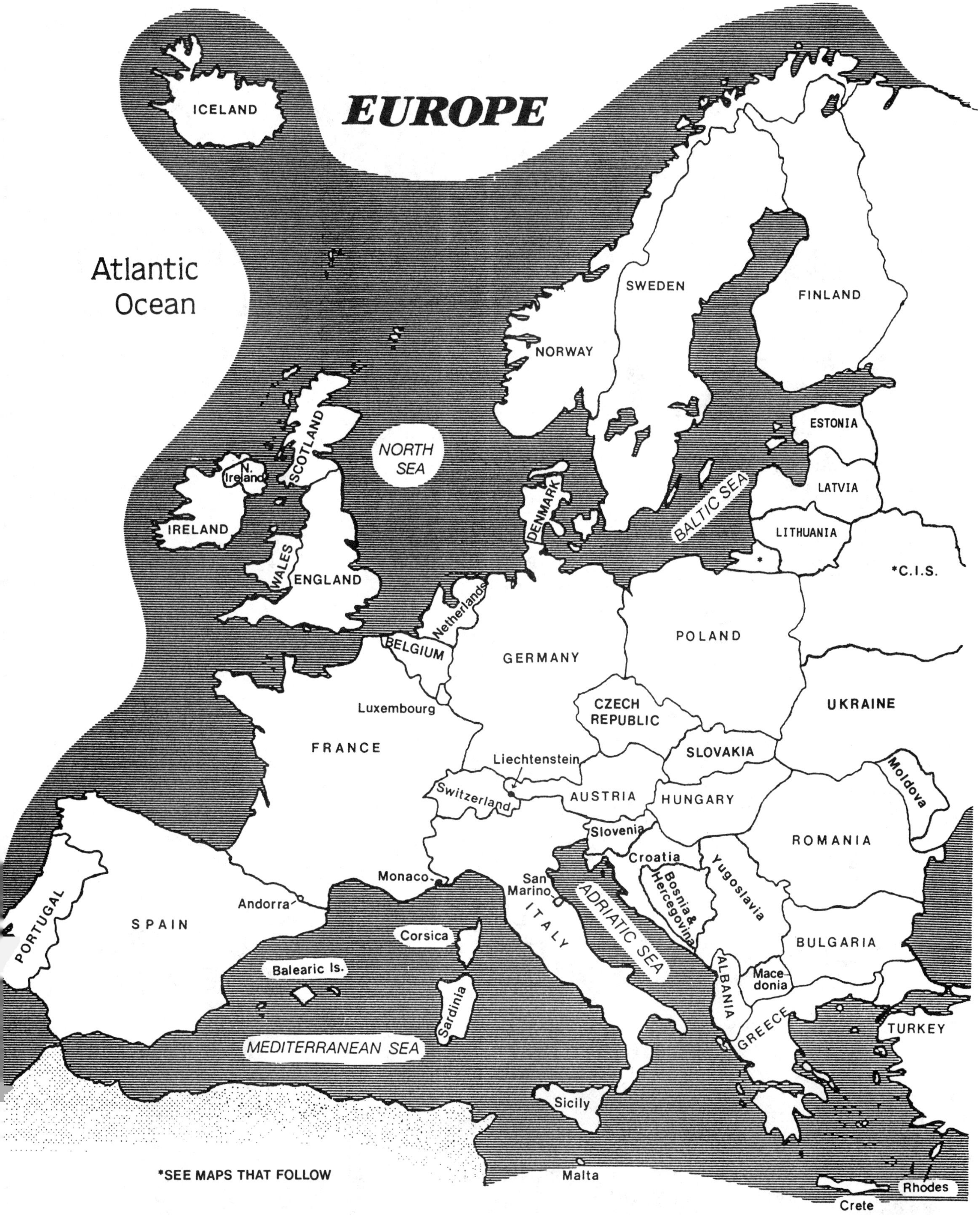
EUROPE
Atlantic Ocean
ICELAND
NORWAY
SWEDEN
FINLAND
ESTONIA
LATVIA
LITHUANIA
*
*C.I.S.
NORTH SEA
BALTIC SEA
SCOTLAND
N. Ireland
IRELAND
WALES
ENGLAND
DENMARK
Netherlands
BELGIUM
Luxembourg
GERMANY
POLAND
UKRAINE
CZECH REPUBLIC
SLOVAKIA
FRANCE
Liechtenstein
Switzerland
AUSTRIA
HUNGARY
Moldova
ROMANIA
Slovenia
Croatia
Bosnia & Hercegovina
Yugoslavia
San Marino
ITALY
ADRIATIC SEA
Monaco
Andorra
PORTUGAL
SPAIN
Corsica
Balearic Is.
Sardinia
MEDITERRANEAN SEA
BULGARIA
ALBANIA
Mace-donia
GREECE
TURKEY
Sicily
Malta
Crete
Rhodes
*SEE MAPS THAT FOLLOW

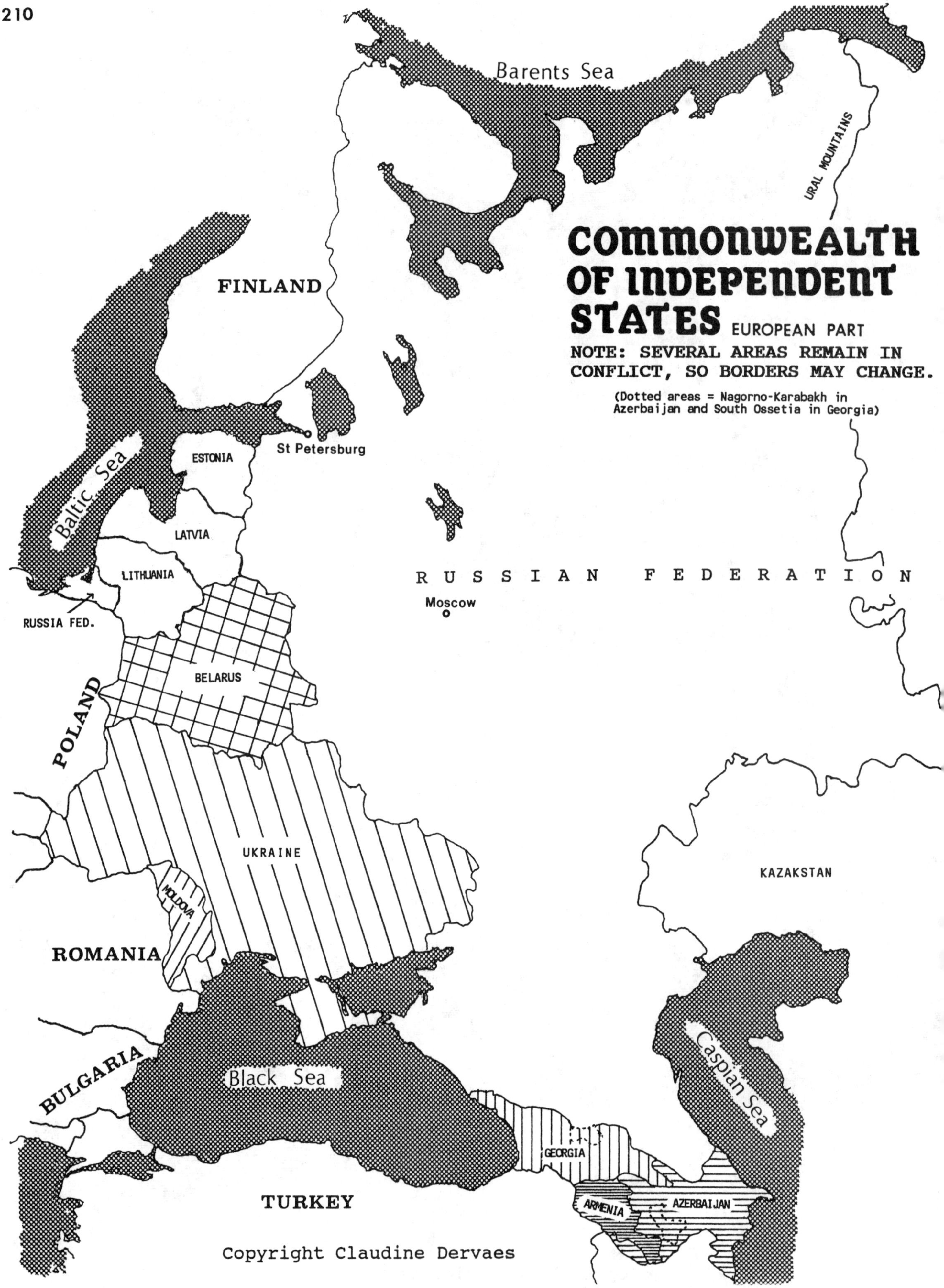

COMMONWEALTH OF INDEPENDENT STATES EUROPEAN PART
NOTE: SEVERAL AREAS REMAIN IN CONFLICT, SO BORDERS MAY CHANGE.
(Dotted areas = Nagorno-Karabakh in Azerbaijan and South Ossetia in Georgia)
Barents Sea
URAL MOUNTAINS
FINLAND
St Petersburg
ESTONIA
Baltic Sea
LATVIA
LITHUANIA
RUSSIA FED.
RUSSIAN FEDERATION
Moscow
BELARUS
POLAND
UKRAINE
MOLDOVA
ROMANIA
KAZAKSTAN
Caspian Sea
Black Sea
BULGARIA
GEORGIA
ARMENIA
AZERBAIJAN
TURKEY

COMMONWEALTH OF INDEPENDENT STATES

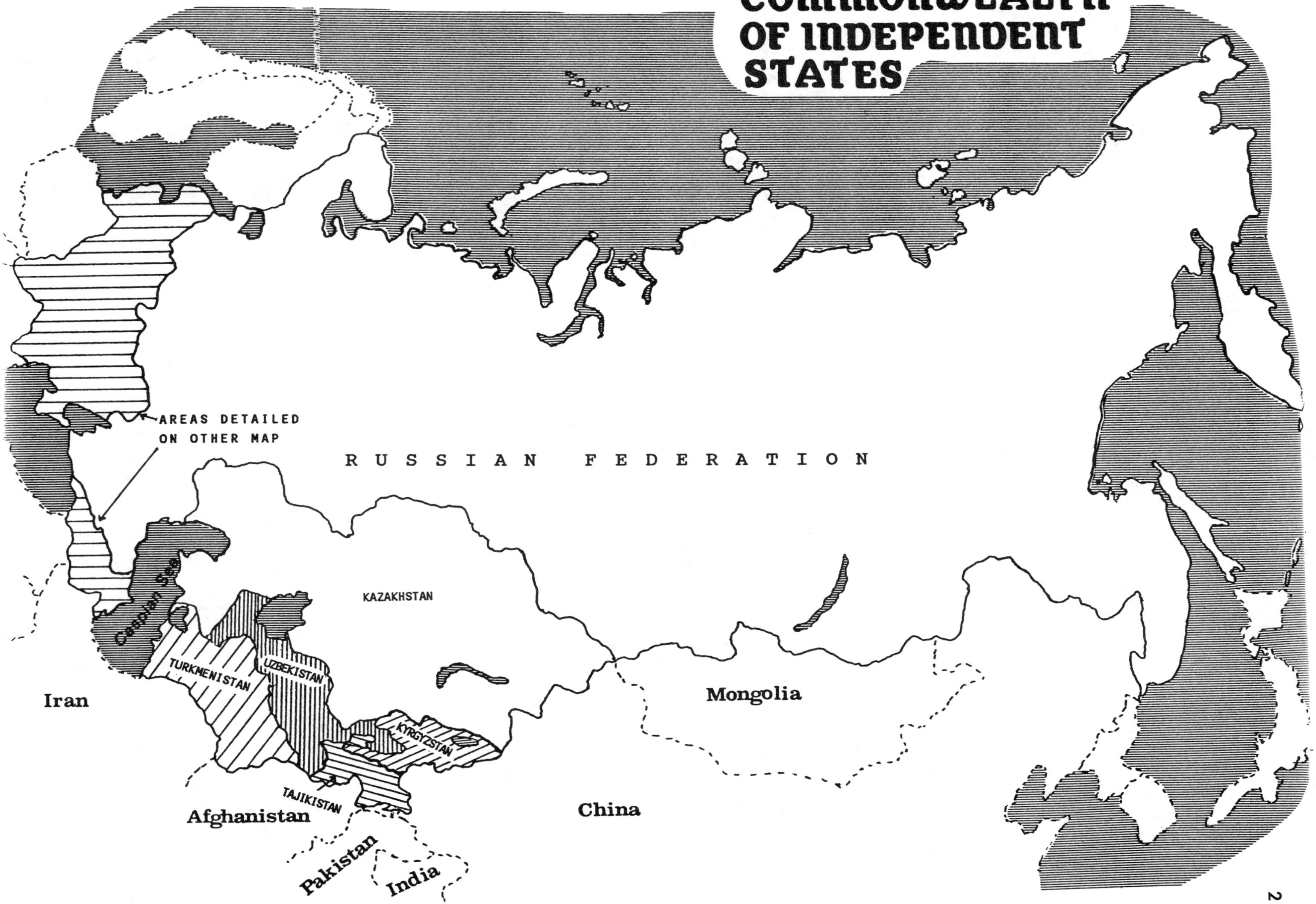

EUROPE - MAJOR CITY/AIRPORT CODES

AUSTRIA
VIE - Vienna
INN - Innsbruck
SZG - Salzburg
GRZ - Graz

BELGIUM
BRU - Brussels

BULGARIA
SOF - Sofia

C.I.S. COMMONWEALTH OF INDEPENDENT STATES
RUSSIA
- MOW - Moscow
- SVO - Moscow (Sheremetyevo)
- VKO - Moscow (Vnukovo)
- DME - Moscow (Domodedovo)
- BKA - Moscow (Bykovo)
- LED - St. Petersburg

UKRAINE
- IEV - Kiev
- KBP - Kiev (Borispol)

BELARUS
- MSQ - Minsk

CZECH REPUBLIC
PRG - Prague

DENMARK
CPH - Copenhagen

ESTONIA
TLL - Tallinn

FINLAND
HEL - Helsinki

FRANCE
PAR - Paris
ORY - Paris/Orly
CDG - Paris/De Gaulle
NCE - Nice
MRS - Marseille

GERMANY
FRA - Frankfurt
DUS - Dusseldorf
HAM - Hamburg
BER - Berlin
MUC - Munich
STR - Stuttgart
CGN - Cologne

GREAT BRITAIN
LON - London
LGW - London/Gatwick
LHR - London/Heathrow
MAN - Manchester
EDI - Edinburgh
BHX - Birmingham
GLA - Glasgow
PIK - Glasgow/Prestwick

GREECE
ATH - Athens
RHO - Rhodes

HUNGARY
BUD - Budapest

ICELAND
REK - Reykjavik

IRELAND
DUB - Dublin
SNN - Shannon

ITALY
ROM - Rome
FCO - Rome/Da Vinci Arpt.
MIL - Milan
VCE - Venice
NAP - Naples

LATVIA
RIX - Riga

LITHUANIA
VNO - Vilnius

LUXEMBOURG
LUX - Luxembourg

NETHERLANDS
AMS - Amsterdam

NORWAY
OSL - Oslo

POLAND
WAW - Warsaw

PORTUGAL
LIS - Lisbon

ROMANIA
BUH - Bucharest

SLOVAKIA/SLOVAK REP.
BTS - Bratislava

SLOVENIA
LJU - Ljubljana

SPAIN
MAD - Madrid
BCN - Barcelona
AGP - Malaga

SWEDEN
STO - Stockholm
BMA - Stockholm (Bromma)
ARN - Stockholm (Arlanda)

SWITZERLAND
ZRH - Zurich
GVA - Geneva
BSL - Basel
BRN - Bern

TURKEY
IST - Istanbul

EUROPE

More than two dozen totally different and contrasting countries make up the continent of Europe - an area less than half the size of North America. The riches of these countries in their museums, churches, cities, landmarks, architecture, history, languages, foods, music, art, and people are an outstanding mix of old and new world elegance. Europe is the "trip of a lifetime" for some, a continual business destination for others, an annual holiday retreat, a journey into history and ancestry, and much, much more.

There is so much to say about each of the countries of Europe, and its popularity as a tourist destination makes it an important area to research and study. Some brief statements about the countries are given here. You should complete profile forms on many of the countries before working through the reviews and tests.

ICELAND - Situated in the North Atlantic, Iceland has fjords, ice fields, volcanoes, hot springs, green valleys - and is not as cold as the name might imply. Its people are some of the most literate in the world; and sagas or storytelling was developed here back in the 12th century. Icelandair is the national airline and the country is just five hours' flight from New York. Reykjavik is the capital and the currency is the krona. The official language is Icelandic, a germanic language that is closely related to Old Norse. English, German, and Danish are widely spoken. The median temperature is 62 degrees Farenheit in July and there is perpetual daylight from May through July. The best buys include: Lopi wool blankets, coats, sweaters, pottery, and souvenirs made of crushed lava. There is no railway system and driving is on the right (Note: roads are mostly gravel rather than paved). Iceland is also the gateway for tours to Greenland and the Faroe Islands (Greenland is only two hours away).

IRELAND - The "Emerald Isle" features destinations such as Dublin, Shannon, Killarney and the Ring of Kerry. There's also Wexford and Waterford, Cork and Blarney (kiss the Blarney Stone at nearby Blarney Castle for the gift of gab). Castle hotels and entertainment, and a country rich in history, folklore, and music - Ireland can be a joy to visit. Ireland is a lush green country, and the capital Dublin contains many outstanding examples of 18th century architecture, wide streets, elegant squares, churches, cathedrals and castles. The River Liffey (spanned by the 165-year-old Halfpenny Bridge) flows through the city to Dublin Bay. The bustling shopping area is around Grafton Street, and the city has many elegant hotels, restaurants, and pubs. Have dinner at the Abbey Tavern - the traditional corned beef or river salmon, followed by lovely Irish ballad music. To the south of the city is the county of Wicklow, the Garden of Ireland, with scenic hills and valleys, quaint villages, classical mansions, and of course, beautiful gardens. Further south and to the east a bit is Kilkenny, a medieval town, with the imposing Kilkenny Castle. The city of Cork in the southwest is an enchanting one, with the River Lee creating two islands in the city's center. Just a few miles from Cork is Blarney Castle. The stone of eloquence is located under the parapet of this ruined castle of the McCarthy clan. One of the legends states that this magical stone exists due to the chivalry of a McCarthy, a worthy but unfortunate man born with a speech impediment. One day while he was walking the grounds of the estate he saw a woman fall into a swift and dangerous stream. He dashed to her rescue and managed to save her. She turned out to be a witch and she granted him one wish - his wish was to speak properly. She told him to go to the stone under the parapet of the castle and kiss it and well, the rest is history. The route along the coast from Cork is particularly scenic - with sheltered harbors and villages flanked by hills and mountains. The Ring of Kerry is a 100 mile route around the Iveragh Peninsula and is one of the great scenic drives. It begins and ends in Killarney, and the Lakes of Killarney live up to their beauty made famous in song and story. The Dingle Peninsula is another natural wonder of the country and is a native Gaelic speaking area. The west of Ireland is the heartland - with stone walled fields, mounds of brown peat, thatched cottages, and red-haired children. Galway is the main city in the west. To the north is the county of Donegal and features the charm of Donegal town, where Donegal tweeds are made - a great buy to bring home. There are famous golf courses that bring many visitors to the country. Other popular sports are fishing and horseback riding (Ireland is famous for its bloodlines and horse racing takes place almost daily from March to September). They say in Ireland that there are no strangers, only friends you haven't met. The country is beautiful, but the attraction for many visitors will be the people - their friendliness, charm, hospitality, lilting speech, and their sense of humor.

NORTHERN IRELAND is part of the United Kingdom, along with England, Scotland, and Wales, and is sometimes referred to as Ulster. The political and religious complexities of the area remain, but the tourist is still welcome here. Visit Giant's Causeway, the astonishing geometric shapes of the basalt rocks, and hear the tale of how they once formed a road for giants. Belfast is the capital - a metropolis of some 400,000 people (nearly a third of the entire population of Northern Ireland). Here's a sample three day tour from Belfast:

DAY 1 - From Belfast harbor quay a ten mile coastal drive ends at medieval Carrickfergus Castle, and then it's 12 miles to Larne. From Larne the scenic Antrim Coast Road winds past the Glens of Antrim and strange rock formations. You'll pass picturesque fishing villages with wayside pubs and tearooms, pretty Murlough Bay (a 4 mile side-trip), Carrick-a-rede Rope Bridge (allow one hour), Giant's Causeway and visitor center. Stay overnight. Total = Approximately 60 miles.

DAY 2 - Your journey now takes you through Roe Valley Country Park, Derry's Walls (allow 40 minutes to walk the walls and 1/2 hour to see Guildhall stained glass), Ulster-American Folk Park, Ulster History Park, Fermanagh Lakeland (call ahead and reserve a late afternoon cruise). Stay overnight around Enniskillen. Total = 105 miles.

DAY 3 - Tour the "plantation" castles at Monea and Tully, Enniskillen Keep (museum), Clogher Valley, Armagh Mall and two cathedrals - both called St. Patrick, and Hillsborough village (with its Georgian town-houses and 18th-century fort). Stay overnight in the Belfast area. Total = 120 miles.

UNITED KINGDOM AND IRELAND

GREAT BRITAIN Q. AND A.

Q. What exactly does the area of Great Britain include?
A. *Great Britain is England, Scotland, and Wales.*

Q. Why is it such a popular destination?
A. *Great Britain offers history and scenery. It is a "heritage" place for many Americans and the language is the same (although there are a lot of different words, expressions, and pronunciations). The countries enjoy a high standard of living, the people are nice, transportation standards and availability are excellent, cities are clean, tourist services and facilities are very good. Health standards are excellent.*

Q. What kind of entertainment is there?
A. *Besides all the restaurants, nightclubs, discos, movie theaters, shopping districts, theaters, and spectator sporting events there are fairs, concerts, and world-famous tournaments, conventions, and shows.*

Q. Are there tourist information centers available?
A. *Yes. While traveling look for the distinctive "i" for information centers that are located throughout the countries.*

Q. Do you have to go through customs between the countries?
A. *There are no formalities between England, Scotland, and Wales.*

Q. Is the electricity the same as the U.S.?
A. *No, U.S. appliances will need transformers. Most outlets are 200 - 250 volts, A.C. 50 cycles. The U.S. generally has 120 volt, 60 cycle electricity.*

Q. What about driving conditions?
A. *Driving is on the left and in major cities or on the M-ways (Motorways) traffic can be really busy. In addition to driving on the left, the steering wheels of almost all cars will be on the right. If driving a stick shift car (not automatic transmission) it can make for a very confusing time at first. Roads can be narrow through small villages. Careful consideration and practice are a must. "Roundabouts" or traffic circles keep the cars moving at intersections - when approaching a roundabout slow down and yield to the traffic on the right. In towns, pedestrians have the right of way at designated crossings.*

Q. Do I have to exchange monies?
A. *Yes. You can exchange monies at banks, airports, train stations, post offices and change bureaus. Banks are usually the best for rates of exchange. You may also want to use a major credit card for purchases as the exchange rates for those purchases may be very good. You may want to call your credit card company first to ask questions about any purchases abroad.*

ENGLAND, SCOTLAND, AND WALES - the area known as Great Britain and part of the United Kingdom, are some of the most popular destinations for U.S. tourists, because of the links to the U.S. in history and culture. London is the New York City of **ENGLAND**, and one of the most expensive capital cities. Even though the sights in London are so numerous, the tourist should allow time for visiting some areas of the countryside - to appreciate more of what the country has to offer. In London there's Big Ben, the Tower of London, Westminster Abbey, the Houses of Parliament, Trafalgar Square, Picadilly Circus, Hyde Park, the British Museum, then shopping on Oxford, Regent, and Bond Streets - it's hard to have time to do it all. Big Ben is the clock tower above Parliament and it is one of the most famous landmarks of the city. The Tower of London, which houses the royal family's crown jewels, dates back to 1066. Among the scores of people who were beheaded in the Tower were Sir Thomas More, two of Henry VIII's wives (Anne Boleyn and Catherine Howard), and the Earl of Essex. Queen Elizabeth I was imprisoned here and Sir Walter Raleigh spent 13 years in the Tower. The traditional Beefeaters, resplendent in their Tudor-style uniforms are the Yeoman Warders of the Tower. During the summer there may be a three or four hour wait to see the jewels. Westminster Abbey is where all but two of England's kings and queens have been crowned. Trafalgar Square, commemorating Nelson's defeat of the French at the Battle of Trafalgar in 1805, is dominated by a statue of that naval hero, atop a column 185 ft. high. The square is also dominated by hoards of pigeons. Picadilly Circus, ablaze with lights and the statue of Eros in bronze, is the Times Square of London. Leading from Picadilly is St. James's Street and the great houses bordering St. James Park. At one end of the park is Buckingham Palace, where the Changing of the Guards ceremony takes place daily at 11:30 am (alternate days in winter) and lasts for about a half-hour. Hyde Park, with its acres of grass, trees, and flowers, is a place to relax. It is also known for the famous Speaker's Corner, where on Sundays, anyone can get on a soapbox, milk crate, ladder or chair and say whatever they want to say! Only treason and obscenity is illegal. The British Museum has one of the world's truly great collections. Oxford Street has the great department stores, Marks & Spencer, Selfridges, C & A, and a multitude of budget shops, clothing boutiques and souvenir shops. Past the junction of Oxford Circus you'll be at the top edge of Mayfair - heart of London's affluent resindents. Here are more attractive squares: Grosvenor and Berkeley Squares. Along the edge facing Hyde Park are the grand hotels: the Dorchester, the Grosvenor, Inn on the Park, Claridges, and more. The Thames River (pronounced "Temz") winds through the city and there is a nice walk to take from Lambeth Palace westward. You'll pass County Hall, the Hayward Gallery and National Film Theater. Then pass under Waterloo Bridge to reach the modern National Theater. From Waterloo Bridge you will have one of the finest views of London.

THE TUBE

The London transport system serves an area of 700 square miles and nearly every house and apartment within the Greater London area is served by public transport. The underground or "tube" is the quickest and easiest way to get around London. Trains run every few minutes between 5:30 am and midnight. Tickets may be bought at station ticket offices or from one of the automatic machines. Most machines list the destinations and cost of the journey. Most stations have automatic barriers - simply insert your ticket to open the gate. Remember to take your ticket if the machine gives it back to you for onward travel. KEEP YOUR TICKET SAFE AS YOU WILL NEED TO HAND IT IN AT YOUR FINAL DESTINATION.

TIPS ABOUT TRAVELING IN THE U.K.

ACCOMMODATIONS: The traveler can pick from a variety of hotels, quaint inns, castles, estates, farmhouses and there are lots of B & B (Bed and Breakfast) properties. Advance reservations for accommodations are recommended if traveling during the summer. If you don't have places reserved, be sure to stop at the information centers (look for distinctive "i" signs) - many times the staff can recommend and reserve accommodations for you there - and they will give directions! If a breakfast is included in the price of accommodations, it can be a Continental breakfast (rolls/toast and coffee/juice) or it can be an English Breakfast.

ENGLISH BREAKFAST - Not short on calories, the typical English breakfast consists of: two eggs, one rasher of bacon, grilled tomatoes, fried mushrooms, baked beans, one black pudding sausage, one British sausage (banger), slice of fried bread, two slices of toast, butter, marmalade, jam and jelly, tea or coffee. Talk about setting you up for the day - wow!

THE PUBS

Pubs are unique British institutions. And like many institutions, they are both admirable and eccentric. They serve beer, wine, liquor, and most have "pub lunches" which offer reasonable fare for the midday meal. Very few pubs will serve food in the evening, however. Children under 14 are not allowed in pubs (pubs that have gardens may allow children). Beer comes in two sizes - pints and half-pints. British beer is famous and there are stouts, porters, lagers, bitters, and ales. And it's not warm - it's simply cellar temperature - about 50 degrees. What is on the pub lunch menu? Bangers and mash (sausages and mashed potatoes), steak and kidney pie (steak and kidney in gravy baked in a pastry), fish and chips (fried fish with french fries), ploughman's lunch (ham, cheese, pickles, garnish, granary bread), prawn salad (shrimps in a mayonnaise type salad), shepherd's pie (ground beef, vegetables, and mashed potatoes cooked in a pastry), and more. Starters (appetizers) or smaller meals can be "jacket potatoes" (baked potatoes filled with a variety of choices - chili, cheese, ground beef, vegetables, etc.), sausage rolls (sausages baked in pastry dough), pates - just to name a few. The popular meal on Sunday is roast beef/pork and gravy, yorkshire pudding (like a popover), roast and mashed potatoes with peas/brussels sprouts. A popular dessert is trifle (a mixture of sponge cake, fruit, wine, jello, custard, and cream). Stopping for a drink in the pubs is very popular. The locals have their "local," the pub they frequent quite often. It really is a form of entertainment for many people who live in Britain - as all the friends and neighbors, fellow workers or business associates can meet and discuss things in a friendly and inviting atmosphere. There may be darts or pool tables, there is often a juke box (CD player), and it can get pretty thick with smoke - depending on the ventilation, Pubs are usually pleasantly decorated with comfortable bar stools, chairs or booths, lots of wood and brass, and wallpaper and carpeting that tend to give a "welcoming" look.

"QUEUES" are lines and "queueing up" is as British as Big Ben. Based on the ancient motto "first come, first served," queueing is an aspect of social democracy. If a Brit wants to catch a bus or take a train or make a call or purchase tickets or merchandise, he queues. So when in London, do as the British do, queue up. And whatever you do, don't queue jump (cut in line)!

YOU MAY BE SURPRISED TO HEAR ALL THE DIFFERENT WORDS AND EXPRESSIONS USED IN GREAT BRITAIN. TRY AND MATCH THE BRITISH ENGLISH WORDS BELOW WITH THE AMERICAN ENGLISH WORDS:

_____1. LIFT	A. WINDSHIELD
_____2. BISCUIT (SWEET)	B. CAR HOOD
_____3. LOO	C. POTATO CHIPS
_____4. FORTNIGHT	D. TELEVISION
_____5. MATE	E. MAIL
_____6. JUMPER	F. PULLOVER SWEATER
_____7. TELLY	G. APARTMENT
_____8. BONNET	H. SOCCER
_____9. FOOTBALL	I. ELEVATOR
____10. BOOT	J. BATHROOM
____11. BOBBY	K. COOKIE
____12. WINDSCREEN	L. BUDDY
____13. CRISPS	M. CHECK
____14. FLAT	N. ROUND TRIP
____15. TICK	O. TWO WEEKS
____16. RETURN	P. BUSY
____17. CALL BOX	Q. POLICE OFFICER
____18. ENGAGED	R. CAR TRUNK
____19. FAG	S. CIGARETTE
____20. POST	T. PHONE BOOTH

Note: If you are interested, Solitaire Publishing has a U.K. to U.S.A Dictionary as a reference for travelers between the U.S. and Britain.

HOW DO YOU SAY...

Bournemouth	=	Borne muth
Derby	=	Darby
Edinburgh	=	Edin boro
Glasgow	=	Glaz go
Gloucester	=	Gloss ter
Harwich	=	Ha ritch
Holyhead	=	Holly head
Leicester	=	Lester
Luton	=	Looten
Norwich	=	Norrich
Peterborough	=	Peter boro
Reading	=	Redding
Salisbury	=	Sols bury
Slough	=	Slou

COMPARISON MEASURES
Imperial pint = approx. 20 ounces
U.S. pint = 16 ounces
Imperial gallon = 160 fluid ounces
U.S. gallon = 128 fluid ounces
The U.S. gallon is about 4/5 of the U.K. gallon

Here is a brief list of places of interest in **ENGLAND:**

SOUTHERN ENGLAND

Canterbury - Canterbury Cathedral and the spiritual center of the Anglican religion. The place where Thomas à Beckett was murdered and the destination of Chaucer's pilgrims.

Dover - Famous for the white cliffs and the port for ferry, hovercraft, and hydrofoil services to the continent of Europe.

Brighton - A seaside resort, often crowded in the summer. The Royal Pavilion, antique shops, nightclubs, and a boardwalk along the shoreline are the resort's features.

Southampton - This ancient and historic port is a busy commercial and industrial center. The New Forest, adjacent to the harbor is one of the best preserved woodland areas with a large variety of birds and is famous for its wild ponies.

Salisbury - The plateau of the Salisbury Plain is dominated by Salisbury Cathedral, with its 404 ft. high spire being visible for miles. Stonehenge is nearby with its prehistoric monuments.

Bournemouth - A popular seaside resort.

Devon and Cornwall - An area of rugged coastline and great scenery.

Bristol and Bath - In the lively port city of Bristol you'll find Cabot Tower - built to commemorate John Cabot's discovery of North America. Bath, a spa town of 18th-century streets and terraces, is famous for its natural hot springs and Roman Baths.

OXFORD AND THE COTSWOLDS

Oxford - This famous university city is worth visiting to walk the grounds of the university's 28 colleges, as well as to visit the town's bookstores, museums, historic buildings, pubs and restaurants.

Windsor - Windsor Castle.

Gloucester - A fine medieval cathedral.

SHAKESPEARE COUNTRY

Stratford-upon-Avon - Second in popularity only to London for visitors, it is here you will see Anne Hathaway's cottage, Shakespeare's birthplace and Trinity Church.

Warwick - Warwick Castle gives you an idea of what life was like in those times - there are wax figures in some of the rooms and dungeon artifacts.

EAST ANGLIA

Norwich - This beautiful city with a fine cathedral, castle (with a museum and art gallery), and medieval houses, is a good center for boating on the Norfolk broads.

Great Yarmouth and Lowestoft - Popular seaside resorts.

Cambridge - A picturesque town also known for its university.

SAMPLE 8 DAY HOSTED TOUR - IN AND OUT OF LONDON

This tour provides several opportunities for exploring sights and shops on your own.

DAY 1 - Arrive at Gatwick airport. After clearing customs and immigration you will be met by our courier (tour escort) and transferred to the London Metropole Hotel where your accommodation has been reserved (a twin-bedded room with bath, continental breakfast, service, and VAT included). The rest of your day is at leisure.

DAY 2 - You will be transported from your hotel at 9:00 am for a morning sightseeing tour of London. The afternoon and evening are free.

DAY 3 - At 9:00 am your motorcoach will depart your hotel for a full day of touring - we will be visiting Windsor and Hampton Court. The evening is free.

DAY 4 - Departing at 8:00 am, today's journey will take you to Stratford-upon-Avon and Warwick Castle. There will be a lunch stop at the famous Shakespeare Hotel. The evening is again free to dine at one of London's great restaurants and enjoy the theater, pubs, or nightclubs.

DAY 5 - Morning and afternoon are free. This evening we will dine at the Cockney Tavern - a four course dinner, plus cabaret and dancing.

DAY 6 - The day is free for you to shop and sightsee. Have afternoon tea. Your host can provide you with suggestions and details on whatever you might wish to do.

DAY 7 - You'll depart the hotel at 9:00 am to be transferred to the Metropole Hotel in Brighton, where accommodations have been reserved (twin-bedded room with private bath, continental breakfast, service and VAT included). At 2:15 pm we will depart for a tour of the Royal Pavilion and a walking tour of The Lanes (famous antique area). This evening will feature a gala dinner (cocktails will be served in the hotel foyer at 7:00 pm).

DAY 8 - The transfer to Gatwick airport for your flight home will pick you up at the hotel at 9:30 am. Please ensure that all extras are settled at the hotel prior to departure.

Thank you for experiencing London and a sample of England with us. We hope that you will return again and again to explore the many other areas of sights of our country, along with Wales and Scotland!

MIDLANDS

Birmingham - An industrial center with an extensive road and rail network, plus cultural buildings such as the Library, Cathedral, and Theater.

Coventry - Rich in history. Visit the new Cathedral.

Nottingham - The Council House, Castle, and Nottingham Playhouse. North of Nottingham is Sherwood Forest (of Robin Hood fame).

MARCHER LANDS

Ludlow - There are hills on either side of the city and a fine castle.

NORTHERN ENGLAND

Special emphasis is given now to Northern England because this area's historic cities, bustling market towns, and some of the country's most inspiring landscapes are worth detail. The National Parks of Northumberland, the Lake District, the North York Moors, the Yorkshire Dales, and the Peak District are designated areas of natural beauty.

Lake District - Rugged mountains, tranquil lakes, sheltered valleys.

North York Moors - Vast expanse of heather moorland with a spectacular coastline.

Yorkshire Dales - Renowned for their impressive limestone scenery.

Northumberland National Park and Hadrian's Wall - Remote hilly country and part of a rich Roman heritage.

Peak District - Contrasting scenery, with wild peat moorland in the north and a softer landscape of pastureland in the south.

CITIES: Chester - Walled city with famous Tudor-style black and white buildings and two-tier shops known as "The Rows."

Helmsley, Keswick, Skipton, and Stockton - Colorful market towns where you will find local goods and produce offered in a way that has changed little over the centuries.

Liverpool - Known because of the Beatles, the city has some worthwhile art galleries and museums.

Manchester - Vibrant city with many attractions.

Durham, Beverly, Ripon, Carlisle, Lancaster. Kendal, Penrith, Alnwick, and Berwick-upon-Tweed - Historic towns and cities that combine modern development with old world charm. Walk the narrow streets and admire the scenery and lifestyle of Britain in this legendary area.

Blackpool - Premier holiday resort and seaside town.

Haworth - Home to the Bronte sisters, who were inspired by the wild, bleak moors of this area.

York - This city preserves many fascinating reminders of its historic past with its cathedrals, abbeys, museums (particularly the Castle Museum). Visit the Shambles, originally the medieval street of butchers which now houses an interesting array of shops.

Off the west coast and accessible by ferry is the Isle of Man, where a 100-mile coastline of towering cliffs and silver sands matches the beauty of a mountainous landscape with river glens inland.

SCOTLAND

Scotland is the northernmost part of Great Britain. Smaller than England and with fewer people, the country is divided geographically into three regions: highlands, lowlands, and southern uplands. The capital is Edinburgh. It's a beautiful city with the imposing 12th-century Edinburgh Castle dominating the heart of the city. The Royal Mile is a cobblestone street which runs from the castle to the Palace of Holyroodhouse. Holyroodhouse was the home of Mary, Queen of Scots for six years and the scene of many dramatic events in her life. Princes Street is lined with shops and many fine buildings. Parallel to Princes Street is Rose Street, which is lined with pubs. To the north is New Town, an area of Georgian streets and squares, preserved in elegant condition. Edinburgh's museums include the National Gallery of Scotland, National Museum of Antiquities, the Royal Scottish Museum, and the Museum of Childhood. While visiting the castle, stop in at the Camera Obscura for a unique experience of viewing the city. Also stop in at the Scotch Whisky Heritage Centre for a guided tour. St. Giles Cathedral and John Knox House are other sights on most tours of the city. In August the city reverberates to the sounds of the spectacular Military Tattoo held every year at the castle. Drawing participants and spectators from all over the world, this display of massed bands and military precision coincides with the Edinburgh International Festival. North of Edinburgh in Fife is St. Andrews - home of golf. Continuing further north along the coast is Aberdeen, a city built largely of granite. Nearby is Braemar, site of the Royal Highland Games. Inverness, situated near the head of Loch Ness, is considered the capital of the highlands. The Scottish Highlands contain some of the most breathtaking scenery in the British Isles. Ben Nevis, at 4,406 ft., is the highest mountain, and round its south and west flanks is Glen Nevis, one of the most beautiful valleys in Scotland. Fort William is one of the best known towns on this coast. The scenic "Road to the Isles" will bring you to Mallaig, where you can take a ferry to the Isle of Skye. The Clan Donald Centre here will give you insight into 13 centuries of clan history. If time permits and you are touring by car, the Northwest Highlands area is one of spectacular scenery - wild and desolate with dramatic mountains and vast sea lochs. See the limestone caverns at Smoo Cave at Durness and the strange shattered tops of Stac Polly just north of Ullapool. Back down the west coast, you can visit Glasgow, Scotland's largest city and a major cultural center. And down near the border with England is Gretna Green. For 100 years Gretna Hall and the blacksmiths at Gretna Green were the first places over the Scottish border that couples could be married without parental consent. Clandestine marriages of this kind were prevented in England by an 18th-century law, but in Scotland it was only necessary for the couple to make a witnessed declaration that they wished to become man and wife. A law passed in 1856 that made a requirement of three weeks' residence in Scotland, and in 1940 a law was passed that prevented the village blacksmiths from performing the ceremony.

WHAT'S HAGGIS?

A food specialty of Scotland is haggis. This dish is made of the heart, liver, lungs, etc. of a sheep minced with oatmeal, suet, and onions, packed into a sheep's stomach and boiled.

WALES
Like Scotland, Wales can be divided into three regions: South Wales, with Cardiff (the capital), Swansea, Newport, Camarthen Bay, and the Brecon Beacons; Mid-Wales, with the Cambrian Mountains and coastal resorts of Cardigan Bay; and North Wales, with the Llandudno and Rhyl resorts, the island of Anglesey, and Snowdonia National Park. Here is a brief outline of cities and sights of the country.

Cardiff - Capital and principal seaport. There are charming Edwardian shopping arcades, many theaters, several museums, and Cardiff Castle.

Swansea - Home town of poet Dylan Thomas. The city of Laugharne is where Dylan spent 16 years of his life.

Carmarthen - Believed to be the oldest town in Wales, it is romantically associated with the Arthurian wizard Merlin.

Fishguard - A ferry port for Ireland.

Aberystwyth - University town with splendid views of the Cardigan Bay coastline.

Portmeirion - The fascinating village that was the setting for the cult television series, The Prisoner.

Llanberis - Starting point for the Snowdon Mountain Railway. Snowdonia National Park is 840 square miles of beautiful countryside.

Caernarfon - Home to the most famous Welsh castle, where Prince Charles was invested as the Prince of Wales in 1969.

Holyhead - Ferry port to Ireland.

Llanfair PG - An abbreviation for its real name, whose 58 letters make it the longest place name in the world.

Beaumaris - Excellent leisure facilities and one of the nicest castles in Wales.

Conwy - Another very impressive castle, complete with medieval town walls. While in the town, check out the smallest house in Britain.

Llandudno and Rhyl - Popular seaside resorts.

Llangollen - Set in a forested landscape overlooking the River Dee, the city is the setting for the International Musical Eisteddfod.

LLANFAIR PG - This abbreviation stands for the longest place name in the world - which is

LLANFAIRPWLLGWYNGYLLGOGERYCHWYRNDROBWLLLLANTYSILIOGOGOGOCH

which stands for : St. Mary's Church in the hollow of the white hazel near to the rapid whirlpool of Llantysilio of the red cave

REVIEW ON IRELAND, NORTHERN IRELAND, ENGLAND, SCOTLAND, AND WALES

1. Give three reasons people might like to visit Great Britain. ______________________
____
____
2. Selfridges and Marks and Spencer are
   A. Castles B. Cathedrals C. Department Stores D. Parks Answer _____
3. Giant's Causeway is in the country of ________________________.
4. What stone do you kiss for the gift of eloquence? ________________
5. The ____________________________ is guarded by the Beefeaters, or Yeoman Warders.
6. Speaker's Corner is in __________ Park, and you can hear people stating their ideas or opinions on _____________ (what day of the week).
7. The city famous for its white cliffs is _______________.
8. Stonehenge is near ____________________, England.
9. The Edinburgh International Festival and Military Tattoo is held in the month of ____________________.
10. The Palace of _______________________ in Edinburgh is where Mary Queen of Scots lived for six years.
11. The largest city in Scotland and a major cultural center is _______________.
12. From Mallaig you can take a ferry to the Isle of __________.
13. The famous street in Edinburgh for shops and fine buildings is _____________ Street.
14. The fascinating village in Wales that provided the setting for the cult television series called *The Prisoner* is _________________________.
15. The Ring of Kerry starts and ends in _________________, Ireland.
16. The river that runs through the city of Dublin is the River _______________.
17. ____________________ is the capital of Northern Ireland.
18. Birmingham is in the Lake District. True or False _____________
19. A walled city with famous Tudor-style black and white buildings and two-tier shops called "The Rows" is the city of _________________.
20. Galway is located on the Irish Sea. True or False ___________
21. The River _______________ runs through the city of London.
22. Name four of the famous sights of London. _________________________
____
23. The Bronte sisters were inspired by the wild, bleak moors in the area of ____________________.
24. The capital of Wales is _____________________.
25. Llanberis is a starting point for excursions into ________________ National Park.

FRANCE

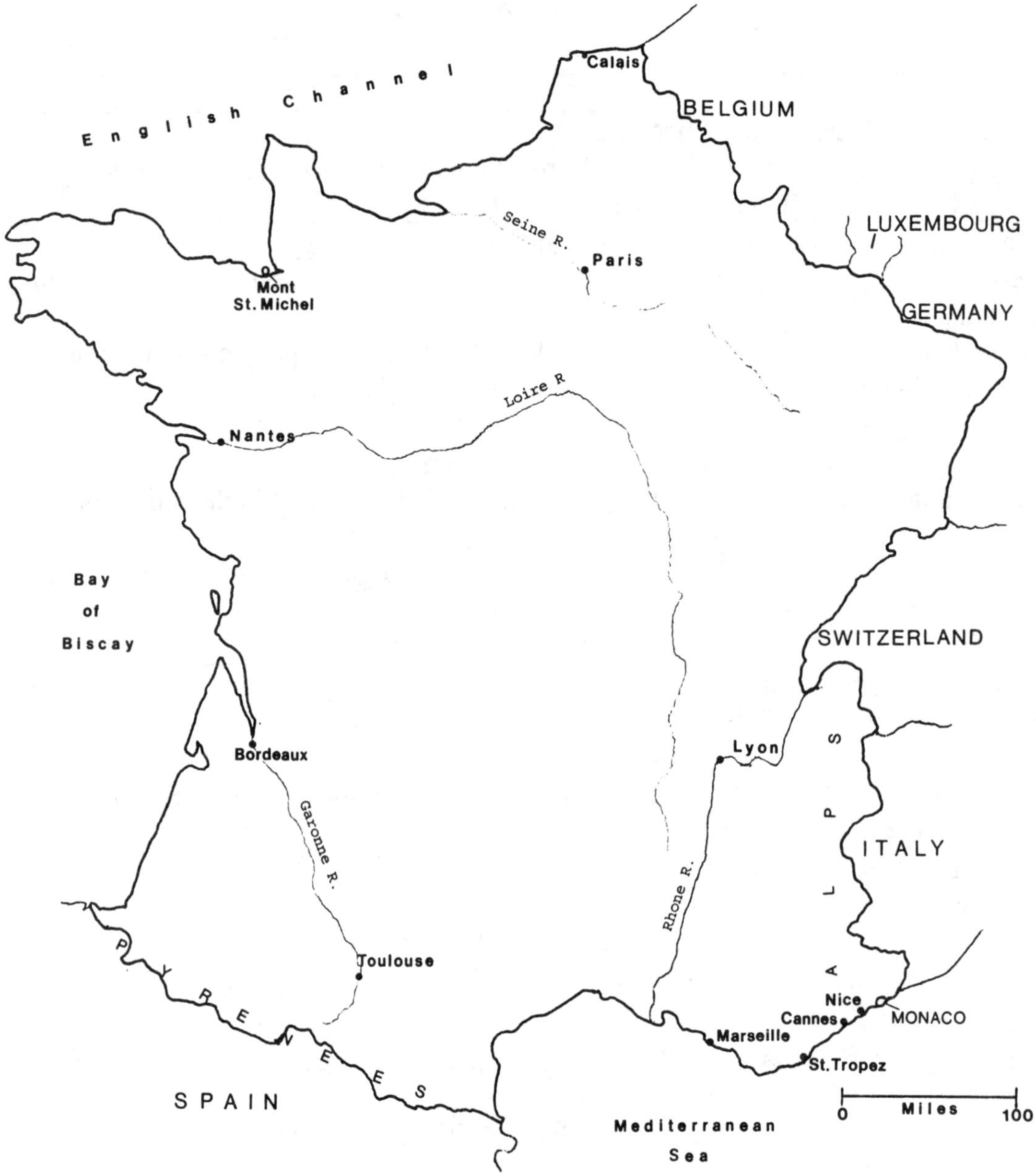

SAMPLE TOUR ITINERARY
Day 1 - Overnight flight to Paris. *Day 2 & 3 - Sightsee in Paris.* *Day 4 - Day trip to Versailles.* *Day 5 - Drive to Mont St. Michel.* *Day 6 - Go through Brittany and the Loire Valley.* *Day 7 - Chateaux Country sightseeing.* *Day 8 - Loire Valley, Chartres, back to Paris.* *Day 9 - Flight home.*

FRANCE certainly cannot be summed up by Paris alone, in the same way that London does not typify the rest of England. Gourmet foods, wines, high fashion, art, and an exciting cosmopolitan city await the tourist who visits Paris. The Eiffel Tower, Cathedral of Notre Dame, the River Seine, the parks and gardens (such as Bois de Boulogne, Bois de Vincennes, Jardin des Tuileries), Louvre Museum, and walking the Champs d'Elysees from the Place de la Concorde to the Arc de Triomphe - after even a few of these sights you'll want to relax at a sidewalk cafe (try the Boulevard St. Michel or Boulevard St. Germain des Pres). The city has an extensive and inexpensive metro/subway network, as well as an efficient rapid transit system. The Rive Gauche (Left Bank) contains the area known as the Latin Quarter - an area of book shops, commercial art galleries and a focus of student activity as the Sorbonne is here. There are more than 80 museums and over 150 art galleries in Paris. Of course the Louvre is the most famous and is home to the Mona Lisa and the Venus de Milo. This huge museum houses more than 350,000 works of art. In the courtyard is the massive plexiglass pyramid designed by I.M. Pei - the well-known American architect. There's also the Georges Pompidou Center, Rodin Museum, Cluny Museum, and the Orsay Museum. A pass that is good at 65 museums and monuments in and around Paris can be purchased at participating museums or the main Paris Tourist Office.

For the first time visitor to Paris with only a couple of days, the organized sightseeing tours are best. After that, however, it is great to explore the city on foot - with a thorough map at your side. The best approach to the Ile de la Cite, the tiny island that began as a village called Lutetia, is by the Pont Neuf, the oldest bridge (completed in 1604). At the statue of Henry IV, turn left at the Place Dauphine, walk around the Palace de Justice and into the court where the Sainte Chapelle stands. A short walk from here will bring you to the Cathedral of Notre Dame. Don't miss a walk through the cathedral garden and across the bridge to the Ile St. Louis for some romantic views of the Seine. It's just a step over to the Rive Gauche (Left Bank) and the Latin Quarter. Deeper into the Left Bank is the Rue Mouffetard market - a madhouse of foodstalls and vendors selling wares. Further west is the Eiffel Tower, 1,000 feet high and the symbol of Paris. Then visit the Church of the Invalides, with its gold dome it is quite beautiful. Over to the Right Bank, visit the Palais-Royal, Paris's Opera House and Museum, the Georges Pompidou Center and the National Museum of Modern Art. The last "must" on your tour of the Right Bank is the Basilica of the Sacre Coeur, which dominates all of Paris from the heights of Montmartre. SAFETY WARNING: Paris is a big and very populated city - and as such your "walking tours" are best taken during the day. Muggings, pickpockets, and roaming gypsies (often ragged-looking children who distract you while their buddies rip you off) are frequent problems for the police.

Getting to France from England has become easier and faster with the "Chunnel" - Channel Tunnel. There is also ferry and hovercraft service from Dover to Calais (and Boulogne). EuroTunnel (a private Anglo-French coporation) owns and operates the Channel Tunnel and Le Shuttle. Le Shuttle is a modern freight train service that provides transportation for people with cars, trucks, and motorcycles. The Eurostar passenger train service (a joint venture of French, British and Belgian rail services) runs between Paris' Gare du Nord, London's Waterloo Station, and Brussels' Midi Terminal. Eurostar service can whisk passengers from London to Paris in three hours.

To the west of Paris is St. Germain-en-Laye, the birthplace of Louis XIV and now a chic suburb. The magnificent Palace of Versailles is another must for visitors. Commissioned by Louis XIV some 40,000 workers built this most lavish dwelling in Europe. Another day trip can be made to Chartres, the site of one of Europe's most famous cathedrals. To the southeast of Paris, Fountainbleau, an official residence to a long line of France's leaders, is filled with history. There may be some tourists who wish to visit Disneyland Paris but be aware that it's more expensive than the Disney theme parks in the U.S. To the north of Paris is St. Denis - the world's first Gothic structure and an important stop on the pilgrim trail. The story is told that after being beheaded by the Romans, St. Denis carried his own head northward until he finally fell and was buried in the spot where the basilica now stands. This is also where Joan of Arc surrendered and Napoleon married Marie-Louise. Chantilly, further north, features a grand chateau next to a man-made lake. Giverny, to the northwest, was home to impressionist Claude Monet for more than 40 years.

One of Europe's best known architectural curiosities is Mont Saint Michel in Normandy. The stunning abbey is located on a bay that has phenomenal tides - with a difference of about 50 feet between the ebb and flow! The sands in the bay are flat and when the tides are at their highest the sea runs over a distance of about 15 miles, forming a wave about 2 feet deep. The Loire Valley and chateaux region is also very popular. A few of the famous chateaux are Blois, Chartres, Lillandry, Chambord, Chenonceaux, and Valencay. Eastern France has the regions of Champagne, Lorraine, Alsace, Franche-Comte, and Burgundy. The Rhone-Alps region has lively contrast, with the craggy north areas of Dauphine and Savoie Mont Blanc to the Rhone Valley villages. Treasure the alpine scenery and visit the country's third largest city, Lyon. The French Riviera - Cote d'Azur gleams with its cities of St. Tropez, Cannes, and Nice. Further west is France's second largest city, Marseilles. Southwestern France has Bordeaux, on the Garonne River, the capital of Aquitaine and a city in the middle of the world's largest wine-producing region. There's also the lovely beach town of Biarritz, the charming village of St. Emilion, Landes National Park, and the Midi-Pyrenees region. Lourdes is located here - the renowned Catholic shrine, as well as the city of Toulouse - called the "Pink City" due to its many pink brick buildings. This is an area of rural, unspoiled medieval villages that are tucked away in the Pyrenees mountains.

Specialty tours have become increasingly popular. Themes include wine, gastronomy, gardens, culture, chateaux and castles, shopping, walking, bicycling, golf, archaeology, language-study, adventure travel, health and spas, ballooning, barging, history, art, antiques, opera and music.

The best time to visit France is May through October, except August (it's the most crowded time to travel since most of the French people - and other Europeans - take their vacation that month). Try and learn a little French - it will help, as French people will appreciate the effort. You may have heard that the French are inhospitable - well the Parisians can be brusque, sometimes even rude, but outside of Paris the people are much more helpful and friendly. French dining is very special but it is also extremely expensive. You can save some by ordering the "fixed price" menu instead of a la carte. Budget accommodations are available in the form of pensions - small guesthouses, usually family-run. A bath may or may not be included. Handshaking as well as kissing on both cheeks are the usual forms of greeting. It may be wise to include Monsieur or Madame when addressing someone as it takes time to get on a first name basis. Best buys include lace, perfumes, wines, crystal, scarves, clothes, antiques, and art.

REVIEW ON FRANCE

1. Give three reasons people might like to visit Paris.____________________________________
____
____
2. The Latin Quarter is on the Left Bank. True or False _________
3. Boulevard ____________________________ and Boulevard ________________________ are two streets mentioned because of their sidewalk cafes.
4. How high is the Eiffel Tower? ________________
5. The Louvre features more than __________________ works of art.
6. The Basilica of the Sacre Coeur dominates all of Paris from the heights of the district called ____________________________.
7. The magnificent Palace of __________________________ was built by 40,000 workers.
8. ______________________ is the capital of Aquitaine and located in the middle of the world's largest wine-producing region.
9. Joan of Arc surrendered and Napoleon married Marie-Louise at ___________________.
10. The city of __________________ is called the "Pink City" due to its many pink brick buildings.
11. The stunning abbey located on a bay that has phenomenal tides is ___________________.
12. Rive Gauche means ______________________.
13. The oldest bridge in Paris, completed in 1604 is the _____________________.
14. To the southeast of Paris is ________________________, an official residence to a long line of France's leaders.
15. Name three of the famous chateaux mentioned in the text. _________________________
____
16. The river that runs through the city of Paris is the _______________.
17. In Paris, the Church of the ______________________ is particularly beautiful because of its gold dome.
18. Three parks and gardens of Paris that were mentioned in the text are _________________
____.
19. Handshaking as well as ____________________________________ are the usual forms of greeting.
20. The Cote d'Azur gleams with its cities of ________________, ________________, and ____________________.

BELGIUM may be small, but it is a charming and friendly country that has a bilingual population (French and Flemish). Brussels (the capital) boasts the Grand Place, the little statue called Manneken Pis, and many museums and churches. You may also want to visit the Atomium - a 335 ft. high replica of an iron molecule (built for 1958 World's Fair). Visit the picturesque canals and narrow, cobblestoned streets of the city of Bruges. Copper, lace, pewterware, tapestries, diamonds, and leather are some of the best buys. Belgium is a producer of a variety of beers - from the Trappist dark beer to the light lagers of Stella Artois and Maes Pils. The Ardennes area of Belgium is famous for its cuisine, forests, lakes, and grottoes. The River Meuse makes its way through important tourist towns such as Dinant and Namur and art treasures from Belgium's history are available in many towns. The site of the Battle of Waterloo is located about 11 miles south of Brussels. The city of Antwerp is the world's diamond capital and its cobbled streets of the old town are great for strolling. There are chocolate shops and pastry shops everywhere and Belgian waffles are a specialty of the country. On street corners there are often counters serving frites - french fries - which may be covered with a dollop of homemade mayonnaise or other exotic sauces. The currency is the Belgian franc and dining and accommodations in this clean country with a high standard of living can be quite expensive.

THE LITTLE STATUE

The little statue of Manneken Pis is treated as the symbol of Brussels' ironic, impudent outlook - a mirror of the cynicism and impiety of its average resident. There are at least a dozen competing legends to explain its origin. One is of a little hero - a boy who used his natural resources to extinguish a bomb thrown into the street. Another is that a little boy startled a witch who saw him in the act of urinating and cursed him to do it forever.

The **NETHERLANDS**, commonly referred to as Holland, is home to tulips, windmills, and the dikes and drainage canals that have reclaimed the land from the sea. Traditional costumes, dances, and folklore, plus the cheese market towns (Edam, Gouda, etc.), the well-preserved city of Amsterdam (the capital) with the official governmental seat - The Hague, the town of Delft - famous for the blue pottery - all this describes Holland. Amsterdam is the city of water - a trip on a boat through the city's picturesque canals is not be missed. There are at least 40 museums (Rijksmuseum, Vincent van Gogh Museum, and the Amsterdam Historical Museum - to name a few). The Anne Frank house, now a museum, is where Anne wrote her famous diary as she and her family hid during World War II. The Spiegel Quarter (near the Rijksmuseum) is an area with a large concentration of antique shops and art galleries. The city is famous for diamonds and there are guided tours of many of the diamond cutters. The currency is the guilder and popular buys include wooden shoes, Delftware, diamonds, cheeses, Indonesian batiks, and local handicrafts. One of the finest airports in the world is Amsterdam's Schipol Airport (located 9 miles from town). Excellent ferry services connect the Netherlands to Great Britain and rail services to the rest of Europe are very extensive.

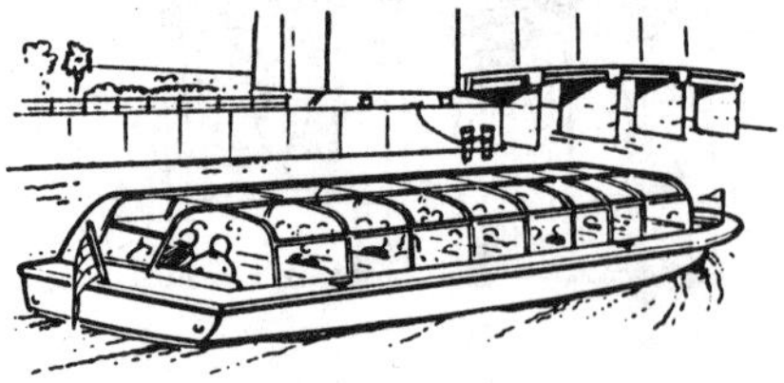

GERMANY'S unification has encouraged the development of facilities in what was East Germany and the city of Berlin, formerly divided into democratic and communist sectors by the Berlin Wall and its armed checkpoints, is a major destination. Germany is a country of sixteen states and one of enormously varied scenery - from sandy beaches to towering mountains, to forests, lakes, medieval villages and great cities. Tour the Black Forest area; cruise down the Rhine River; sightsee in medieval towns like Wurzburg, Rothenburg, etc.; celebrate Octoberfest in Munich; visit Cologne, Heidelberg, Bremen, Mainz, Mannheim, Frankfurt, Dresden, Leipzig, Weisbaden, Stuttgart; ski in the German Alps - there are many activities to choose from in Germany.

Bavaria is the most popular tourist destination for visitors. Its four main areas are: the Bavarian Forest and east Bavaria, Swabia and Allgau in the southwest, Upper Bavaria (with the German part of the Alps in the south), and Franconia. The Bavarian Forest is an unspoiled and peaceful region, with historic towns such as Passau and Regensburg. Well-known cities in Upper Bavaria are Garmisch-Partenkirchen, Mittenwald, and Oberammergau (home of the famous Passion Play, performed during the summer). One of the spectacular feats of architecture that symbolizes the fairytale landscape of Bavaria is Neuschwanstein Castle, built by King Ludwig II. High on the ridge of a mountain and surrounded by snow-capped peaks, it is probably the most famous landmark of Germany. Bavaria's capital is Munich - a major business and international artistic center. The city's most famous beer cellar is the Hofbrauhaus, and there are many museums, gardens, and shopping areas to explore. Connecting the north end of Bavaria with the south is the most notable of all German scenic roads - the Romantic Road. The towns along the way give travelers insight into the area's art, history and culture and places of particular interest are Wurzburg, Rothenberg, Dinkelsbuhl, and Nordlingen.

GERMANY'S SOCIAL PROFILE

Handshaking is customary. Normal courtesies should be observed and it is common to be offered food and refreshments when visiting someone's home. When eating a meal it is considered impolite to leave your left hand on your lap when using your right hand to eat - leave your other hand resting lightly on the table. Before eating, it is customary to say Guten Appetit to the other people at the table, and the correct reply is Ebenfalls. The main meal of the day is lunch and a light snack is eaten in the evening. Breakfast usually consists of a boiled egg, bread rolls with jam, honey, cold cuts, and cheese. Bratwurst (grilled, fried, or boiled sausages) is a specialty. Strudel is a baked pastry with fruit filling (apple filling is most traditional). Local and regional specialties cover an enormous variety. Bars can either have table or counter service, although customers will often find that drinks bought are just marked down on a beer mat and then paid for when leaving. German wines are among the finest in the world. Nightlife opportunities include opera, theater, nightclubs, discos, and bars with live music. Hundreds of festivals are celebrated throughout the country and sports include swimming, hiking, cycling, horseriding, golf, fishing, tennis, squash, walking, and of course, all winter sports.

Berlin and Bonn will both be administrative capitals by the year 2000. Germany's currency is the Deutsche Mark. The national airline is Lufthansa and major airports are located in Frankfurt, Munich, and Berlin (which has two main airports - Tegel and Schonefeld).

SPAIN and PORTUGAL

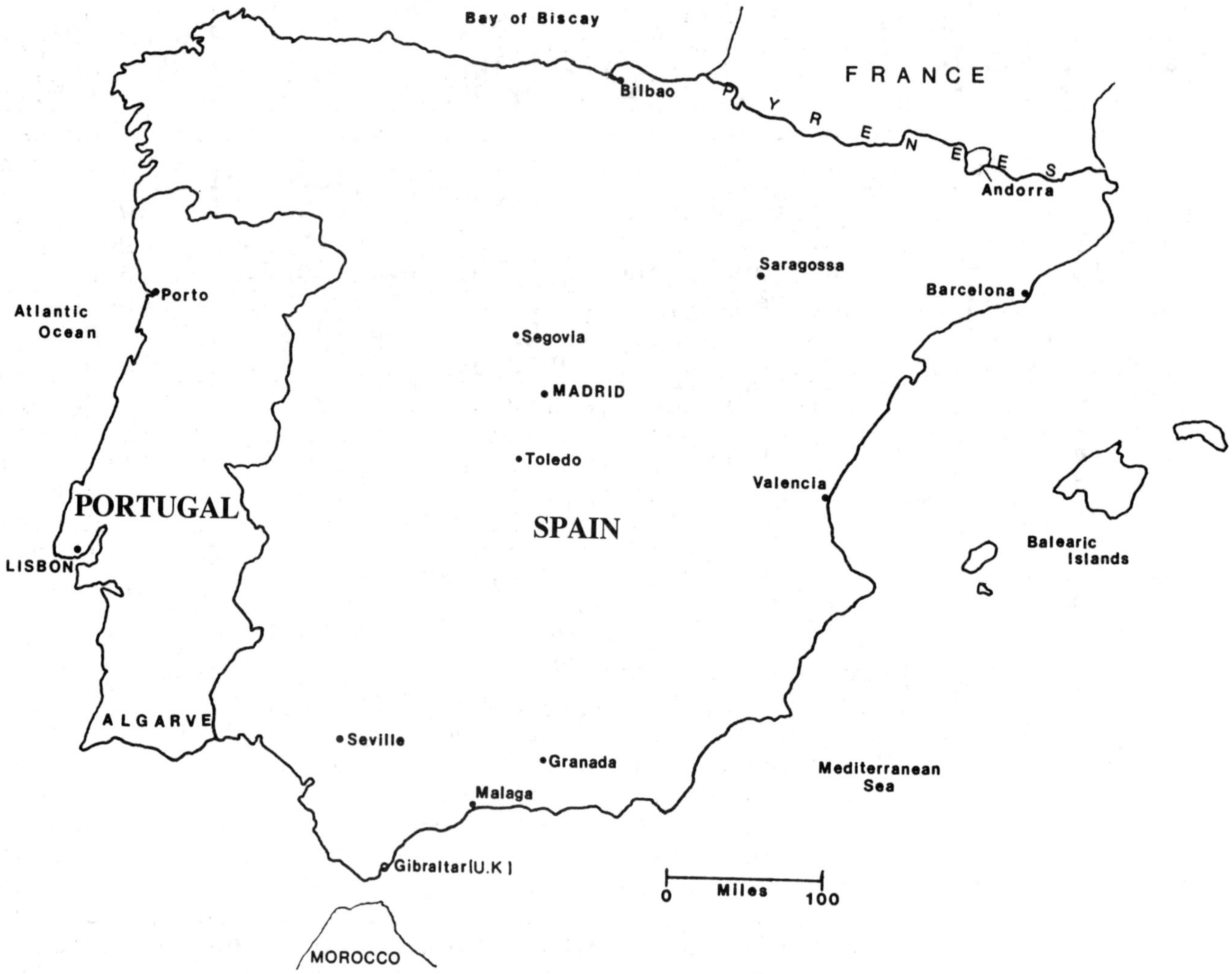

TRAVEL TIPS ABOUT SPAIN

Siesta is from 1:30 pm to 4:30 pm and stores, offices, museums, and even churches can be closed. Always dress respectably in churches. Meal times are late, especially in Madrid - lunch is between 1:30 pm and 4:00 pm and dinner is from 8:30 pm to 11:30 pm. Before dinner drinks are usually accompanied by tapas, which are specialty appetizers. The national dish of paella can be prepared in many ways, based on meat or seafood. It is usually a mixture of chicken and seafood baked with yellow rice, tomatoes, and spices. Gazpacho is chilled vegetable soup. Spain is wine drinking country and sangria is a fruity chilled wine and soda mixture. Flamenco dancing/shows are traditional forms of entertainment, and there are also nightclubs and discos. There are many regional and local fiestas, fairs, and special events, and stumbling upon a local fiesta in a small village or town can be a highlight of your trip (of course you can contact the national tourist office to find out all the major scheduled events as well!). The climate varies from temperate in the north to dry and hot in the south. The best months to visit are April to October. Note: August is usually very crowded because Europeans have chosen to come here for their month vacation. Best buys include leather goods, olive oil, spices, cooking items, leather goods, wood carvings, damascened steel and gold from Toledo, ceramics, glassware, embroidered linen, lace, and antiques. The currency is the peseta, divided into centimes.

SPAIN borders France and within the border, nestled in the Pyrenees Mountains, is the small country of **ANDORRA** (worth a visit to buy some duty-free goods). Spain shares the Iberian peninsula with Portugal and the regions of Spain vary in their topography, from the Basque region at the foothills of the Pyrenees to the Andalusian region of southern Spain. There have been many influences on architecture here - Roman, Visigoth, Romanesque, Moorish, Byzantine, Medieval, Renaissance, Baroque, and Art Nouveau. The historical traditions that have shaped the country are reflected in the many castles, churches, monuments and houses. Spain's 50 provinces are also home to enormously diverse wildlife - from the many species of birds to exotic mammals such as ibexes, chamois, lynxes, wild boars, etc. Andalucia is a mountainous region, rich in minerals and a major producer of olives, grapes, lemons and oranges. The capital of this region is Seville, a city with one of the world's largest Gothic cathedrals. The bell tower is a Moorish minaret topped by a large bronze statue so acurately balanced that it acts as a weather vane. The Alcazar (royal residence of Spain's former Muslim leaders) is a classic example of Arab-Christian architecture. Visit also Cordoba - with a spectacular 8th century mosque, and Granada - for the famous Alhambra Palace (allow a day to tour it). Costa Brava is the area from the French border south to a few miles north of Barcelona; the Costa Blanca is the coastline in the province of Alicante; and the Costa del Sol, a most important tourist area, stretches to either side of the city of Malaga and includes the resorts of Marbella and Torremolinos. Madrid, the country's capital, is a cosmopolitan city with sights such as the famous Prado Museum, the Royal Palace, the Plaza Mayor, and Retiro Park. To the north and northwest of Madrid is the inland region of Castile and Leon - a region that is hot and dry most of the year, but this area's extensive plains make it an important agricultural asset for a country as mountainous as Spain. Toledo, situated on a granite hill surrounded by a loop of the Tagus River, is not to be missed. Visit also the city of Segovia - to see a working Roman aqueduct - one of the best preserved Roman structures, and the many unspoiled Romanesque churches. Barcelona is the second largest city in Spain, located in the region of Catalonia. Sights in Barcelona include: the Picasso Museum, the Old Town, the Ramblas, and the unusual Sagrada Familia church (an incomplete work of visionary Catalon architect, Antonio Gaudi). The Balearic and Canary Islands are both possessions of Spain. The Balearic Islands (Mallorca, Ibiza, Formentera, and Menorca) are in the Mediterranean Sea (about a 45 min. flight from Barcelona). The Canary Islands are off the northwest coast of Africa. Gran Canaria is the most visited and Las Palmas is the major city.

PORTUGAL, one of the world's largest suppliers of cork and a producer of Port wines, has quite a different atmosphere than Spain. From Lisbon, the capital, tourists flock to seaside resorts such as Estoril and Cascais, and to the coast in the south of Portugal, the Algarve. The Algarve coast includes beaches, big hotels, casinos, amusements, sports facilities, as well as family-style tourist villages and camping. A center for pilgrimages is the city of Fatima - where it is believed the Virgin Mary appeared in 1917. Coimbra is Portugal's third largest city and an ancient university town. Enjoy its winding streets, terraced houses, and a particular style of Fado (the melancholy but moving music that is distinctively Portuguese). Madeira, off the coast of Africa, is a Portuguese island known for Madeira wines and its strikingly beautiful scenery and gardens.

REVIEW ON BELGIUM, NETHERLANDS, AND GERMANY

1. Name three cities in Belgium besides Brussels. ________________________________
2. Berlin and Munich will both be administrative capitals of Germany by the year 2000. True or False _________
3. ___________ is a city in Holland that is famous for its pottery.
4. Neuschwanstein Castle is in Bavaria. True or False ___________
5. _______________________ , Germany is the city famous for its Passion Play.
6. There are _____ states in Germany.
7. Amsterdam's _______________ airport is one of the finest airports in the world.
8. Waterloo is in the Netherlands. True or False __________
9. The 335 ft. high replica of an iron molecule is called the ______________ and is located in Brussels.
10. In Germany it is customary to say ____________________ to the people at your table before beginning a meal.

REVIEW ON SPAIN AND PORTUGAL

1. Spain shares the ________________ Peninsula with Portugal.
2. The capital of Portugal is __________________.
3. The city of ______________ is situated on a granite hill, surrounded by a loop of the Tagus River.
4. Name three Balearic Islands. ____
5. What is the name of the famous museum in Madrid? ____________________
6. Andalucia is a mountainous region of Spain and a major region for the production of olives. What is the capital city of this region? ___________________
7. The Costa del Sol stretches to either side of the city of ______________________.
8. In what city is the unusual Sagrada Familia church? _______________________
9. The popular coast of Portugal that features beaches, big hotels, casinos, and sports facilities is the ________________.
10. You can see a working Roman aqueduct in the city of _________________.
11. The famous Alhambra Palace can be toured when visiting the city of ____________.
12. What is the melancholy but moving music that is distinctly Portuguese? __________
13. A center for pilgrimages in Portugal is the city of ________________.
14. The Canary Islands are in the Mediterranean Sea. True or False ___________
15. The small country of _________________ is nestled in the Pyrenees Mountains region of Spain.

LIECHTENSTEIN, the postage stamp country (small and famous for its popular collector's item stamps) is situated on the border between Austria and Switzerland. It is also known for its vineyards and there are a number of ski resorts.

Ah **SWITZERLAND**! The Alps and the Jura Mountains, the high standard of living, quality watches and knives, the creamy variety of chocolates, the international banking and financial center, and the medieval and scenic towns of Lucerne, Geneva, Basel, Bern, and Zurich - all are reasons to visit Switzerland. The highest peaks in the country are Monta Rosa, the Dom, the Matterhorn, and the Jungfrau. The most popular areas are the Engadine, the Bernese Oberland, the Valais, and the Ticino. Switzerland encompasses four cultures: French (Geneva area), Swiss-German (Zurich area), Italian (Lugano area), and Romansh (the south-eastern region). Immaculate and stunning scenery, deluxe accommodations and standards of service, extensive transportation and touring services - this country is a great (although expensive) place to visit. Bern is the capital and the currency is the Swiss franc. The specialty food of Switzerland is fondue - skewered chunks of meat, bread, or fruit that is dipped into a delicious concoction of melted cheeses mixed with wine and other ingredients (the meat is cooked first and there may be other "dips"). Note: It is not an inexpensive dinner.

AUSTRIA and the city of Vienna are famous for offering beautiful scenery and music. Mozart, Beethoven, Brahms, Strauss are just some of the legendary musical geniuses of the Austrian culture. The Danube River and the lovely lakes of the region east of Salzburg provide scenic highlights, along with the ski resorts of Kitzbuhel, Lienz, Innsbruck, etc. Carinthia is Austria's southernmost province and is becoming more popular due to its mild climate, scenic mountains, attractive lakes, fine churches, monasteries, palaces, castles, and resorts. Tours often combine Austria with Switzerland and Germany, spending a couple of nights in Vienna and one in Salzburg. In Vienna the sights include touring the Terraced Gardens of Prince Eugene's Belvedere Palace, driving along Ring Boulevard past Emperor Franz Josef's Hofburg Palace and the State Opera, visiting Prater amusement park, visiting St. Stephen's Cathedral and witnessing the midday parade of historical figures at the musical Anker Clock. The capital is Vienna and the country's currency is the schilling. It is also an expensive country with a high standard of living.

REVIEW ON SWITZERLAND AND AUSTRIA

1. Name three of the legendary musical geniuses of the Austrian culture. ________________
   ____
2. The capital of Austria is ____________________.
3. ________________ is the food specialty of Switzerland.
4. What are two of Austria's ski resorts? ________________________________
5. The ______________ River and the lovely lakes of the region east of Salzburg provide scenic highlights when touring Austria.
6. The capital of Switzerland is ______________.
7. Name two of the highest peaks in Switzerland. ______________________________
8. Two of the best buys of Switzerland are ______________ and ______________.
9. Sights of Vienna include the Terraced Gardens of Prince Eugene's ______________ Palace and Emperor Franz Josef's ____________ Palace.
10. The currency of Switzerland is the ____________________.

GREECE

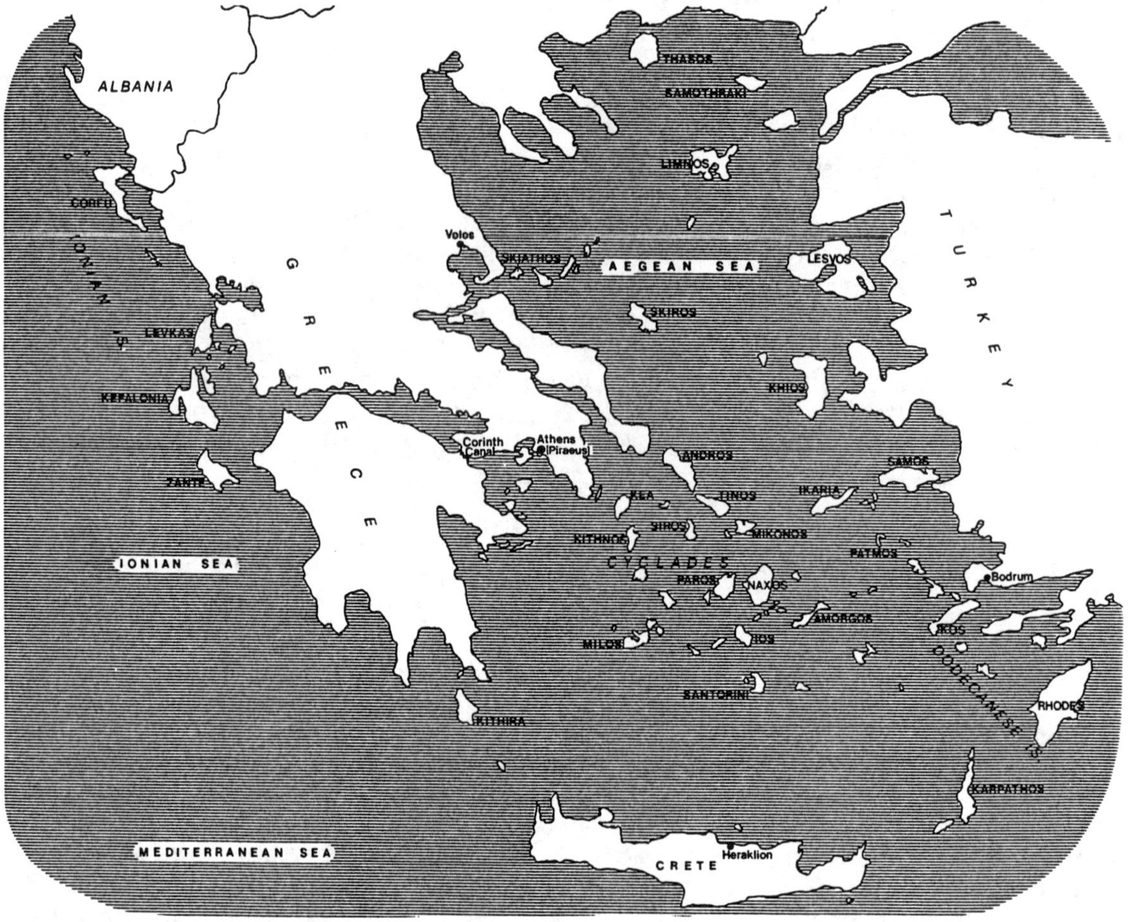

GREECE is a country that has a variety of archaeological treasures and insight into ancient history and culture, plus the natural beauty and vibrancy of being one of the most appealing tourist destinations. Bring along a book on mythology in order to appreciate the sights and points of interest, such as: the Acropolis, Theatre of Dionysus, the Parthenon, the Temple of Olympian Zeus, Arch of Hadrian, and the Monument of Lysicrates. Athens, the capital, is a lively city - especially at night in the old Plaka District where visitors dine in the tavernas and enjoy bouzouki or folk music or see the ruins illuminated. The islands of Greece account for one-fifth the land area of the country and are hosts to thousands of tourists. The majority are located in the Aegean - between the Greek and Turkish coasts. The Ionian Islands are the exception and are scattered along the west coast in the Ionian Sea. There are regular sailings from the port of Athens (Piraeus) to many of the islands. Islands to visit include: Rhodes, Mykonos, Santorini, Crete, Hios, Kos, Lesbos, Corfu, and Samos - just to name a few. You may want to try ouzo - the potent national drink or retsina - Greek wine, and sample Greek food specialties - moussaka, dolmades, souvlaki, and giros. The Greeks have a strong historical and cultural heritage and the Greek Orthodox Church has a big influence on the way of life, particularly in more rural areas. The currency is the drachma and best buys of the country are jewelry, pottery and ceramics, wines flokati (rugs in vivid colors), embroidered clothes, local handicrafts, and icons (religious paintings or mosaics). It is customary to bargain in the markets. Greece is crowded with tourists in July and August.

ITALY

ITALY attracts the attentions of artists, lovers, historians and many others because of cities such as Venice, Florence, Rome, Naples, Milan, Pisa, Bologna, Assisi, Genoa, and islands such as Capri, Sicily, and Sardinia. Vatican City, the world's smallest country, is surrounded by Rome and contains the impressive St. Peter's Basilica, the Sistine Chapel (Michelangelo painted its ceiling), and the offices and residence of the Pope of the Catholic religion. Florence (locally spelled Firenze) is a city of Renaissance art and architecture. Visit the Piazza del Duomo (Cathedral Square) and climb the 463 steps to the top to view the city and countryside. The Uffizi Gallery - one of the most famous museums is here. Stroll through the city's gardens and shop in the city's markets and shops - look for leather goods, lacquer trays, jewelry, pottery and ceramics, and local crafts. Note: Always safeguard valuables and purses so they are less likely to be stolen. Never leave a car unlocked or valuables in it.

Rome is the "Eternal City," with broad streets, outrageous traffic, beautiful courtyards, statues, and fountains. From the Colosseum to the Pantheon, the Catacombs and the Baths - Rome is a favorite destination for those interested in art and architecture, plus ancient, medieval and Renaissance history. Throw a coin in the Trevi Fountain if you want to return to Rome one day or throw two to make a second wish. The Spanish Steps are particularly beautiful in spring because of the blooming flowers. The Borghese Gardens and the scenic Appian Way are other sights. Roma (local spelling) sprawls among seven hills and it is best to plan to divide your days there to concentrate on certain sections of the city.

Pisa - yes, home to the Leaning Tower - is a stop on most tours. And then, of course, there's Venice (Venezia). Divided by 177 canals and crossed by 400 bridges, the city is both picturesque and dirty. But it is unique and the attractions include St. Mark's Square, the Doges' Palace, the Campanile, and the Bridge of Sighs. Hire a gondola to sightsee the city. Naples (Napoli) impresses visitors with its beautiful bay and the towering Mt. Vesuvius. When Vesuvius erupted in AD 79 it covered the city of Pompeii - see this preserved city. South of Naples is the Sorrento Peninsula, which is one of the most beautiful and romantic areas of the country. Catch the ferry to Capri to see the shimmering Blue Grotto. The Lake District of Italy is near the Swiss border and features Lake Como, Lake Maggiore, and Lake Orta. Milan is a center of business, fashion and manufacturing. The Italian Riviera stretches from the French border to Livorno in the region of Tuscany. This is an area of enchanting scenery, quaint and secluded beaches, and unique villages. Italy's ski resorts are in the Alps and Dolomites, although there are also a few in the Apennines, and it is possible to ski on the slopes of Mt. Etna in Sicily. Sicily is a mountainous yet arid island and in the center of the north coast is the ancient capital city of Palermo.

REVIEW ON GREECE AND ITALY

1. The capital of Greece is ______________.
2. Name four islands of Greece that tourists visit. ________________________________

   ____
3. _____________ is the port of Athens.
4. Rome is called "The ____________________ City."
5. The Uffizi Gallery is one of the famous museums in Florence. True or False _________
6. The Italian Riviera stretches from the French border to Livorno in _______________.
7. In Venice you can see the Doges' Palace and the Bridge of __________________.
8. The ancient capital city of Palermo is on the island of __________________.
9. What mountain erupted in AD 79 and covered the city of Pompeii? ________________
10. The world's smallest country is _________________________.
11. In what city is the Piazza del Duomo? __________________
12. Name three best buys of Italy. ____
13. ________________, ___________________, and ________________ are three food specialties of Greece.
14. What is an icon? ____
15. The Blue Grotto is an attraction of the island of Capri. True or False ______________

NEW REPUBLICS (FORMER YUGOSLAVIA)

YUGOSLAVIA has been divided into a number of republics and particular areas are undergoing extreme political instability and civil war. Travel to **SLOVENIA** and **CROATIA** has been somewhat resumed, as these areas are more removed from the conflict areas. However, the situation remains extremely volatile in the Republic of **BOSNIA**, whose population is divided between Muslims, Serbs, and Croats. The history of the entire Balkan area is very complex - as it is a region that has fallen prey to acquisition attempts by its neighbors, from the ancient Greeks to the Austro-Hungarian empire of the Hapsburgs. This region of vastly differing climates and temperatures as well as decidedly differing peoples is dispersed into republics such as **SLOVENIA, CROATIA, SERBIA, BOSNIA & HERCEGOVINA, MACEDONIA**, and **MONTENEGRO**. There are three major languages (Slovenian, Macedonian, and Serbo-Croatian), two different alphabets (Cyrillic and Roman), and three major religions (Orthodox, Catholic, and Muslim). The Dalmatian coast offers the beaches and seaside towns that are popular with Europeans.

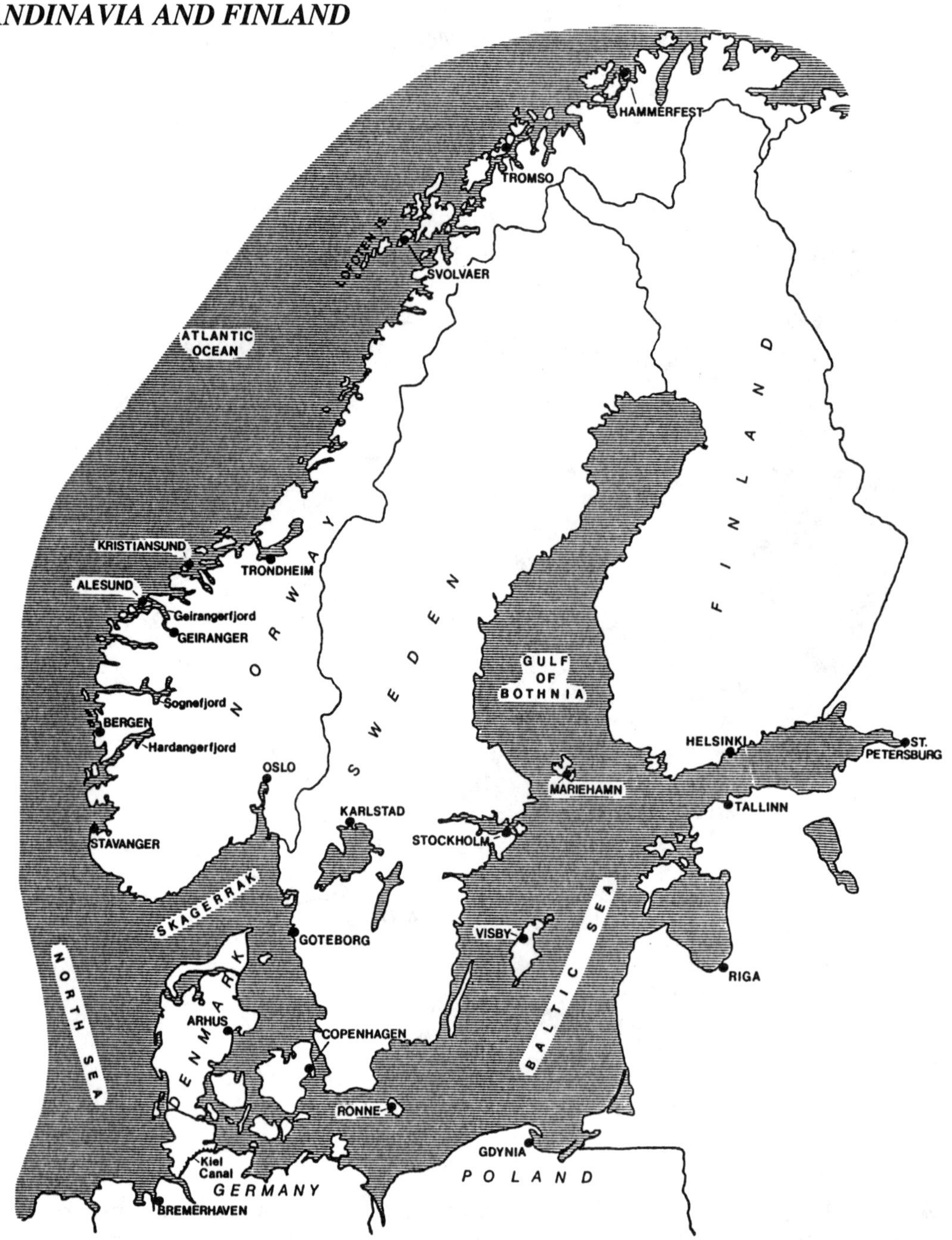

Scandinavia includes **NORWAY, SWEDEN, and DENMARK.** Geographically, the Scandinavian peninsula even excludes Denmark, but historically the three have been grouped together. Some tours to the area will also visit **FINLAND, ICELAND, and the Faroe Islands.**

NORWAY's scenery is one of the most beautiful in the world - with the coastline of fjords or inlets opening to thousands of islands; and in the north, one can see the nomadic Lapp people bringing their reindeer herds to graze. Although half of Norway lies above the Arctic Circle, the Gulf Stream tempers the climate along the coast. Major cities to visit include: Oslo, Bergen, Stavanger, Trondheim, and Tromso. Besides sightseeing, skiing and fishing are very popular activities. Most towns and resorts have shops for typical Norwegian handicrafts and the best buys include furs, woven goods, knitwear, woodcarvings, silver, enamel, pewter, glass, and porcelain. The fjord country covers the area from Stavanger to Kristiansund and from the North Sea to the mountain ranges in the east. The longest, Sognefjord, runs for about 125 miles into the interior. Others include the Ryfylke Fjords, Hardanger Fjord, Sunn Fjord, Nord Fjord, Geiranger Fjord, and Romsdal Fjord. In mountainous West Norway, the glaciers sometimes even reach down into the bottom of the adjacent valley.

SWEDEN ranks as a leading industrial country and is the richest and biggest of the Scandinavian countries. The capital, Stockholm, is built on a string of islands. Start at the Old Town (Gamla Stan) - a cluster of old buildings and cobblestone streets. Visit historic churches, the Royal Palace, Stockholm's elegant City Hall (Stadshuset), and the many museums. Goteborg (also spelled Gothenburg) is a major port city with spacious streets and a network of canals. It is a starting point for popular 3-day trips through Sweden's great lakes and the historic Gota Canal. The province of Skane, at the tip of Sweden is an area of fertile fields and meadows. You can see constant reminders of the days of Danish rule (Skane was ruled by the Danes until 1658) in the more than 200 castles and manors. If you visit the city of Malmo, buy the Malmo-kortet (Malmo card) which entitles you to free travel on buses, free admission to museums and discounts on a wide variety of purchases. The province of Smaland is home to Swedish glass-making, with three-quarters of all Swedish glassworks located in the counties of Kronoberg and Kalmar. Smaland is also an area of vast forests and pleasant lakes, with many coastal towns that stretch along the Baltic. Sweden's largest islands, Gotland and Oland offer a fascinating mixture of ancient history and natural beauty. On Gotland there are the Lummelunda caves with spectacular stalagmites and stalactites and a preserved medieval town at Kattlundsgard. The Swedish Lakeland region is dominated by the largest, Lake Vanern, and the whole region is considered the center of Swedish culture, and it is where the majority of Swedes live. Visit the university city of Uppsala, and the folklore and craft center, Dalarna. The Swedish smorgasbord, a table covered with a variety of cold and hot dishes, takes so long to prepare that most Swedish families have it only on special occasions. Shopping in Sweden means finding some of the finest glassware, sweaters, wood objects, clothes, and furs.

DENMARK's center of fun is Copenhagen, one of the biggest and liveliest capitals of Europe. See the Little Mermaid Statue in the harbor, visit museums, palaces, churches, and have dinner at Tivoli Gardens. Go to Odense, birthplace of Hans Christian Anderson. The country's landscape consists mainly of low-lying fertile countryside interspersed with beech woods, small lakes, and fjords. Jutland comprises the greater part of the country. There are nice sandy beaches, but changing winds and tides may make swimming unsafe. Alborg contains the largest Viking burial ground, plus a cathedral, monastery, and castle. Funen is known as the "Garden of Denmark" and has picturesque castles and manor houses set in beautifully landscaped parks and gardens. Tour the islands and medieval towns, and share laughter and conversation with the friendly and hospitable Danish people.

FINLAND is one of the larger European countries in size, but small in population. In Lapland, the winter sports season lasts until May, and the Midnight Sun shines night and day throughout June and part of July. The capital city, Helsinki, has historic landmarks, parks, and streets along with gleaming modern buildings. Finland's coastline is very indented and around the coast is an archipelago of thousands of islands varying in size. This land of 60,000 lakes is known for beautiful china, glassware, furs, and jewelry. The world famous Finnish bath, the sauna, is a part of most Finnish homes.

SAMPLE TOUR ITINERARY - SCANDINAVIA AND FINLAND
Day 1 - Overnight flight to Copenhagen.
Day 2 - Time to rest or start exploring the city of Copenhagen.
Day 3 - Guided tour of the city, with optional excursions available for the afternoon.
Day 4 - Take the ferry to the fairy-tale island of Funen. Overnight in Aalborg.
Day 5 - A three hour ferry ride will take you to Goteburg/Gothenburg, Sweden. Then tour the coastline to arrive in Oslo, Norway for the night.
Day 6 - Spend the day in Oslo.
Day 7 - Tour the area and overnight in Hardangerfjord.
Day 8 - Take the ferry from here to Bergen.
Day 9 - A fjord cruise followed by motorcoach trip will take you to Valdres for your overnight stay.
Day 10 - Head for Lillehammer, where you will stay the night.
Day 11 - From Lillehammer you'll tour back to Sweden and stay in Karlstad.
Day 12 - On to Stockholm for the night.
Day 13 - A night cruise will take you to Turku, Finland.
Day 14 - Spend the day in Turku.
Day 15 - Head for Tampere, where you'll stay the night.
Day 16 - Board your Silverline boat for a lake cruise, then head south to the capital of Finland, Helsinki.
Day 17 - Sightseeing in Helsinki with time for some last minute purchases before you head home.
Day 18 - Flight to your home.

REVIEW ON NORWAY, SWEDEN, DENMARK AND FINLAND

1. There are nice, sandy beaches in Denmark. Why is it not so safe for swimming? _______
   ____
2. ______________________ comprises the greater part of Denmark.
3. The longest fjord in Norway, ____________________ runs for about 125 miles into the interior.
4. Name three major cities in Norway. ____
5. What is the capital of Sweden? _____________________
6. The city of __________________ in Denmark contains the largest Viking burial ground, plus a cathedral, monastery, and castle.
7. Sweden's province of _______________ is home to glass-making.
8. In what city is the Little Mermaid Statue? ___________________________
9. The major port city of ________________________ is a starting point for popular three day trips through Sweden's great lakes and the historic _______ Canal.
10. The Swedish Lakeland region is dominated by the largest, Lake ______________.
11. Helsinki is the capital of Finland. True or False ____________
12. What city features the birthplace of Hans Christian Anderson? ___________________
13. ________________, ___________________, and ________________ are three best buys of Sweden.
14. The nomadic people of Norway are the _______________.
15. The world famous Finnish bath, the ________, is a part of most Finnish homes.

THE BALTICS

LATVIA is a Baltic country that has experienced rapid economic development and increased trading since its independence. The capital is Riga, a beautiful city with a diversity of architectural styles and numerous historical buildings. Latvians are generally reserved and somewhat formal but very hospitable. They are proud of their culture and national heritage.

LITHUANIA is another independent country. The historic capital city Vilnius offers an adequate range of good accommodations that includes large hotels and smaller pensions/guest houses. About 18 miles from Vilnius is Trakai - an ancient capital of Lithuania. The city has a 14th century castle and is situated on Lake Galve - where boat rides are available.

ESTONIA is the most northerly of the Baltic Republics and has great scenic beauty - with over 1,200 lakes, 800 islands, and many forests. Economic ties with Scandinavia continue to grow, as well as with the European Community. Tallinn, the capital of Estonia, is dominated by the soaring steeple of the medieval Town Hall, and offers a number of other historical landmarks and monuments.

C.I.S.

The **C.I.S. - COMMONWEALTH OF INDEPENDENT STATES** includes quite a number of newly formed republics from the break up of the Soviet Union. The C.I.S. encompasses one-sixth of the land area of the world. The topography consists of an immense plain framed by mountains, interspersed with plateaus, lakes, and rivers. The Aral Sea, Caspian Sea, and Lake Baikal are the most important. The state of **Belarus** contains many ancient Russian cities and agriculture and industry are well developed. **Moldova** is a small state located between the Ukraine and the River Prut. The state of **Ukraine** has Kiev as its capital. Also in this state is the port of Odessa and the city of Yalta, the Pearl of the Crimea.

The **RUSSIAN FEDERATION** encompasses an area almost twice the size of the United States. The Ural Mountains form the border between European Russia and Siberia (Asia). Moscow, the capital, is a major cultural, industrial, and transportation center, and has a population of more than 8 million people. The focal point of the city is Red Square with the Kremlin located on one side. Other sights in Moscow include St. Basil's Cathedral, with its particularly striking onion-shaped domes, the many palaces, museums, churches, plus the subway (unusually beautiful) and the Bolshoi Theater. Browse in the shops for the country's best buys (fur caps, caviar, vodka, wood and metal sculptures, hand-painted lacquerware, and the popular "nesting dolls"). The second largest city is St. Petersburg, a quaint city known as the "Venice of the North" because of its hundreds of bridges criss-crossing the Neva River. This is where you can see the fortress of Peter and Paul, the Hermitage Museum, and many parks, gardens, and tree-lined avenues.

The state of **Armenia** has the capital Yerevan, one of the oldest cities in the world - founded nearly 2800 years ago at the time of ancient Babylon and Rome. The state of **Azerbaijan** presently is experiencing some civil and ethnic conflicts in the Nagorno-Karabakh region. The state of **Georgia** has Tbilisi as its capital, set in the midst of several mountain ranges in the valley of the River Kura. Gori, the birthplace of Stalin, is also located in this state.

Kazakstan is the second largest state in the Commonwealth and the relatively young city of Alma-Ata is the capital. **Kyrgyzstan** is a state located in Central Asia, north of Afghanistan, offering spectacular mountain ranges and valleys plus warm, sandy beaches and thermal springs. **Tajikistan** is a state dominated by the Pamir Mountains - containing the highest peaks of the C.I.S.

Turkmenistan is a state that is mostly desert and the capital is Ashkhabad - a green and sprawling city. **Uzbekistan** with its colorful and varied countryside features major cities such as Samarkand, Tashkent, and Bukhara. Because certain areas of the C.I.S. are experiencing political unrest, those intending to visit regions should contact the U.S. Department of State and seek up-to-date advice from foreign government offices.

The end of Communism has turned Russia and the other states into lands of unprecedented opportunity, but the change to a market economy has also brought problems. There is daily confusion and frustration, paralyzing political struggles, rampant inflation, local and ethnic conflicts, monetary chaos, and rising crime. Soaring inflation has reached double digits - usually 20-30 percent per month. Although most of the states have set up their own currencies, the U.S. dollar is used everywhere, as the republics do not have the revenues nor even the paper to print new bills. Credit cards may be accepted at major hotels, but U.S. dollars are generally preferred - and they should be "crisp" bills, as older dollar bills can sometimes be rejected as counterfeit! Visa regulations for travel to Russia, the Baltic States, and the C.I.S. are constantly changing, so check with consulates or embassies for current requirements. Regarding weather conditions, Moscow and St. Petersburg are warm from about mid-May to early September. Generally the republics experience long, dark, cold winters. Aeroflot, once the only Soviet airline, has broken up into several companies that use Aeroflot equipment and crews. Be aware that there has been an alarming drop in safety and maintenance standards. On all forms of transportation there may be delays and glitches - the key is to be flexible, patient and tolerant.

REVIEW ON THE BALTICS AND THE C.I.S.

1. The capital of Estonia is ________________.
2. What mountains form the border between European Russia and Siberia (Asia)? ________
3. Name three of the best buys of Russia. ______________________________________
4. Vilnius is the capital of Latvia. True or False. ___________
5. Kiev is the capital of ________________.
6. C.I.S. stands for ____.
7. 1,200 lakes, 800 islands and many forests describes the topography of the country of ________________.
8. The cathedral in Moscow with the onion-shaped domes is St. ___________'s.
9. A state that is mostly desert with the capital Ashkhabad is ________________________.
10. The port of Odessa and the city of Yalta are in the state of ________________.

OTHER EUROPEAN COUNTRIES

GIBRALTAR, at the tip of Spain, is a British rock fortress and is one of the few places you can see two continents at once. This British Crown Colony's sources of income include the British bases, ship repair and docking facilities plus tourism and offshore financial services. The construction industry is also important. At present, border crossings are relatively unrestricted and as such, many Gibraltar residents work in Spain and a significant number of Spaniards work in Gibraltar.

MONACO, near the border of France and Italy, is famous for the casino at Monte Carlo and a gathering place for the wealthy and aristocratic. The Palace is home of the Grimaldi family (the oldest ruling house in Europe).

LUXEMBOURG provides a visit through an area of castles, scenic forests, hills, plateaus, and gorges. It is a prosperous country with a high standard of living. Banking and steel are mainstays of this country's economy.

SAN MARINO is a tiny state situated on the east coast of Italy. It is the only surviving city-state. Like Andorra, Liechtenstein, and Monaco it is a reminder of times when Europe was made up of tiny political units. Tourism provides most of the state's income and the landscape is mostly green rolling hills dominated by the three peaks of Mount Titano.

ALBANIA, famed for its fierce tribal people, has been alternately ruled by Soviet and Chinese Communists and later independently. The country has recently opened up more to tourism. Most of the country is wild and mountainous, but there are fine sandy beaches and some beautiful lakes.

ROMANIA has the Black Sea, the Danube Delta, beach, health and ski resorts, the Transylvania region of Dracula fame, and a capital city, Bucharest, that has been called the "Paris of the Balkans." The Carpathian Mountains provide a beautiful and densely forested area with many health and winter resorts that are open year round. The Danube Delta is a vast expanse of watery wilderness containing numerous little waterways, wetlands, patches of forest and varied wildlife and birds. The Black Sea coast is the principal tourist area and has fine, white sandy beaches.

BULGARIA is a major exporter of wine, and its jams are much appreciated abroad. The national food, yogurt, is featured in many recipes and is claimed to contribute to a long and pleasant life. The ancient capital of Sofia has a wealth of architectural styles, many museums, theaters, art galleries, and opera houses.

Visit **POLAND** to see the historic districts of Warsaw, museums, old palaces; and to sit in the cafes that are a way of life for the Polish people. This is the land where Chopin and Copernicus lived, a land and people that continually strive to preserve an independent heritage. The Mazurian Lake District is particularly beautiful and Zakopane is a popular ski resort located in the Tatra Mountains.

The **CZECH and SLOVAK REPUBLICS** lie at the heart of central Europe. In January 1993 Czechoslovakia legally split into these two republics. The two republics together have three main regions - western Bohemia, the rich agricultural region of Moravia, and the easternmost region of Slovakia. Bohemia contains the Czech capital, Prague - built on hills and spanning the river Vltava. Tourists are also drawn to this region to visit the spa towns of Carlsbad and Marienbad and to stay in the beautiful region of gentle hills and woodlands known as the Bohemian Forest. The Elbe River flows through Bohemia from the Giant Mountains - a popular skiing region. Brno is Moravia's administrative and cultural center, an area of wooded highlands, vineyards, folk art and castles. In Slovakia or the Slovak Republic, the Tatra Mountains dominate and Bratislava is the capital.

HUNGARY, with its capital city Budapest, has attracted more and more tourists because of its fairly developed facilities. Divided by the Danube into two parts (Buda and Pest), the capital has museums, cafes, theaters, and much more. Hungary has hundreds of thermal springs, contains Europe's largest freshwater lake, Lake Balaton, and is famous for specialties such as goulash, a local wine called "Bull's Blood," and for a variety of local arts and crafts.

Europe and Asia meet in **TURKEY**, with influences and ruins dating back to the Greeks, Romans, Turks, and other civilizations. Istanbul is one of the world's most intriguing cities. It was Byzantium, the seat of a huge empire; and it was Constantinople, the capital of the Roman Empire. Of over 400 mosques in Istanbul, the most famous is the Blue Mosque. Other attractions in Istanbul include Topkapi Palace, St. Sophia Mosque, Galata Bridge, the parks, gardens, and covered bazaars. Many sights and ruins are located along the Aegean coast, such as the remains of Troy, Izmir (the birthplace of Homer), and the spectacular ruins at Ephesus. Kusadasi is an attractive resort. Pamukkale is famous for its calcified waterfall and thermal waters and there are some ruins of the Roman city of Hierapolis. The capital of the country, Ankara, is located in Central Anatolia. The Cappadocia region is a spectacular area with some unique landscape features of rocks and cones. There are elaborate cave systems and underground cities to explore, and a must see is the surrealist landscape of rock churches, cones, frescoes, and houses hollowed out of the sides of cliffs at Goreme.

ISLAND DESTINATIONS

The **BALEARIC ISLANDS** are a possession of Spain. Of Mallorca, Menorca, Ibiza, and Formentera, Mallorca has the most to see and explore.

The **CANARY ISLANDS** are also a possession of Spain. Although they are located off the coast of Africa, they are often visited from the European continent. Tenerife is the largest and is dominated by mountains and several spectacular valleys. Gran Canaria is the most visited and Las Palmas is the major city.

MALTA is the largest inhabited island of the Maltese Archipelago; Gozo and Comino are the other inhabited islands. Clear blue waters, secluded bays, sandy beaches, medieval towns - these features attract tourists. Valletta is the capital.

CORSICA - a possession of France - is a charming, unspoiled and rugged island that consists of forests, mountains, granite, snow, sandy beaches, and orange trees.

SARDINIA AND SICILY are part of Italy. Palermo is the capital of Sicily and Europe's largest and most active volcano, Mt. Etna, is located on Sicily. Sardinia is the second largest island in the Mediterranean. Much of Sardinia's interior is uninhabited and undeveloped.

Using other resources (guidebooks, maps, tour brochures, etc.), fill out profile forms on many of the countries, then complete the reviews and tests.

You may wish to contact the tourist offices for useful maps, information and brochures to help in your research.

If this manual is used in a school curriculum, the instructor may want to assign students to do a project on a country. Students may have to create a poster, a collage, bring in handicraft items and present 10-15 minutes of information on a specific country.

COUNTRY: ____________________ CAPITAL: ____________________
DOCUMENTARY REQUIREMENTS (U.S. CITIZENS): ____________________
CURRENCY: __________ CURRENCY CODE: ______ EXCHANGE RATE: ______
LANGUAGE(S): ____________________
SIZE: ____________________ POPULATION: ____________________
CLIMATE: ____________________
BEST TIME TO VISIT: ____________________
MAJOR CITIES/PLACES OF INTEREST: ____________________
____
____
____
SPORTS: ____________________
RELIGION(S): ____________________ GOVERNMENT: ____________________
FOOD SPECIALTIES: ____________________
BEST BUYS: ____________________
SPECIAL INFORMATION: ____________________
AIRLINES: ____________________ CITY/AIRPORT CODES: ____________________
TRANSPORTATION: ____________________
SPECIAL HOTELS/RESORTS/MISCELLANEOUS INFO ____________________
____

COUNTRY: ____________________ CAPITAL: ____________________
DOCUMENTARY REQUIREMENTS (U.S. CITIZENS): ____________________
CURRENCY: __________ CURRENCY CODE: ______ EXCHANGE RATE: ______
LANGUAGE(S): ____________________
SIZE: ____________________ POPULATION: ____________________
CLIMATE: ____________________
BEST TIME TO VISIT: ____________________
MAJOR CITIES/PLACES OF INTEREST: ____________________
____
____
____
SPORTS: ____________________
RELIGION(S): ____________________ GOVERNMENT: ____________________
FOOD SPECIALTIES: ____________________
BEST BUYS: ____________________
SPECIAL INFORMATION: ____________________
AIRLINES: ____________________ CITY/AIRPORT CODES: ____________________
TRANSPORTATION: ____________________
SPECIAL HOTELS/RESORTS/MISCELLANEOUS INFO ____________________
____

COUNTRY: ____________________ CAPITAL: ____________________
DOCUMENTARY REQUIREMENTS (U.S. CITIZENS): ____________________
CURRENCY: __________ CURRENCY CODE: ______ EXCHANGE RATE: ______
LANGUAGE(S): ____________________
SIZE: ____________________ POPULATION: ____________________
CLIMATE: ____________________
BEST TIME TO VISIT: ____________________
MAJOR CITIES/PLACES OF INTEREST: ____________________
____
____
____
SPORTS: ____________________
RELIGION(S): ____________________ GOVERNMENT: ____________________
FOOD SPECIALTIES: ____________________
BEST BUYS: ____________________
SPECIAL INFORMATION: ____________________
AIRLINES: ____________________ CITY/AIRPORT CODES: ____________________
TRANSPORTATION: ____________________
SPECIAL HOTELS/RESORTS/MISCELLANEOUS INFO ____________________
____

COUNTRY: ____________________ CAPITAL: ____________________
DOCUMENTARY REQUIREMENTS (U.S. CITIZENS): ____________________
CURRENCY: __________ CURRENCY CODE: ______ EXCHANGE RATE: ______
LANGUAGE(S): ____________________
SIZE: ____________________ POPULATION: ____________________
CLIMATE: ____________________
BEST TIME TO VISIT: ____________________
MAJOR CITIES/PLACES OF INTEREST: ____________________
____
____
____
SPORTS: ____________________
RELIGION(S): ____________________ GOVERNMENT: ____________________
FOOD SPECIALTIES: ____________________
BEST BUYS: ____________________
SPECIAL INFORMATION: ____________________
AIRLINES: ____________________ CITY/AIRPORT CODES: ____________________
TRANSPORTATION: ____________________
SPECIAL HOTELS/RESORTS/MISCELLANEOUS INFO ____________________
____

COUNTRY: ____________________ CAPITAL: ____________________
DOCUMENTARY REQUIREMENTS (U.S. CITIZENS): ____________________
CURRENCY: __________ CURRENCY CODE: ______ EXCHANGE RATE: ______
LANGUAGE(S): ____________________
SIZE: ____________________ POPULATION: ____________________
CLIMATE: ____________________
BEST TIME TO VISIT: ____________________
MAJOR CITIES/PLACES OF INTEREST: ____________________
____
____
____
SPORTS: ____________________
RELIGION(S): ____________________ GOVERNMENT: ____________________
FOOD SPECIALTIES: ____________________
BEST BUYS: ____________________
SPECIAL INFORMATION: ____________________
AIRLINES: ____________________ CITY/AIRPORT CODES: ____________________
TRANSPORTATION: ____________________
SPECIAL HOTELS/RESORTS/MISCELLANEOUS INFO ____________________
____

COUNTRY: ____________________ CAPITAL: ____________________
DOCUMENTARY REQUIREMENTS (U.S. CITIZENS): ____________________
CURRENCY: __________ CURRENCY CODE: ______ EXCHANGE RATE: ______
LANGUAGE(S): ____________________
SIZE: ____________________ POPULATION: ____________________
CLIMATE: ____________________
BEST TIME TO VISIT: ____________________
MAJOR CITIES/PLACES OF INTEREST: ____________________
____
____
____
SPORTS: ____________________
RELIGION(S): ____________________ GOVERNMENT: ____________________
FOOD SPECIALTIES: ____________________
BEST BUYS: ____________________
SPECIAL INFORMATION: ____________________
AIRLINES: ____________________ CITY/AIRPORT CODES: ____________________
TRANSPORTATION: ____________________
SPECIAL HOTELS/RESORTS/MISCELLANEOUS INFO ____________________
____

COUNTRY:____________________ CAPITAL:____________________
DOCUMENTARY REQUIREMENTS (U.S. CITIZENS):____________________
CURRENCY:____________________ CURRENCY CODE:__________ EXCHANGE RATE:__________
LANGUAGE(S):____________________
SIZE:____________________ POPULATION:____________________
CLIMATE:____________________
BEST TIME TO VISIT:____________________
MAJOR CITIES/PLACES OF INTEREST:____________________
____
____
____
SPORTS:____________________
RELIGION(S):____________________ GOVERNMENT:____________________
FOOD SPECIALTIES:____________________
BEST BUYS:____________________
SPECIAL INFORMATION:____________________
AIRLINES:____________________ CITY/AIRPORT CODES:____________________
TRANSPORTATION:____________________
SPECIAL HOTELS/RESORTS/MISCELLANEOUS INFO____________________
____

COUNTRY:____________________ CAPITAL:____________________
DOCUMENTARY REQUIREMENTS (U.S. CITIZENS):____________________
CURRENCY:____________________ CURRENCY CODE:__________ EXCHANGE RATE:__________
LANGUAGE(S):____________________
SIZE:____________________ POPULATION:____________________
CLIMATE:____________________
BEST TIME TO VISIT:____________________
MAJOR CITIES/PLACES OF INTEREST:____________________
____
____
____
SPORTS:____________________
RELIGION(S):____________________ GOVERNMENT:____________________
FOOD SPECIALTIES:____________________
BEST BUYS:____________________
SPECIAL INFORMATION:____________________
AIRLINES:____________________ CITY/AIRPORT CODES:____________________
TRANSPORTATION:____________________
SPECIAL HOTELS/RESORTS/MISCELLANEOUS INFO____________________
____

COUNTRY:____________________ CAPITAL:____________________
DOCUMENTARY REQUIREMENTS (U.S. CITIZENS):____________________
CURRENCY:____________________ CURRENCY CODE:__________ EXCHANGE RATE:__________
LANGUAGE(S):____________________
SIZE:____________________ POPULATION:____________________
CLIMATE:____________________
BEST TIME TO VISIT:____________________
MAJOR CITIES/PLACES OF INTEREST:____________________
____
____
____
SPORTS:____________________
RELIGION(S):____________________ GOVERNMENT:____________________
FOOD SPECIALTIES:____________________
BEST BUYS:____________________
SPECIAL INFORMATION:____________________
AIRLINES:____________________ CITY/AIRPORT CODES:____________________
TRANSPORTATION:____________________
SPECIAL HOTELS/RESORTS/MISCELLANEOUS INFO____________________
____

COUNTRY: ______________________ CAPITAL: ______________________
DOCUMENTARY REQUIREMENTS (U.S. CITIZENS): ______________________
CURRENCY: __________ CURRENCY CODE: ______ EXCHANGE RATE: ________
LANGUAGE(S): ______________________
SIZE: ______________________ POPULATION: ______________________
CLIMATE: ______________________
BEST TIME TO VISIT: ______________________
MAJOR CITIES/PLACES OF INTEREST: ______________________
____
____
____
SPORTS: ______________________
RELIGION(S): ______________________ GOVERNMENT: ______________________
FOOD SPECIALTIES: ______________________
BEST BUYS: ______________________
SPECIAL INFORMATION: ______________________
AIRLINES: ______________________ CITY/AIRPORT CODES: ______________________
TRANSPORTATION: ______________________
SPECIAL HOTELS/RESORTS/MISCELLANEOUS INFO ______________________
____

COUNTRY: ______________________ CAPITAL: ______________________
DOCUMENTARY REQUIREMENTS (U.S. CITIZENS): ______________________
CURRENCY: __________ CURRENCY CODE: ______ EXCHANGE RATE: ________
LANGUAGE(S): ______________________
SIZE: ______________________ POPULATION: ______________________
CLIMATE: ______________________
BEST TIME TO VISIT: ______________________
MAJOR CITIES/PLACES OF INTEREST: ______________________
____
____
____
SPORTS: ______________________
RELIGION(S): ______________________ GOVERNMENT: ______________________
FOOD SPECIALTIES: ______________________
BEST BUYS: ______________________
SPECIAL INFORMATION: ______________________
AIRLINES: ______________________ CITY/AIRPORT CODES: ______________________
TRANSPORTATION: ______________________
SPECIAL HOTELS/RESORTS/MISCELLANEOUS INFO ______________________
____

COUNTRY: ______________________ CAPITAL: ______________________
DOCUMENTARY REQUIREMENTS (U.S. CITIZENS): ______________________
CURRENCY: __________ CURRENCY CODE: ______ EXCHANGE RATE: ________
LANGUAGE(S): ______________________
SIZE: ______________________ POPULATION: ______________________
CLIMATE: ______________________
BEST TIME TO VISIT: ______________________
MAJOR CITIES/PLACES OF INTEREST: ______________________
____
____
____
SPORTS: ______________________
RELIGION(S): ______________________ GOVERNMENT: ______________________
FOOD SPECIALTIES: ______________________
BEST BUYS: ______________________
SPECIAL INFORMATION: ______________________
AIRLINES: ______________________ CITY/AIRPORT CODES: ______________________
TRANSPORTATION: ______________________
SPECIAL HOTELS/RESORTS/MISCELLANEOUS INFO ______________________
____

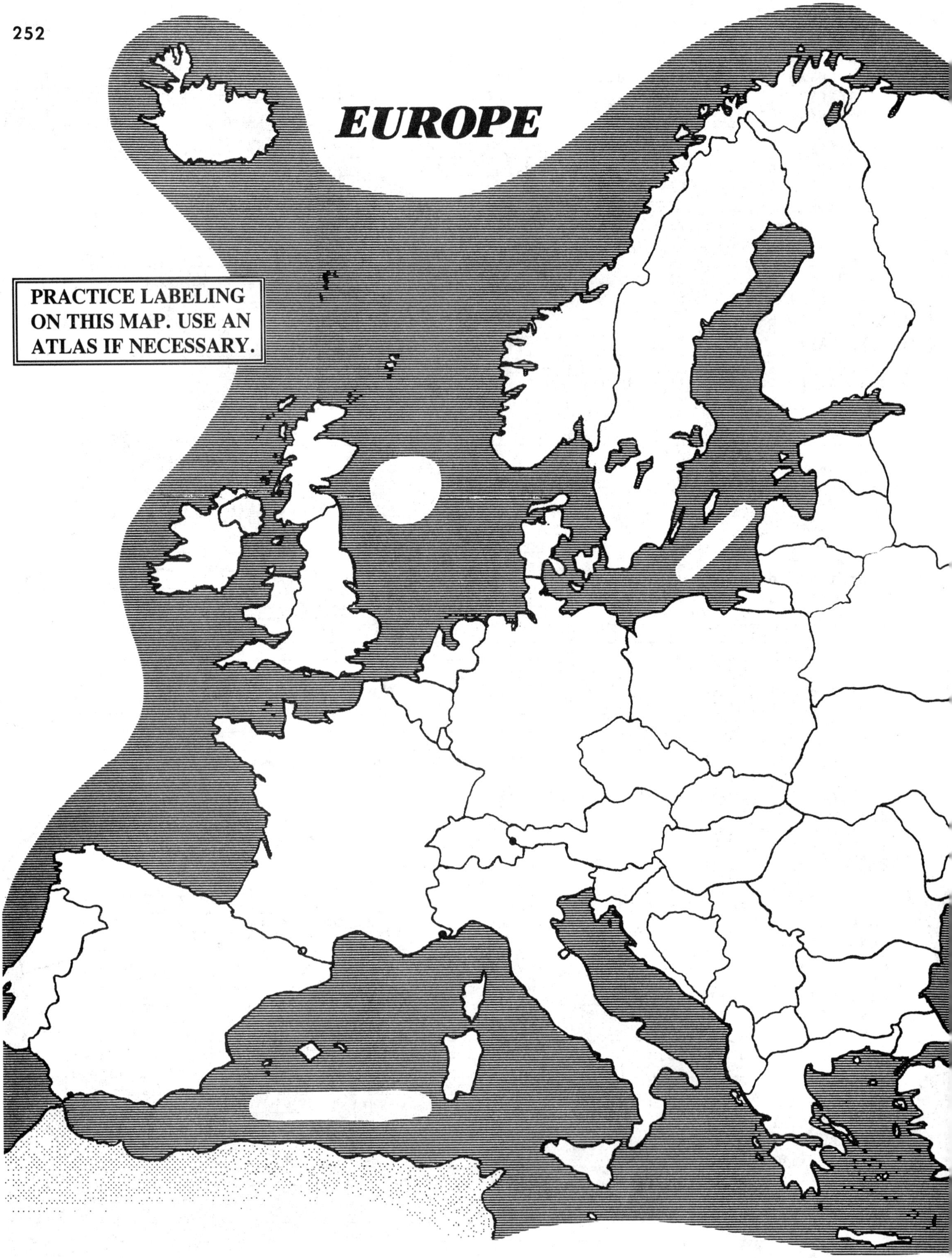
EUROPE
PRACTICE LABELING ON THIS MAP. USE AN ATLAS IF NECESSARY.

EUROPE

PRACTICE LABELING ON THIS MAP. USE AN ATLAS IF NECESSARY.

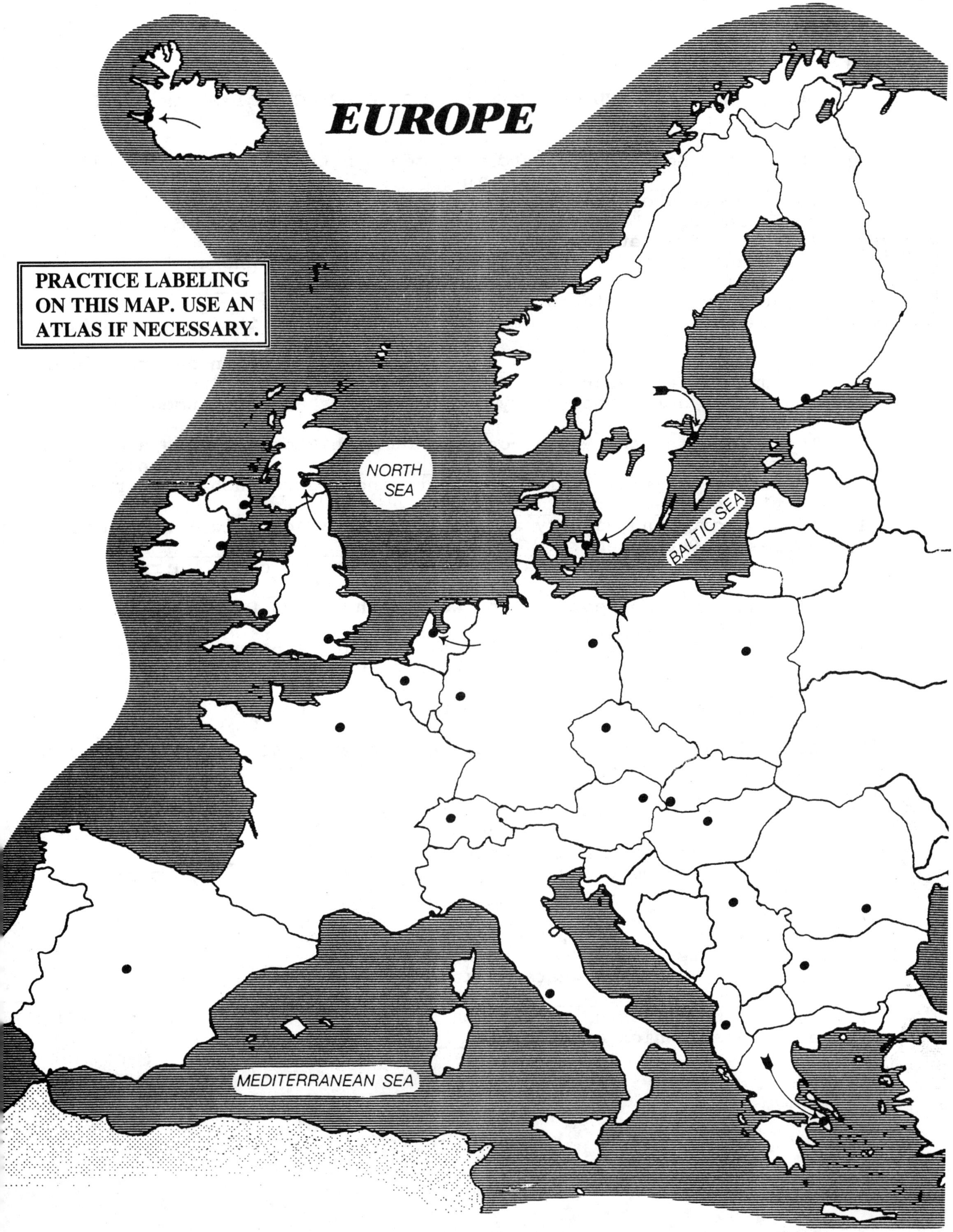

EUROPE REVIEW

USE MAPS, COUNTRIES AND CAPITALS LIST OR CURRENCIES LIST IF NECESSARY.

1. The Little Mermaid Statue can be seen in the harbor of the city of ____________________________ in ____________________________________.
2. The country where the drachma is the currency is ________________.
3. Music and art, beautiful scenery, and cities such as Salzburg and Innsbruck are details describing ______________________________.
4. The Grand Place and the little statue called Manneken Pis are sights in _____________________, ________________________(country).
5. Country of 60,000 lakes and capital Helsinki is _________________.
6. Wedged between Belgium, Germany, and France is the small country of ____________________________.
7. _______________, ________________ is where you can see the Louvre Museum, Eiffel Tower, and Notre Dame Cathedral.
8. Goulash is a food specialty and paprika is an often used spice in ______________________________.
9. The Acropolis, the Parthenon, and other historic sights are in the city of __________________ in ______________________(country).
10. Called the "Emerald Isle" and featuring sights such as Blarney Castle is _________________________.
11. In what city and country are Buckingham Palace, Big Ben, and the Houses of Parliament? ____________________, ____________________
12. Vatican City, the smallest country in the world, is surrounded by the city of _______________, __________________(country).
13. One can find the best buys of wooden shoes and Delftware in the country of ______________________.
14. City of canals and highlighted by St. Mark's Square (Piazza San Marco) and the Doges' Palace (Palazzo Ducale) is _________________, _______________(country).
15. Oslo is the capital and reindeer herds may be seen in the northern part of ____________________.
16. Capital city of the country where volcanoes, hot springs, and ice fields can be found is ____________________ in ___________________.
17. ____________________is the capital of _________________, an island located in the Mediterranean, and where Maltese is spoken.
18. ________________________is actually two cities, separated by the Danube River, and is the capital of _____________________________.
19. What country has the currency called the zloty and the capital, Warsaw? ____________________
20. Sofia is the capital of ___________________________.
21. Castles, beer gardens, the Rhine River, a major car manufacturing area - these things describe the country of _____________________.
22. The city in England where Shakespeare was born is ________________ _____________________________.
23. One of the cities on the French Riviera has a huge film festival every year? Which city is it? ___________________

24. ____________________is the capital of _______________________, the country described by windmills, tulips, cheese market towns and a land reclaimed from the sea by a series of dikes.
25. A capital city, formerly divided into East and West sections and now part of a unified Germany is ____________________________.
26. _______________________ is Romania's capital city.
27. Fantastic alpine scenery and best buys of watches, knives, cameras, and chocolates are in ______________________________.
28. The capital city of the Czech Republic is __________________________
29. The _____________ is the currency of the Austria.
30. _____________, a specialty of Switzerland, features skewered chunks of bread/fruit dipped into a pot of a melted cheese mixture.
31. Vilnius is the capital of Lithuania. True or False _____________
32. Sweden's famous food specialty is ______________________, a table of a variety of hot and cold dishes.
33. Three of the best buys in Russia are ______________________, _______________________, and ____________________________________.
34. In what city are the Kremlin and Red Square? ______________________
35. Monte Carlo, known for its famous casino, is in ___________________.
36. Cordoba, Barcelona, Granada, and Toledo are cities in ____________.
37. Lisbon is the capital of ______________________.
38. The country at the tip of Spain famous for its rock fortress is ____________________________________.
39. A popular form of entertainment in Portugal that features songs and lamenting ballads is the _______________.
40. One of the most literate countries in the world and where sagas, or storytelling, originated is _______________________.
41. The country that has two national languages (French and Flemish) and has cities such as Ghent, Bruges, Liege, Namur, and Antwerp is ____________________.
42. Edinburgh is the capital of _______________________.
43. Ouzo is a popular drink and tavernas are popular nightspots in the country of ____________________.
44. The _________________ Islands, situated in the Atlantic Ocean off the coast of North Africa, are a possession of Spain.
45. Naples and Florence are popular cities to visit in _______________.
46. In the Pyrenees Mountains on the border between Spain and France is the country of ___________________________.
47. The escudo is the currency of ________________________.
48. The name of the chapel located in Vatican City that features a ceiling painted by Michelangelo is the __________________ Chapel.
49. What was once the only Soviet airline? ______________________
50. Killarney, Limerick, Shannon, and Dublin are in __________________.

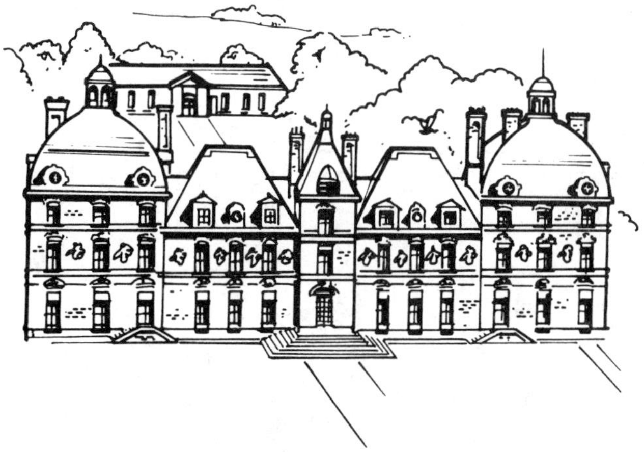

EUROPE REVIEW

Answer "T" for True or "F" for False to the following statements.

_______ 1. Portugal is on the Mediterranean Sea.
_______ 2. The Balearic Islands are a possession of Spain.
_______ 3. Portugal is a large producer of cork.
_______ 4. The Prado is a famous museum in Madrid.
_______ 5. The Black Forest is in Belgium.
_______ 6. Stonehenge is located in Ireland.
_______ 7. The coastal area that includes Torremolinos is called the Costa Brava.
_______ 8. Ouzo is the national drink of Bulgaria.
_______ 9. The name of the mountain range on the border of Spain and France is the Jura Mountains.
_______10. Corsica is a possession of Italy.
_______11. Bergen, Norway is above the Arctic Circle.
_______12. "Bull's Blood" is a local wine of Austria.
_______13. The Apennines are mountains spanning the peninsula of Italy.
_______14. Beaumaris Castle can be found in Germany.
_______15. Zurich is the capital of Switzerland.

EUROPE REVIEW

1. Flamenco shows are popular in the country of ____________________.
2. Goteburg/Gothenburg is a major port city of ____________________.
3. ________________________ is called the "postage stamp" country.
4. Name three cities in Germany. ____________________________
5. What English coastal city is known for its famous white cliffs?

   ____
6. The area known as Scandinavia includes ________________________

   ____.
7. ______________ is Moscow's famous cathedral with the onion-shaped domes.
8. The Ural Mountains are in Italy. True or False ___________
9. Normandy, Brittany, and Burgundy are regions of _________________.
10. Edam and Gouda are two types of cheeses made in _________________.
11. The Danube River is a main artery for transportation within the country of Ireland. True or False ____________
12. Giant's Causeway, an unusual area of geometrically-shaped basalt rocks, is in ___________________________.
13. The United Kingdom is made up of _____________________________

    ____.
14. The resort area called the Algarve is in ______________________.
15. Two major islands in the Mediterranean Sea that are possessions of Italy are _______________ and __________________.

EUROPE REVIEW

1. Cardiff is the capital of ______________________________.
2. The ________________ Islands (Mallorca, Menorca, and Ibiza) in the Mediterranean Sea are a possession of Spain.
3. In what city are the famous Tivoli Gardens and the Little Mermaid Statue? ______________________
4. What country offers beautiful scenery and has the capital, Vienna? ________________
5. Gran Canaria is one of the _______________ Islands.
6. The country that has best buys of lace, leather, diamonds, cookies, pewterware, and tapestries is ______________________.
7. The schilling is the currency of ________________________.
8. Spain's Costa del Sol stretches to either side of ______________.
9. In the country of ________________, it is popular to tour the Black Forest, cruise down the Rhine River, and perhaps go skiing at Garmisch.
10. If you were in the city of ____________________ you could walk through the Jardin des Tuileries, cruise on the Seine River, or see a lavish show at the Lido or the Moulin Rouge.
11. Name three places of interest in London. ________________________, __________________________, and _____________________________
12. You would go to the Danish city of __________________ to see the birthplace of Hans Christian Anderson.
13. Budapest is the capital of Romania. True or False ____________
14. The country of ___________________ has Oslo as its capital.
15. The city known as the "Venice of the North" is _________________.
16. Three languages spoken in Switzerland are ______________________, ___________________, and ____________________.
17. The famous fairytale castles in Germany were built by the eccentric monarch named ________________________.
18. The currency of Spain is the ____________________.
19. The city in Italy famous for its Leaning Tower is ______________.
20. The ___________________ is the currency of Turkey.
21. What is the name of the famous palace of Louis XIV located outside of Paris? ______________________
22. In what city would you walk down the Via Veneto and throw a coin in Trevi Fountain? _________________
23. The city of Budapest is on the _____________ River.
24. The largest freshwater lake in Europe is Lake _________________ in ______________________.
25. The nickname for the country of Ireland is ____________________.

EUROPE REVIEW

MATCH THE CAPITAL CITIES TO THEIR COUNTRIES (not all answers may be used). Use the list of capitals and countries if you are unable to locate the answers within the text.

1.	_______Madrid	A. Ireland
2.	_______London	B. Russia
3.	_______Budapest	C. Spain
4.	_______Rome	D. Portugal
5.	_______Bern	E. Iceland
6.	_______Brussels	F. England
7.	_______Dublin	G. Switzerland
8.	_______Athens	H. Romania
9.	_______Berlin	I. Hungary
10.	_______Paris	J. Turkey
11.	_______Copenhagen	K. Germany
12.	_______Vienna	L. Finland
13.	_______Helsinki	M. Wales
14.	_______Amsterdam	N. Poland
15.	_______Warsaw	O. Sweden
16.	_______Cardiff	P. Belgium
17.	_______Sofia	Q. Austria
18.	_______Bucharest	R. Netherlands/Holland
19.	_______Ankara	S. Bulgaria
20.	_______Belfast	T. Italy
21.	_______Prague	U. Czech Republic
22.	_______Moscow	V. France
23.	_______Reykjavik	W. Northern Ireland
24.	_______Lisbon	X. Liechtenstein
25.	_______Stockholm	Y. Denmark
		Z. Greece

MATCH CURRENCIES TO COUNTRIES. Use the currencies list if necessary.

1.	_______Peseta	A. Russia
2.	_______Escudo	B. England
3.	_______Belgian Franc	C. Hungary
4.	_______Drachma	D. Spain
5.	_______Forint	E. Italy
6.	_______Italian Lire(a)	F. Switzerland
7.	_______Mark	G. Germany
8.	_______Zloty	H. Portugal
9.	_______Norwegian Krone	I. Iceland
10.	_______Guilder	J. Greece
11.	_______Schilling	K. Turkey
12.	_______Lei	L. Bulgaria
13.	_______French Franc	M. Poland
14.	_______Swiss Franc	N. Norway
15.	_______Turkish Lira	O. Netherlands
16.	_______Pound Sterling	P. Austria
17.	_______Irish Pound (Punt)	Q. Romania
18.	_______Iceland Krona	R. Ireland
19.	_______Ruble	S. France
20.	_______Lev	T. Belgium

NOW SEE IF YOU CAN IDENTIFY THESE SIGHTS OF EUROPE:

Give names, cities, and/or countries, as they apply to the statements.

1. The Arc de Triomphe, shown here, is located in ________________.
   city

2. This is Neuschwanstein, a castle built by the eccentric monarch,

   King ____________________________.
   It is located in the country of

   ____________________________.

3. This is the famous Tower Bridge, a sight to see in the city of

   ____________________________.

4. If you are in ______________, Italy you're sure to see this famous landmark,

   the ____________________________.

5. This is the ______________________
Statue that is located in the

city of ___________________________

in _________________________________.
country

6. Visitors to Athens, Greece are likely to see

the ______________________________
pictured here.

7. This might be a common sight if you were in the country of

______________________________.

8. Tourists in the city of canals,

______________________________,
can sightsee from a gondola.

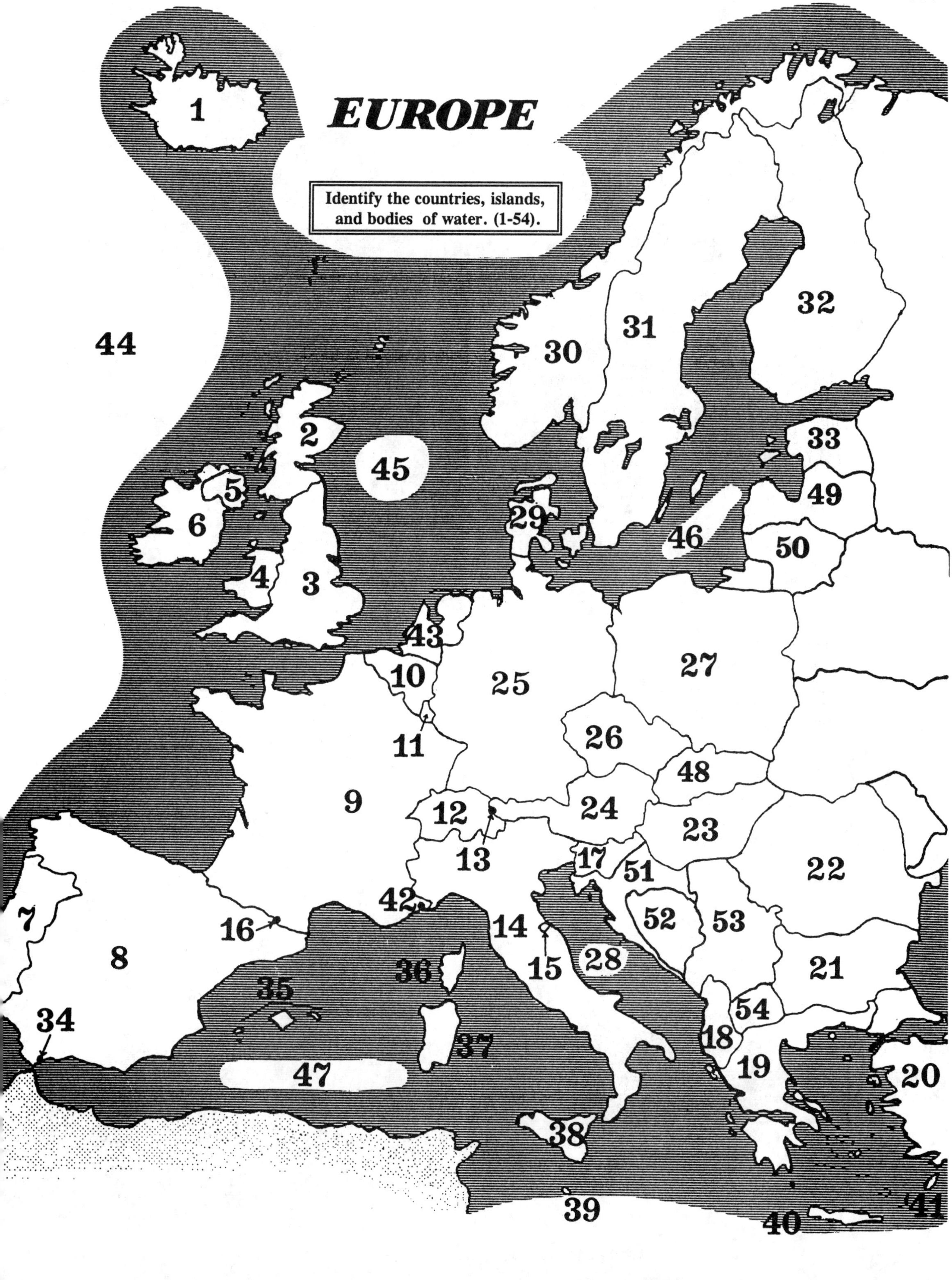
EUROPE
Identify the countries, islands, and bodies of water. (1-54).
1
2
3
4
5
6
7
8
9
10
11
12
13
14
15
16
17
18
19
20
21
22
23
24
25
26
27
28
29
30
31
32
33
34
35
36
37
38
39
40
41
42
43
44
45
46
47
48
49
50
51
52
53
54

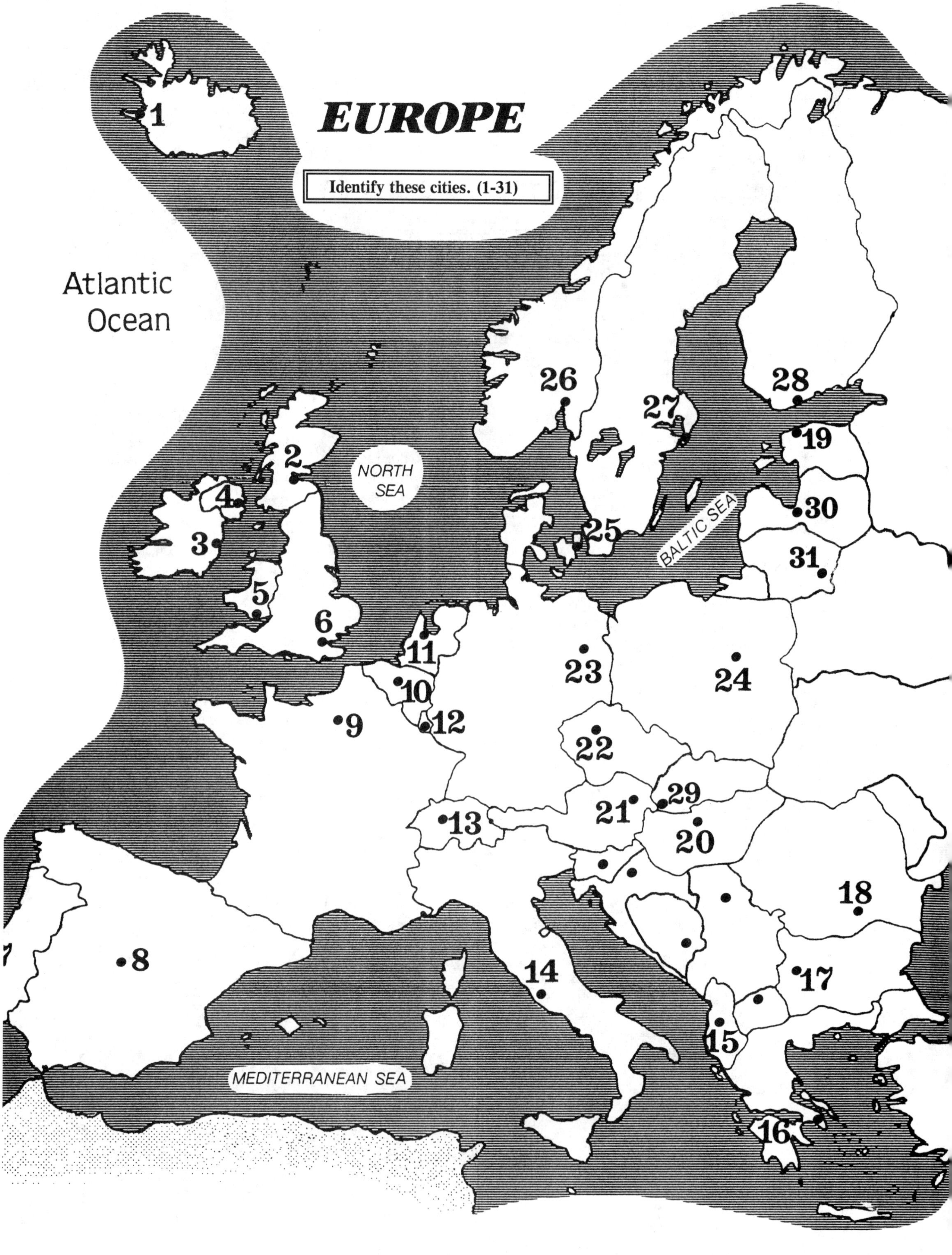
EUROPE
Identify these cities. (1-31)
Atlantic Ocean
NORTH SEA
BALTIC SEA
MEDITERRANEAN SEA
1
2
3
4
5
6
8
9
10
11
12
13
14
15
16
17
18
19
20
21
22
23
24
25
26
27
28
29
30
31

EUROPEAN DESTINATIONS - FURTHER ACTIVITIES

1. Plan an eight day itinerary for a couple who are planning a trip to Switzerland in July. They are active, in their 50's, and have never been to Europe before.

2. Two college students, Carla and Stephanie, are planning on going to Europe for three weeks. They want to get a Eurailpass and travel through France, Spain, Italy, and maybe Greece. They will be flying in and out of Luxembourg. They are particularly interested in seeing the cities of Paris, St. Tropez, Nice, Cannes, Madrid, Barcelona, Malaga, Torremolinos, Rome, Pisa, Naples, Venice, Athens, Rhodes, and Mykonos. Suggest an itinerary, using approximate travel times by train, and consider omitting cities or altering the order in which they are visited.

3. Mr. and Mrs. John Hunter are planning a two week trip to Great Britain. They have both been to London and southern England and would like to sightsee in Wales and Scotland. They find that the airfare into London is the least expensive so they will use it as their gateway and rent a car. What would be a possible itinerary? They like the outdoors and are an active young couple.

4. Two ladies in their late 40's are going to Italy in April. They have never been to Europe before. Provide a day-by-day itinerary for a ten day stay, visiting Rome, Florence, Naples, Capri, Pisa, Venice, Pompeii, etc. They will fly in and out of Rome and want to travel by train between cities.

5. A couple and their two children, aged 10 and 7, would like to go to Europe for ten days. They would like mainly to visit Germany, Austria, and Switzerland, but they are concerned about costs and would like to spend about $5000.00 total on the trip. What are your suggestions for the trip and its itinerary?

ABOUT ACCOMMODATIONS

Accommodations in Europe range widely. There are hotels, inns, resorts, castles, pensions, paradors, guest houses, youth hostels, and more.

The types of rooms vary. In many European cities, rooms will be relatively small with twin beds. In some hotels and inns, there are rooms without private baths. You may want to ask to see the room at an inn or hotel prior to registering.

Meal plans included with the room price also vary. There is the bed and breakfast accommodation, with usually a meal of eggs, toast, and coffee/tea included. CP (Continental Plan) means a continental breakfast is included, which may be just rolls and coffee. Other meal plans are: AP (American Plan) - all three meals, MAP (Modified American Plan) - two meals, usually breakfast and dinner, and EP (European Plan) - no meals.

NOTES

CHAPTER 13

Africa

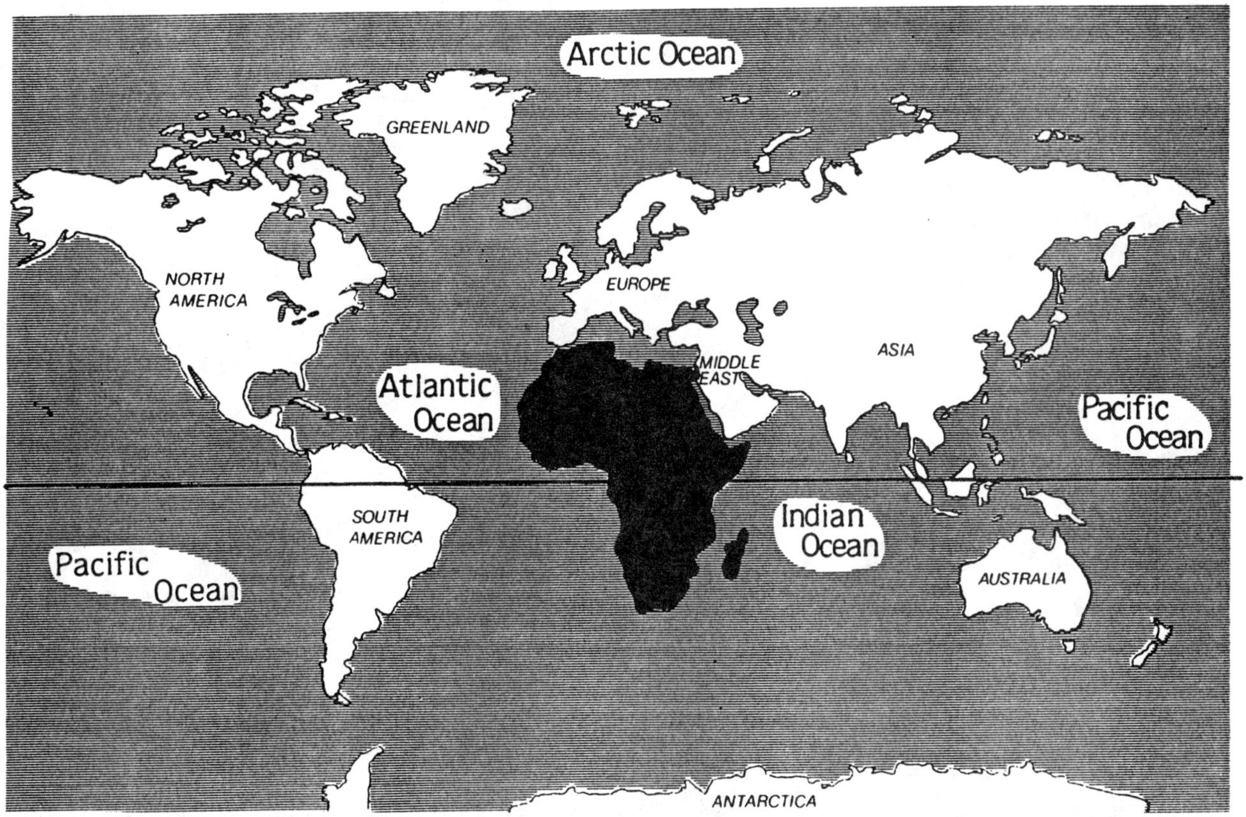

NOTES

COUNTRIES OF AFRICA

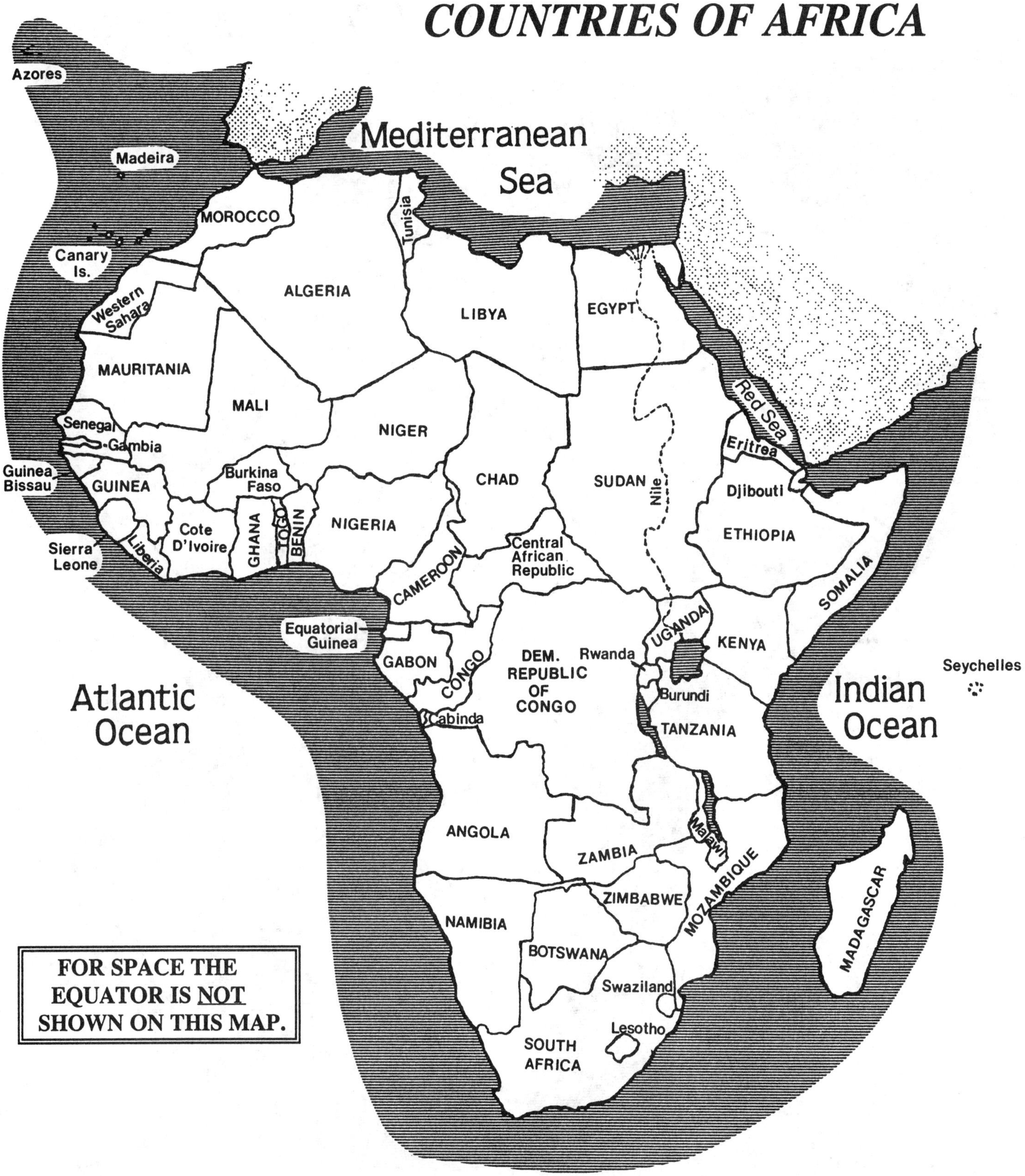

FOR SPACE THE EQUATOR IS NOT SHOWN ON THIS MAP.

SOME CITIES IN AFRICA

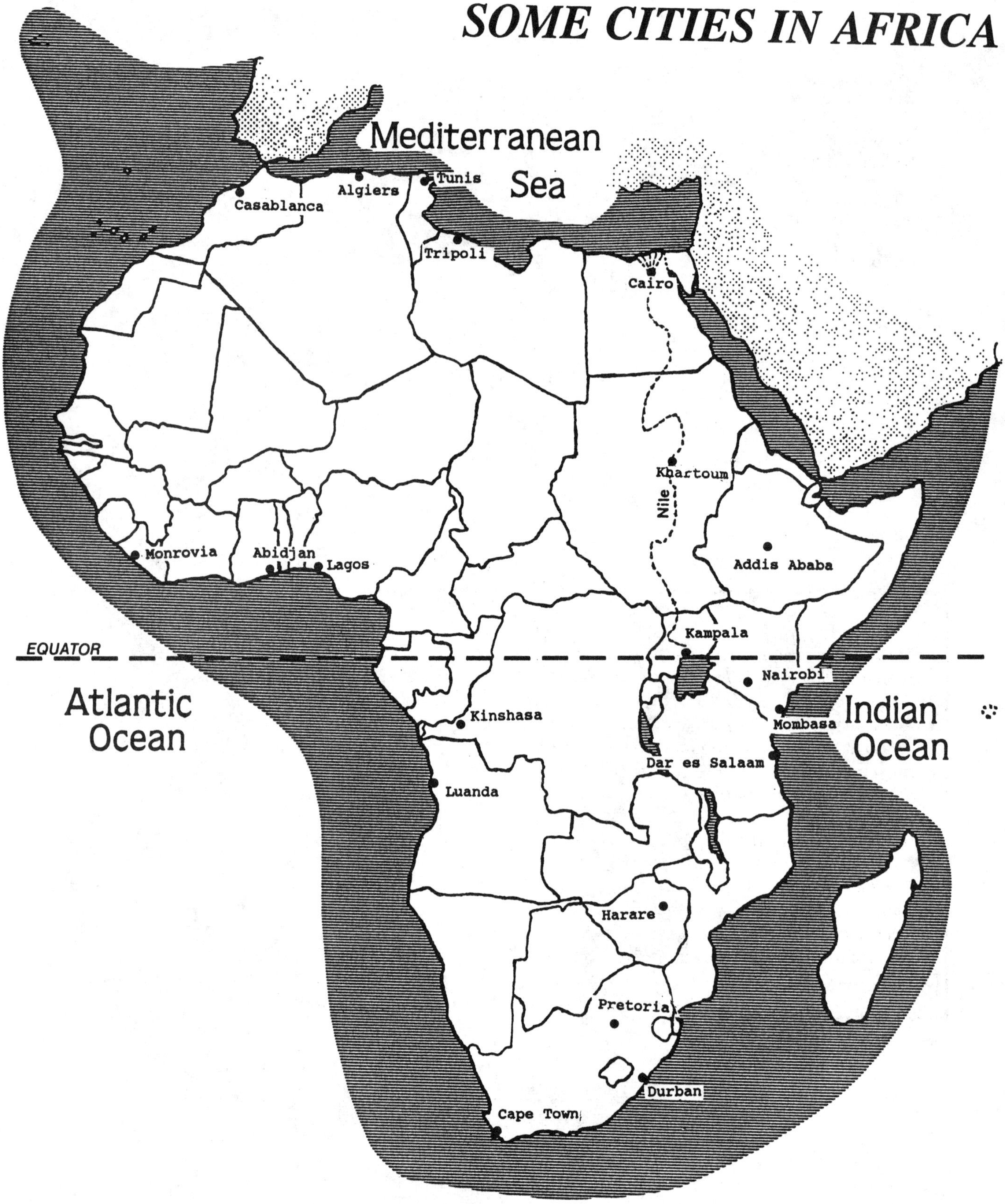
Mediterranean
Sea
Tunis
Algiers
Casablanca
Tripoli
Cairo
Khartoum
Nile
Addis Ababa
Monrovia
Abidjan
Lagos
Kampala
EQUATOR
Nairobi
Atlantic
Ocean
Kinshasa
Mombasa
Indian
Ocean
Dar es Salaam
Luanda
Harare
Pretoria
Durban
Cape Town

AFRICA - MAJOR CITY/AIRPORT CODES

ALGERIA
ALG - Algiers

BOTSWANA
GBE - Gaborone

CHAD
NDJ - N'djamena

COTE D'IVOIRE
ABJ - Abidjan

EGYPT
CAI - Cairo
LXR - Luxor

ETHIOPIA
ADD - Addis Ababa

GHANA
ACC - Accra

KENYA
NBO - Nairobi
MBA - Mombasa

LIBERIA
MLW - Monrovia

MOROCCO
RBA - Rabat
RAK - Marrakech
TNG - Tangier

MOZAMBIQUE
MPM - Maputo

NIGERIA
LOS - Lagos

SENEGAL
DKR - Dakar

SEYCHELLES
SEZ - Mahe Island

SOUTH AFRICA
JNB - Johannesburg
CPT - Cape Town
DUR - Durban

TANZANIA
DAR - Dar es Salaam

TUNISIA
TUN - Tunis

ZAMBIA
LUN - Lusaka

ZIMBABWE
HRE - Harare

TIPS ON TRAVEL TO AFRICA

1. *Check with the U.S. Department of State for advisories and the consulates/embassies of the countries for requirements and the CDC (Centers for Disease Control) for health and medical recommendations.*
2. *Find out the best time to travel and use a reputable company for the travel arrangements.*
3. *Know that Africa appeals to the more adventurous, and is not for travelers who expect high standards, thorough reliable transportation and other particulars.*
4. *Bring plenty of film. Carry bottled water with you, and perhaps some packaged snacks.*
5. *Always ask permission before taking photographs.*
6. *Guard your possessions.*
7. *Don't be surprised if you are treated with hostility or searched at border crossings.*
8. *Don't swim at any beach where others aren't swimming.*
9. *Don't assume that you can enter any mosque. Always ask.*
10. *Drug laws are taken very seriously. Never purchase or use illegal drugs.*
11. *Dress conservatively in the cities.*
12. *Handshaking is the customary form of greeting.*
13. *You may find yourself caught in the center of unsolicited attention. Young children will try to sell you things; unofficial guides will offer advice/services. Be courteous but wary and firm when necessary.*

AFRICA

The size of the continent of Africa, the number of countries, and the variety of influences (European colonialism and numerous tribal groups) are all indicators of the tremendous diversity and potential of this area of the world. The equator splits this great continent, and the enormous Sahara Desert spans the northern countries. Africa is also a land of great rivers - the Nile, Niger, Orange, Zambezi, Zaire - just to name a few. It is a place to see wildlife - elephants, zebras, lions, wildebeests, giraffes, hippos, rhinoceroses, antelopes, etc. Many areas are subject to famine, poverty, disease, illiteracy, and political conflicts and struggles. The tourist may visit Kenya and Tanzania to go on a safari; Egypt to see the Nile River, the Sphinx, and the Great Pyramids; Morocco to shop in the bazaars; or Cote D'Ivoire for a resort vacation. But even with some countries' increased revenues from tourism and agricultural exports, there remain generally difficult conditions. What were once local problems (famine, droughts, friction between tribal groups, health conditions) have now reached international attention and the business traveler and the tourist should be aware of the possible instability of many African nations. U.S. travelers should check with the Department of State for travel advisories and current information. Most countries will be outlined here. Complete profile forms on major tourist destinations and countries before working on the reviews and tests.

MOROCCO lies across from Spain and tourists visit cities such as Fez, Rabat, Tangier, Casablanca, and Marrakech - gateway to the Sahara. The souks (marketplaces) are where tourists bargain for the colorful native crafts, copperware, gold and silver jewelry, and leather goods. Mint tea is the national drink and couscous (spiced semolina and meat sauce cooked over broth) is the national dish.

ALGERIA and TUNISIA are countries to which tourist travel is somewhat limited. They are French influenced countries, with histories that involved French colonialism, and the national languages are French and Arabic. Tunisia, the site of the ancient city of Carthage, attracts some European tourists to its beach resort areas.

Few Westerners visit **LIBYA, SUDAN, ETHIOPIA, ERITREA, DJIBOUTI, SOMALIA, CHAD, NIGER, MAURITANIA, and WESTERN SAHARA.**

MALI may be a stop on tours to see the tribal culture of the Dogon people and to visit the city of Timbuktu.

EGYPT, one of the most popular tourist countries of Africa, is sometimes combined with tours of Israel or the Middle East. The modern city of Cairo is a mass of people, noise, poverty, dust and dirt, mixed with splendid monuments, museums, mosques and city sights. From Tahrir Square buses depart for the Great Pyramids of Giza, the Sphinx, the Step Pyramid of King Zoser, and many other ancient sites. There are cruises on the Nile River, excursions to the Aswan Dam (one of the world's highest and largest), tours to the Temples of Karnak and Luxor and the Valley of the Kings. The relics of an ancient past and a history dating back over 5,000 years will attract those with an interest in art, architecture, archaeology, Middle Eastern study and religions, agriculture, desert research, Islamic culture, folklore, etc. Sport activities include yachting, diving, deep sea fishing, horseback riding, golf, along with spectator sports like soccer and horse racing.

BURKINA FASO used to be called Upper Volta, and three great rivers, the White, Red, and Black Volta, water the country's plains. Ouagadougou is the capital and within the urban areas French customs prevail and French is the official language.

A French heritage is evident in **SENEGAL** and **COTE D'IVOIRE.** Although the national language is French, both have other local languages (in Senegal the people widely speak Wolof and 20 other local languages). Dakar, the capital of Senegal, is a major port and industrial center. Foreign investment and agricultural exports have made Cote d'Ivoire's economy fairly high and stable. The capital is Yamoussoukro and Abidjan is a major city.

GAMBIA is a narrow strip of land almost completely surrounded by Senegal and has beaches and facilities that cater to some Europeans.

Continuing along the west coast of Africa are the countries of **GUINEA-BISSAU, GUINEA, and SIERRA LEONE**, with economies primarily based on agriculture.

In 1821 the American Colonization Society purchased land in **LIBERIA** for the resettling of freed American Negro slaves. The Liberian Dollar is pegged against the U.S. Dollar and U.S. notes are circulated. The capital, Monrovia, is named after President Monroe. Western firms have developed major economic activities around the country's resources of rubber and iron-ore. Other economic assistance comes from a large merchant fleet registered under the Liberian flag, some light industry, and U.S. economic aid.

GHANA has a variety of natural resources which include gold, diamonds, manganese ore, bauxite, cocoa, timber, oil, and agricultural products, and there is a rising interest in tourism.

TOGO's economy is mostly agriculturally based, and the country has a large reserve of phosphate. A fishing industry operates along the coast.

BENIN, which used to be called Dahomey, is largely undeveloped.

NIGERIA is a country of potential because of its oil reserves and its untapped resources of natural gas and coal, but it is hampered by a largely unskilled labor force, diverse and competitive ethnic groups, poor health conditions, few power facilities, and other internal and political tensions.

CAMEROON's official languages are English and French, but the people form a diverse population made up of hundreds of groups that speak a variety of major African languages.

CENTRAL AFRICAN REPUBLIC is another country having a variety of ethnic groups, further diversified by migrations during slave-trading times.

EQUATORIAL GUINEA is the only African country with Spanish as the official language, and it is composed of Rio Muni and five islands (Bioko is the largest and the capital is located there).

GABON has more than forty ethnic groups which include the Fang, the Eshira, the Bapounou, and the Teke. French is the official language.

CONGO is another French influenced republic, and the capital city of Brazzaville was the commercial center for the former colony called French Equatorial Africa.

DEMOCRATIC REPUBLIC OF CONGO was formerly Zaire. This country's earliest inhabitants were probably the Pygmies, who settled there thousands of years ago. Before being called Zaire it was the Belgian Congo. Today it is a country with hundreds of indigenous languages and peoples, with the Bantu peoples accounting for the majority. A recent uprising has changed the leadership of the country and thus the name change as well.

UGANDA suffered under the dictatorship of Major General Idi Amin, whose rule was largely corrupt, economically devastating and filled with a total disregard for human rights. Amin was driven from Uganda by a force of Tanzanian troops and Ugandan exiles.

KENYA is a popular tourist destination and its national parks and game reserves have long been famous for their variety and wealth of flora and fauna. Tourist facilities are well developed and there are many organized safaris. Aberdare National Park is adjacent to Mt. Kenya, and two of the park's popular lodges, Treetops and the Ark, are built on platforms overlooking clearings and feeding areas that are lit up for viewing at night. Amboseli National Park affords a fine view of Mt. Kilimanjaro (located across the border in Tanzania). Masai Mara National Reserve; Mt. Kenya, Meru, and Tsavo National Parks; Samburu Game Park; and the Lake Turkana region are some possible touring areas. Swahili is the national language - say "Jambo" to mean "how are you?" and "Ahsante" to mean "thank you."

TANZANIA has Africa's highest mountain, Mt. Kilimanjaro, and its largest game reserve, the Selous Game Reserve. On its western border is Lake Tanganyika, and along its northern border is Lake Victoria. The national parks include: Serengeti (featuring the spectacular migration), Lake Manyara, Arusha, Mikumi, Ruaha, Gome, Tarangire, and the Selous Game Reserve. The Ngorongoro Crater, a collapsed volcano almost ten miles across and 1,900 feet deep, is home to herds of zebras, wildebeests, elephants, rhinos, gazelles, and buffaloes. The country also includes the islands of Zanzibar ("island of cloves/spices") and Pemba.

RWANDA and BURUNDI border Tanzania, and there are some organized safaris to Rwanda's Kagera National Park.

ZAMBIA is home to the "smoke that thunders," Victoria Falls, as well as a number of national parks.

MALAWI's largest ethnic group is the Chewa, and it is these people who speak Chichewa, the national language. The official language is English and the currency is the kwacha (Zambia's currency is also called the kwacha).

The Zambezi River flows through **MOZAMBIQUE** into the Indian Ocean. The influence of Portugal is evident here, as Portuguese is the official language, along with many dialects of Swahili.

The tableland of the Kalahari Desert covers most of **BOTSWANA** and there are some national parks and game reserves.

ZIMBABWE's capital, Harare, was formerly called Salisbury, and is the usual starting point for any visit. From this clean and sophisticated city, tour some of the national parks, gardens, and sanctuaries that have emerged as some of Africa's most beautiful.

NAMIBIA was formerly known as South West Africa, and the official languages are Afrikaans and English (like South Africa). The country's attractions include national parks and game reserves, sights such as the Namib Desert (with its towering sand dunes - some up to 1000 feet high), and the attractive capital city of Windhoek (featuring German colonial architecture, three castles, fashionable shops and German cafes).

Tourist travel to **ANGOLA** is generally not allowed; some business travel is permitted.

SOUTH AFRICA's climate is generally sunny, with mild winters, except for an occasional cold spell when snow might fall. Because it is in the Southern Hemisphere, the seasons are the reverse of those North of the Equator. There are three major geographical regions: plateau, mountains, and the coastal belt. The two major rivers are the Orange and the Limpopo, and major cities include Pretoria, Cape Town, Johannesburg, and Durban. Seeing Kruger National Park and the "diamond capital of the world," city of Kimberley, are popular tourist activities, as well as taking the famous Blue Train from Pretoria or Johannesburg to Cape Town. Around Cape Town see the Castle of Good Hope, the History Museum, and ride the cable car to the top of Table Mountain. Gold, diamonds, and wool are major exports of South Africa and there are good wines and brandies locally produced. The policy of apartheid, the separation of whites from non-whites, was an establishment cemented by the National Party, which came into power in 1948. The abolishment of the apartheid policy has brought many changes. Some trouble in the political and social life of South Africa continues. There are three capitals: Cape Town is the legislative capital, Pretoria is the administrative, and Bloemfontein is the judicial capital. The currency is the rand.

LESOTHO and SWAZILAND are two countries within the overall borders of South Africa. Both offer casinos to interest the visitor and some natural beauty as well.

MADAGASCAR, off the coast of Mozambique, is the fourth largest island in the world, and includes several much smaller islands. Much of the flora and fauna found here is endemic to Madagascar, and the island is a large producer of cloves, vanilla, sugar cane and bananas.

Other islands off the coast of Africa include: Canary Is. (a Spanish possession), the Azores (Portuguese), Cape Verde Is. (a republic), the republic of Sao Tome and Principe, the island nation of Comoros, the former French possession Mauritius, and the Seychelles (a republic).

Complete profiles on countries such as Egypt, Kenya, Tanzania, Gambia, Cote d'Ivoire, Morocco, South Africa, Zambia, Ghana, and Rwanda. After you have researched and read about the destinations, complete the reviews and tests.

COUNTRY: ____________ CAPITAL: ____________
DOCUMENTARY REQUIREMENTS (U.S. CITIZENS): ____________
SHOTS, OTHER INFO: ____________
CURRENCY: ____________ CURRENCY CODE: ________ EXCHANGE RATE: ____________
LANGUAGE(S): ____________
SIZE: ____________ POPULATION: ____________
BEST TIME TO VISIT: ____________
MAJOR CITIES/PLACES OF INTEREST/PARKS AND RESERVES: ____________
____
____
____
SPORTS: ____________
RELIGIONS: ____________ GOVERNMENT: ____________
FOOD SPECIALTIES: ____________
BEST BUYS: ____________
SPECIAL INFORMATION: ____________
____
AIRLINES: ____________ CITY/AIRPORT CODES: ____________
TRANSPORTATION: ____________
OTHER INFO: ____________

COUNTRY: ____________ CAPITAL: ____________
DOCUMENTARY REQUIREMENTS (U.S. CITIZENS): ____________
SHOTS, OTHER INFO: ____________
CURRENCY: ____________ CURRENCY CODE: ________ EXCHANGE RATE: ____________
LANGUAGE(S): ____________
SIZE: ____________ POPULATION: ____________
BEST TIME TO VISIT: ____________
MAJOR CITIES/PLACES OF INTEREST/PARKS AND RESERVES: ____________
____
____
____
SPORTS: ____________
RELIGIONS: ____________ GOVERNMENT: ____________
FOOD SPECIALTIES: ____________
BEST BUYS: ____________
SPECIAL INFORMATION: ____________
____
AIRLINES: ____________ CITY/AIRPORT CODES: ____________
TRANSPORTATION: ____________
OTHER INFO: ____________

COUNTRY: ____________ CAPITAL: ____________
DOCUMENTARY REQUIREMENTS (U.S. CITIZENS): ____________
SHOTS, OTHER INFO: ____________
CURRENCY: ____________ CURRENCY CODE: ________ EXCHANGE RATE: ____________
LANGUAGE(S): ____________
SIZE: ____________ POPULATION: ____________
BEST TIME TO VISIT: ____________
MAJOR CITIES/PLACES OF INTEREST/PARKS AND RESERVES: ____________
____
____
____
SPORTS: ____________
RELIGIONS: ____________ GOVERNMENT: ____________
FOOD SPECIALTIES: ____________
BEST BUYS: ____________
SPECIAL INFORMATION: ____________
____
AIRLINES: ____________ CITY/AIRPORT CODES: ____________
TRANSPORTATION: ____________
OTHER INFO: ____________

COUNTRY: ____________ CAPITAL: ____________
DOCUMENTARY REQUIREMENTS (U.S. CITIZENS): ____________
SHOTS, OTHER INFO: ____________
CURRENCY: ____________ CURRENCY CODE: ________ EXCHANGE RATE: ____________
LANGUAGE(S): ____________
SIZE: ____________ POPULATION: ____________
BEST TIME TO VISIT: ____________
MAJOR CITIES/PLACES OF INTEREST/PARKS AND RESERVES: ____________
SPORTS: ____________
RELIGIONS: ____________ GOVERNMENT: ____________
FOOD SPECIALTIES: ____________
BEST BUYS: ____________
SPECIAL INFORMATION: ____________
AIRLINES: ____________ CITY/AIRPORT CODES: ____________
TRANSPORTATION: ____________
OTHER INFO: ____________

COUNTRY: ____________ CAPITAL: ____________
DOCUMENTARY REQUIREMENTS (U.S. CITIZENS): ____________
SHOTS, OTHER INFO: ____________
CURRENCY: ____________ CURRENCY CODE: ________ EXCHANGE RATE: ____________
LANGUAGE(S): ____________
SIZE: ____________ POPULATION: ____________
BEST TIME TO VISIT: ____________
MAJOR CITIES/PLACES OF INTEREST/PARKS AND RESERVES: ____________
SPORTS: ____________
RELIGIONS: ____________ GOVERNMENT: ____________
FOOD SPECIALTIES: ____________
BEST BUYS: ____________
SPECIAL INFORMATION: ____________
AIRLINES: ____________ CITY/AIRPORT CODES: ____________
TRANSPORTATION: ____________
OTHER INFO: ____________

COUNTRY: ____________ CAPITAL: ____________
DOCUMENTARY REQUIREMENTS (U.S. CITIZENS): ____________
SHOTS, OTHER INFO: ____________
CURRENCY: ____________ CURRENCY CODE: ________ EXCHANGE RATE: ____________
LANGUAGE(S): ____________
SIZE: ____________ POPULATION: ____________
BEST TIME TO VISIT: ____________
MAJOR CITIES/PLACES OF INTEREST/PARKS AND RESERVES: ____________
SPORTS: ____________
RELIGIONS: ____________ GOVERNMENT: ____________
FOOD SPECIALTIES: ____________
BEST BUYS: ____________
SPECIAL INFORMATION: ____________
AIRLINES: ____________ CITY/AIRPORT CODES: ____________
TRANSPORTATION: ____________
OTHER INFO: ____________

COUNTRY: ____________ CAPITAL: ____________
DOCUMENTARY REQUIREMENTS (U.S. CITIZENS): ____________
SHOTS, OTHER INFO: ____________
CURRENCY: ____________ CURRENCY CODE: ________ EXCHANGE RATE: ____________
LANGUAGE(S): ____________
SIZE: ____________ POPULATION: ____________
BEST TIME TO VISIT: ____________
MAJOR CITIES/PLACES OF INTEREST/PARKS AND RESERVES: ____________
____
____
____
SPORTS: ____________
RELIGIONS: ____________ GOVERNMENT: ____________
FOOD SPECIALTIES: ____________
BEST BUYS: ____________
SPECIAL INFORMATION: ____________
____
AIRLINES: ____________ CITY/AIRPORT CODES: ____________
TRANSPORTATION: ____________
OTHER INFO: ____________

COUNTRY: ____________ CAPITAL: ____________
DOCUMENTARY REQUIREMENTS (U.S. CITIZENS): ____________
SHOTS, OTHER INFO: ____________
CURRENCY: ____________ CURRENCY CODE: ________ EXCHANGE RATE: ____________
LANGUAGE(S): ____________
SIZE: ____________ POPULATION: ____________
BEST TIME TO VISIT: ____________
MAJOR CITIES/PLACES OF INTEREST/PARKS AND RESERVES: ____________
____
____
____
SPORTS: ____________
RELIGIONS: ____________ GOVERNMENT: ____________
FOOD SPECIALTIES: ____________
BEST BUYS: ____________
SPECIAL INFORMATION: ____________
____
AIRLINES: ____________ CITY/AIRPORT CODES: ____________
TRANSPORTATION: ____________
OTHER INFO: ____________

COUNTRY: ____________ CAPITAL: ____________
DOCUMENTARY REQUIREMENTS (U.S. CITIZENS): ____________
SHOTS, OTHER INFO: ____________
CURRENCY: ____________ CURRENCY CODE: ________ EXCHANGE RATE: ____________
LANGUAGE(S): ____________
SIZE: ____________ POPULATION: ____________
BEST TIME TO VISIT: ____________
MAJOR CITIES/PLACES OF INTEREST/PARKS AND RESERVES: ____________
____
____
____
SPORTS: ____________
RELIGIONS: ____________ GOVERNMENT: ____________
FOOD SPECIALTIES: ____________
BEST BUYS: ____________
SPECIAL INFORMATION: ____________
____
AIRLINES: ____________ CITY/AIRPORT CODES: ____________
TRANSPORTATION: ____________
OTHER INFO: ____________

AFRICA

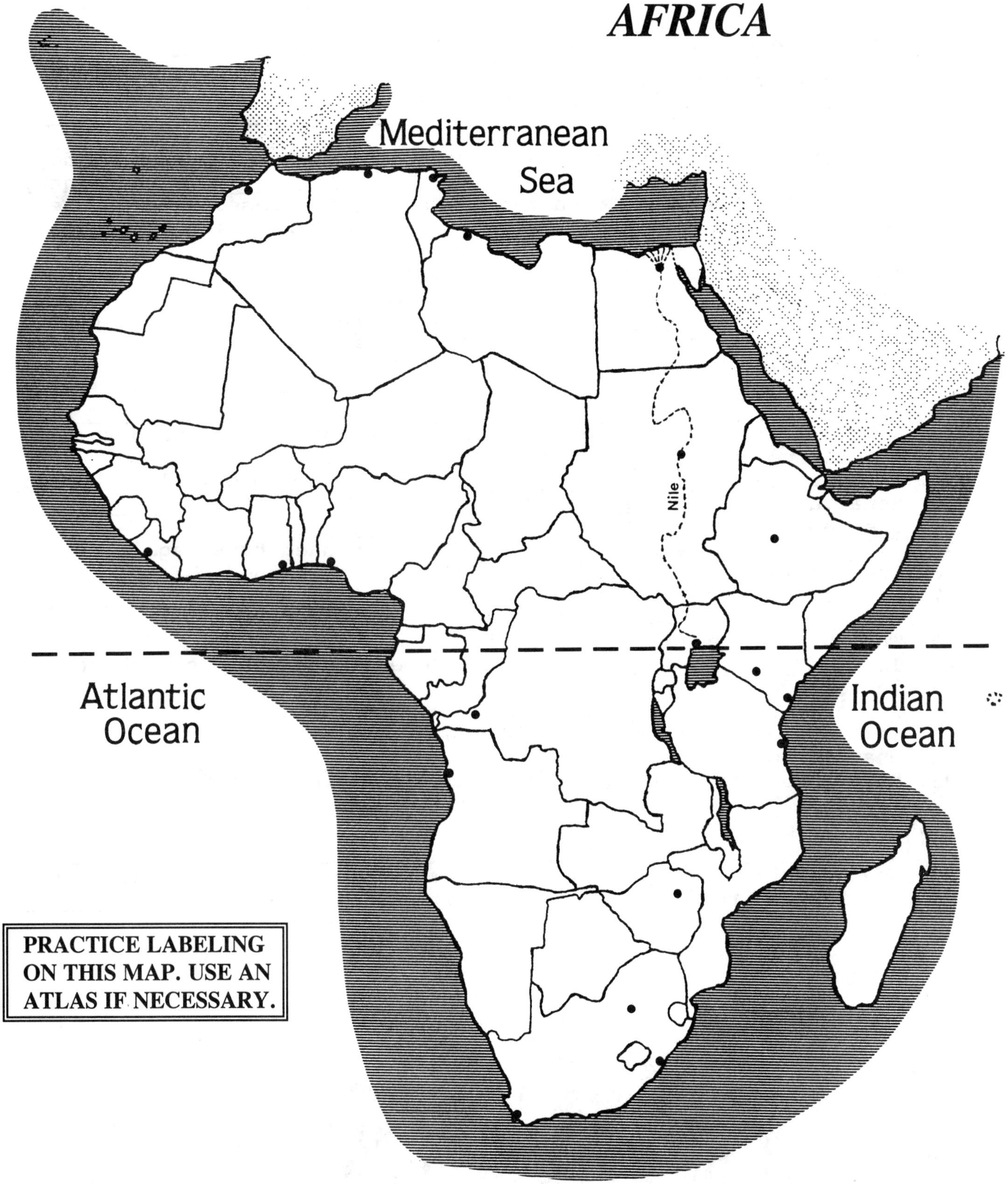

PRACTICE LABELING ON THIS MAP. USE AN ATLAS IF NECESSARY.

AFRICA REVIEW

1. Name three national parks located in Kenya. ______________________, ______________________, and ______________________.
2. The capital of Egypt is ______________________.
3. Three places of interest in Egypt are ______________________, ______________________, and ______________________.
4. The site of the ancient city of Carthage is near the present day city of ______________________ in ______________________(country).
5. In 1821 the American Colonization Society purchased land in the country of ______________________ for the resettling of freed American Negro slaves.
6. The capital of that country was named for ______________________, and is called ______________________.
7. Famous ______________________ Falls, called "the smoke that thunders" is located on the border of Zambia and Zimbabwe.
8. The legislative capital of South Africa is ______________________,
9. ______________________ is the capital of Ethiopia.
10. The country that has Tripoli as its capital is ______________________.
11. ______________________ is a spiced semolina and meat sauce dish and a food specialty of Morocco.
12. The country of ______________________ used to be called Dahomey.
13. Somalia is on the west coast of Africa. True or False __________
14. The capital of Algeria is ______________________.
15. ______________ is almost completely surrounded by Senegal.
16. The massive desert that spans North Africa is the ______________.
17. The famous river that flows through Egypt is the ______________.
18. ________________is a major city in Cote D'Ivoire.
19. The national drink in Morocco is ______________________.
20. The ______________ Dam in Egypt is one of the world's highest and largest dams.
21. Formerly called Salisbury, Zimbabwe's capital, ______________________, is the usual starting point for any visit.
22. What is the capital of Kenya? ______________________
23. Name five animals that can be commonly viewed on safaris in Africa. ____
24. What does apartheid mean? ____ ____
25. What country has Africa's highest mountain, Mt. Kilimanjaro, and the largest reserve, the Selous Game Reserve? ______________________

AFRICA REVIEW

USE THE LIST OF CAPITALS OR AN ATLAS FOR ASSISTANCE:

MATCH THE CITIES TO THEIR COUNTRIES:

1.	_______Accra	A. Tanzania
2.	_______Dar es Salaam	B. South Africa
3.	_______Abidjan	C. Namibia
4.	_______Windhoek	D. Morocco
5.	_______Ouagadougou	E. Kenya
6.	_______Lagos	F. Ghana
7.	_______Cairo	G. Senegal
8.	_______Maputo	H. Dem. Republic of Congo
9.	_______Lusaka	I. Burkina Faso
10.	_______Kinshasa	J. Zambia
11.	_______Brazzaville	K. Angola
12.	_______Dakar	L. Congo
13.	_______Tunis	M. Sierra Leone
14.	_______Rabat	N. Egypt
15.	_______Freetown	O. Cote D'Ivoire
16.	_______Monrovia	P. Mozambique
17.	_______Banjul	Q. Tunisia
18.	_______Luanda	R. Nigeria
19.	_______Pretoria & Cape Town	S. Liberia
20.	_______Nairobi	T. Gambia

AFRICA REVIEW

USE THE TEXT, MARKED MAPS AND AN ATLAS IF NECESSARY:

1. Name three countries who colonized parts of Africa. ______________
____
2. The Equator passes through the African countries of Gabon, Congo, Dem. Republic of Congo, Uganda, ________________________ and Somalia.
3. Egypt's north border is the ____________________________ Sea and its eastern border is the ______________________________ Sea.
4. The city of Timbuktu is in _____________________________________.
5. What is a souk? ____
6. Windhoek, Namibia features colonial architecture and cafes that are of what European country's influence? ____________________________
7. What two countries are located within the borders of South Africa? ____________________________ and ______________________________
8. The fourth largest island in the world, located off the coast of Mozambique, is ____.
9. If you say "Jambo" when you are in Kenya, what language are you speaking? __________________________________
10. ____________________________ is the only African country with Spanish as the official language, and the country is composed of Rio Muni and five islands.
11. The currency of South Africa is the _____________.
12. Name three major cities in South Africa. ___________________________
____
13. Dakar is a major port and industrial center and the capital of ____________________________.
14. Name two major cities in Morocco that tourists visit. _____________
____
15. The Kalahari Desert is in _____________________________________.
16. The island of _________________________ is located just north of Dar es Salaam, Tanzania and is known as the "island of spices."
17. Tourists may want to take the famous ___________________ Train to go from Pretoria or Johannesburg to Cape Town in South Africa.
18. Formerly known as the Belgian Congo and a country whose earliest inhabitants were probably the Pygmies is__________________________.
19. Treetops and the Ark are popular lodges in Kenya's national park called __________________________.
20. The ___________________________________, a collapsed volcano crater that is nearly ten miles across and 2,000 feet deep, is one of the sights of Tanzania.
21. The city airport code for Nairobi is ______.
22. The country that used be called Upper Volta is ___________________ ____________________.
23. Two major exports of South Africa are ____________________________ and ____________________________________.
24. The _________________________ Islands are located in the Indian Ocean about 1,000 miles east of Kenya.
25. About 450 miles west of Senegal in the Atlantic Ocean are the ______________________________ Islands (use an atlas for reference).

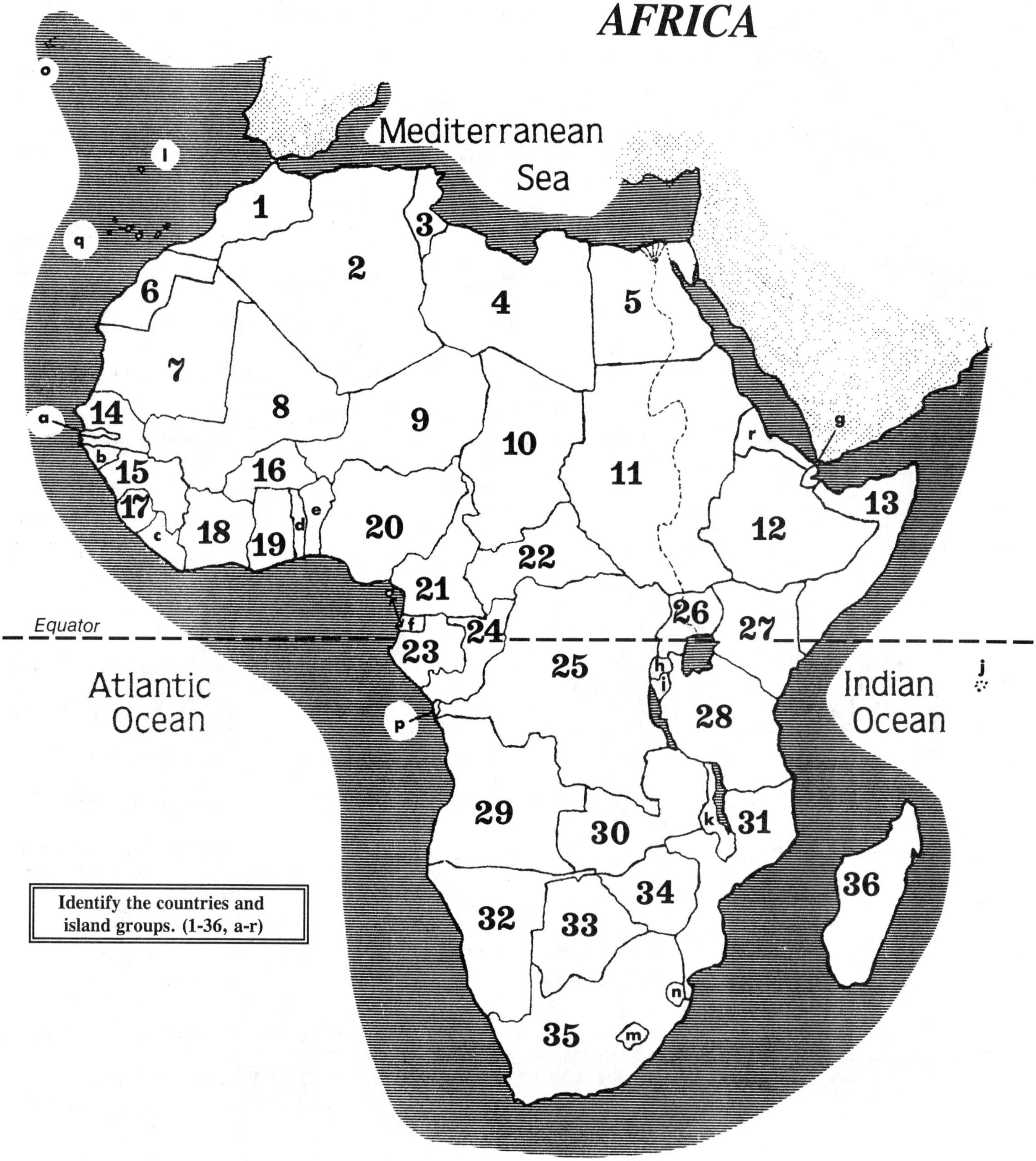

Identify the countries and island groups. (1-36, a-r)

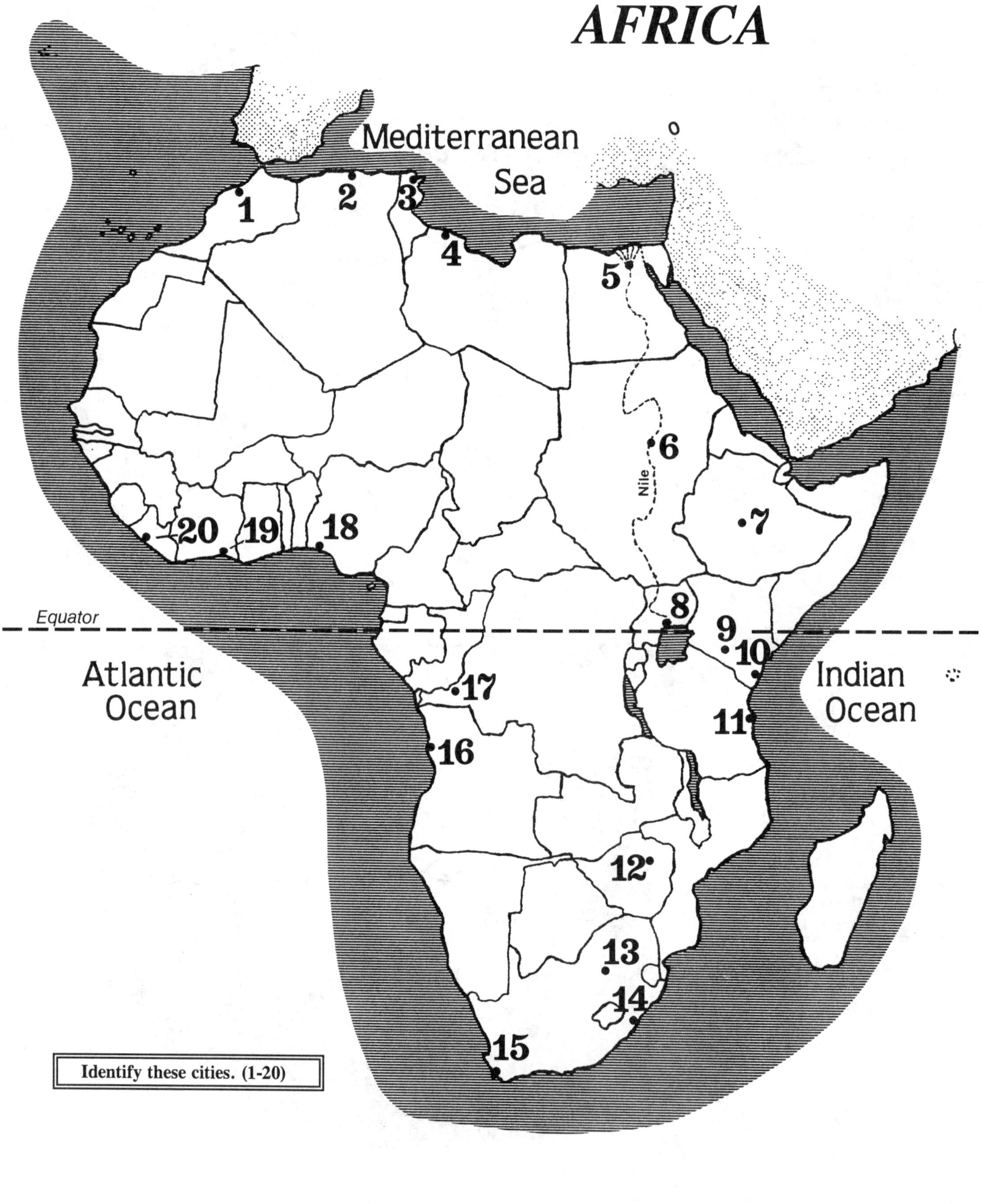
AFRICA
Mediterranean
Sea
Nile
Equator
Atlantic
Ocean
Indian
Ocean
1
2
3
4
5
6
7
8
9
10
11
12
13
14
15
16
17
18
19
20
Identify these cities. (1-20)

CHAPTER 14

Middle East and Asia

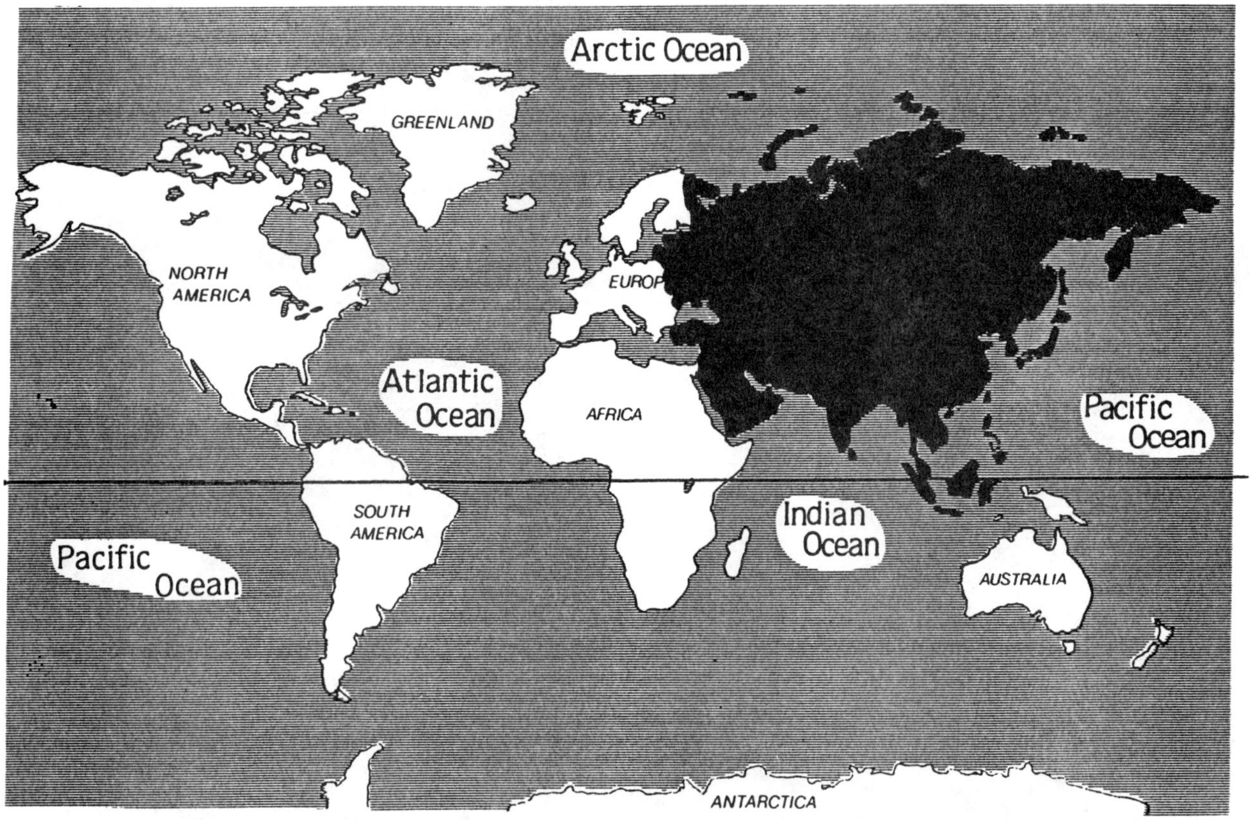

NOTES

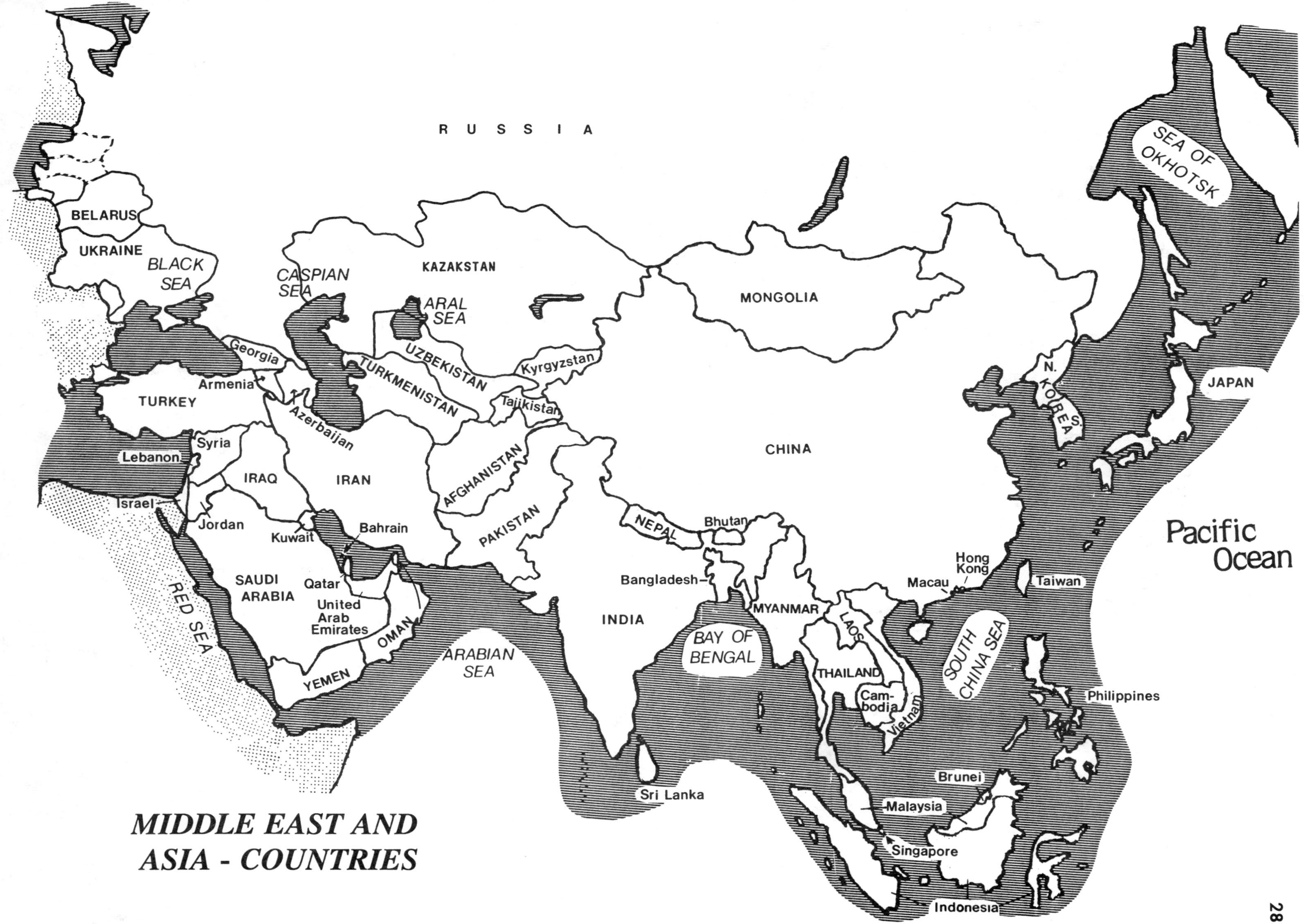

MIDDLE EAST AND ASIA - COUNTRIES

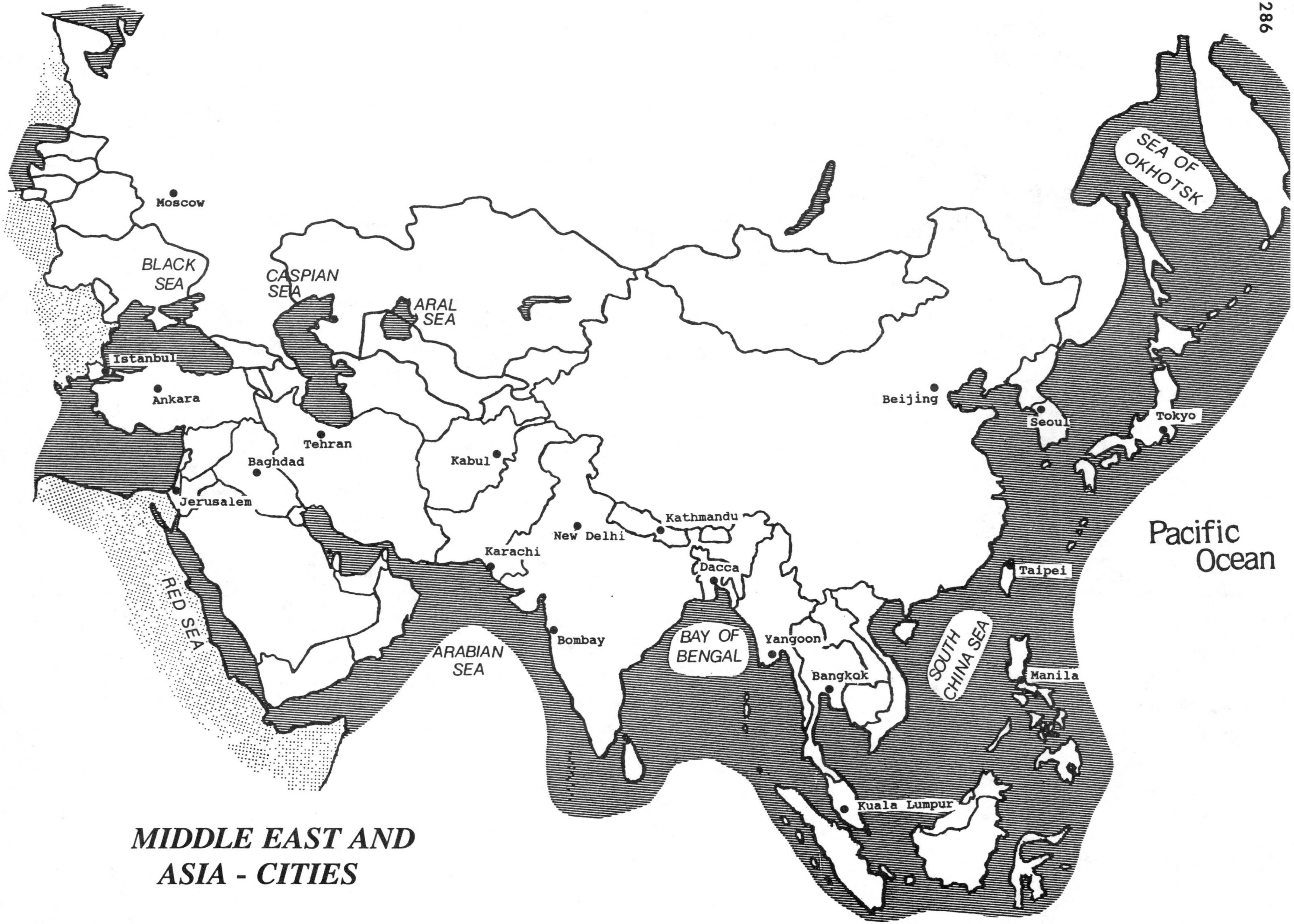

MIDDLE EAST AND ASIA - CITIES

MIDDLE EAST AND ASIA - MAJOR CITY/AIRPORT CODES

BAHRAIN
BAH - Bahrain

ISRAEL
TLV - Tel Aviv
JRS - Jerusalem
HFA - Haifa
ETH - Elat

JORDAN
AMM - Amman

SAUDI ARABIA
RUH - Riyadh

SYRIA
DAM - Damascus

UNITED ARAB EMIRATES
DXB - Dubai

CHINA
BJS - Beijing
PEK - Beijing/Capital

HONG KONG
HKG - Hong Kong

INDIA
DEL - Delhi
BOM - Bombay
CCU - Calcutta
MAA - Madras

INDONESIA
JKT - Jakarta
DPS - Denpensar Bali

JAPAN
TYO - Tokyo
HND - Tokyo/Haneda
NRT - Tokyo/Narita
OSA - Osaka

KOREA
SEL - Seoul

MALAYSIA
KUL - Kuala Lumpur

NEPAL
KTM - Kathmandu

PHILIPPINES
MNL - Manila

SINGAPORE
SIN - Singapore

TAIWAN
TPE - Taipei

THAILAND
BKK - Bangkok

TIPS ON TRAVEL TO MIDDLE EAST AND ASIA

1. Check with the U.S. Department of State for advisories and the consulates/embassies of the countries for requirements and the CDC (Centers for Disease Control) for health and medical recommendations.
2. Avoid travel to any problem areas. Find out the best time to travel and use a reputable company.
3. Know that many countries in this area of the world have political problems, poverty, crime, drug traffic, poor health standards, unreliable transportation, and cultural and social taboos. Travel to many of these countries will appeal only to the more adventurous. Be flexible, tolerant, and patient.
4. Read about the countries you plan to visit to be aware of cultural and social conventions and specifics.
5. Purchase medical insurance. Bring plenty of film and tissues to use in rest rooms. Guard your possessions.
6. Always ask permission before taking photographs.
7. Drink bottled water if uncertain. Avoid drinks with ice and foods from street vendors.
8. Find out when it's appropriate to tip and when it's not.
9. Don't assume that you can enter any mosque. Always ask. Remove your shoes before entering.
10. Drug laws are taken very seriously. Never purchase or use illegal drugs.
11. Dress conservatively in the cities.
12. Young children may try to sell you things, unofficial guides will offer services. Be firm but courteous.

MIDDLE EAST

The region of the Middle East includes a northern tier of nations on the Eurasian mainland (Turkey, Iran, Afghanistan), a cluster of nations (Israel, Jordan, Syria, Lebanon, Iraq), the Arabian Peninsula countries of Saudi Arabia, Bahrain, Kuwait, Yemen, Oman, Qatar and the United Arab Emirates, and parts of North Africa (Egypt, Sudan, Libya, Tunisia, and Morocco). The distinctive characteristics of Middle East countries are: Islam is a major religion, the Arab language and culture is widespread, and many have enormous oil reserves. Israel is quite the exception with a government and nation that is primarily Jewish and a national language of Hebrew. Political unrest in this area of the world requires that the traveler check with current news sources for any travel advisories.

ISRAEL
One of the most popular countries tourists visit is Israel, home to three world religions (Christianity, Judaism, and Islam). The capital is Jerusalem and it features sights such as the Wailing (or Western) Wall, Church of the Holy Sepulchre, and the Dome of the Rock. You can see the famous Chagall windows and the Old City, with its Arab, Christian, and Jewish quarters and markets. Biblical cities include Bethlehem and Nazareth. Tel Aviv is the leading commercial city and major gateway (several non-stop flights are available from the U.S. to Tel Aviv's Ben Gurion airport). Tours to Israel will visit the Dead Sea (the lowest point on earth), the Negev Desert, and Eilat (a resort city). Native born Israelis are known as sabras (from the Hebrew word for a fruit that is tough on the outside and soft inside). Best buys include brass and copperware goods, furs, silver, painted tiles, glasswork, religious items, antiques, and local handicrafts. The Sabbath begins at sunset on Friday and ends Saturday at sunset - this is the day set aside to rest. El Al, the national airline, is extremely strict on security - you will need to check in for flights about three hours prior to departure time.

ASIA

The large continent of Asia offers a variety of cultures, climates, and sights. The Indian subcontinent, which includes Pakistan, India, Nepal, Sri Lanka, Bangladesh, and Bhutan, has a monsoon climate characterized by distinct wet and dry seasons.

INDIA
India is one of the world's most populated countries and Hinduism is the dominant religion. Islam, Buddhism, and many other religions are practiced. The main language is Hindi, but other languages are spoken and English remains a language of the government, higher education and international business. The British influence is still present in many aspects of the society and culture of India. Tea is India's favorite drink, but there is also a variety of Indian beer. There is generally little nightlife in India, although a few major cities have clubs and discos. Indian crafts are quite numerous and every region has its own specialties. Silks, spices, jewelry, bronze and brasswork,

papier mache products, wood carvings, leather goods, clothes, carpets, fabrics - there is a lot to buy and much of it is very inexpensive. The economy is undeveloped, and poverty and disease are part of the life of many of India's people. The complex cultures, religious temples, festivals, and pilgrimages are a big part of visiting this country that has a mystique all its own.

Air and train travel is available between many cities, and India's rail network is the largest in Asia. Express train services link many major cities and train travel is relatively inexpensive. Buses connect many cities but local bus services are crowded and not very tolerable. It is not advisable to rent a car and to avoid hassles it's best to take an escorted tour of the country.

Agra is home to the Taj Mahal, a magnificent mausoleum and one of the most notable sights. If time permits schedule two days in order to see it twice. Bombay is the "Gateway to India." Its main attraction is Elephanta Island out in the Arabian Sea. Calcutta, India's largest city, has temples and shrines to visit, but the poverty and filth can be very disturbing. Jaipur is called the "Pink City" because of its rose-colored sandstone architecture. Varanasi is the holiest site in the country and thousands of Hindu pilgrims bathe in the Ganges River as a religious ritual to purify themselves (however, the river is one of the most polluted in the world). Goa is a city popular for its nice beaches. Other cities include Srinagar, Madras, and New Delhi (which includes the old city, Delhi).

NOTE: BOMBAY OFFICIALLY CHANGED ITS NAME TO MUMBAI AND MADRAS WILL BE CHANGED TO CHENNAI.

NEPAL

Nepal is visited by those interested in seeing Mt. Everest as well as for hiking and mountain climbing. The trekking season is generally from September to May, but the best time is actually from October to December and March to April. Regarding social conventions here, superstition and religion are combined. As far as a foreigner is concerned, there are several customs associated with the attitude that visitors are "polluted." Never step over the feet of a person - always walk around. Never offer food or drink that you have tasted. Use both hands to offer or accept anything - never use just the left hand. And it is rude to point a finger at a person or a statue.

SRI LANKA (formerly Ceylon) is a beautiful island to visit, but there have been numerous outbreaks of violence between the Tamil and Sinhalese population.

MYANMAR, formerly Burma, is a country that has been closed to tourists for many years, but now has a more open policy.

THAILAND
Thailand is a popular destination - an exotic country filled with temples housing giant statues of Buddha. Bangkok is known as the "Venice of the Orient" because of its network of canals. It's a city offering exciting nightlife, unique shopping and dining experiences. Pattaya Beach and Phuket Island are popular resort areas. Chiang Mai is an ancient city and the moat around the city is still intact. It is a starting point for exploring the Golden Triangle. Organized treks are very popular - usually stopping for four nights in various villages. An elephant ride and river rafting are often included in the adventure. Choose a company carefully, however, as there have been some horror stories of travelers who have been victimized and/or hurt.

INDONESIA, a country of more than 13,000 islands, has the capital, Jakarta, on the island of Java. Sumatra, Borneo, and the most popular island, Bali, are some of the tourist destinations. The city of Jakarta on Java offers sightseeing from the colonial Dutch and British periods. The modern Istiglal Mosque in the city center is one of the largest in the world. In Jakarta and many other towns the helecak, a motorized rickshaw, can be used for inexpensive transportation. Sumatra is the second largest island and has hot springs, unexplored jungle, vast plantations, and many wildlife reserves. Bali, the "Island of the Gods," is comprised of volcanic mountains, lakes and rivers, terraced rice fields, giant banyans, and palm groves. The island has thousands of temples and bays ringed with white, sandy beaches on the coast. Dancing is considered an art in Indonesia and performances are given in village halls and squares. The dances vary greatly in both style and number of performers (the "Monkey Dance" calls for about 100 agile participants).

MALAYSIA, a country composed of the peninsula region south of Thailand and the top part of the island of Borneo (except for **BRUNEI**), reflects a mixture of Malay, Indian, Chinese, and European cultures. Places to visit include the capital, Kuala Lumpur, the islands of Penang, Pangkor, and Langkawi, several resorts in the hills and east coast areas, and the unusual and undeveloped states of Sabah and Sarawak on Borneo.

SINGAPORE
On the tip of the Malaysian peninsula is a tiny country but a major financial center and tourist destination - Singapore. Clean, modern, industrialized, stable - cosmopolitan Singapore boasts world class restaurants, nightlife, and fantastic shopping (the best buys include crafts, electronics, luggage, jade, jewelry, silks, clothing).

The **PHILIPPINES**, an archipelago of more than 7,000 islands, has a tropical climate tempered by constant sea breezes. The capital is Manila and the national language is Filipino, but there are many island dialects spoken and English is widely taught.

CHINA

Back on the Asian mainland is the vast region of China and its northern neighbor, Mongolia. Travel to China became extremely popular in the 1980s but has since declined because of the government's crackdown and violence that surfaced in the massacre of students who gathered to protest in May 1989 in Tiananmen Square. China is a huge country and the most populated in the world - with over one billion people (and there are more than 32 Chinese cities that have over one million population). Beijing, the capital, contains the Forbidden City, a museum and public park that was once the residence of the emperors. There are six palaces and 800 smaller buildings, containing 9,000 rooms. Other sights in the city include the zoo, the Grand View Garden, and the Temple of Heaven. Take a day trip from Beijing to walk atop the Great Wall of China, one of the wonders of the world. It is said that more than 300,000 men worked for more than 10 years to complete it and it was built wide enough for carriages and transportation of supplies.

Xian was the starting point for the Silk Road, and is one of the most popular tourist attractions because of its Tomb of the Emperor Qin Shi Huangdi and its terra-cotta figures (over 6,000 life-size warriors and horses buried along with the emperor). Shanghai, Guilin, and Guangzhou are other cities included on most tours. The area of Tibet, known as the "Roof of the World," was formerly closed to tourists and visas are still limited. The attraction of Tibet is its isolation from the rest of the world and the preservation of its own way of life and religious traditions.

TRAVEL TO CHINA TIPS

The Chinese are generally reserved with courtesy rather than familiarity being preferred. The full title "People's Republic of China" should be used instead of China. Although handshaking is customary, a visitor may be greeted with a bow or a round of applause (the usual response is to bow or applaud back). In China, the family name is always mentioned first. Tipping is officially not allowed and can be considered insulting. Discussing business during a meal is inappropriate. White is the color for mourning and should be avoided. It's a good idea to visit the government-run Friendship Store in any city for best buys. Learn how to count from one to ten in Chinese. Chew foods carefully - as bones may be cut up into the food. Prepare yourself to see people spitting in public - it's acceptable. Many cities have a problem with air pollution, and when coupled with stress from traveling, cold weather, and high altitude some travelers can develop respiratory problems. The Chinese do not usually volunteer information and travelers are advised to ask questions. Generosity is important, so small gifts are recommended when you are visiting someone's home.

HONG KONG is a fabulous destination for shopping. Tailor-made clothes, silks, jade, crafts, electronics, and many other goods are best buys. It is still too early to know but there may be some changes as this former British Crown Colony reverted to Chinese rule on June 30, 1997. Hong Kong consists of numerous islands and several hundred square miles of territory on the mainland. Most travelers will stay in Kowloon - a peninsula that juts out into Victoria Harbor from the mainland.

A side trip from Hong Kong is by hydrofoil to **MACAU** - to see a bit of Portugal in Asia and a popular destination for gamblers.

JAPAN
Japan consists of four main islands: Hokkaido, Honshu, Shikoku and Kyushu. On Honshu is the city of Tokyo, where visitors flock to the Emperor's Palace, the Meiji Shrine, Ueno Park, and the Ginza district. Most of the country is covered by hills and mountains; the highest is Mt. Fuji - at about 12,300 feet. Lowlands and plains are mainly scattered along the coast and there are deeply indented bays with good natural harbors. Kyoto on Honshu Island attracts many visitors to see the temples, palaces and shrines, and to walk the quiet streets - maybe stopping to see the textile weavers in their workshops. Ogawamachi is home to paper-making, and the city of Nikko has splendid temples and mausoleums and is set in a national park. Japanese manners and customs are generally very formal and polite. It is considered impolite to say "no," they will often say "maybe" or "it is very difficult." When entering a Japanese home or restaurant it is customary to remove one's shoes and leave them pointing to the outside door. Tipping is not customary. As the Japanese have many unique and important customs, read up on the culture prior to your visit.

Traditional Japanese theater features the arts of Kabuki, Noh, and Bunraku (puppet shows). Best buys include pearls, lacquerware, silks, pottery, china, crystal, cloisonne, cameras, weavings, coral items, and local handicrafts. Plan your expenditures carefully however, as accommodations, meals, and services are very expensive (a cab from Narita Airport to Tokyo will cost about $265.00, so take the train).

Accommodations range from the very deluxe to family inns and pensions. Minshuku (family-owned bed and breakfast type properties) are good for people wanting to become more familiar with Japanese culture. Ryokans are larger, Japanese-style accommodations that range from inexpensive to expensive. In the traditional inns, the guests remove their shoes and put on slippers, and the beds are thin mattresses spread on the floor. Japanese-style baths (often used by both men and women) are also part of the experience.

KOREA is presently divided into North and South republics. There are indications of an eventual rapprochement between the two parties. South Korea is open to tourism, and visitors often start in Seoul, the capital, and continue to Kyongju, Pusan, and maybe an excursion to Cheju Island. Korea has its own cuisine, quite different from Chinese or Japanese. Rice is of course the staple food and a typical Korean meal consists of rice, soup, rice water and 8-20 side dishes of vegetables, poultry, fish, eggs, bean curd, and sea plants. Most Korean dishes are laced heavily with red pepper.

TAIWAN is also known as Formosa, and this island's people enjoy a high standard of living. Taiwan is the main island of a group of 78 islands. Taipei is the capital and major sights include: the National Museum of History, the Taipei Fine Arts Museum, and Chung Cheng (Chiang Kai-shek) Memorial Hall. Yangmingshan Park is famous for its cherry and azalea trees that attract thousands of visitors at blossom time.

RESEARCH COUNTRIES, PRACTICE THE MAP, AND COMPLETE THE REVIEWS.

COUNTRY: ________________ CAPITAL: ________________
DOCUMENTARY REQUIREMENTS (U.S. CITIZENS): ________________
SHOTS, OTHER INFO: ________________
CURRENCY: ________ CURRENCY CODE: ________ EXCHANGE RATE: ________
LANGUAGE(S): ________________
SIZE: ________________ POPULATION: ________________
BEST TIME TO VISIT: ________________
MAJOR CITIES AND PLACES OF INTEREST: ________________
____
____
____
SPORTS: ________________
RELIGIONS: ________________ GOVERNMENT: ________________
FOOD SPECIALTIES: ________________
BEST BUYS: ________________
SPECIAL INFORMATION: ________________
____
AIRLINES: ________________ CITY/AIRPORT CODES: ________________
TRANSPORTATION: ________________
OTHER INFO: ________________

COUNTRY: ________________ CAPITAL: ________________
DOCUMENTARY REQUIREMENTS (U.S. CITIZENS): ________________
SHOTS, OTHER INFO: ________________
CURRENCY: ________ CURRENCY CODE: ________ EXCHANGE RATE: ________
LANGUAGE(S): ________________
SIZE: ________________ POPULATION: ________________
BEST TIME TO VISIT: ________________
MAJOR CITIES AND PLACES OF INTEREST: ________________
____
____
____
SPORTS: ________________
RELIGIONS: ________________ GOVERNMENT: ________________
FOOD SPECIALTIES: ________________
BEST BUYS: ________________
SPECIAL INFORMATION: ________________
____
AIRLINES: ________________ CITY/AIRPORT CODES: ________________
TRANSPORTATION: ________________
OTHER INFO: ________________

COUNTRY: ________________ CAPITAL: ________________
DOCUMENTARY REQUIREMENTS (U.S. CITIZENS): ________________
SHOTS, OTHER INFO: ________________
CURRENCY: ________ CURRENCY CODE: ________ EXCHANGE RATE: ________
LANGUAGE(S): ________________
SIZE: ________________ POPULATION: ________________
BEST TIME TO VISIT: ________________
MAJOR CITIES AND PLACES OF INTEREST: ________________
____
____
____
SPORTS: ________________
RELIGIONS: ________________ GOVERNMENT: ________________
FOOD SPECIALTIES: ________________
BEST BUYS: ________________
SPECIAL INFORMATION: ________________
____
AIRLINES: ________________ CITY/AIRPORT CODES: ________________
TRANSPORTATION: ________________
OTHER INFO: ________________

COUNTRY: ____ CAPITAL: ____
DOCUMENTARY REQUIREMENTS (U.S. CITIZENS): ____
SHOTS, OTHER INFO: ____
CURRENCY: ____ CURRENCY CODE: ____ EXCHANGE RATE: ____
LANGUAGE(S): ____
SIZE: ____ POPULATION: ____
BEST TIME TO VISIT: ____
MAJOR CITIES AND PLACES OF INTEREST: ____
SPORTS: ____
RELIGIONS: ____ GOVERNMENT: ____
FOOD SPECIALTIES: ____
BEST BUYS: ____
SPECIAL INFORMATION: ____
AIRLINES: ____ CITY/AIRPORT CODES: ____
TRANSPORTATION: ____
OTHER INFO: ____

COUNTRY: ____ CAPITAL: ____
DOCUMENTARY REQUIREMENTS (U.S. CITIZENS): ____
SHOTS, OTHER INFO: ____
CURRENCY: ____ CURRENCY CODE: ____ EXCHANGE RATE: ____
LANGUAGE(S): ____
SIZE: ____ POPULATION: ____
BEST TIME TO VISIT: ____
MAJOR CITIES AND PLACES OF INTEREST: ____
SPORTS: ____
RELIGIONS: ____ GOVERNMENT: ____
FOOD SPECIALTIES: ____
BEST BUYS: ____
SPECIAL INFORMATION: ____
AIRLINES: ____ CITY/AIRPORT CODES: ____
TRANSPORTATION: ____
OTHER INFO: ____

COUNTRY: ____ CAPITAL: ____
DOCUMENTARY REQUIREMENTS (U.S. CITIZENS): ____
SHOTS, OTHER INFO: ____
CURRENCY: ____ CURRENCY CODE: ____ EXCHANGE RATE: ____
LANGUAGE(S): ____
SIZE: ____ POPULATION: ____
BEST TIME TO VISIT: ____
MAJOR CITIES AND PLACES OF INTEREST: ____
SPORTS: ____
RELIGIONS: ____ GOVERNMENT: ____
FOOD SPECIALTIES: ____
BEST BUYS: ____
SPECIAL INFORMATION: ____
AIRLINES: ____ CITY/AIRPORT CODES: ____
TRANSPORTATION: ____
OTHER INFO: ____

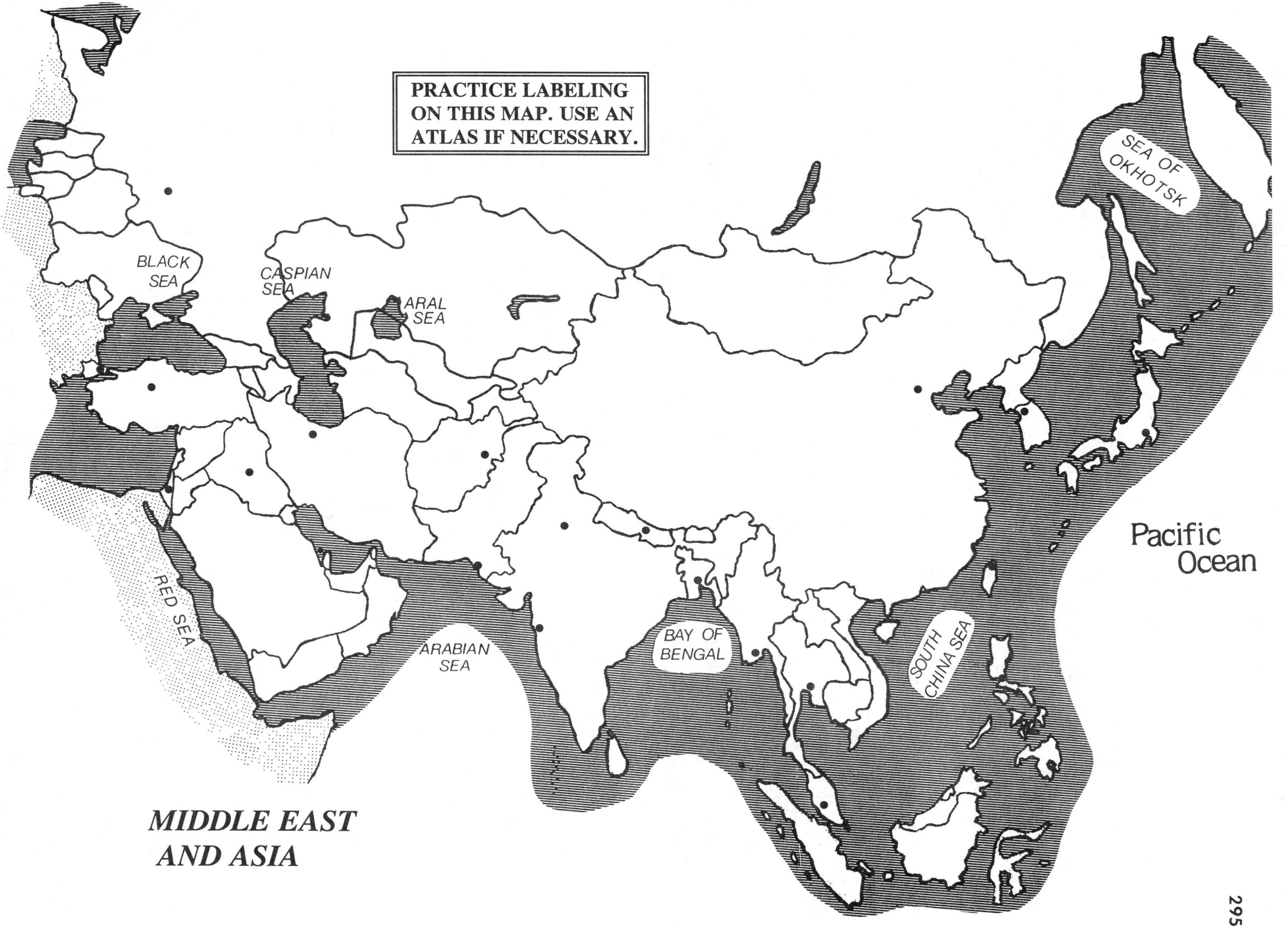

MIDDLE EAST AND ASIA

MIDDLE EAST AND ASIA REVIEW

USE THE CAPITALS LIST AND THE CURRENCIES LIST IF NECESSARY.

1. Name three cities in Israel. ______________________________
   ____
2. In what city is the Wailing or Western Wall? ______________
3. What three world religions have their foundations in Israel? ______
   ____
4. The ____________________ is an extremely salty body of water and the lowest point on earth - 1200 feet below sea level.
5. When does the Shabbat or Jewish Sabbath begin and end? _________
   ____
6. Two of the best buys of Israel are ________________________.
7. Name five countries in the region of the Middle East. __________
   ____
8. The Taj Mahal is located in __________________________ (name city and country).
9. ______________________ is the capital of Malaysia.
10. Two types of theater popular in Japan are __________________ and ________________________.
11. The currency of Israel is the __________________.
12. Macau has an influence of the country of __________________.
13. Mt. Everest is in the country of ____________________.
14. Name three countries that use the dinar as their currency name.
    ____
15. Name five cities in India. _________________________________
    ____
16. Name two resort areas of Thailand. __________________________
    ____
17. The four major islands of Japan are _________________________
    ____.
18. Three of the best buys of India are __________________________
    ____.
19. The city of ____________ is the capital of Afghanistan.
20. The archipelago of the Philippines is made up of over _________ islands.
21. The island republic also known as Formosa is _________________.
22. ____________________ is the main language of India.
23. Most Korean dishes are laced heavily with what spice? _________
24. ____________ was formerly Ceylon.
25. The ____________ is India's currency.
26. ____________ is known as the "Pink City."
27. The starting point for exploring the Golden Triangle in Thailand is the city of _______________.
28. Elephanta Island is a main attraction when visiting the city of ____________, India.
29. In China, it's customary to discuss business at a meal. True or False _________
30. Ryokans are large Japanese vans that offer inexpensive transportation. True or False ________

MIDDLE EAST AND ASIA REVIEW

MATCH THE FOLLOWING CITIES TO COUNTRIES:

USE AN ATLAS IF NECESSARY, AS NOT ALL CITIES ARE MENTIONED IN THE TEXT.

Note: Some answers may not be used and some may be used more than once.

1. ______Tokyo
2. ______Shanghai
3. ______Seoul
4. ______Taipei
5. ______Islamabad
6. ______Kabul
7. ______Dacca
8. ______New Delhi
9. ______Hiroshima
10. ______Manila
11. ______Kuala Lumpur
12. ______Riyadh
13. ______Beirut
14. ______Jerusalem
15. ______Amman
16. ______Baghdad
17. ______Bangkok
18. ______Colombo
19. ______Madras
20. ______Jakarta
21. ______Beijing
22. ______Eilat
23. ______Guangzhou
24. ______Kathmandu
25. ______Calcutta

A. India
B. Taiwan
C. Lebanon
D. Israel
E. China
F. Syria
G. Jordan
H. Iraq
I. Afghanistan
J. South Korea
K. Thailand
L. Indonesia
M. Bangladesh
N. Philippines
O. Sri Lanka
P. Nepal
Q. Saudi Arabia
R. Mongolia
S. Yemen
T. Myanmar
U. Iran
V. Pakistan
W. Malaysia
X. Japan
Y. Bahrain

MATCH THE FOLLOWING SIGHTS OR PLACES TO THE COUNTRIES:

Note: Some answers may not be used and some may be used more than once.

1. ______Mt. Fuji
2. ______Taj Mahal
3. ______Forbidden City
4. ______Dome of the Rock
5. ______Great Wall
6. ______Mt. Everest
7. ______Pattaya Beach
8. ______Repulse Bay
9. ______Balinese dancers
10. ______Kyoto
11. ______Langkawi Island
12. ______Phuket Island
13. ______Cheju Island
14. ______Kowloon
15. ______Sabah and Sarawak
16. ______Nikko
17. ______Nazareth
18. ______Tiananmen Square
19. ______Ginza District
20. ______Ming Tombs

A. Malaysia
B. Indonesia
C. Nepal
D. China
E. Thailand
F. Philippines
G. Hong Kong
H. Israel
I. Japan
J. Sri Lanka
K. Afghanistan
L. Taiwan
M. Singapore
N. South Korea
O. India

Identify the countries. (1-52)

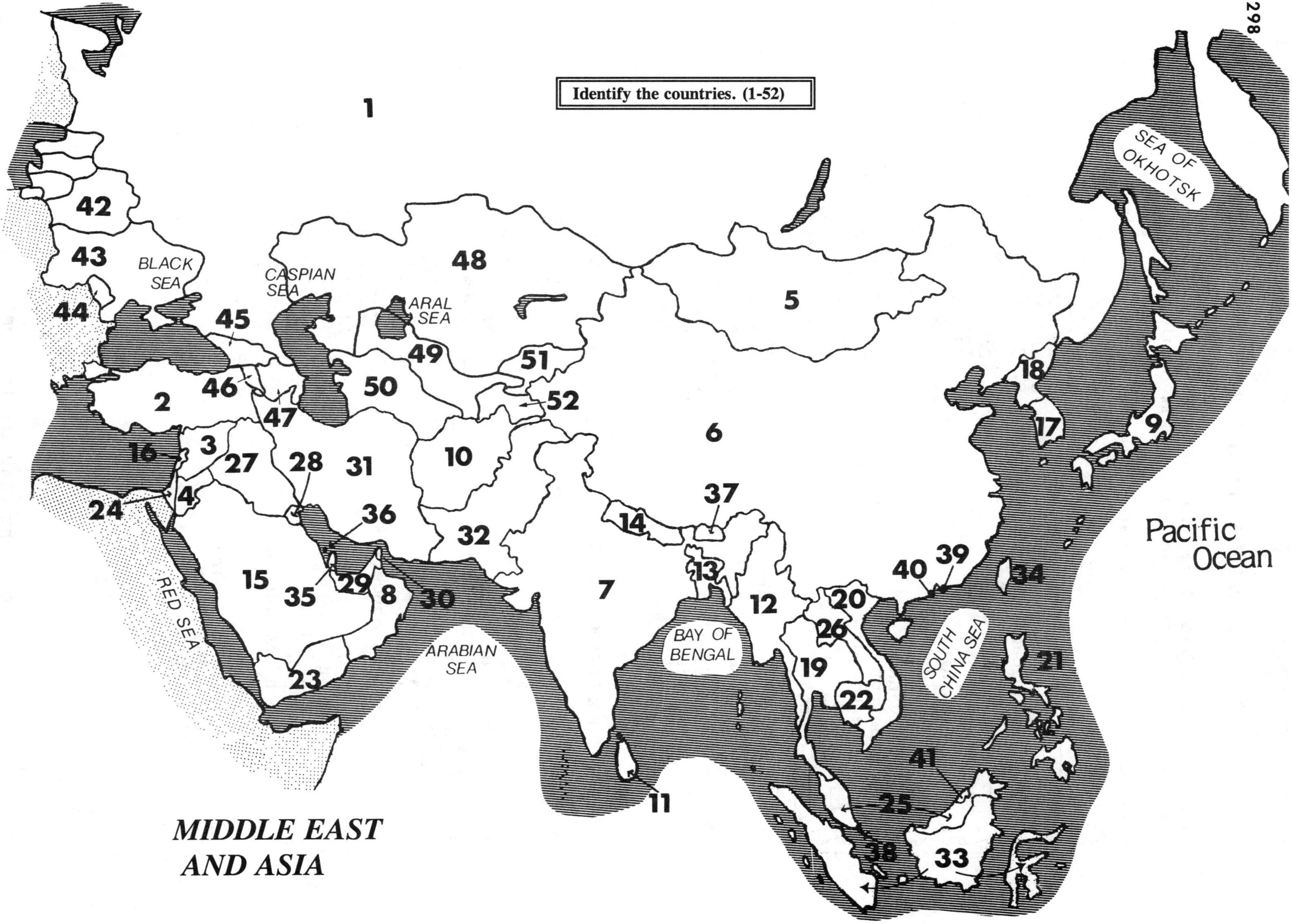

MIDDLE EAST AND ASIA

Identify these cities. (1-20)

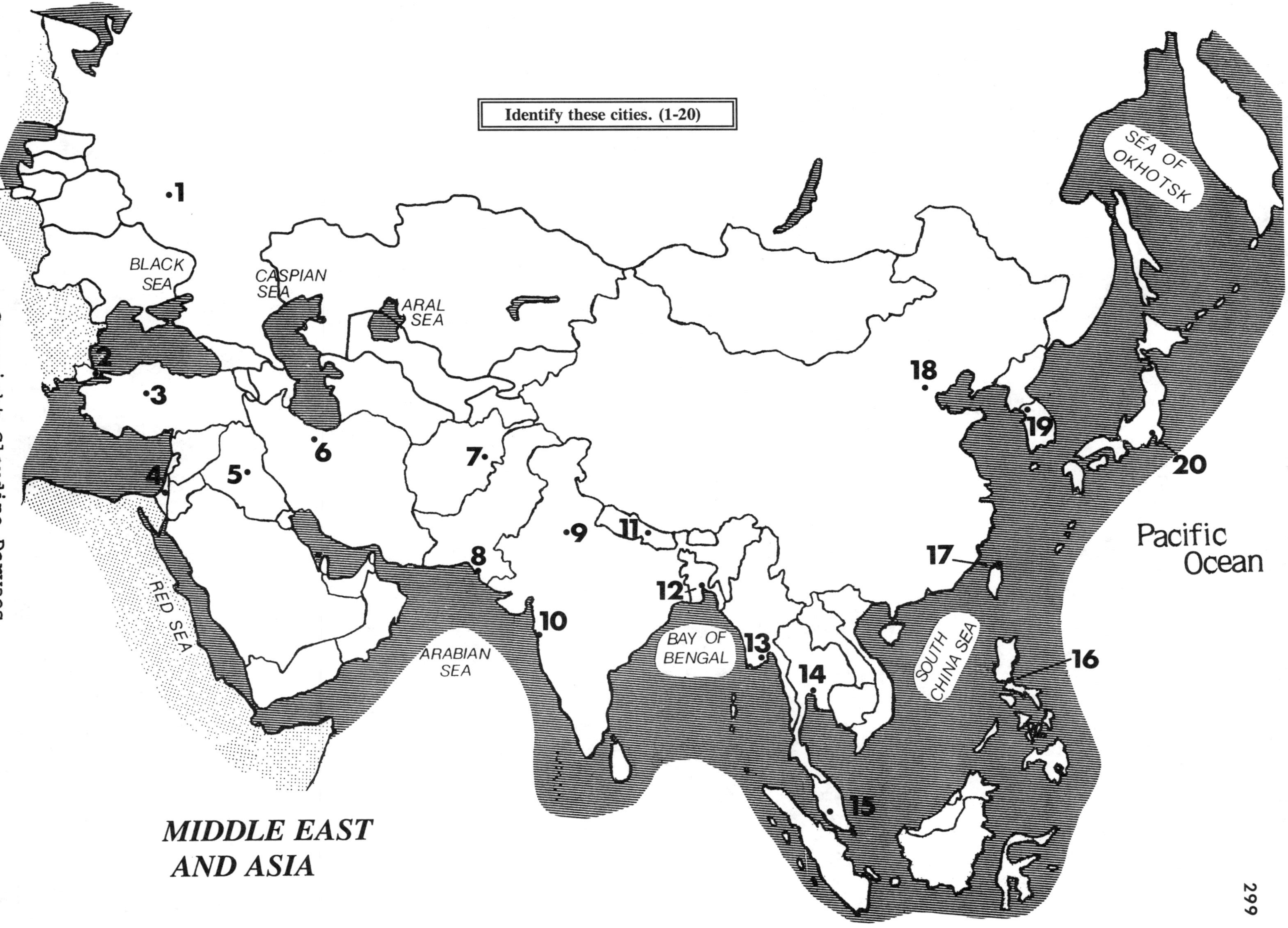

MIDDLE EAST AND ASIA

NOTES

CHAPTER 15

Australia, New Zealand and the Pacific Ocean

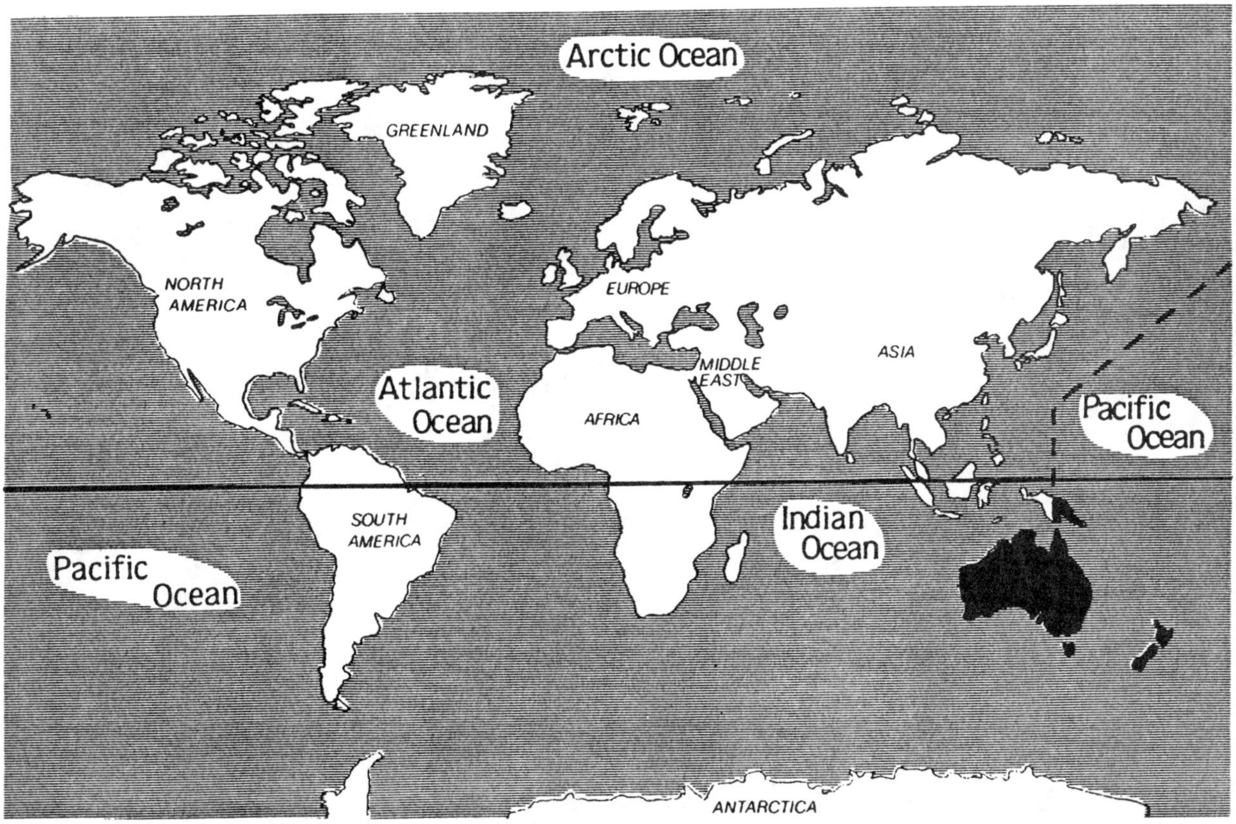

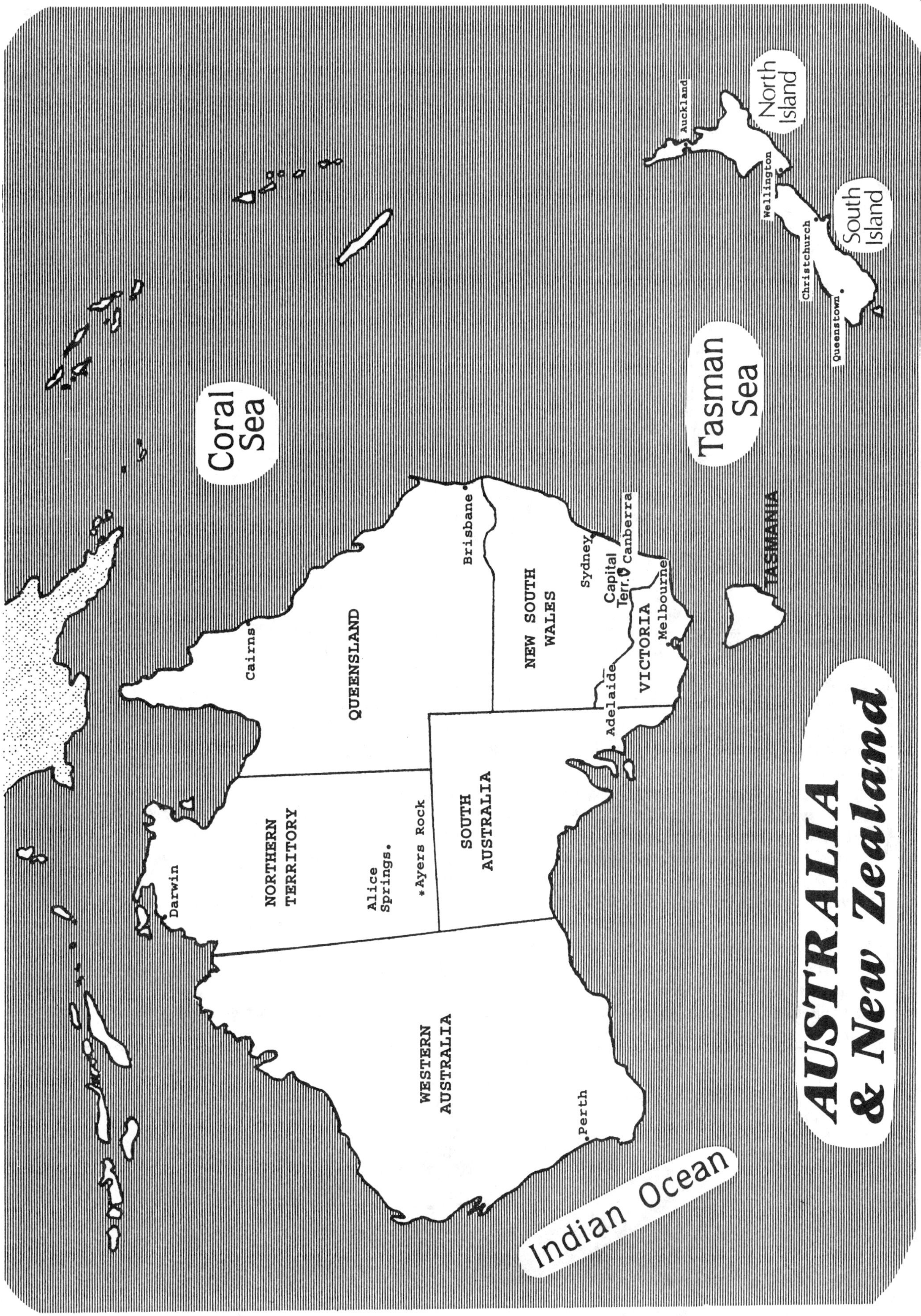
AUSTRALIA
& New Zealand
Coral Sea
Tasman Sea
Indian Ocean
North Island
South Island
Auckland
Wellington
Christchurch
Queenstown
TASMANIA
QUEENSLAND
NEW SOUTH WALES
VICTORIA
SOUTH AUSTRALIA
NORTHERN TERRITORY
WESTERN AUSTRALIA
Capital Terr.
Canberra
Sydney
Melbourne
Adelaide
Brisbane
Cairns
Darwin
Alice Springs.
*Ayers Rock
Perth

AUSTRALIA, NEW ZEALAND AND PACIFIC OCEAN - MAJOR CITY/AIRPORT CODES

AUSTRALIA
SYD - Sydney
MEL - Melbourne
BNE - Brisbane
PER - Perth
CBR - Canberra
DRW - Darwin
ASP - Alice Springs
HBA - Hobart

NEW ZEALAND
AKL - Auckland
WLG - Wellington
CHC - Christchurch

AMERICAN SAMOA
APW - Apia

COOK ISLANDS
RAR - Rarotonga

FIJI
SUV - Suva
NAN - Nandi

FRENCH POLYNESIA
PPT - Papeete, Tahiti
MOZ - Moorea
BOB - Bora Bora

GUAM
GUM - Guam

PAPUA NEW GUINEA
POM - Port Moresby

TONGA
TBU - Tongatapu

TRUK
TKK - Truk

VANUATU
VLI - Port Vila

WESTERN SAMOA
PPG - Pago Pago

YAP
YAP - Yap

TRAVELING TO AUSTRALIA? HERE ARE SOME IMPORTANT POINTS:

Driving is on the left. Water is safe to drink and health standards are excellent.

The wet season is from November to February, but somewhere in Australia the weather will be wonderful for touring no matter when you visit. Of course, the seasons are reversed from the Northern Hemisphere.

Check out the various "passes" available for touring the country by air, coach or train - they can save a bundle.

Tipping is not required but may be welcome in certain circumstances.

Every type of accommodation is available - from youth hostels to farmhouses, B & Bs, campgrounds, motels, hotels, luxurious resorts, apartments, and home exchanges.

Best buys include opals. sheepskin products, boomerangs, pearls, gold items, Aboriginal crafts, leather goods, wines, diamonds, toy koalas, and local handicrafts.

Although English is the official language, there are many colorful Australian expressions as well as the Australian accent that may confuse you. Don't hesitate to ask questions - the people are very friendly.

You will need adaptors and voltage convertors for your U.S. electrical appliances.

Lightweight and casual clothing is suitable; a sweater or jacket should be handy for cooler nights or seasons. Business meetings and fine restaurants will call for more formal attire.

Read guidebooks (Lonely Planet, Fodor's, Frommer's, etc.) to find out more about what you will see or what you might like to visit.

AUSTRALIA AND NEW ZEALAND

Travel to Australia and New Zealand is very popular and the facilities and transportation to and within these countries are quite extensive. First, let's take a look at Australia.

AUSTRALIA

Australia is about as large as the mainland of the United States and therefore offers a vast area with an extremely varied terrain. Along its northeast coast stretches the Great Barrier Reef - over 1200 miles of beautiful water and unique plant and animal life. This area is dotted with island resorts, lying on or between the reef and the Queensland coast.

Queensland

Brisbane is the state capital of Queensland and has a year-round warm subtropical climate. It's the gateway to sun, sand, surf, and coral and is Australia's fastest growing city. The attractions in the city include: Lone Pine Koala Sanctuary, the Botanic Gardens, Bunya Park, the Queensland Maritime Museum, the City Hall and State Parliament House, and South Bank Park. Located in the southeast corner of the state, about an hour's drive from Brisbane is the Gold Coast - just about the best beach area of the country. Surfing and swimming are particularly popular at Surfers Paradise. Along the Gold Coast Highway visit Currumbin Bird Sanctuary to see the flocks of brilliantly colored lorikeets (a type of parrot) that fly in each day to be fed. About an hour west of the Gold Coast is Lamington National Park with rugged mountains and jungle-like rainforest. An hour north of Brisbane is the Sunshine Coast - an area of unspoiled beaches and lakes and mountains (Noosa Heads is a superb resort here). Townsville is an ideal starting point for those wanting to see the Great Barrier Reef. Charter launches visit nearby islands and the Outer Reef daily (if weather permits). Scenic flights over the reef can also be arranged. The city of Cairns is a gateway to the northern part of the reef and there are sugarcane plantations and cattle stations to visit as well. The Great Barrier Reef is a diver's paradise and there are holiday islands (Hayman Island, Lizard Island, Green Island, Magnetic Island, Heron Island, Dunk Island - to name a few). Facilities range from modest accommodations to extensive resorts.

Northern Territory

Darwin is the territorial capital and sits at the "Top End" - an area of lush tropical vegetation, national parks, and wildlife habitats. Alice Springs is set in the red desert area and is a popular tourist resort. It is the base for tours to the Outback and Ayers Rock - the world's largest monolith and a sacred site for the Aborigines. Visitors can climb the rock or explore the caves at its base. The rock's color changes from bright red or purple to blazing orange - depending on the time and atmospheric conditions.

South Australia
Except for the capital of the state, Adelaide, South Australia is not very populated. It is a wine-producing area along with vast expanses of desert, plus craggy mountains, meandering rivers, and some nice beach resorts. Adelaide has a European atmosphere and there is a large European (particularly German) population here.

New South Wales
The state of New South Wales has perhaps the most varied of landscapes - from snow-capped mountains to long, golden sandy beaches. Sydney is the state capital and has one of the most famous harbors in the world - distinctive with the architecture of the Sydney Opera House. The sky-line rivals that of Manhattan and it's a major commercial and business center. Sights besides the Opera House and harbor include Taronga Zoo, Sydney Tower (a 1000 ft. tower above the Centrepoint Shopping Complex), the Royal Botanic Gardens, the Australian Museum, and The Rocks area (a restored section with cobbled streets, gas lamps, craft shops, and tiny restaurants).

Australian Capital Territory
This territory contains Canberra, the country's capital, an elegant city of wide streets, gardens and parks.

Victoria
The state of Victoria at Australia's eastern base has the cosmopolitan capital city of Melbourne, a city with sizable Italian, Greek, and Chinese minority populations, each with their own quarter. Outside the city - about 22 miles away are the Dandenong Ranges. Great views of the city are possible from the Summit Lookout. This region also has beaches, lakes, rivers, and national parks to explore.

Western Australia
Western Australia's most popular and capital city is Perth, a boom city with modern skyscrapers which overshadow the colonial buildings of the past. The Swan River winds through the city and provides for swimming and cruising activities. A popular resort is Rottnest Island. East of Perth is Kalgoorlie - a gold mining town and in the north of the state are the Kimberleys, a region rich in Aboriginal legends and a diamond-producing center.

Tasmania
The island of Tasmania features Hobart, a yacht and sailing center. There is ferry service to the island from Melbourne as well as flights from Melbourne and Sydney.

The vast distances between major cities in Australia make air the most convenient method of travel, although train journeys are an interesting (however slower) alternative. Australia offers so much - in scenery, in many sports activities, in the unique plants and animals, and in its culture.

NEW ZEALAND is composed of North Island and South Island and is a somewhat more formal country than Australia. The largest city and business center is Auckland (on North Island). Situated on a narrow isthmus that divides the Waitemata Harbor from the Manukau Harbor, the city's landscape features fourteen extinct volcanoes - with each summit offering panoramic views. A delightful way to experience the "City of Sails" is to take a lunchtime cruise on a catamaran. A must to visit is Kelly Tarlton's Underwater World to walk down the world's largest acrylic tunnel for underwater viewing of sharks, sting rays, and all sorts of sea creatures. Art galleries, shops, fine hotels, the scenic harbor, historic buildings, museums, theaters and restaurants - the city has a variety of sights and activities. Stretching from Auckland along the Northland Peninsula to Cape Reinga is a region of golden beaches, great scenery, and unlimited natural recreational attractions. Heading south of Auckland you can visit the incredible Waitomo Caves and the Glow Worm Grotto - a cavern illuminated by millions of tiny glow worms. Lake Taupo, at the geographic center of North Island, is the country's largest lake. Rotorua is the premier tourist spot with attractions of incredible thermal activity, the Maori people and their traditions, world famous trout fishing and beautiful lakes. Hot springs, boiling mud, erupting geysers, steaming terraces of sulphur and colorful silica deposits combine for an eerie and wonderful sightseeing experience (the pungent odor of hydrogen sulphide is a constant companion). More scenic, but inclined to poor weather is the country's capital, Wellington, located at the southern tip of North Island.

A flight will take you to Queenstown on South Island - your base city for touring this part of the country. This delightful Alpine resort is an all year holiday center. Jet boating, whitewater rafting, scenic flightseeing, horseriding, golfing, hiking, climbing, safari trips, and of course skiing make for an active time. Above the city a gondola lift rises over 1312 feet to a restaurant perched on Bob's Peak offering a spectacular view. The gateway to Fjordland National Park is Te Anau - a city nestled beside a placid lake of the same name. Highlights of the area are the glow worm caves at Te Anau, plus day trips to Milford Sound and Doubtful Sound. At Milford Sound, you can cruise the fjord to the 540 foot high Bowen Falls, mile-high Mitre Peak, and the edge of the Tasman Sea. Mount Cook National Park is another attraction of South Island - a splendor of snow-clad peaks (Mt. Cook is the highest at 12,350 ft.). Flights will take you to land directly on Tasman Glacier nearby. Another city on most tours of South Island is Christchurch. Often described as the "most English city outside England" the city is delightful - with its public gardens, fine old buildings, parks, museums, architecture, and tree-lined streets.

New Zealand offers scenic and unusual beauty in caves, geysers, mountains, glaciers, waterfalls, parks, forests, valleys, coastal bays and inlets. The Maoris (pronounced "mourees") were the first settlers. A Polynesian, well-ordered, tribal society, their arts, crafts, and culture are part of the experience of visiting the country. Should a visitor be invited to a formal Maori occasion, the pressing of noses (hongi) is a common greeting. Besides the wonderful and varied Maori crafts, distinctive jewelry and items made from the paua shell and New Zealand greenstone are popular purchases. Woolen and sheepskin goods, rugs, and leather products are also good buys. The nation's symbol, the kiwi (a flightless nocturnal bird), is rarely seen outside a zoo. New Zealanders are known as "Kiwis" and kiwi is also a native fruit of the country.

Now, complete a profile form - first on Australia and then New Zealand.

COUNTRY: ____________ CAPITAL: ____________
DOCUMENTARY REQUIREMENTS (U.S. CITIZENS): ____________
SHOTS, OTHER INFO: ____________
CURRENCY: ____________ CURRENCY CODE: ________ EXCHANGE RATE: ____________
LANGUAGE(S): ____________
SIZE: ____________ POPULATION: ____________
BEST TIME TO VISIT: ____________
TERRITORY: ____________ MAJOR CITIES/SIGHTS: ____________
TERRITORY: ____________ MAJOR CITIES/SIGHTS: ____________
TERRITORY: ____________ MAJOR CITIES/SIGHTS: ____________
TERRITORY: ____________ MAJOR CITIES/SIGHTS: ____________
TERRITORY: ____________ MAJOR CITIES/SIGHTS: ____________
SPORTS: ____________
RELIGIONS: ____________ GOVERNMENT: ____________
FOOD SPECIALTIES: ____________
BEST BUYS: ____________
SPECIAL INFORMATION: ____________
AIRLINES: ____________ CITY/AIRPORT CODES: ____________
TRANSPORTATION: ____________
OTHER INFO: ____________

COUNTRY: ____________ CAPITAL: ____________
DOCUMENTARY REQUIREMENTS (U.S. CITIZENS): ____________
SHOTS, OTHER INFO: ____________
CURRENCY: ____________ CURRENCY CODE: ________ EXCHANGE RATE: ____________
LANGUAGE(S): ____________
SIZE: ____________ POPULATION: ____________
BEST TIME TO VISIT: ____________
MAJOR CITIES/SIGHTS: ____________
SPORTS: ____________
RELIGIONS: ____________ GOVERNMENT: ____________
FOOD SPECIALTIES: ____________
BEST BUYS: ____________
SPECIAL INFORMATION: ____________
AIRLINES: ____________ CITY/AIRPORT CODES: ____________
TRANSPORTATION: ____________
OTHER INFO: ____________

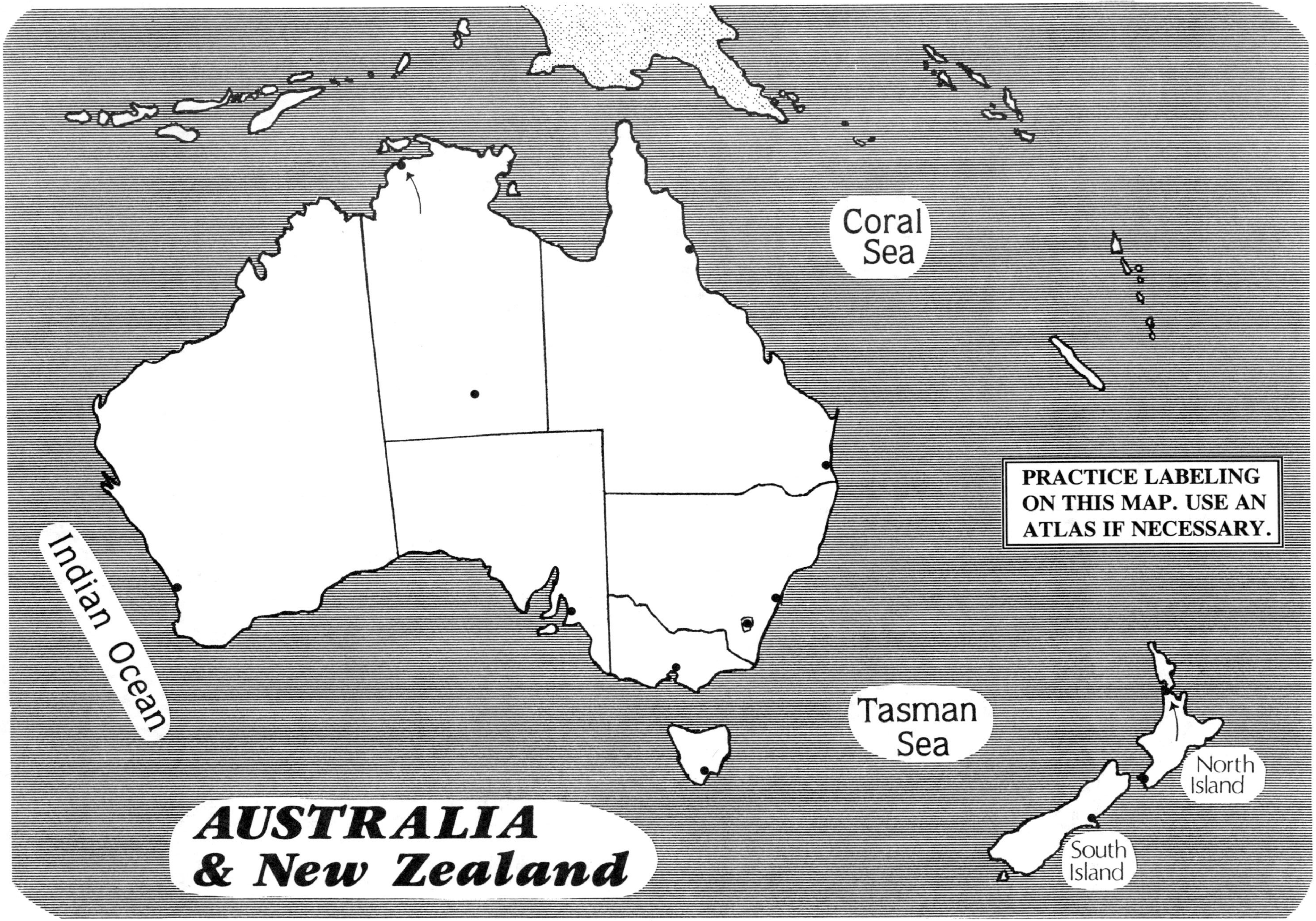
AUSTRALIA
& New Zealand
PRACTICE LABELING ON THIS MAP. USE AN ATLAS IF NECESSARY.
Coral Sea
Tasman Sea
Indian Ocean
North Island
South Island

AUSTRALIA AND NEW ZEALAND REVIEW

1. The coral reef stretching for 1200 miles along the northeast coast of Australia is called the ______________________________.
2. In the southeast corner of the state of ____________________ is the Gold Coast - an area of fine beaches.
3. _______________________ is the great red monolith in the Northern Territory that is a "must see."
4. The city of __________________________ in the Northern Territory is a starting point for many of the tours to the "Outback."
5. Currumbin Bird Sanctuary is in New South Wales. True or False ___________
6. What is hongi? ____
7. The landmark building known for its distinctive architecture and located in Sydney's harbor is the ________________________________.
8. The popular resort island located near Perth is ________________ ________________________________.
9. __________________________ is a major city in the wine-producing area of Australia.
10. What are some of the best buys of Australia? _____________________ ____

MATCH THE CITIES TO THE TERRITORIES:

11.	_____Perth	A. Western Australia
12.	_____Darwin	B. South Australia
13.	_____Adelaide	C. Victoria
14.	_____Melbourne	D. Northern Territory
15.	_____Cairns	E. Queensland

16. Name three cities in New Zealand. ______________________________ ____
17. Milford Sound is on South Island. True or False __________
18. Name three sports activities popular in New Zealand. ____________ ____
19. Name three topographical features found in New Zealand. __________ ____
20. __________________________ is New Zealand's capital.
21. What unusual bird (also a fruit) is the nation's symbol? _________
22. The native tribespeople of New Zealand are the __________________.
23. Distinctive jewelry and items made from the ________________ shell are popular buys.
24. ______________________ is known as the "City of Sails."
25. The highest mountain in New Zealand is Mt. _____________.

OPTIONAL ASSIGNMENT:
Two women are planning a trip to New Zealand. They want to see all the sights of New Zealand, using a rented motorhome. They each have about $8,000.00 USD to spend on the trip. Plan out a sample list of costs for airfare, motorhome rental, gas expenses, etc. Give a day-by-day sample itinerary and other helpful information.

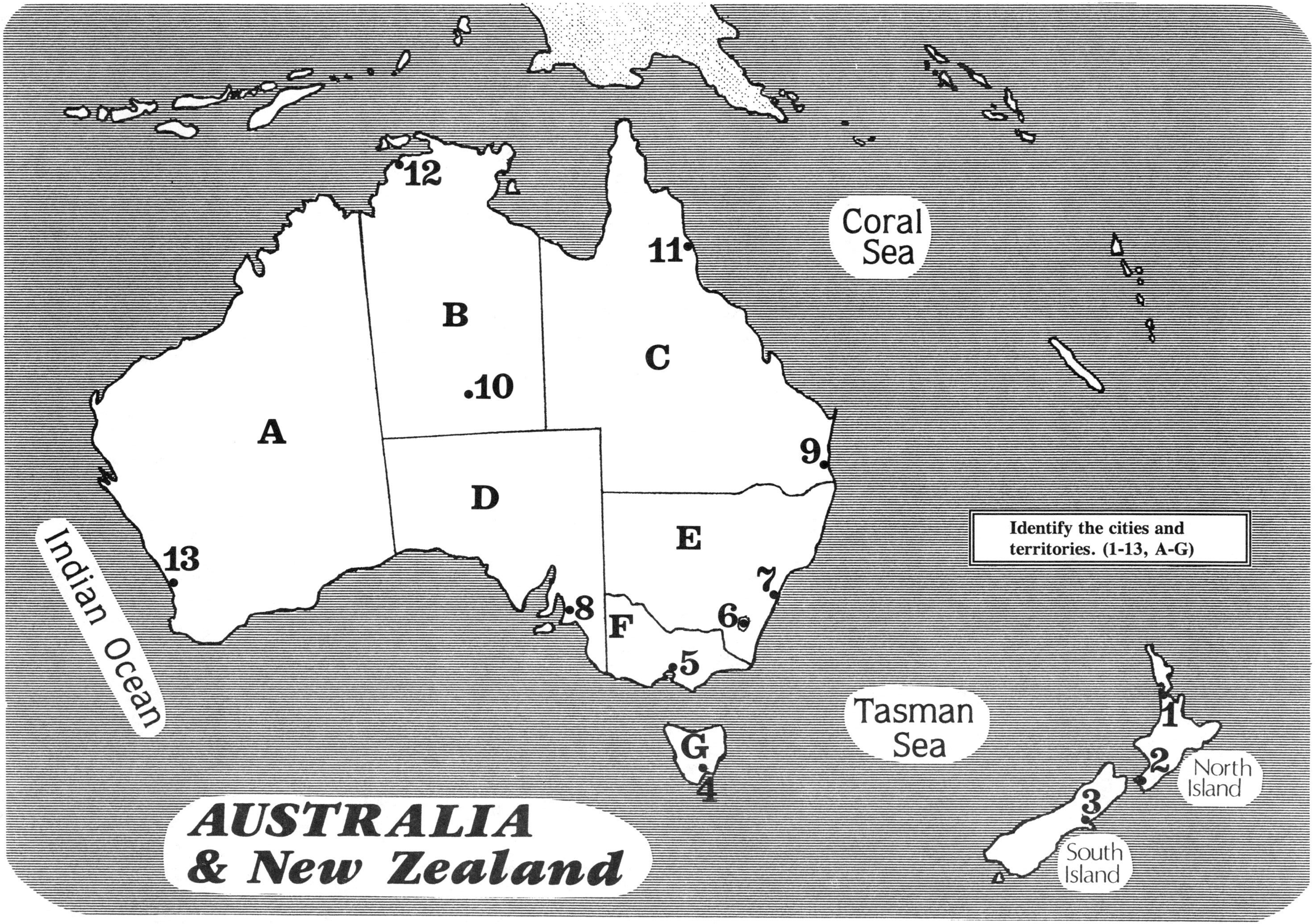
Coral Sea
Tasman Sea
Indian Ocean
North Island
South Island
A
B
C
D
E
F
G
1
2
3
4
5
6
7
8
9
10
11
12
13
Identify the cities and territories. (1-13, A-G)
AUSTRALIA & New Zealand

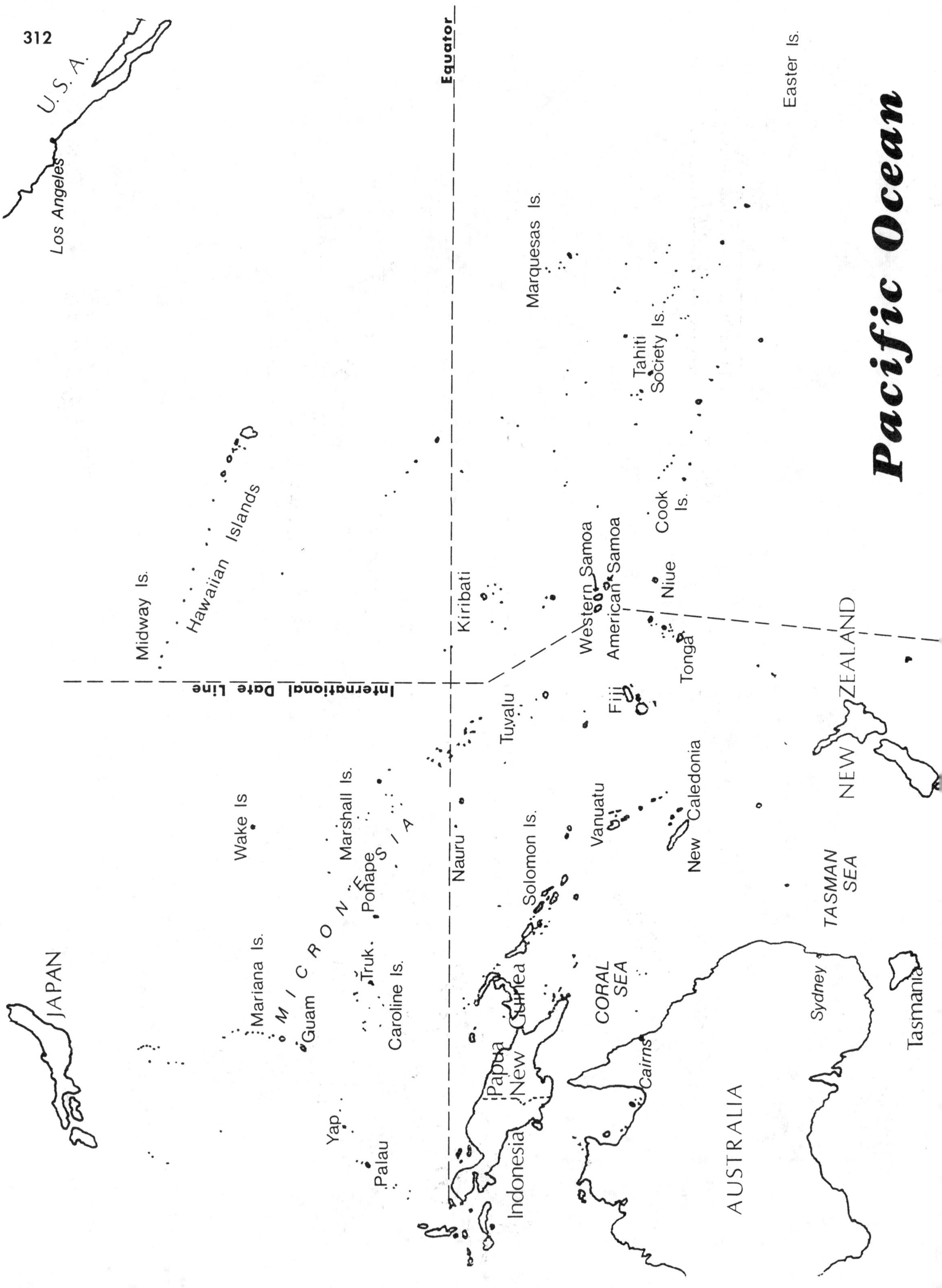
Pacific Ocean
U.S.A.
Los Angeles
Equator
Easter Is.
Marquesas Is.
Tahiti
Society Is.
Hawaiian Islands
Midway Is.
Cook Is.
Western Samoa
American Samoa
Niue
Kiribati
Tonga
International Date Line
NEW ZEALAND
Fiji
Tuvalu
New Caledonia
Vanuatu
Wake Is.
Marshall Is.
Nauru
Solomon Is.
TASMAN SEA
MICRONESIA
Ponape
Truk
Mariana Is.
Guam
Caroline Is.
JAPAN
CORAL SEA
Papua New Guinea
Tasmania
Sydney
Cairns
AUSTRALIA
Yap
Palau
Indonesia

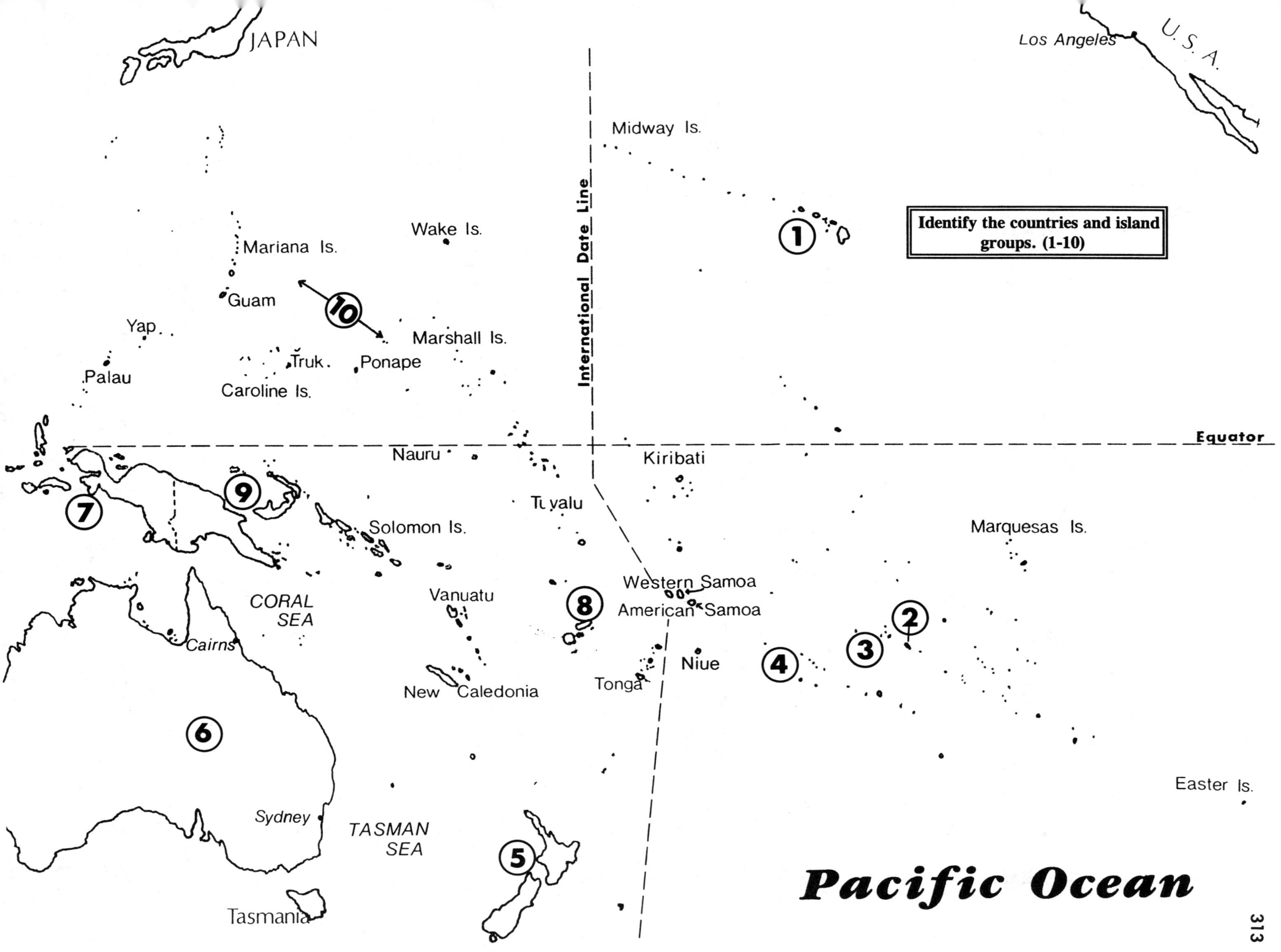
Identify the countries and island groups. (1-10)
JAPAN
U.S.A.
Los Angeles
Midway Is.
International Date Line
Equator
Wake Is.
Mariana Is.
Guam
Yap
Palau
Truk
Ponape
Caroline Is.
Marshall Is.
Nauru
Kiribati
Tuvalu
Solomon Is.
Marquesas Is.
Western Samoa
American Samoa
Vanuatu
New Caledonia
Tonga
Niue
CORAL SEA
Cairns
TASMAN SEA
Sydney
Tasmania
Easter Is.
Pacific Ocean
1
2
3
4
5
6
7
8
9
10

PACIFIC OCEAN

The **PACIFIC OCEAN** encompasses a vast area with many different island groups.

The **HAWAIIAN ISLANDS** were previously studied as a major U.S. destination. You may wish to review the information.

Located south of the Equator are the **MARQUESAS ISLANDS**, the northernmost group of French Polynesia. The **SOCIETY ISLANDS**, which include Tahiti, Bora Bora, and Moorea, are also part of French Polynesia, along with the Tuamotu Archipelago, Gambier Islands, and Austral Islands.

EASTER ISLAND, a possession of Chile, is most famous for the Moai, gigantic stone figures which are found all over the island.

The **COOK ISLANDS** honor the great explorer, Captain James Cook, who himself had discovered some of the islands.

WESTERN SAMOA (independent) and **AMERICAN SAMOA** (a U.S. territory) are located at about 173 longitude, near the IDL (International Date Line). Apia is the capital of Western Samoa, and the capital of American Samoa is Pago Pago (pronounced "Pangou Pangou").

The republic of **KIRIBATI** (pronounced "Kiribass"), formerly the Gilbert Islands, is a remote destination with a hot and humid climate. One of the islands, Christmas Island, has extensive populations of birdlife and a wildlife sanctuary.

Over 2,100 islands make up the area known as Micronesia. The main groups are the **MARIANA ISLANDS, MARSHALL ISLANDS, CAROLINE ISLANDS, and Federated States of Micronesia (which include Yap, Truk, and Ponape). GUAM** is the major gateway to the area and is a U.S. territory.

PAPUA NEW GUINEA consists of over 600 islands and lies in the middle of the long chain of islands that stretch from the mainland of Southeast Asia. The main island (actually the eastern half) shares a border with Indonesia. A fantastic wildlife (38 species of the bird of paradise, 450 species of butterfly), a great variety of ecosystems (rainforests, mangrove swamps, etc.), and tremendous tribal diversity (a country of over 700 local languages) - this country cannot be easily summarized. Port Moresby is the capital. Tours along the Sepik River are common, as it enables the visitor to stop at the many settlements and tribal villages along its banks.

The **SOLOMON ISLANDS**, site of some of the fiercest battles of World War II, are also home to some of the most beautiful of South Pacific peoples.

VANUATU was formerly the New Hebrides, and this island offers the many sports that interest tourists, as well as a richness and vitality in the arts, crafts, and culture of its people.

NEW CALEDONIA has been experiencing some tensions between the French settlers and indigenous Melanesians, so check for current advisories and information. Noumea is the capital - a busy little city with a mixed population (French, Arab, Melanesian, Indonesian, etc.).

The **FIJI ISLANDS** are hospitable islands, home to more than 700,000 people. They enjoy a warm, sunny climate with a mild, dry season from May to October and a warm, wetter season from November to April. The two largest islands are Viti Levu and Vanua Levu. The capital is Suva and the major international airport is at Nadi (pronounced "Nandi").

TUVALU is one of the world's smallest and most isolated island groups and is also one of the least developed.

TONGA's craftsmen and women are famous for their weaving, carving, and cloth-making. Nuku'alofa, on Tongatapu Island, is the capital, and the archipelago is made up of 172 islands, many of which are uninhabited.

NIUE - an island not part of any other group of islands - offers a wide variety of sports activities, some historic sights, marine and national parks, and native festivals, events, and crafts.

These are just some of the islands of the Pacific Ocean. If you look at a detailed map in an atlas, you will see the myriad of names and islands that spread across this vast ocean area.

Complete profiles on as many islands/groups as possible before filling in the reviews and tests that follow.

ISLAND/GROUP:__________________________ CAPITAL:____________________
DOCUMENTARY REQUIREMENTS (U.S. CITIZENS):_____________________________
SHOTS, OTHER INFO:____
CURRENCY:________________ CURRENCY CODE:______ EXCHANGE RATE:__________
LANGUAGE(S):____
SIZE:_____________________________ POPULATION:________________________
MAJOR CITIES AND PLACES OF INTEREST:_________________________________
____
____
____
____
SPORTS:____
RELIGIONS:_______________________________GOVERNMENT:__________________
FOOD SPECIALTIES:____
BEST BUYS:____
SPECIAL INFORMATION:____
____
AIRLINES:_____________________________CITY/AIRPORT CODES:______________
TRANSPORTATION:____
OTHER INFO:____

ISLAND/GROUP: ____________________ CAPITAL: ____________________
DOCUMENTARY REQUIREMENTS (U.S. CITIZENS): ____________________
SHOTS, OTHER INFO: ____________________
CURRENCY: ____________ CURRENCY CODE: ________ EXCHANGE RATE: ____________
LANGUAGE(S): ____________________
SIZE: ____________________ POPULATION: ____________________
MAJOR CITIES AND PLACES OF INTEREST: ____________________
____
____
____
SPORTS: ____________________
RELIGIONS: ____________________ GOVERNMENT: ____________________
FOOD SPECIALTIES: ____________________
BEST BUYS: ____________________
SPECIAL INFORMATION: ____________________
____
AIRLINES: ____________________ CITY/AIRPORT CODES: ____________________
TRANSPORTATION: ____________________
OTHER INFO: ____________________

ISLAND/GROUP: ____________________ CAPITAL: ____________________
DOCUMENTARY REQUIREMENTS (U.S. CITIZENS): ____________________
SHOTS, OTHER INFO: ____________________
CURRENCY: ____________ CURRENCY CODE: ________ EXCHANGE RATE: ____________
LANGUAGE(S): ____________________
SIZE: ____________________ POPULATION: ____________________
MAJOR CITIES AND PLACES OF INTEREST: ____________________
____
____
____
SPORTS: ____________________
RELIGIONS: ____________________ GOVERNMENT: ____________________
FOOD SPECIALTIES: ____________________
BEST BUYS: ____________________
SPECIAL INFORMATION: ____________________
____
AIRLINES: ____________________ CITY/AIRPORT CODES: ____________________
TRANSPORTATION: ____________________
OTHER INFO: ____________________

ISLAND/GROUP: ____________________ CAPITAL: ____________________
DOCUMENTARY REQUIREMENTS (U.S. CITIZENS): ____________________
SHOTS, OTHER INFO: ____________________
CURRENCY: ____________ CURRENCY CODE: ________ EXCHANGE RATE: ____________
LANGUAGE(S): ____________________
SIZE: ____________________ POPULATION: ____________________
MAJOR CITIES AND PLACES OF INTEREST: ____________________
____
____
____
SPORTS: ____________________
RELIGIONS: ____________________ GOVERNMENT: ____________________
FOOD SPECIALTIES: ____________________
BEST BUYS: ____________________
SPECIAL INFORMATION: ____________________
____
AIRLINES: ____________________ CITY/AIRPORT CODES: ____________________
TRANSPORTATION: ____________________
OTHER INFO: ____________________

PACIFIC OCEAN REVIEW

Using the brief descriptions of islands/groups provided in this manual, complete the following sentences.

1. The Society Islands include the popular destinations of Tahiti, Bora Bora, and ___________________.
2. Easter Island is a possession of the country of ________________.
3. Over 2,100 islands make up the area known as ___________________, with the main groups of the Mariana Islands, Caroline Islands, Yap, Truk, Ponape, and others.
4. Western Samoa is _______________________, while American Samoa is a U.S. territory.
5. The gigantic stone figures found all over Easter Island are called __________________.
6. Site of some of the fiercest battles of World War II and also home to some of the most beautiful South Pacific peoples are the _________________________ Islands.
7. The _____________ Islands honor the great explorer who discovered many South Pacific areas.
8. French Polynesia includes the Marquesas Islands, Society Islands, Tuamotu Archipelago, Gambier Islands, and _______________ Islands.
9. Formerly New Hebrides, ________________________________ offers a rich variety of arts, crafts, and culture.
10. The two largest islands of ____________________ are Viti Levu and Vanua Levu.
11. ____________________ was formerly the Gilbert Islands.
12. Papua New Guinea's main island, Borneo, shares a border with the country of ____________________.
13. One of the world's smallest and most isolated groups of islands is ____________________, located northwest of Fiji.
14. An archipelago made up of 172 islands, mostly uninhabited, and whose people are famous for their weaving, carving, and cloth-making, is ____________________.
15. The U.S. territory that is the gateway to Micronesia is the island of __________________________.

Match the following cities to islands/island groups:

16. ______Papeete
17. ______Pago Pago
18. ______Noumea
19. ______Agana
20. ______Suva
21. ______Nuku'alofa
22. ______Apia
23. ______Port Moresby
24. ______Vila
25. ______Rarotonga

A. Western Samoa
B. Tonga
C. Vanuatu
D. Tahiti, French Polynesia
E. Cook Islands
F. American Samoa
G. Guam
H. New Caledonia
I. Borneo, Papua New Guinea
J. Fiji Islands

NOTES

CHAPTER 16

FINAL REVIEWS AND DESTINATION EVALUATION FORMS

NOTES

GENERAL GEOGRAPHY REVIEW

24 HOUR CLOCK AND GENERAL GEOGRAPHY TEST

Convert into AM or PM

1. 0010 = ____________
2. 1752 = ____________
3. 1345 = ____________
4. 0532 = ____________
5. 1421 = ____________

Convert into 24 HOUR CLOCK

6. 10:12 AM = ____________
7. 12:20 PM = ____________
8. 9:15 AM = ____________
9. 8:45 PM = ____________
10. 6:20 AM = ____________

MATCH THE COUNTRIES TO THEIR CONTINENT:

11. _____Morocco
12. _____Mexico
13. _____Indonesia
14. _____Albania
15. _____Philippines
16. _____Venezuela
17. _____Luxembourg
18. _____Egypt

A. NORTH AMERICA
B. SOUTH AMERICA
C. EUROPE
D. AFRICA
E. ASIA
F. AUSTRALIA
G. ANTARCTICA

MATCH THE ISLANDS TO THE OCEANS IN WHICH THEY ARE LOCATED:

19. _____Bermuda
20. _____Galapagos
21. _____Seychelles
22. _____Canary
23. _____Maldive Is.

A. ATLANTIC OCEAN
B. PACIFIC OCEAN
C. INDIAN OCEAN
D. ARCTIC OCEAN

MATCH THE PLACE OF INTEREST TO THE APPROPRIATE COUNTRY:

24. _____Ayers Rock
25. _____Taj Mahal
26. _____Machu Picchu
27. _____Sugarloaf Mountain
28. _____Notre Dame Cathedral
29. _____Neuchwanstein Castle
30. _____Anne Hathaway's Cottage
31. _____Xian Statues
32. _____Aswan Dam
33. _____Blue Mosque

A. FRANCE
B. TURKEY
C. CHINA
D. ENGLAND
E. GERMANY
F. EGYPT
G. AUSTRALIA
H. INDIA
I. PERU
J. BRAZIL

GENERAL GEOGRAPHY REVIEW

MATCH THE FOLLOWING CAPITALS TO U.S. STATES:

1. ____Jefferson City	A. Illinois
2. ____Sacramento	B. Kentucky
3. ____Carson City	C. South Dakota
4. ____Springfield	D. Virginia
5. ____Pierre	E. Missouri
6. ____Salem	F. Wyoming
7. ____Richmond	G. Oregon
8. ____Madison	H. California
9. ____Cheyenne	I. Wisconsin
10. ____Frankfort	J. Nevada

MATCH THE FOLLOWING CAPITALS TO CENTRAL AMERICAN COUNTRIES:

11. ____Tegucigalpa	K. Honduras
12. ____Belmopan	L. Nicaragua
13. ____Managua	M. Costa Rica
14. ____San Jose	N. Belize

MATCH THE FOLLOWING CITIES TO CARIBBEAN ISLANDS:

15. ____Nassau	O. St. Thomas
16. ____Fort-de-France	P. St. Maarten
17. ____Santo Domingo	Q. Jamaica
18. ____Kingston	R. New Providence Is.
19. ____San Juan	S. St. Croix
20. ____Georgetown	T. Grand Cayman
21. ____Philipsburg	U. St. Martin
22. ____Marigot	V. Puerto Rico
23. ____Orangestad	W. Martinique
24. ____Charlotte Amalie	X. Aruba
25. ____Christiansted	Y. Dominican Republic

MATCH THE FOLLOWING CAPITALS TO SOUTH AMERICAN COUNTRIES:

26. ____Bogota	A. Suriname
27. ____Buenos Aires	B. Chile
28. ____Quito	C. Colombia
29. ____Santiago	D. Ecuador
30. ____Paramaribo	E. Argentina

MATCH THE FOLLOWING CAPITALS TO EUROPEAN COUNTRIES:

31. ____Bucharest	F. Poland
32. ____Copenhagen	G. Finland
33. ____Oslo	H. Greece
34. ____Warsaw	I. Romania
35. ____Budapest	J. Belgium
36. ____Prague	K. Norway
37. ____Vienna	L. Denmark
38. ____Helsinki	M. Austria
39. ____Athens	N. Czech Republic
40. ____Brussels	O. Hungary

MATCH THE FOLLOWING CITIES TO AFRICAN COUNTRIES:

41. ____Abidjan	P. Egypt
42. ____Cairo	Q. Kenya
43. ____Kinshasa	R. Zimbabwe
44. ____Dar es Salaam	S. Senegal
45. ____Harare	T. Cote d'Ivoire
46. ____Tripoli	U. Dem. Republic of Congo
47. ____Monrovia	V. Tanzania
48. ____Accra	W. Ghana
49. ____Nairobi	X. Liberia
50. ____Dakar	Y. Libya

MATCH THE FOLLOWING CAPITALS TO MIDDLE EAST AND ASIA COUNTRIES:

1.	____Tehran	A. Indonesia
2.	____Damascus	B. Japan
3.	____Beirut	C. Nepal
4.	____Tokyo	D. Syria
5.	____Jakarta	E. Pakistan
6.	____Dacca	F. Lebanon
7.	____Kabul	G. Bangladesh
8.	____Kathmandu	H. Iran
9.	____Islamabad	I. Afghanistan
10.	____Port Moresby	J. Papua New Guinea

MATCH THE FOLLOWING CITIES TO COUNTRIES/PACIFIC ISLANDS:

11.	____Wellington	K. New Zealand (N. Island)
12.	____Perth	L. Tasmania
13.	____Papeete	M. New Zealand (S. Island)
14.	____Hobart	N. Tahiti
15.	____Agana	O. Australia
16.	____Christchurch	P. Guam
17.	____Honolulu	Q. Tonga
18.	____Noumea	R. Viti Levu (Fiji Is.)
19.	____Suva	S. New Caledonia
20.	____Pago Pago	T. American Samoa
21.	____Taipei	U. U.S. - Oahu, Hawaii
22.	____Nuku'alofa	V. Taiwan
23.	____Vila	W. Western Samoa
24.	____Kahului	X. U.S. - Maui, Hawaii
25.	____Apia	Y. Vanuatu

NOW SEE IF YOU CAN IDENTIFY THESE DRAWINGS OF U.S. CITIES:

1. ______________________________

2. ______________________________

3. ______________________________

4. ______________________________

5. ______________________________

6. ______________________________

NAME THREE PLACES OF INTEREST IN EACH OF THE FOLLOWING CITIES:

1. NEW YORK________________________________

2. LONDON________________________________

3. PARIS________________________________

4. ROME________________________________

5. LOS ANGELES________________________________

6. BEIJING________________________________

7. TOKYO________________________________

8. NEW ORLEANS________________________________

9. SAN FRANCISCO________________________________

10. MEXICO CITY________________________________

11. RIO DE JANEIRO________________________________

12. SYDNEY________________________________

13. MADRID________________________________

14. MOSCOW________________________________

15. ATHENS________________________________

NOW NAME THESE SIGHTS AND WHERE THEY ARE LOCATED:

Note: On the top line state the attraction's name and on the bottom line the city and country.

1. ______________________________

____

2. ______________________________

____

3. ______________________________

____

4. ______________________________

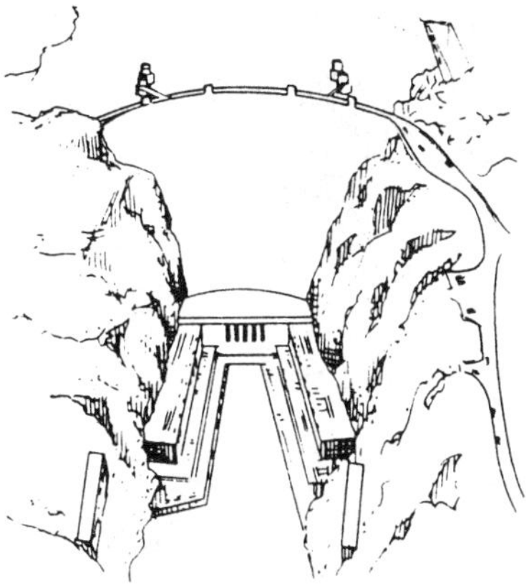

____

5. ______________________________

____

6. ______________________________

____

NOW NAME THESE SIGHTS AND WHERE THEY ARE LOCATED:

Note: On the top line state the attraction's name and on the bottom line the city (if applicable) and country.

1. ______________________________

____

2. ______________________________

____

3. ______________________________

____

4. ______________________________

____

5. ______________________________

____

6. ______________________________

____

GENERAL GEOGRAPHY REVIEW

USE AN ATLAS FOR ASSISTANCE:

1. The body of water located between Italy and Yugoslavia is the ____.
2. The __________________________ Sea is located between Saudi Arabia and India.
3. The Azores are located in the Pacific Ocean. True or False __________________
4. Auckland and Wellington are both located on the North Island of New Zealand. True or False ______________________
5. Istanbul is the capital of Turkey. True or False _______________
6. Munich is in the northern part of Germany. True or False _______
7. Corsica is a possession of Italy. True or False ________________
8. The Baltic Sea is located between Great Britain and the coast of France. True or False __________________
9. Rotterdam is a city in Belgium. True or False __________________
10. Split and Dubrovnik are coastal cities of Yugoslavia, located on the Adriatic Sea. True or False _______________________
11. Quebec is a province with very few lakes and rivers. True or False ___________________
12. Yellowknife is one of the few cities in the Northwest Territories of Canada. True or False ____________________
13. The capital of Barbados is Bridgetown. True or False ____________
14. The equator goes through the South American countries of Ecuador, Colombia, and _______________________.
15. The Tropic of _____________________________ goes right through the middle of Australia.

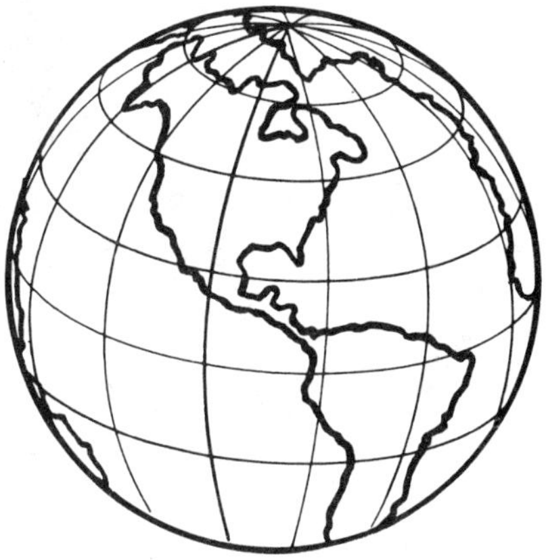

NOW THAT YOU HAVE COMPLETED THIS MANUAL, YOUR FURTHER RESEARCH CAN BE ORGANIZED BY COMPLETING DESTINATION EVALUATION FORMS WHEN YOU TRAVEL. THE FOLLOWING PAGES PROVIDE BLANK FORMS THAT WILL BE HELPFUL FOR THE ORGANIZATION OF DETAILS. THANK YOU FOR PURCHASING SOLITAIRE PUBLISHING MATERIALS. WE WELCOME YOUR QUESTIONS OR COMMENTS AT ANY TIME. YOU CAN CONTACT US BY E-MAIL AT PSolitaire@aol.com

NOTES

DESTINATION EVALUATION FORM

DATE:____________________ COMPLETED BY:_________________________

CITY,STATE or PROVINCE,COUNTRY:____

LANGUAGES:____ English widely spoken?_____

APPROXIMATE FLYING TIME_________________________FROM____________________________

ROUTING____

AIRPORT CODE AND NAME_______________________________ Rate 1 to 5 (5 is best):
Cleanliness____ Appearance____ Baggage Handling____ Staff Efficiency____
Safety____ Efficient Facility____ Staff Courteous____ Signs Well Posted____

DISTANCE FROM AIRPORT TO DESTINATION_____________ TRANSPORTATION AVAILABLE:
___rental cars ___train ___bus ___taxi ___subway OTHER____________________
Costs of transportation:____
Advantages/Disadvantages of transportation:____________________________________
____

NAMES OF SOME HOTELS, THEIR LOCATIONS, PRICE RANGES, COMMENTS:
(or use hotel evaluation form for thorough details)

____
____
____
____
____

OTHER TYPES OF ACCOMMODATIONS (Bed and Breakfast, Campgrounds, Guest Houses, etc.)

____

NAMES OF RESTAURANTS, LOCATIONS, PRICES, AND COMMENTS:

____
____
____
____

NAMES OF NIGHTCLUBS, DISCOS, ATTRACTIONS, LOCATIONS, PRICES, AND COMMENTS:

____
____
____
____

DESCRIBE BEACHES (if applicable):
____

SHOPPING:
Best Buys, prices, comments____
Local Handicrafts____
Best Places To Shop____
Bargaining Policies____
Shops Accept Local Currency____ U.S.Dollars____ Credit Cards____(__________)

SAFETY:
Safe To Walk Around At Night? To Go Alone? Any Special Concerns for Men/Women?
Lock Valuables? Wear Jewelry? Carry A Purse? Park Anywhere? Comments:
____
____
Special Hints/Information:____
Remarks About Visitors/Residents:____

DESTINATION EVALUATION FORM

DATE:____________________ COMPLETED BY:_________________________

CITY,STATE or PROVINCE,COUNTRY:____

LANGUAGES:____ English widely spoken?_____

APPROXIMATE FLYING TIME_________________________FROM___________________________

ROUTING____

AIRPORT CODE AND NAME________________________________ Rate 1 to 5 (5 is best):
Cleanliness____ Appearance____ Baggage Handling____ Staff Efficiency____
Safety____ Efficient Facility____ Staff Courteous____ Signs Well Posted____

DISTANCE FROM AIRPORT TO DESTINATION____________ TRANSPORTATION AVAILABLE:
___rental cars ___train ___bus ___taxi ___subway OTHER____________________
Costs of transportation:____
Advantages/Disadvantages of transportation:______________________________________
____

NAMES OF SOME HOTELS, THEIR LOCATIONS, PRICE RANGES, COMMENTS:
(or use hotel evaluation form for thorough details)

____
____
____
____
____

OTHER TYPES OF ACCOMMODATIONS (Bed and Breakfast, Campgrounds, Guest Houses, etc.)

____

NAMES OF RESTAURANTS, LOCATIONS, PRICES, AND COMMENTS:

____
____
____
____

NAMES OF NIGHTCLUBS, DISCOS, ATTRACTIONS, LOCATIONS, PRICES, AND COMMENTS:

____
____
____
____

DESCRIBE BEACHES (if applicable):
____

SHOPPING:
Best Buys, prices, comments____
Local Handicrafts____
Best Places To Shop____
Bargaining Policies____
Shops Accept Local Currency____ U.S.Dollars____ Credit Cards____(__________)

SAFETY:
Safe To Walk Around At Night? To Go Alone? Any Special Concerns for Men/Women?
Lock Valuables? Wear Jewelry? Carry A Purse? Park Anywhere? Comments:
____
____
Special Hints/Information:____
Remarks About Visitors/Residents:____

DESTINATION EVALUATION FORM

DATE:____________________ COMPLETED BY:__________________________

CITY,STATE or PROVINCE,COUNTRY:____

LANGUAGES:____ English widely spoken?_____

APPROXIMATE FLYING TIME_________________________FROM____________________________

ROUTING____

AIRPORT CODE AND NAME________________________________ Rate 1 to 5 (5 is best):
Cleanliness____ Appearance____ Baggage Handling____ Staff Efficiency____
Safety____ Efficient Facility____ Staff Courteous____ Signs Well Posted____

DISTANCE FROM AIRPORT TO DESTINATION_____________ TRANSPORTATION AVAILABLE:
___rental cars ___train ___bus ___taxi ___subway OTHER____________________
Costs of transportation:____
Advantages/Disadvantages of transportation:_______________________________
____

NAMES OF SOME HOTELS, THEIR LOCATIONS, PRICE RANGES, COMMENTS:
(or use hotel evaluation form for thorough details)

____
____
____
____
____

OTHER TYPES OF ACCOMMODATIONS (Bed and Breakfast, Campgrounds, Guest Houses, etc.)

____

NAMES OF RESTAURANTS, LOCATIONS, PRICES, AND COMMENTS:

____
____
____
____

NAMES OF NIGHTCLUBS, DISCOS, ATTRACTIONS, LOCATIONS, PRICES, AND COMMENTS:

____
____
____
____

DESCRIBE BEACHES (if applicable):
____

SHOPPING:
Best Buys, prices, comments____
Local Handicrafts____
Best Places To Shop____
Bargaining Policies____
Shops Accept Local Currency____ U.S.Dollars____ Credit Cards____(__________)

SAFETY:
Safe To Walk Around At Night? To Go Alone? Any Special Concerns for Men/Women?
Lock Valuables? Wear Jewelry? Carry A Purse? Park Anywhere? Comments:
____
____
Special Hints/Information:____
Remarks About Visitors/Residents:____

DESTINATION EVALUATION FORM

DATE:______________________ COMPLETED BY:___________________________

CITY,STATE or PROVINCE,COUNTRY:____

LANGUAGES:____ English widely spoken?_____

APPROXIMATE FLYING TIME___________________________FROM______________________________

ROUTING____

AIRPORT CODE AND NAME___________________________________ Rate 1 to 5 (5 is best):
Cleanliness____ Appearance____ Baggage Handling____ Staff Efficiency____
Safety____ Efficient Facility____ Staff Courteous____ Signs Well Posted____

DISTANCE FROM AIRPORT TO DESTINATION_____________ TRANSPORTATION AVAILABLE:
___rental cars ___train ___bus ___taxi ___subway OTHER____________________
Costs of transportation:____
Advantages/Disadvantages of transportation:____
____

NAMES OF SOME HOTELS, THEIR LOCATIONS, PRICE RANGES, COMMENTS:
(or use hotel evaluation form for thorough details)

____
____
____
____
____

OTHER TYPES OF ACCOMMODATIONS (Bed and Breakfast, Campgrounds, Guest Houses, etc.)

____

NAMES OF RESTAURANTS, LOCATIONS, PRICES, AND COMMENTS:

____
____
____
____

NAMES OF NIGHTCLUBS, DISCOS, ATTRACTIONS, LOCATIONS, PRICES, AND COMMENTS:

____
____
____
____

DESCRIBE BEACHES (if applicable):
____

SHOPPING:
Best Buys, prices, comments____
Local Handicrafts____
Best Places To Shop____
Bargaining Policies____
Shops Accept Local Currency____ U.S.Dollars____ Credit Cards____(__________)

SAFETY:
Safe To Walk Around At Night? To Go Alone? Any Special Concerns for Men/Women?
Lock Valuables? Wear Jewelry? Carry A Purse? Park Anywhere? Comments:
____
____
Special Hints/Information:____
Remarks About Visitors/Residents:____

ANSWER KEY

PAGE 14
NO ANSWER KEY AS RESPONSES WILL VARY.

PAGE 18
1. J
2. M
3. D
4. H
5. B
6. R
7. G
8. K
9. L
10. N
11. O
12. T
13. P
14. F
15. Q
16. E
17. C
18. I
19. A
20. S

PAGE 27
1. 6:00 pm, Jun. 1
2. 9:00 pm, Jan. 15
3. 1:00 am, Aug. 4
4. 9:00 pm, Jul. 5
5. 11:30 am, Feb. 4
6. 10:30 am, Sept. 9
7. 7:30 am, May 1
8. 10:00 am, Oct. 29
9. 8:45 pm, Mar. 28
10. 3:30 am, May 1

PAGE 34
1. Grassy portion of land with few trees.
2. A hurricane occurring in the Pacific, usually during the summer and fall.
3. One of the two times a year that the sun is directly overhead at midday on the equator. The vernal equinox occurs on approximately Mar. 21.
4. The general rule that for every 1,000 feet of altitude the temperature will be 3.5 degrees Farenheit cooler.
5. The side towards the wind.
6. A high, steep-sided, rock plateau.
7. A major ocean current that carries the warmer waters of the Atlantic Ocean and helps moderate the temperatures as far away as Great Britain.
8. A map that concentrates on the boundaries of countries, states, etc., with very little, if any, details on the surface features.
9. A line drawn on a map connecting places where the barometric pressure is the same.
10. The area between the Tropic of Cancer and the Tropic of Capricorn.
11. An island made of a ring or strip of coral.
12. A land area formed by the sediment of a river.
13. A group of islands.
14. A marshy creek or sluggish river tributary.
15. A narrow strip of land between two larger land masses.

PAGE 35
1. South America, Europe, Asia, North America, Africa, and Australia
2. Pacific, Indian, Atlantic, Pacific, Arctic
3. Greenland, Iceland, Madagascar (Malagasy Republic), New Zealand (North and South Island)
4. Aral, Caspian, Black, Mediterranean
5. Rocky, Andes, Himalaya
6. Sahara
7. Ecuador, Colombia, Brazil

PAGE 36
1. Pacific
2. North Sea
3. Bay of Bengal
4. Tasman
5. Black, Aegean, Mediterranean
6. Irish
7. Greenland
8. Africa, Europe, North America, South America, Australia, Asia, and Antarctica
9. Latitude
10. Longitude
11. Gulf Stream & Humboldt
12. Mercator
13. False
14. 25, 25
15. False
16. 1,000, 3.5
17. dry
18. A place of mosses, lichens, and stunted trees and plants. Beneath the surface the ground remains frozen year round.
19. Typhoons, June to November
20. Temperature, precipitation, humidity, wind, barometric pressure

PAGE 37
1. 1656
2. 1918
3. 2323
4. 1222
5. 2140
6. 2307
7. 1950
8. 0312
9. 1029
10. 0044
11. 12:22 pm
12. 2:58 pm
13. 6:18 pm
14. 10:03 pm
15. 3:14 pm
16. 4:55 am
17. 11:11 am
18. 8:15 am
19. 1:08 am
20. 12:26 am

PAGE 38
1. 12:10 am
2. 5:52 pm
3. 1:45 pm
4. 5:32 am
5. 2:21 pm
6. 7:03 pm
7. 10:12 pm
8. 8:09 pm
9. 4:01 pm
10. 9:41 am
11. 11:15 am
12. 1:10 pm
13. 9:05 pm
14. 8:32 pm
15. 12:18 pm
16. 1012
17. 1220
18. 0915
19. 2045
20. 0620
21. 1343
22. 2314
23. 0723
24. 1652
25. 2150
26. 0001
27. 1116
28. 1742
29. 1835
30. 2005

PAGE 55
1. Grand Canyon, Arizona
2. Everglades, Florida
3. Yellowstone, Wyoming (mostly)
4. Arches, Utah
5. Redwoods, California

PAGE 59
1. Vermont
2. Nantucket and Martha's Vineyard
3. White
4. New Haven
5. Rhode Island
6. Maine
7. Freedom Trail
8. False
9. Bronx, Brooklyn, Manhattan, Queens, Staten Island
10. Cooperstown
11. True
12. False
13. Rhode Island
14. Massachusetts
15. Vermont
16. Maine
17. Connecticut
18. Vermont
19. Massachusetts
20. New Hamsphire

PAGE 62
1. Brunswick
2. Savannah
3. Atlanta
4. Charleston
5. Richmond
6. Lexington
7. Nashville
8. Memphis
9. Asheville
10. Hilton Head

PAGE 63
1. Ohio
2. Baltimore
3. Pisgah
4. South Carolina
5. Brandywine
6. Sea Island, Brunswick
7. North Carolina
8. Gen. "Stonewall" Jackson, Gen. Robert E. Lee
9. Kentucky
10. Arlington
11. True
12. Biltmore
13. Savannah
14. North Carolina, Tennessee
15. Virginia
16. 100
17. Williamsburg, Yorktown
18. False
19. False
20. False

PAGE 66

1. False
2. False
3. False
4. False
5. Cocoa
6. False
7. Arkansas
8. False
9. Biloxi
10. San Antonio
11. False
12. February
13. French Quarter
14. False
15. Arkansas

A. 4
B. 5
C. 6
D. 1
E. 2
F. 3

PAGE 68

1. 11,000
2. Wisconsin
3. Dubuque, Cedar Rapids, Davenport
4. False
5. 630
6. Jefferson, Lincoln, Theodore Roosevelt
7. Missouri
8. St. Paul
9. True
10. May
11. Rush
12. John G. Shedd
13. Badlands
14. Jamestown
15. O'Hare

PAGE 74

1. Denver
2. True
3. Sante Fe
4. Arizona
5. Salt Lake City
6. True
7. Wasatch
8. 1,149
9. Bitterroot
10. Arizona
11. False
12. Arizona, New Mexico, Utah
13. Jackson
14. 200
15. False
16. False
17. Oregon
18. Malibu, Redondo, Venice, Santa Monica
19. Sacramento
20. False
21. New Mexico
22. Sangre de Cristo
23. South
24. Mann's Chinese Theater
25. Alcatraz
26. False
27. False
28. False
29. Phoenix
30. Colorado

PAGE 81

1. D
2. G
3. A
4. C
5. F
6. E
7. H
8. B
9. I
10. J
11. P
12. N
13. M
14. K
15. O
16. L
17. Q
18. R
19. T
20. S

1. South Dakota
2. Texas
3. Detroit
4. Chicago
5. Capitol, White House, FBI Building, House & Senate, Lincoln Memorial, Jefferson Memorial, Washington Monument, Potomac River, Georgetown, Smithsonian
6. St. Louis
7. Boston, Massachusetts
8. Hollywood, Spruce Goose, Disneyland, Knotts Berry Farm, Universal Studios, Rodeo Drive, Queen Mary, Burbank, stars' homes
9. Nashville, Tennessee
10. Las Vegas

PAGE 82-83

1. Maine, New Hampshire, Vermont, Massachusetts, Rhode Island, Connecticut
2. New Orleans
3. Golden Gate Bridge, Union Square, Fisherman's Wharf, North Beach, cable cars, Lombard Street, Chinatown
4. Mt. McKinley (Denali), in Alaska
5. Philadelphia
6. Broadway, Empire State Bldg., Central Park, Times Square, World Trade Center, Statue of Liberty, United Nations Bldg.
7. Alaska
8. Seattle
9. Denver
10. Arizona
11. California
12. Maine
13. New Jersey
14. Salt Lake City
15. Buffalo
16. Ohio
17. Iowa
18. Idaho
19. Minnesota
20. Mississippi
21. Reno
22. True
23. Colorado, Brazos, Pecos, Trinity, Guadalupe
24. E
25. F
26. G
27. C
28. D
29. B
30. A
31. G
32. I
33. H

PAGE 83 CULINARY DELIGHTS

1. H
2. E
3. F
4. I
5. K
6. G
7. B
8. C
9. A
10. D

PAGE 84

1. G	11. R
2. Q	12. F
3. K	13. J
4. T	14. N
5. D	15. O
6. E	16. P
7. B	17. S
8. I	18. L
9. H	19. C
10. M	20. A

1. Seattle, WA
2. Washington, DC
3. St. Louis, MO

PAGE 85

Note: Extra credit can be given for naming capital cities.

1. Texas (TX) - Austin
2. Louisiana (LA) - Baton Rouge
3. Kansas (KS) - Topeka
4. Wisconsin (WI) - Madison
5. Colorado (CO) - Denver
6. New Mexico (NM) - Santa Fe
7. Kentucky (KY) - Frankfort
8. North Carolina (NC) - Raleigh
9. South Carolina (SC) - Columbia
10. Florida (FL) - Tallahassee
11. Alabama (AL) - Montgomery
12. Virginia (VA) - Richmond
13. Tennessee (TN) - Nashville
14. Arkansas (AR) - Little Rock
15. Mississippi (MS) - Jackson
16. Georgia (GA) - Atlanta
17. Oklahoma (OK) - Oklahoma City
18. Nebraska (NE) - Lincoln
19. Pennsylvania (PA) - Harrisburg
20. Delaware (DE) - Dover
21. West Virginia (WV) - Charleston
22. District of Columbia (DC) - Washington
23. Maine (ME) - Augusta
24. New Hampshire (NH) - Concord
25. Rhode Island (RI) - Providence
26. New York (NY) - Albany
27. Ohio (OH) - Columbus
28. Missouri (MO) - Jefferson City
29. Arizona (AZ) - Phoenix
30. California (CA) - Sacramento
31. Wyoming (WY) - Cheyenne
32. Indiana (IN) - Indianapolis
33. South Dakota (SD) - Pierre
34. Washington (WA) - Olympia
35. Iowa (IA) - Des Moines
36. New Jersey (NJ) - Trenton
37. North Dakota (ND) - Bismarck
38. Massachusetts (MA) - Boston
39. Illinois (IL) - Springfield
40. Maryland (MD) - Annapolis
41. Utah (UT) - Salt Lake City
42. Minnesota (MN) - St. Paul
43. Michigan (MI) - Lansing
44. Nevada (NV) - Carson City
45. Montana (MT) - Helena
46. Oregon (OR) - Salem
47. Idaho (ID) - Boise
48. Connecticut (CT) - Hartford
49. Vermont (VT) - Montpelier
50. Alaska (AK) - Juneau

Note: Listed in parentheses are the three-letter codes for the airport(s) serving these destinations.

1. Tampa, FL (TPA)
2. Miami, FL (MIA)
3. Atlanta, GA (ATL)
4. Cleveland, OH (CLE)
5. Los Angeles, CA (LAX, ONT, LGB, BUR)
6. Phoenix, AZ (PHX)
7. Dallas, TX (DAL, DFW)
8. Houston, TX (HOU, IAH)
9. Albuquerque, NM (ABQ)
10. Washington, DC (WAS, DCA, IAD, BWI)
11. Denver, CO (DEN)
12. Seattle, WA (SEA, LKE)
13. Boise, ID (BOI)
14. San Francisco, CA (SFO, OAK)
15. Minneapolis, MN (MSP)
16. Milwaukee, WI (MKE)
17. Kansas City, MO (MKC, MCI)
18. St. Louis, MO (STL)
19. Pittsburgh, PA (PIT)
20. New York City, NY (NYC, LGA, JFK, EWR)
21. Boston, MA (BOS)
22. Hartford, CT (BDL)
23. Cincinnati, OH (CVG)
24. Indianapolis, IN (IND)
25. Salt Lake City, UT (SLC)
26. Las Vegas, NV (LAS)
27. Portland, OR (PDX)
28. New Orleans, LA (MSY)
29. Philadelphia, PA (PHL)
30. Baltimore, MD (BWI)
31. Detroit, MI (DET,DTT,DTW)
32. Chicago, IL (CHI,ORD,MDW, CGX)
33. Buffalo, NY (BUF)

PAGE 100

1. H
2. D
3. A
4. C
5. A
6. H
7. D
8. A
9. H
10. C
11. H
12. A
13. D
14. H
15. B
16. C
17. A
18. H
19. C
20. D
21. E
22. C
23. C
24. H
25. G
26. Muumuus, coral, perfumes, carvings, local crafts, silks
27. Mahalo
28. A porch or veranda
29. False
30. Kane, Wahini

PAGE 101

1. Hawaii
2. Maui
3. Lanai
4. Molokai
5. Oahu
6. Kauai
7. Niihau
8. Hilo
9. Kona
10. Honolulu
11. Lihue
12. Waimea
13. Kahului
14. Kaunakakai
15. Lanai City
16. Kahoolawe
17. Hana
18. Kahuku
19. Lahaina
20. Wailuku

PAGE 110

1. Anchorage, Fairbanks, Nome, Juneau, Valdez, Pt. Barrow (Barrow), Sitka, Kotzebue
2. True
3. Prudhoe Bay; Valdez
4. Hunting, fishing, camping, mountaineering, exploring, shopping, sightseeing, skiing, wildlife viewing and photography, cruising through the Inside Passage
5. Kotzebue
6. Juneau
7. Brooks Range
8. Yukon River
9. Aleutian
10. Kodiak
11. Matanuska
12. Russian Orthodox
13. Alyeska
14. Denali
15. Native crafts, gold nuggets, soapstone articles
16. 59
17. Wasilla
18. Katmai
19. True
20. It means a chunk has broken off and created an iceberg
21. False
22. 64
23. Chugach
24. Ptarmigan
25. False

PAGE 111

1. Fairbanks
2. Kotzebue
3. Pt. Barrow (Barrow
4. Kodiak
5. Anchorage
6. Nome
7. Skagway
8. Juneau
9. Ketchikan
10. Sitka

PAGE 118-119

These are sample replies.

1. You may find some New Yorkers to be abrupt and aggressive - probably due to their harried pace of life. The city has a lot of crime - like many big cities - you just need to take the proper precautions. To cut down on expenses, look for weekend bargains and packages, use public transportation such as buses and subways, and eat at coffee shops and delis rather than full service restaurants.
2. There are some self-contained resorts where the tourist is much more insulated from many such problems. Some newer developed areas, such as Ixtapa and Cancun, are also less subject to the poor appearance and poverty lifestyle of rural areas.
3. The fact that some islands are very undeveloped means they offer a truly relaxing vacation and that is what appeals to some people. However, there are many islands to choose from, and they differ dramatically. Some have casinos, some are much larger than others with several places to sightsee, and some have a more lively atmosphere. There are extensive resorts available on some islands, which offer all kinds of activities for guests.
4. Some areas should be avoided. It is important to check with the Center for Disease Control and the tourist or government offices for current advisories, precautions, shots necessary and any recommendations. Certain individuals with particular health problems should check with their doctor for advice.
5. You may encounter some French people who may not be particularly friendly, especially if you are in a busy, huge city like Paris. Make an effort to be considerate and perhaps study some French prior to your trip so that you can communicate better.
6. Your trip doesn't have to be inundated with churches and museums. There are many sports activities to enjoy - hiking, fishing, camping, bicycling, skiing, golfing, etc. The countryside offers beautiful and differing scenery. There are beaches, rivers, lakes, mountains and islands. How about the shopping, dining, and nightlife? There are casinos, spas, and resorts. Visit the quaint villages, the big cities, castles, and experience the different culture and lifestyle of Europe.
7. England may not be the place you'll get a suntan, but the the weather is "unpredictable" and it can be quite nice and sunny. It doesn't usually get extremely cold, and the rain is what contributes to that beautiful green countryside. Take an umbrella and a mackintosh so sightseeing is not curtailed entirely.
8. The standard of living is high in Scandinavian countries, but you can always look to stay in modest inns, bed and breakfast hotels, or other inexpensive accommodations. Perhaps limit your stay in Europe - make the trip length eight days instead of two weeks. Travel in low season and use bargain packages.
9. The standards of health may be much lower than you are used to. Take proper precautions and medicines, follow health recommendations so that you can safely visit many areas. Of course, your own health and physical condition must be considered and your own physician can advise you best.
10. Africa is a huge continent and the climate varies greatly. There are seasons to consider and best times to travel - depending on the country/countries you intend to visit. Take repellents and protective clothing to guard against the insects and bugs.
11. It is always advisable to check on current conditions of the country you are going to visit. Some countries in Africa are more stable than others.
12. I don't know if that is a problem confined to travel to Africa because it can happen when you travel anywhere. If you are traveling from the U.S., try using a U.S. airline or an airline that has an office in the U.S., so that if there are any problems you can contact them easily.

PAGE 132

1. 4
2. 5000
3. CN Tower
4. False
5. Ottawa
6. Prince Edward Island
7. Nova Scotia
8. Montreal
9. True
10. Ontario, Quebec
11. Fredericton
12. Rideau
13. True
14. Saskatchewan
15. Calgary
16. Banff, Jasper
17. Regina, Saskatchewan
18. Butchart
19. St. John, New Brunswick
20. Yellowknife

PAGE 133

1. Nova Scotia
2. Prince Edward Island
3. Ontario
4. Manitoba
5. Northwest Territories
6. British Columbia
7. Quebec
8. Saskatchewan
9. New Brunswick
10. Yukon
11. Newfoundland
12. Alberta

PAGE 134

1. Halifax
2. Quebec
3. Montreal
4. Ottawa
5. Toronto
6. Winnipeg
7. Regina
8. Saskatoon
9. Calgary
10. Edmonton
11. Vancouver
12. Victoria

PAGE 144

1. Morelia, Puebla, Guadalajara
2. Cuernavaca
3. Mexico City, Taxco, Acapulco
4. D
5. Cabo San Lucas
6. Tijuana
7. C
8. D
9. D
10. 31

PAGE 145

1. Nuevo Peso
2. Tacos, enchilades
3. Ceramics, embroidered clothes, blankets
4. Mexicali, Tijuana, Ciudad Juarez
5. Taxco
6. Chapultepec Castle, National Museum of Anthropology, National Palace
7. C
8. Acapulco
9. Los Mochis
10. Tequila, Kahlua
11. Ixtapa
12. PV
13. Tarahumara
14. Cancun
15. Merida
16. False
17. Tulum
18. Cozumel
19. 11,000
20. Cholula

PAGE 146

1. Mexico City
2. Acapulco
3. Manzanillo
4. Cabo San Lucas
5. Mazatlan
6. Cozumel
7. Guadalajara
8. Merida
9. La Paz
10. Puerto Vallarta

PAGE 155

1. C
2. E
3. A
4. G
5. D
6. F
7. B
8. J
9. H
10. K
11. I
12. Belize
13. Costa Rica
14. Balboa
15. Guatemala
16. Belize
17. Guatemala
18. Panama
19. Honduras
20. Nicaragua

PAGE 170

1. False
2. False
3. False
4. Boonoonoonoos
5. Dorada
6. Port-au-Prince, Haiti
7. SDQ
8. Cap Haitien
9. Port-au-Prince
10. False
11. Rio Grande
12. True
13. False
14. Larimar
15. 5

1. El Yunque
2. St. Thomas
3. St. John
4. 30
5. Que Pasa
6. False
7. Paradores Puertorriquenos
8. Culebra and Vieques
9. Christiansted, Fredericksted
10. False
11. True
12. Blackbeard's
13. False
14. SJU
15. True

PAGE 156

1. Panama
2. Mexico
3. Guatemala
4. El Salvador
5. Belize
6. Costa Rica
7. Nicaragua
8. Honduras
9. Caribbean Sea
10. Pacific Ocean

PAGE 164

1. 700
2. 26, 1
3. Lucaya
4. Georgetown
5. Abaco
6. San Salvador
7. Alvernia, Cat
8. Eleuthera
9. Abaco
10. Paradise
11. Ardastra
12. June, July, August
13. Marsh Harbour, Abaco
14. NAS
15. San Salvador

1. Grand Turk, Salt Cay
2. Canada, Bahamas
3. Providenciales
4. False, 3,000
5. True
6. False
7. True
8. Creole
9. Grand Cayman
10. Cayman Brac

PAGE 181

1. O
2. B
3. C
4. K
5. E
6. I
7. J
8. L
9. F
10. H
11. P
12. H
13. G
14. D
15. J
16. A
17. N
18. M
19. Q
20. H
21. C
22. B
23. H
24. I
25. H
26. A
27. N
28. R
29. Q
30. S

PAGE 182-183

1. Nassau and Freeport
2. St. Thomas, St. John, St. Croix
3. False
4. Aruba, Bonaire, Curacao
5. Jamaica
6. Liquor, electronic equipment, jewelry
7. Havana
8. Rum
9. $1200.00
10. 4 liters
11. San Juan
12. Cayman Islands
13. Guadeloupe
14. St. Martin/St. Maarten
15. Aruba, Puerto Rico
16. Dominican Republic, Haiti
17. Swimming, diving, snorkeling, tennis, golf, sightseeing, relaxing
18. Divi divi
19. Tortola, Virgin Gorda
20. French goods, perfumes, china
21. Georgetown
22. False
23. St. Eustatius
24. Grenada
25. MBJ
26. Martinique
27. Jamaica
28. 85,000
29. Trinidad
30. Philipsburg, Marigot
31. AUA
32. 110, 1
33. Santo Domingo, Dominican Republic
34. 35
35. Vieques, Culebra
36. Trinidad
37. Barbados
38. Bonaire
39. False
40. False
41. False
42. False
43. False
44. False
45. Antigua
46. Grand Cayman
47. False
48. False
49. False
50. Dominica

PAGE 184

1. B
2. C
3. I
4. G
5. H
6. A
7. D
8. J
9. F
10. K
11. L
12. P
13. O
14. N
15. M

PAGE 185

1. Cuba
2. Jamaica
3. Grand Cayman
4. San Blas Islands
5. Vieques
6. Haiti
7. Dominican Republic
8. Puerto Rico
9. St. Thomas
10. Aruba
11. Curacao
12. Bonaire
13. Trinidad
14. Tobago
15. New Providence Island (capital: Nassau)
16. Grand Bahama Island (main city: Freeport)
17. St. Croix
18. St. John
19. St. Martin/St. Maarten
20. Guadeloupe
21. Isla Margarita
22. Grenada
23. St. Vincent
24. St. Lucia
25. Martinique
26. Dominica
27. Marie Galante
28. Montserrat
29. Antigua
30. Barbuda
31. Nevis
32. St. Kitts
33. St. Barthelemy
34. St. Eustatius
35. Anguilla
36. Tortola
37. Crooked Island
38. Mona
39. Great Inagua Island
40. Turks & Caicos Island
41. Little Inagua Island
42. Mayaguana Island
43. Acklins Island
44. Rum Cay
45. San Salvador Island
46. Cat Island
47. Long Island
48. Great Exuma Island
49. Eleuthera
50. Great Abaco Island
51. Bimini
52. Andros
53. Isle of Youth or Isle of Pines
54. Roques
55. Orchilla
56. Tortuga
57. Blanquilla
58. Barbados

PAGE 188

1. Hamilton
2. Hamilton
3. 7
4. Parishes
5. Harrington
6. True
7. 600
8. Somerset
9. Front Street
10. Immaculate, very friendly, no rainy season, wide variety of accommodations, excellent shopping, fine restaurants, lots of sports

PAGE 201

1. Simon Bolivar
2. Piranha
3. Tango
4. Figa
5. Portuguese
6. Portillo
7. Paraguay
8. Angel
9. Punta del Este
10. Vicuna
11. Gaucho
12. Bariloche
13. La Paz
14. Kaieteur Falls
15. Easter Island
16. Manaus
17. Galapagos
18. Quechua
19. Real
20. Cuzco

PAGE 202

1. A
2. B
3. D
4. B
5. D
6. B
7. D
8. D
9. B
10. B
11. D
12. B
13. D
14. A
15. A

PAGE 203

1. C
2. D
3. E
4. M
5. L
6. G
7. A
8. K
9. J
10. H
11. F
12. B
13. I
14. N
15. S
16. R
17. T
18. O
19. P
20. Q
21. Because of the altitude
22. A clenched fist that is a symbol of good luck
23. Wall hangings, carvings, weavings, trinkets
24. Parillada
25. Nausea, dizziness, and headache

PAGE 204

1. Rio de Janeiro, Brasilia, Sao Paulo
2. South American Cowboy
3. Guyana
4. Devil's Island
5. Iguassu
6. Andes
7. Guayaquil
8. Calle Florida, Calle Santa Fe
9. Lake Titicaca
10. Ipanema, Copacabana
11. Margarita Island
12. Peru
13. Brazil
14. Bariloche
15. Iguanas, giant tortoises, red-footed and blue-footed boobies, flightless cormorants
16. Simon Bolivar
17. Manaus
18. Venezuela
19. Colombia
20. Vina del Mar, Valparaiso
21. Uruguay
22. La Guaira
23. Paraguay and Bolivia
24. Venezuela
25. Guyana
26. Easter Island
27. Cajas
28. Cuzco
29. La Boca
30. 13

PAGE 205

1. Colombia
2. Venezuela
3. Bolivia
4. Argentina
5. Uruguay
6. Paraguay
7. Brazil
8. Peru
9. French Guiana
10. Ecuador
11. Guyana
12. Chile
13. Suriname
14. Falkland Islands
15. Galapagos Islands

PAGE 206

1. Brasilia, Brazil
2. Asuncion, Paraguay
3. Santiago, Chile
4. La Paz, Bolivia
5. Caracas, Venezuela
6. Montevideo, Uruguay
7. Lima, Peru
8. Bogota, Colombia
9. Buenos Aires, Argentina
10. Quito, Ecuador

PAGE 219 As quiz is just for fun - no answer key is provided.

PAGE 225

1. History and scenery, the language is the same, the people are nice
2. C
3. Northern Ireland
4. Blarney
5. Tower of London
6. Hyde, Sunday
7. Dover
8. Salisbury
9. August
10. Holyroodhouse
11. Glasgow
12. Man
13. Princes
14. Portmeirion
15. Dublin
16. Liffey
17. Belfast
18. False
19. Chester
20. False
21. Thames
22. Big Ben, Houses of Parliament, Trafalgar Square, Westminster Abbey
23. Haworth
24. Cardiff
25. Snowdonia

PAGE 229

1. See the famous sights, experience French culture, buy French goods, visit famous museums
2. True
3. St. Michel, St. Germain des Pres
4. 1,000 ft.
5. 350,000
6. Montmartre
7. Versailles
8. Bordeaux
9. St. Denis
10. Toulouse
11. Mont St. Michel
12. Left Bank
13. Pont Neuf
14. Fountainbleau
15. Blois, Chartres, Chenonceaux
16. Seine
17. Invalides
18. Bois de Boulogne, Bois de Vincennes, Jardin des Tuileries
19. Kissing on both cheeks
20. St. Tropez, Nice, Cannes

PAGE 234

1. Bruges, Namur, Dinant
2. False
3. Delft
4. True
5. Oberammergau
6. 16
7. Schipol
8. False
9. Atomium
10. Guten Appetit

1. Iberian
2. Lisbon
3. Toledo
4. Formentera, Ibiza, Mallorca
5. Prado
6. Seville
7. Malaga
8. Barcelona
9. Algarve
10. Segovia
11. Granada
12. Fado
13. Fatima
14. False
15. Andorra

PAGE 235

1. Mozart, Brahms, Beethoven
2. Vienna
3. Fondue
4. Innsbruck and Kitzbuhel
5. Danube
6. Bern
7. Jungfrau and the Matterhorn
8. Watches, chocolates
9. Belvedere, Hofburg
10. Swiss franc

PAGE 238

1. Athens
2. Mikonos, Rhodes, Santorini
3. Piraeus
4. Eternal
5. True
6. Tuscany
7. Sighs
8. Sicily
9. Vesuvius
10. Vatican City
11. Florence
12. Pottery, leather goods, jewelry
13. Souvlaki, moussaka, giros
14. Religious paintings or mosaics
15. True

PAGE 242

1. Changing winds and tides
2. Jutland
3. Sognefjord
4. Oslo, Bergen, Tromso
5. Stockholm
6. Alborg
7. Smaland
8. Copenhagen
9. Goteborg, Gota
10. Vanern
11. True
12. Odense
13. Glassware, sweaters, furs
14. Lapp
15. Sauna

PAGE 244

1. Tallinn
2. Ural
3. Nesting dolls, vodka, wood and metal sculptures
4. False
5. Ukraine
6. Commonwealth of Independent States
7. Estonia
8. Basil
9. Turkmenistan
10. Ukraine

PAGE 254-255

1. Copenhagen, Denmark
2. Greece
3. Austria
4. Brussels, Belgium
5. Finland
6. Luxembourg
7. Paris, France
8. Hungary
9. Athens, Greece
10. Ireland
11. London, England
12. Rome, Italy
13. Netherlands
14. Venice, Italy
15. Norway
16. Reykjavik, Iceland
17. Valletta, Malta
18. Budapest, Hungary
19. Poland
20. Bulgaria
21. Germany
22. Stratford-upon-Avon
23. Cannes
24. Amsterdam, Netherlands
25. Berlin
26. Bucharest
27. Switzerland
28. Prague
29. Schilling
30. Fondue
31. True
32. Smorgasbord
33. Furs, caviar, vodka
34. Moscow
35. Monaco
36. Spain
37. Portugal
38. Gibraltar
39. Fado
40. Iceland
41. Belgium
42. Scotland
43. Greece
44. Canary
45. Italy
46. Andorra
47. Portugal
48. Sistine
49. Aeroflot
50. Ireland

PAGE 256

1. F
2. T
3. T
4. T
5. F
6. F
7. F
8. F
9. F
10. F
11. F
12. F
13. T
14. F
15. F

1. Spain
2. Sweden
3. Liechtenstein
4. Munich, Frankfurt, Berlin
5. Dover
6. Norway, Sweden, and Denmark
7. St. Basil's
8. False
9. France
10. Netherlands
11. False
12. Northern Ireland
13. England, Scotland, Wales, and Northern Ireland
14. Portugal
15. Sicily and Sardinia

PAGE 257

1. Wales
2. Balearic
3. Copenhagen
4. Austria
5. Canary
6. Belgium
7. Austria
8. Malaga
9. Germany
10. Paris
11. Tower of London, Buckingham Palace, Hyde Park
12. Odense
13. False
14. Norway
15. St. Petersburg
16. French, Italian, German
17. King Ludwig II
18. Peseta
19. Pisa
20. Lira
21. Versailles
22. Rome
23. Danube
24. Lake Balaton, Hungary
25. Emerald Isle

PAGE 258

1. C
2. F
3. I
4. T
5. G
6. P
7. A
8. Z
9. K
10. V
11. Y
12. Q
13. L
14. R
15. N
16. M
17. S
18. H
19. J
20. W
21. U
22. B
23. E
24. D
25. O

1. D
2. H
3. T
4. J
5. C
6. E
7. G
8. M
9. N
10. O
11. P
12. Q
13. S
14. F
15. K
16. B
17. R
18. I
19. A
20. L

PAGE 259-260

1. Paris
2. Ludwig, Germany
3. London
4. Rome, Colosseum
5. Little Mermaid, Copenhagen, Denmark
6. Parthenon
7. Netherlands/Holland
8. Venice

PAGE 261

1. Iceland
2. Scotland
3. England
4. Wales
5. N. Ireland
6. Ireland
7. Portugal
8. Spain
9. France
10. Belgium
11. Luxembourg
12. Switzerland
13. Liechtenstein
14. Italy
15. San Marino
16. Andorra
17. Slovenia
18. Albania
19. Greece
20. Turkey
21. Bulgaria
22. Romania
23. Hungary
24. Austria
25. Germany
26. Czech Republic
27. Poland
28. Adriatic Sea
29. Denmark
30. Norway
31. Sweden
32. Finland
33. Estonia
34. Gibraltar
35. Balearic Islands
36. Corsica
37. Sardinia
38. Sicily
39. Malta
40. Crete
41. Rhodes
42. Monaco
43. Holland/ Netherlands
44. Atlantic Ocean
45. North Sea
46. Baltic Sea
47. Mediterranean Sea
48. Slovakia/Slovak Republic
49. Latvia
50. Lithuania
51. Croatia
52. Bosnia & Hercegovina
53. Yugoslavia
54. Macedonia

PAGE 262

1. Reykjavik
2. Edinburgh
3. Dublin
4. Belfast
5. Cardiff
6. London
7. Lisbon
8. Madrid
9. Paris
10. Brussels
11. Amsterdam
12. Luxembourg
13. Bern
14. Rome
15. Tirane/Tirana
16. Athens
17. Sofia
18. Bucharest
19. Tallinn
20. Budapest
21. Vienna
22. Prague
23. Berlin
24. Warsaw
25. Copenhagen
26. Oslo
27. Stokholm
28. Helsinki
29. Bratislava
30. Riga
31. Vilnius

PAGE 278

1. Aberdare, Amboseli, Mt. Kenya
2. Cairo
3. Aswan Dam, Sphinx, Great Pyramids of Giza
4. Tunis, Tunisia
5. Liberia
6. President Monroe, Monrovia
7. Victoria
8. Cape Town
9. Addis Ababa
10. Libya
11. Cous Cous
12. Benin
13. False
14. Algiers
15. Gambia
16. Sahara
17. Nile
18. Abidjan
19. Mint tea
20. Aswan
21. Harare
22. Nairobi
23. Wildebeests, lions, cheetahs, zebras, hyenas
24. Separation of whites from non-whites
25. Tanzania

PAGE 279

1. F
2. A
3. O
4. C
5. I
6. R
7. N
8. P
9. J
10. H
11. L
12. G
13. Q
14. D
15. M
16. S
17. T
18. K
19. B
20. E

PAGE 280

1. Portugal, Great Britain, Spain, France, Germany
2. Kenya
3. Mediterranean, Red
4. Mali
5. A marketplace
6. Germany
7. Lesotho, Swaziland
8. Madagascar
9. Swahili
10. Equatorial Guinea
11. Rand
12. Pretoria, Cape Town, Johannesburg
13. Senegal
14. Rabat, Fez
15. Botswana
16. Zanzibar
17. Blue
18. Dem. Republic of Congo
19. Aberdare
20. Ngorongoro Crater
21. NBO
22. Burkina Faso
23. Diamonds, gold
24. Seychelles
25. Cape Verde

PAGE 281

1. Morocco
2. Algeria
3. Tunisia
4. Libya
5. Egypt
6. Western Sahara
7. Mauritania
8. Mali
9. Niger
10. Chad
11. Sudan
12. Ethiopia
13. Somalia
14. Senegal
15. Guinea
16. Burkina Faso
17. Sierra Leone
18. Cote d'Ivoire
19. Ghana
20. Nigeria
21. Cameroon
22. Central African Republic
23. Gabon
24. Congo
25. Zaire
26. Uganda
27. Kenya
28. Tanzania
29. Angola
30. Zambia
31. Mozambique
32. Namibia
33. Botswana
34. Zimbabwe
35. South Africa
36. Madagascar

a. Gambia
b. Guinea-Bissau
c. Liberia
d. Togo
e. Benin
f. Equatorial Guinea
g. Djibouti
h. Rwanda
i. Burundi
j. Seychelles
k. Malawi
l. Madeira
m. Lesotho
n. Swaziland
o. Azores
p. Cabinda
q. Canary Islands
r. Eritrea

PAGE 282

1. Casablanca
2. Algiers
3. Tunis
4. Tripoli
5. Cairo
6. Khartoum
7. Addis Ababa
8. Kampala
9. Nairobi
10. Mombasa
11. Dar es Salaam
12. Harare
13. Pretoria
14. Durban
15. Cape Town
16. Luanda
17. Kinshasa
18. Lagos
19. Abidjan
20. Monrovia

PAGE 296

1. Jerusalem, Nazareth, Bethlehem
2. Jerusalem
3. Christianity, Islam, Judaism
4. Dead Sea
5. It begins on Friday at sunset and lasts until Saturday at sunset
6. Religious articles, jewelry, glasswork
7. Israel, Jordan, Syria, Kuwait, Lebanon
8. Agra, India
9. Kuala Lumpur
10. Noh, Kabuki
11. Shekel
12. Portugal
13. Nepal
14. Jordan, Iraq, Tunisia
15. Agra, Bombay (Mumbai), Goa, Calcutta, Jaipur
16. Phuket Island, Pattaya Beach
17. Honshu, Hokkaido, Kyushu, Shikoku
18. Papier mache goods, brassware, silks, rugs, clothes
19. Kabul
20. 7,000
21. Taiwan
22. Hindi
23. Red pepper
24. Sri Lanka
25. Rupee
26. Jaipur
27. Chiang Mai
28. Bombay (Mumbai)
29. False
30. False

PAGE 297

1. X	8. A	14. D	20. L
2. E	9. X	15. G	21. E
3. J	10. N	16. H	22. D
4. B	11. W	17. K	23. E
5. V	12. Q	18. O	24. P
6. I	13. C	19. A	25. A
7. M			

1. I	11. A
2. O	12. E
3. D	13. N
4. H	14. G
5. D	15. A
6. C	16. I
7. E	17. H
8. G	18. D
9. B	19. I

PAGE 298

1. C.I.S.
2. Turkey
3. Syria
4. Jordan
5. Mongolia
6. China
7. India
8. Oman
9. Japan
10. Afghanistan
11. Sri Lanka
12. Myanmar
13. Bangladesh
14. Nepal
15. Saudi Arabia
16. Lebanon
17. South Korea
18. North Korea
19. Thailand
20. Vietnam
21. Philippines
22. Kampuchea
23. Yemen
24. Israel
25. Malaysia
26. Laos
27. Iraq
28. Kuwait
29. United Arab Emirates
30. Oman (another part)
31. Iran
32. Pakistan
33. Indonesia
34. Taiwan
35. Qatar
36. Bahrain
37. Bhutan
38. Singapore
39. Hong Kong
40. Macau
41. Brunei
42. Belarus
43. Ukraine
44. Moldova
45. Georgia
46. Armenia
47. Azerbaijan
48. Kazakstan
49. Uzebekistan
50. Turkmenistan
51. Kyrgyzstan
52. Tajikistan

PAGE 299

1. Moscow
2. Istanbul
3. Ankara
4. Jerusalem
5. Baghdad
6. Tehran
7. Kabul
8. Karachi
9. New Delhi
10. Bombay
11. Kathmandu
12. Dacca
13. Yangoon
14. Bangkok
15. Kuala Lumpur
16. Manila
17. Taipei
18. Beijing
19. Seoul
20. Tokyo

PAGE 310

1. Great Barrier Reef
2. Queensland
3. Ayers Rock
4. Alice Springs
5. False
6. The pressing of noses
7. Opera House
8. Rottnest Island
9. Adelaide
10. Boomerangs, toy koalas, opals, local crafts
11. A
12. D
13. B
14. C
15. E
16. Auckland, Wellington, Christchurch
17. True
18. Fishing, hiking, whitewater rafting
19. Geysers, glaciers, mountains
20. Wellington
21. Kiwi
22. Maoris
23. Paua
24. Auckland
25. Cook

PAGE 311

1.	Auckland	A.	Western Australia
2.	Wellington	B.	Northern Territories
3.	Christchurch	C.	Queensland
4.	Hobart	D.	South Australia
5.	Melbourne	E.	New South Wales
6.	Canberra	F.	Victoria
7.	Sydney	G.	Tasmania
8.	Adelaide		
9.	Brisbane		
10.	Alice Springs		
11.	Cairns		
12.	Darwin		
13.	Perth		

PAGE 313

1. Hawaii
2. Tahiti
3. Society Islands
4. Cook Islands
5. New Zealand
6. Australia
7. Indonesia
8. Fiji
9. Papua New Guinea
10. Micronesia

PAGE 317

1. Moorea
2. Chile
3. Micronesia
4. Independent
5. Maoi
6. Solomon
7. Cook
8. Austral
9. Vanuatu
10. Fiji
11. Kiribati
12. Indonesia
13. Tuvalu
14. Tonga
15. Guam
16. D
17. F
18. H
19. G
20. J
21. B
22. A
23. I
24. C
25. E

PAGE 321

1. 12:10 am	18. D
2. 5:52 pm	19. A
3. 1:45 pm	20. B
4. 5:32 am	21. C
5. 2:21 pm	22. A
6. 1012	23. C
7. 1220	24. G
8. 0915	25. H
9. 2045	26. I
10. 0620	27. J
11. D	28. A
12. A	29. E
13. E	30. D
14. C	31. C
15. E	32. F
16. B	33. B
17. C	

PAGE 322-323

1. E	26. C
2. H	27. E
3. J	28. D
4. A	29. B
5. C	30. A
6. G	31. I
7. D	32. L
8. I	33. K
9. F	34. F
10. B	35. O
11. K	36. N
12. N	37. M
13. L	38. G
14. M	39. H
15. R	40. J
16. W	41. T
17. Y	42. P
18. Q	43. U
19. V	44. V
20. T	45. R
21. P	46. Y
22. U	47. X
23. X	48. W
24. O	49. Q
25. S	50. S

PAGE 324

1. H
2. D
3. F
4. B
5. A
6. G
7. I
8. C
9. E
10. J
11. K
12. O
13. N
14. L
15. P
16. M
17. U
18. S
19. R
20. T
21. V
22. Q
23. Y
24. X
25. W

PAGE 325

1. New York
2. San Francisco
3. New Orleans
4. Los Angeles
5. Washington, DC
6. Las Vegas

PAGE 326

1. Empire State Bldg., Statue of Liberty, World Trade Center, Central Park, Rockefeller Center, Times Square, etc.
2. Buckingham Palace, Big Ben, Houses of Parliament, Tower of London, Picadilly Circus, Soho, Downing Street, etc.
3. Eiffel Tower, Louvre Museum, Champs d'Elysees, Arc de Triomphe, Latin Quarter, Notre Dame Cathedral, Pantheon, Montmartre, etc.
4. Colosseum, Trevi Fountain, Capitoline Hill, Vatican City, St. Peter's Cathedral, Sistine Chapel, Catacombs, etc.
5. Queen Mary, Disneyland, Knott's Berry Farm, Catalina Is., Griffith Park, Hollywood, Old Mission Church, etc.
6. Forbidden City, Tien An Men Square, Great Wall of China, Summer Palace, etc.
7. Ginza District, Emperor's Palace, Diet Building, Meiji Shrine, Ueno Park, Iris Garden, Tokyo Tower, etc.
8. French Quarter, Superdome, Jackson Square, Canal Street, Audubon Zoo, Cafe du Monde, Mississippi River, Cities of the Dead, etc.
9. Fisherman's Wharf, Telegraph Hill, Golden Gate Bridge, Ghirardelli Square, Nob Hill, the Cannery, Lombard Street, Chinatown, etc.
10. Alameda Park, Zocalo, Shrine of Guadeloupe, Chapultepec Park and Castle, Floating Gardens of Xochimilco, Zona Rosa, Palacio des Belles Artes, Aztec Ruins, Museum of Anthropology, National Palace
11. Ipanema and Copacabana beaches, Sugarloaf Mountain, Corcovado Mountain, Candelaria Church, Flamengo Park, etc.
12. Opera House, Harbor Bridge, Taronga Zoo Park, Australian Museum, Bondi and other beaches, Cadman's Cottage, Paddington District, etc.
13. Prado Museum, Royal Palace, Museo Taurino, Retiro Park, etc.
14. Red Square, St. Basil's Cathedral, Kremlin, the subway, Gum and Tsum Department stores, Armory Museum, Gorky Park, Mausoleum, etc.
15. Parthenon, Acropolis, Theatre of Dionysus, Roman Forum, Arch of Hadrian, Apteros Nike, Temple of Zeus, Tower of Winds, etc.

PAGE 327

1. Taj Mahal
   Agra, India
2. Sydney Opera House
   Sydney, Australia
3. Sphinx
   near Cairo, Egypt
4. Hoover Dam
   near Las Vegas, NV, U.S.
5. Eiffel Tower
   Paris, France
6. Cliff Divers
   near Acapulco, Mexico

PAGE 328

1. Zermatt, Switzerland
2. Big Ben and Houses of Parliament in London, England
3. Notre Dame Cathedral in Paris, France
4. Mt. Rushmore near Rapid City, SD, U.S.
5. Great Wall in China
6. Diamond Head at the end of Waikiki Beach in Honolulu, Oahu, HI, U.S.

PAGE 329

1. Adriatic
2. Arabian
3. False
4. True
5. False
6. False
7. False
8. False
9. False
10. True
11. False
12. True
13. True
14. Brazil
15. Capricorn

SOLITAIRE PUBLISHING
P.O. BOX 14508
TAMPA, FL 33690-4508
(813) 876-0286 or (800) 226-0286 (U.S.)
E-mail: PSolitaire@aol.com

Thank you for having purchased Solitaire Publishing materials. If you would like to receive other items, use the form below or contact us for a current catalog.

- -

I would like to receive:

The Travel Training Series		
Travel Geography	$24.95	________
Domestic Travel and Ticketing	$29.95	________
Selling Tours and Independent Travel	$18.95	________
International Travel	$24.95	________
Selling Cruises	$15.95	________
Sales and Marketing Techniques	$24.95	________
The Travel Dictionary	$15.95	________
COMPLETE SET WITH TOTE BAG AND ATLAS	$129.95	________

ADDITIONAL MATERIALS DISTRIBUTED BY SOLITAIRE PUBLISHING:

Hammond Headline Atlas	$4.50	________
How to Open Your Own Travel Agency	$39.95	________
How to Get a Job with a Cruise Line	$14.95	________
Building Profits With Group Travel	$29.95	________
Incentive Travel: The Complete Guide	$45.00	________
Travel Industry Personnel Directory	$31.00	________
A Coach Full of Fun	$19.95	________
Home-Based Travel Agent	$24.95	________
Air Courier Bargains	$14.95	________
Tour Designing and Packaging	$59.95	________
Travel Agency Bookkeeping Made Simple	$45.00	________
VIDEO on CAREERS IN TRAVEL	$39.95	________
VIDEO on TOUR WELCOME	$29.95	________

Florida residents please add 7% sales tax. +________

Shipping charges: Orders to $60.00 (Contiguous U.S.) - add 10% (minimum $4.00), over $60.00 add 8%. For AK, HI, and Int'l - add $5.00 for each item ordered. For quantities and other questions, please contact us.

SHIPPING +____________

TOTAL ENCLOSED =____________

Name: ______________________________________

School/Company______________________________

Address: ___________________________________

City/State/Zip: ____________________________

Phone: (______)_____________________________

______ Please mail me a current catalog on all your publications.